INDUCTION AND JUSTIFICATION

*An Investigation of Cartesian Procedure
in the Philosophy of Knowledge*

INDUCTION AND JUSTIFICATION

*An Investigation of Cartesian Procedure
in the Philosophy of Knowledge*

FREDERICK L. WILL

Cornell University Press

ITHACA AND LONDON

First published 1974 by Cornell University Press.
Published in the United Kingdom by Cornell University Press Ltd., 2–4 Brook Street, London W1Y 1AA.

International Standard Book Number 0-8014-0823-7
Library of Congress Catalog Card Number 73-19079

Printed in the United States of America by Vail-Ballou Press, Inc.

To Louise
Not Just
"Present at the Creation"

Contents

MOTTO, AND ASPIRATION

"I have from the first felt sure that the writer, when he sits down to commence his novel, should do so, not because he has to tell a story, but because he has a story to tell."

ANTHONY TROLLOPE

Preface

In this book one broad point of view in the theory of knowledge is criticized, the case for an alternative is advanced, and some features of that alternative are briefly outlined. The case for the alternative is not argued in a primarily deductive way, that is, by means of an intended demonstration designed to extract the main theses of the view in question from a close inspection of certain basic philosophical notions: knowledge, evidence, reason, and the rest. The issues to which the case is directed are much too controversial in relation to these notions to be amenable to a procedure like this, which relies so heavily upon principles, theses, suppositions concerning the matters at hand already accepted, explicitly or implicitly, in certain philosophical views or in common sense and present as intellectual deposits in the rules of discourse employed in these domains. The case can be made, if it can be made at all, only when one does not limit himself to the elucidation of salient features of certain philosophical conceptions, but, passing beyond this, subjects these conceptions to searching criticism, in the hope that out of the results it may be possible to develop, if not new conceptions, at least improved versions of the old. In a philosophical context in which this kind of critical examination is needed, the advantages of definiteness and precision afforded by some techniques are more than offset by their tendency to fix, to freeze, to render less rather than more accessible to critical appraisal the fundamental philosophical preconceptions with which all our basic philosophical notions are deeply impregnated. In the course of a review of Max Black's *Models and Metaphors* some years ago I cited the reminder in that book that "philosophical arguments do not stand to their reasons as the conclusion of a deductive argument to its sufficient premises. The success of any philosophical investigation must be judged by the extent to which it dispels initial perplexity and permits a perspicuous view of a complex territory." According to the view advanced in this present book the contrast between deductive argument and the elaboration of theory is not so sharp as Black's comment may suggest, such sharpness fitting better if what is contrasted with the elaboration and support of theory is calculation and the formal derivation of conclusions, rather than deduction itself. That, however, is one detail of a larger view, the whole of which is offered here in the hope that it will contribute in some degree to the joint cause of reducing perplexities in the theory of knowledge and achieving a more realistic and enlightening view of the complex territory of human life and achievement with which that theory generally is concerned.

Readers aware of my work on induction over the years may identify the present work with an earlier projected book of mine on the problem of induction, and may then find its character puzzling for a variety of reasons, among them, the fact that this problem, in its proper character, plays so small a part in it. The simple answer to this puzzle is that this book is not the one with which I was earlier engaged. It is rather a sequel to and consequence of that earlier work, long since completed but never published.

That work was an extended study in the philosophy of induction, about twice the length of the present book, about half devoted to a positive theory of inductive inference and the rest to a critical study of major contemporary views in the field. After completing a draft of that work, and in the process of critically examining the views set forth in it in preparation for publication, I gradually came to realize that the positive view of induction advanced in it was flawed in a way that resisted emendation. What was chiefly wrong with my philosophy of induction was, I finally concluded, that it *was* a philosophy of induction, a kind of philosophy which—Prichard's phraseology seems to fit here—rests upon a mistake. The heart of that mistake is the supposition that the problem of induction is what it appears to be, namely, to revert to the idiom of that philosophy, a problem about the validity of general contingent propositions by which our knowledge is extended from the supposed data of experience, a problem, as Hume put it, about "the foundation of all conclusions from experience." The writing of that earlier manuscript and the efforts to emend it were important though arduous steps in an educative process by which I became progressively aware of and progressively capable of breaking free from this supposition and the broad philosophical preconceptions it represents. But in consequence, I then found that, in order to say what I thought about the problem of induction, an entirely new book was needed, one in which the focus was not upon this problem, but upon something much deeper and pervasive, which in a certain matrix expresses itself in terms of this particular apparent puzzle or difficulty. The result is the present book, now bearing the title *Induction and Justification*.

In speaking deprecatingly of something I have referred to broadly as a "philosophy of induction" I perhaps run some risk of being understood as deprecating in principle and universally all philosophical study of inductive procedures. Nothing so extreme is intended. Inductive procedures, that is, disciplined methods of drawing conclusions from instances, developing and testing statistical hypotheses from samples, and so on, are in themselves no more alien to philosophy, no less the object of proper philosophical inquiry, than the procedures we employ in seeing objects or casting sums. Philosophical questions arise when we explore various aspects of all these procedures. But, with respect to the questions concerning inductive ones, beyond noting briefly something of their character and variety (Chapter 2, Sections 19–20; Chapter 4), no further attention is paid to them in this book. My primary object in this regard is not to explore these questions but rather to expose what has been a huge impediment to their exploration, namely, the transmutation of the questions and the diversion of attention from them to a certain grand and perennially absorbing philosophical project which I have called the "justification operation."

Here again, just as criticism may be directed against something properly referred to as a "philosophy of induction," without disparaging all philosophical study of inductive procedures, so criticism may be directed at something properly referred to as "justification philosophy," without disparaging everything that might properly be referred to as justification, or as a theory of justification, in the philosophy of knowledge, in ethics, or in philosophy generally. In the book I try repeatedly to make this point clear with respect to justification, and have striven to dissociate myself from any position which would exclude from the catalogue of legitimate and valuable philosophical activities all those properly thought of as of a justifying nature. In contrast, I have advanced in Part III a view of the philosophy of knowledge in which justification takes a proper, though less exaggerated place, *unum inter pares,* among the activities in which we engage in the philosophical examination, understanding, criticism, validation, invalidation, emendation, and development of features or items of the collective institution that is human knowledge. Even so, perhaps it is well to give this notice at the outset that what, under the title of "justification," is the subject of criticism in this book is a particular kind of justification operation and result, incorporated in a particular kind of justification program, conceived in a particular kind of theory about justification, and defended by a particular kind of justification argument.

Problems encountered in the program in question have a striking capacity, like young cuckoos, to displace others in the philosophical nest, a capacity which is not least effective when their philosophical character is not clearly discerned. Efforts to solve them then present themselves principally as attempts to explore, illuminate, and regularize our conceptions of evidence and evidential support, disclosing their deeper character only in the quite particular means or resources they countenance as suitable for this purpose. For example, in the past half century the applications of the mathematical theory of probability to problems of statistical inference have yielded a rich store of techniques and principles capable of illuminating, regularizing, and improving conceptions and rules of evidence in the domain of statistical practice. This domain is far removed, and the problems vastly different, from the traditional problems about justification studied by philosophers. But if one disregards these differences, he may be led to conclude that, as the solution of very concrete problems lies in the discovery of means of applying the mathematical theory to concrete, complex situations, so the solution of abstract, philosophical problems lies in the discovery of ways to apply the theory to similarly abstract ones. A natural result of this is treatments of the "logical" or "philosophical" foundations of probability theory which are ill-suited to the discussion of philosophical problems pertinent to characteristic statistical methods and in which, in consequence, the discussion of these problems tends to be replaced by the discussion of justification problems, now carried on in a statistical idiom.

It may be expected that the study of philosophical problems concerning inductive methods will be advanced by increased understanding and vigilance toward this and like tendencies. That, however, is not the principal goal to which the book as a whole is directed. As the ensuing discussion attempts to make clear, the impeding effect which justification theory has upon the philosophical study of inductive practices is but one example of the similar effect it has generally in the philosophy of knowledge, and through that, upon the investigation of what constitutes rational procedures in the philosophical appraisal, criticism, and reform of human practices in all domains of human life, including those far beyond the common rubrics of science and knowledge.

I am glad to have the opportunity here to acknowledge some of my debts to various individuals and agencies who have assisted my work on this book. First I wish to mention the students in my graduate seminars at the University of Illinois during the past few years. They provided me with a special incentive and occasion to develop some of the views set forth in the book, and helped me to eliminate some genuine difficulties as well as sources of misunderstanding. Next, I wish to express my deep appreciation of the support my philosophical studies have received from this University. The beginning pages of the book reproduce an observation of Anthony Trollope about the writing of novels which has seemed to me to apply also to works in philosophy. The generous and enlightened character of the support of my studies by the

University of Illinois helped me to live up, to the extent that I have, to the sentiment of Trollope's remark. Further, when it became clear that completion of the book required some special assistance in the way of free time for research and writing, I was fortunate to receive for this purpose a grant from the National Science Foundation. My work in producing the manuscript and preparing it for publication was greatly lightened by the willing, efficient help of the secretarial staff of my department.

Upon completion of the first draft of the manuscript I was able to enlist the services of a number of individuals to read portions or all of it and give me their advice. I am pleased to think that I was able to use with profit comments from all these people, leaving my readers and me in varying degrees in their debt. The names of those to whom the debt is owed are, in no order except alphabetical: B. J. Diggs, J. A. Easley, Jr., Nicholas Georgalis, Nelson Goodman, William H. Hay, Wilfrid Sellars, Thomas B. Settle, David S. Shwayder, Robert C. Stalnaker, and Frederick R. Suppe. Also of assistance to me in this regard was a careful, critical assessment of the manuscript procured and transmitted to me by Cornell University Press.

Like many authors in similar circumstances I am intimidated by the difficulty of finding words to express the special debt this book owes to the one to whom it is dedicated. Not just, in the phrase of Alfonso the Wise used in the dedication, "present at the creation," my wife Louise read the various versions of the manuscript, and contributed editorial advice at every stage, helping me to eliminate from it both errors and infelicities. She also shared with me the work in the preparation of the Bibliography and the Index. These items of assistance, however, considerable as they are, represent but a small portion of the extensive, devoted, and in all ways enduring contribution she has made over many years in support of the philosophical studies from which this book has emerged.

FREDERICK L. WILL

Urbana, Illinois

INDUCTION AND JUSTIFICATION

*An Investigation of Cartesian Procedure
in the Philosophy of Knowledge*

The Plan of This Work

1. The main theme of this book is that a certain kind of approach in the philosophy of knowledge, exemplified in what is referred to in the book as "Cartesian" or "justification" theory, is seriously mistaken and overdue for replacement with a radically different, more adequate, and, at the same time, more realistic view.

2. This theme is first developed in connection with a discussion of the philosophical problem of induction. The discussion aims to show that certain features of justification theory are responsible for a cluster of frustrating and debilitating difficulties like this problem which have for years attended work in the philosophy of knowledge carried on from the point of view of the theory. The sources of these difficulties, it is argued, lie very deep in the theory of knowledge, in certain philosophical preconceptions about knowledge and the nature of the authority of cognitive claims which decisively affect the manner in which one sets out to make a philosophical appraisal of such claims. The problem of induction is one of the better known and more studied of these difficulties, all of which in different ways reflect the inadequacy of these preconceptions. Much of the frustration encountered in philosophical thought about all these difficulties is due to the circumstance that they are generated by a nest of philosophical preconceptions which also renders them insoluble.

3. The first two chapters of the book, the only ones directed primarily to induction and related topics, expand upon this point. Chapter 1 traces the problem to its source in the general view of knowledge that resulted from the empiricist criticism and

17

revision of the basic Cartesian view that knowledge is a kind of vision or intuition, that there are certain first intuitions (first cognitions), and that further knowledge consists of consequent intuitions elicited from or founded upon these. The problem of induction was one of the difficulties encountered in the development of this view when sensuous intuition replaced rational intuition as the means by which knowledge was achieved, the other main features of the view remaining substantially unchanged. When, within the framework of such a philosophy, one asks concerning the means by which, beginning with first intuitions of sense, one can arrive at a body of knowledge resembling what we now have or accept as knowledge, the position of general principles of inference, of what Hume called "the relation of cause and effect," becomes crucial. If as Hume said, in his own language, all expansion of immediate sensuous intuition is founded upon these general principles, how are they themselves to be known? For certain reasons which are set forth, the problem of showing how these general relations or connections can be achieved becomes a first, necessary step in showing how the view can be successfully maintained that knowledge consists of sensory intuition and its expansions. The problem of accounting for the expansion becomes the problem of accounting for our knowledge of these general connections, and in this way the expansion problem assumes the typical form it exhibits in the philosophical problem of induction, that of some kind of gargantuan logical problem about the validity of "generalizations from experience."

4. One consequence of this development has been a permanent confusion installed in the philosophy of knowledge between the study of this encompassing problem and the study of the actual processes in which in the sciences, the technical arts, and other areas we do make and appraise generalizations of various sorts. When the topic of how laws are discerned and established in the physical sciences, or of how more or less secure generalizations are attained in these sciences and in other areas, is identified with the topic of how in general two or a hundred instances have more weight than one—whether these be instances of birds, eggs, planets, or whatever—the technical appearance of the topic has the doubly unfortunate effect of, first, obscuring what is of pri-

mary philosophical interest in the topic, which is not essentially a matter of generalization, and, second, by its philosophical generality and abstractness, excluding what is of interest in the procedures of generalization in the various areas in which they are successfully applied. In a word, the transformation of a philosophical question about the expansion of knowledge into a quasi-technical question about generalization, has tended to obscure the philosophical character of the question, while, on the other hand, the philosophical preconceptions embedded in the question have seriously impeded understanding of the technical procedures with which the expansion has been identified. The career of the philosophical problem of induction seems to show sufficiently well that an understanding of what is philosophically interesting in the practice of generalization will not be achieved by a preoccupation with the kinds of questions about the colors of birds or the character of eggs, or even drawing balls from urns, that have typified discussions of this problem. And similar conclusions may now be drawn concerning two further satellite topics which have been the topics of extensive discussion in recent years, namely, laws and probability. In order to preserve certain philosophical doctrines about knowledge central to the empiricist version of Cartesianism, it has seemed to many that it is necessary to think of laws in a certain way, and, by consequence, of conditional statements; and there have been similar consequences affecting the interpretation of statements and other expressions of probability. The encompassing difficulty of understanding how the expansion of knowledge can be understood within the confines of this philosophy is accompanied by similar difficulties, in the same confining philosophy, with these topics, difficulties traceable more to the philosophy than to the topics themselves. These matters are dealt with in some detail in Chapter 2, under the title of "The Shaping of the Problem." Because, in keeping with the doctrine of the book, the philosophical problem of induction is not regarded as essentially a problem about either induction or probability, the comment in the chapter on probability is intentionally brief. For those wishing a more extensive account from the point of the view taken in the book of some of the main issues that have been debated about probability, an Appendix on that topic is provided at the end of the volume.

5. If the problem of induction is not primarily about induction, what *is* it about? It is about "justification." It is the form, taken in the empiricist version of the Cartesian philosophy, of a more general philosophical problem, endemic to the Cartesian philosophy and very plain in the philosophy of Descartes himself, about how our knowledge can be viewed as a sound expansion of certain limited and altogether sure revelations or deliverances to us. These may or may not be revelations or deliverances of sense. Probing further into the problem and inquiring why it should be thought that knowledge has the character attributed to it by implication in this problem, one finds a most important source to be one which Descartes himself emphasized, namely, the intention to meet the challenges of philosophical skepticism by accepting the propriety of the large-scale questions which that view seeks to raise concerning our knowledge and then answering them. The chief philosophical significance of the problem of induction is the way it makes plain in its own context what Descartes's metaphysical justification of reason (*malgré lui*) illustrates in its own, namely, that this way of meeting the skeptical challenge cannot succeed. The problem of induction is the Cartesian circle without God, or, perhaps better, with a very prosaic, secular God whose name is "Induction," and whom the philosophy that conceives it is unable to show is a good God rather than a mischievous demon.

6. This view is set forth in Chapter 3, and, with this, the center of attention shifts from the problem of induction to the general justification problem. The view taken of that problem is that the difficulties and bafflements encountered in achieving justification—of induction, scientific conclusions, moral judgments, and so on—are not due, as some have thought, to unclarity of thought about justification, to a misconception of what justification "really is." Much more is involved here than some large semantic slip. "Justification," as it is conceived in justification theory, is an expression of a certain view of the nature of well-ordered knowledge; it is, among other things, the name given to a certain kind of backing which, according to the theory, a genu-

ine item of knowledge, a rationally acceptable truth claim must have. The name itself is not of great importance. Backing of this kind would be as difficult to secure under any other name for most that we at any time take ourselves to know or to reasonably hold to be true in one way or another. It should now be painfully clear that philosophers devoted to achieving this kind of backing for items or domains which they take to be knowledge are not going to receive gratefully an offer of something radically different in its place, so long as we are willing to call it "justification." In the sense intended we cannot justify inductive conclusions, and therewith the claim that the sun will rise tomorrow, or did rise yesterday, or that the earth is a satellite of the sun, and the moon of the earth. Justification is a very special article, and in very short supply. The question is not whether it is scarce, but rather whether we should regard ourselves as unfortunate in consequence of this scarcity. Why should one want it? The answer, already given, is that it is wanted for the purpose of answering skeptical questions about knowledge by those who judge that the challenge of these questions is to be met in this way.

Bafflement in solving the justification problem is bafflement in doing just this. It is not bafflement in engaging in the practices followed in the sciences, the technical arts and disciplines, and in everyday life, when we are concerned to find out and know. It is bafflement in showing in a certain particular way that we know what we take ourselves to know, do reasonably accept what we take ourselves so to accept, in these and other domains. As a way of making clear the specific nature of what is required in Cartesian theory under the title of justification, a good portion of Chapter 4 is devoted to drawing the contrast between the demands of this theory and what is actual practice in certain areas of inquiry and practical life when we have occasion to appraise the acceptability of truth claims. The three major aspects of cognitive practice stressed in drawing the contrast are (1) the variety of grounds appealed to in support of claims advanced, (2) the variety of procedures employed in appraising the strength of such grounds, and (3) the variety of response or stance to the claims sanctioned, in view of the grounds, in a variety of cognitive situations. The contrast seems to make very plain that the source of

the demands of the theory lies very little in the attempt to construct a philosophical view of knowledge that will be a refined
reflection of actual practices, and much more in an attempt to
provide something that to its advocates seems to be required for
certain distinctive philosophical purposes. Adopting the language
of this philosophy, one may say that something like this may be
required if what we take to be knowledge of ourselves and the
world is in general in need of *justification,* if it is open to some
serious and encompassing charges concerning its validity. Such
extreme charges would seem to call for the kind of extreme measures dictated by the theory, if only they could be carried out in
such a way as to meet the demand.

7. Up to this point in the book, in treating the obviously close
connections between justification theory and philosophical skepticism, the primary emphasis is on the motives of advocates of
the theory to meet the challenges represented in that skeptical
position by accepting the questions raised in it as legitimate ones
and showing that they can be answered. Though not so much
emphasized, the further point is argued that the acceptance of
the questions themselves already represents a great degree of
skepticism about the accepted practices and institutions of knowledge. Indeed, one of the principal appeals of first cognitions and
the endeavor to rationalize knowledge as a structure founded on
them is the apparent independence which such intended cognitions promise to have with respect to accepted practices and institutions. They represent an attempt to secure some basis protected from general doubts and dissatisfactions concerning these
practices and institutions, which may serve as an utterly safe basis
from which an entirely independent examination or audit of
these practices and institutions can be carried out. As a preface
to the critical examination of justification theory offered in Part
II of the book, a general discussion of this aspect of the theory
seems desirable. Such a discussion, emphasizing briefly the extreme alienation expressed by the theory with respect to cognitive practices, and institutions, and the extreme utopianism of
the program it dictates for the philosophical improvement, is
given in Chapter 5.

A view sometimes expressed of the difficulties encountered by
justification theory is that they are due to a misguided desire for

certainty on the part of many engaged in its development, and might consequently be avoided, or at least ameliorated, if this appetite were sensibly abated. If the trouble is certainty, it is certainty of a very special kind. If by "certainty" is meant absolute fixity and incorrigibility in everything we take ourselves to detect by some kind of observation or inspection, and in the elaborations of relations of necessity or probability between these and other items, such diagnosis of fault seems supportable, though it is somewhat misleading and the projected remedy infeasible. It is misleading to identify certainty in this way with the kind of extreme, large-scale and long-run incorrigibility which the theory seeks. And, even if this were not so, when that quest is subtracted, the result is not a revision of justification theory, but its rejection.

8. Corresponding to the distinctive view embodied in justification theory of the nature of the rationality of truth claims, there is a typical argument advanced by advocates in support of the view. Chapter 6 is devoted to the elucidation of one such argument. The argument in question, presented by R. M. Chisholm, sets out to establish by careful reasoning one phase of the theory, namely, the thesis, with respect to what it is now usual to mark off as "empirical" or "factual" knowledge, that the rationality of all genuine items of such knowledge can be traced back to and hence requires a foundation in what are called "self-justifying statements" or "self-presenting states of affairs." Examination of the argument reveals it to be what the preceding discussion would lead one to expect, an elaboration in reverse order of what is essentially the Cartesian view of the nature of the authority of these truth claims which it is proper for us to accept as knowledge or as in any degree reasonable.

The examination of the argument for such foundations in the alleged data of inner or outer sense provides the occasion for raising the correlated questions whether there are or can be immediate, incorrigible, and infallible deliverances of sense, such as justification theory requires, and whether most of our knowledge can be viewed as irreversible and hence irrevisable inferences or constructions made upon such foundations. Justification arguments are ways in which advocates of that theory demonstrate these requirements of what in the theory is conceived of as "justification." Appraisal of the arguments and the theory expressed in the arguments is not fruitfully a matter of determining whether these are requirements, for the theory is designed to make them so. It is rather a matter of determining whether what is conceived in the theory as justification can be secured for items of knowledge generally, and, supposing that it cannot, explaining the wide appeal of a theory that views what is not available as nevertheless indispensable.

9. The kinds of difficulty associated with the two requirements of the theory just discriminated can be usefully segregated into two classes: foundation difficulties, and construction difficulties. The first of these are the difficulties in supposing that there are first, direct, infallible cognitions, cognitions that in the empiricist interpretations of the theory are the data or direct apprehensions of inner and outer sense. Extensive considerations are advanced in Chapter 7 against this supposition. Though the case against such cognitions is an extensive and complex one, and the main theme not simple, it may be briefly stated. It is that in the very formulation of such alleged immediate apprehensions much mediation is necessarily involved: mediation in the form of dependence upon resources which extend far beyond what is encompassed in the conception of such cognitions. The very terms we employ in formulating, in *having* these apprehensions, have the significance they have only because of our complex relations with entities, states, conditions, practices that extend far beyond us. All these things are liable to change and do change. The possibility of change is alone sufficient to render the supposition that there are incorrigible apprehensions of sense untenable.

10. In keeping with the general teaching of the book, the problem of induction is noted in Chapter 8 to be one among a variety of construction difficulties; that is, difficulties encountered in the theory, supposing that the foundation difficulties could be surmounted, of showing how our knowledge in various domains could be accounted for as inferences or constructions made upon these alleged foundations. Not pausing for comment upon such essentially similar problems in the theory as those of "other minds," of "abstract entities," and of "value," the chapter urges as a lesser attended but in the end more significant difficulty, that

posed by what is called in the discussion the "revision phenomena." The aspects of corrigibility and revision are somewhat different in the phases of knowledge that are less directly connected with observation and direct inspection, though something very much like the duck-rabbit phenomenon occurs in reasoning, theorizing, in conception, as well as in perception, as any reader of detective novels should be able to confirm. The revision phenomena reveal at a different level the lesson to be derived from an examination of the first cognitions of sense, namely, that at the alleged secondary and further stages of knowledge, no more than at the alleged primary ones, can the supposition that there are unrevisable cognitions be maintained.

11. One of the most important intellectual dividends accruing from the examination of the motives and fortunes of justification theory is a progressive clarification of the kind of theory it is intended to be, the kind of service in the intellectual economy it is designed to perform. It is designed to provide a systematic view of our knowledge that will expose its grounds, the sources of its authority, to be more than equal to the challenges to this authority made by philosophers with skeptical intent. The skeptical attack proceeds by persistently asking questions about grounds or authority until the supply of answers is exhausted. The design of justification theory is to show that those philosophers who proceeded with skeptical intent in this matter are mistaken in supposing that the supply of answers is not equal to the demand.

In the process of criticizing this one view of knowledge and its grounds, the outlines of an alternative view of a very different kind begin to emerge. The most prominent contrasting feature of this view is that in it knowledge is regarded as a complex social institution, or, better, as a vast complex of such institutions. Since knowledge is achieved and expanded by all of us by first being indoctrinated in this collective institution, by operating in it and through it, and in some cases by assisting in its development, the kind of questions that some philosophers seek to raise from an alleged position outside the collective institution cannot coherently be raised, and the by-product of these conceived questions which is the project of justification theory cannot succeed.

12. This immediately suggests the question, which serious

critics of such a position have not delayed to ask, of how the kind of critical examination that philosophy professes to be able to make of our cognitive practices and institutions is then possible. The career of justification theory is a demonstration of the frustrations encountered when one conceives the conduct of this examination in one way, dominated by one particular purpose. The characteristic breadth and significance of philosophical questions about knowledge—and they *are* questions of large scale—easily lead in philosophical imagination to an expansion of this scale to the maximum degree, as if it were possible to do with respect to the totality of our cognitive institutions and practices what we can do for some, and at some time no doubt for any.

It is a sound principle that what is not possible is also not necessary. In elaborating the character of "The Philosophical Scrutiny of Knowledge," Chapters 9 and 10 attempt to illuminate the way in which philosophical questions may be about the legitimacy of fundamental features of our cognitive practices and institutions without in consequence of this being in principle rendered intractable to treatment of a kind that considers the features in question in their place in the broad system of practices and the broad collection of institutions, including sometimes, most helpfully, institutions which themselves are not primarily cognitive ones. Philosophical questions about practices and domains in the area of human knowledge may be illuminatingly conceived as constitutional questions about the conduct of affairs in that intellectual polity. Decisions concerning proper procedure in affairs of knowledge, no more than corresponding decisions in political and legal affairs, demand that all features of the constitution be put into question at once and a decision reached, as Hobbes reached his decision about the sovereignty of the king, by beginning afresh with the state of nature and attempting to elucidate the decision from the progressive illumination of what that state and some overriding imperative, like that for self-preservation, require.

There is an influential view in the philosophy of science, corresponding to a similar view in political philosophy, according to which fundamental constitutional decisions, because they are themselves questions about what shall count as proper, reasonable procedure in a certain domain, cannot be expected to be dealt with by such procedures, always require in the end extraordinary, arational means. In arguing against this view, in arguing that we do sometimes have institutional means for dealing with questions basic to the character of our institutions, Chapter 10 carefully emphasizes that the grounds for this claim of undeniable competence with respect to *some* questions is not a claim with respect to *all.* The case for the philosophical examination of basic issues concerning human institutions, cognitive and otherwise, is not based upon any guarantee of uniform success.

13. In conformity with its name, the Epilogue adds a final word to the extensive discussion of the two contrary ways of proceeding in the theory of knowledge which, beginning with the early discussion of the problem of induction, is extended and deepened in the main body of the book. This final word concerns the connection between justification theory and the view that the validity of everything we properly take to be knowledge, ultimately depends upon a phase in the cognitive process in which things are known by direct revelation. Briefly, and in a somewhat different manner from Part III of the book, the Epilogue argues that the straitened alternative offered by this theory, namely, revelation or disaster, is a false alternative. The homely analogy of seeing, which we do with eyes, spectacles, and other optical instruments, is employed to make the very simple point that, just as there is no vicious circle and hence no skeptical consequence entailed by our employing lenses or eyes while testing their veracity, so there are no necessary difficulties in determining the veracity of other features of what may be viewed as our intellectual optics. Literal seeing and intellectual seeing are alike in this respect. In both we are subject to illusion, obscurity, and error. In both there are different kinds of vision, different ways our eyes can be trained to make different discriminations, for different purposes. In both, when we are at a loss to determine whether what we seem to see is actually what we do see, we do not, or at least should not, pluck out our eyes on the curious supposition that by this deprivation we shall somehow enable ourselves to see whatever we see direct and bare.

PART I

INDUCTION, AND THE JUSTIFICATION PROBLEM

CHAPTER 1

The Philosophical Matrix
of the Problem of Induction

1. The problem of induction represents a skeptical attack upon a large domain of accepted belief and opinion that is ordinarily taken to be knowledge. The domain encompasses all that we take ourselves to know about ourselves and the world, except for that tiny segment of objects or phenomena that we are alleged to have some kind of "direct" or "immediate" knowledge of in experience. The philosophical problem is that of repulsing the skeptical attack. That means meeting and disarming the philosophical argument that is claimed by some to lead inexorably, from sound beginnings, to the conclusion that no belief or opinion in the wide domain referred to can count as knowledge; that, indeed, when any such belief is subjected to the most careful scrutiny and just standards that philosophical inquiry can bring, it must be judged in the end as without any real justification whatsoever.

2. If we begin with the supposition that this conclusion is as extravagant as it sounds, we are led to the conclusion that the fault must be, not induction, but in ourselves; not in the grounds that can be adduced for our alleged knowledge in the disputed domain, but in the philosophical standards by which the grounds have been appraised. If the scale shows a sack of feathers to have the same weight as a sack of lead shot, we may well look for unsuspected features, not in feathers or lead, but in the scale.

The scale in this case is a philosophical theory about knowledge. Specifically, in the era of modern philosophy in which this problem has flourished, it is that version of the Cartesian view of knowledge known as empiricism.

3. If Hume is the father of this problem, Descartes, frequently named as the father of modern philosophy, is surely a grandfather. Peirce, contrasting "the spirit of Cartesianism" with scholasticism, which it displaced, identified as one of the four main features of the Cartesian spirit the doctrine "that the ultimate test of certainty is to be found in the individual consciousness; whereas scholasticism had rested on the testimony of sages and of the Catholic church." Against this Peirce maintained the thesis that "we have no power of Intuition, but every cognition is determined logically by previous cognitions." [1]

For a central feature of the philosophical matrix from which the problem of induction springs is the Cartesian doctrine that knowledge is achieved by intuition and developed by expanding intuition. The association of Descartes's name with this doctrine should not be taken to imply that Descartes invented the doctrine, even among modern philosophers, though in his thought he did illustrate it. Much of the same doctrine, though by no means in so clear and unequivocal form, is to be found, for example, in the views of Hobbes concerning the development of knowledge by definition and ratiocination from definition. Hobbes, a contemporary and sometimes rival of Descartes, was in this respect a "Cartesian," not because he was a follower of Descartes, but because at some important points his views about knowledge coincided with ones set forth with extraordinary force and clarity, and given wide currency, in Descartes's philosophical writings.

4. The view about knowledge and intuition referred to here is not simply, to use Peirce's words, that there is in us a "power of intuition"; it is that *all* knowledge is attained by the exercise of this power. And intuition, as Descartes said, is not to be identified with "the fluctuating testimony of the senses, nor [with] the misleading judgment of a wrongly combining imagination." It is, instead, "the apprehension which the mind, pure and attentive, gives us so easily and distinctly that we are thereby freed from all doubt as to what it is that we are apprehending." [2]

[1] *Collected Papers*, 5.264, 265.   [2] *Regulae*, III (N. Kemp Smith, trans.).

Knowing is "seeing" or "apprehending" by the natural light of reason; and knowledge, the issue or result of this activity, is what is seen or apprehended. It is "sights" and the consolidation of these sights in more extensive views, more penetrating visions.

The strategy for attaining knowledge was thus for Descartes the strategy for cultivating the certain apprehensions in which knowing consists. This means pursuing these apprehensions rigorously, not letting oneself be satisfied with such poor substitutes as the fluctuating testimony of the senses, hasty judgment, or alleged truths offered us by the educative benevolence of others. And it means also following the kind of order in one's investigations—essentially that proceeding from the simplest matters to the more complex—that will enable one to exploit most efficiently the capacity that already-attained intuitions have to make new, hitherto unattainable ones possible. For little that we wish to know can be comprehended in one simple apprehension. More, and indeed much more than we commonly suspect, can be comprehended in a succession of intuitions each capitalizing upon preceding ones.[3] Thus, though we may not be able to apprehend immediately, in one single intuition, that 2 and 2 amount to the same as 3 and 1, we may apprehend this mediately, says Descartes, by intuiting "that 2 and 2 amount to 4 and that 3 and 1 also amount to 4, . . . [and] also that the first-mentioned proposition is a necessary conclusion from these two." [4] This procedure of progressively expanding intuition, consolidating and advancing its results, Descartes called "deduction." The Cartesian formula that all knowledge is by intuition and deduction thus does not contravene, but rather further defines, the basic tenet of this theory of knowledge that knowledge is achieved by intuition and developed by expanding this power.[5]

5. A feature of this general view of knowledge whose importance can hardly be overemphasized is the progressive, steplike procedure in which it conceives the advancement of knowledge to proceed. Items of knowledge are validated by the accomplish-

---

[3] Cf. Hobbes's, "By God, this is impossible!"   [4] *Regulae*, III.
[5] For the purposes of the present study we may leave aside the question, important for the full interpretation of Descartes's own philosophy, of the role played by memory in deduction.

ment of steps of intuitive clarity and absolute security. Increase and development of knowledge must therefore be accomplished by addition to the results achieved, never by the revision, transformation, revaluation of them. Once an item of information is apprehended, any question concerning its validity is settled permanently. With that question behind him, one can pursue further intuitions, secure in the trust that the question will remain behind, will never need to be reopened, indeed cannot properly be reopened. What is established, if it is established at all, is established absolutely. Item *A,* once won, remains a hard, indestructible atom of knowledge. The winning of it may be forgotten, but never impugned. Further intuitions may add to it. One may secure *B,* and *C,* and *D,* the last of which may be to the effect that, given *B* and *C, E* follows, thus making possible the mediate intuition of *E* itself. However slow and small the advances one may make, following this procedure, they are all absolute, inexpugnable ones. There is indeed no guarantee of advance at any particular point in this campaign into the territory of ignorance. But there is a guarantee against retreat. Any move made, however small, is quite indefeasible.

6. Put in this bold way the view about the way knowledge is developed may seem an unusual and extreme one, one that can be attributed to Descartes and other confident rationalists, but little further. The trust of the early rationalists in intuition, and the fundamental position it occupied in their theories of knowledge, are well known. What is not so well understood, but is nevertheless essential for understanding the way in which the problem of induction arises, is that, in the respects just emphasized, the empiricist philosophy in which it arose, was and is Cartesian. Validation of knowledge claims for Locke, or Hume, for example, is as exclusively a matter of the attainment and accretion of intuitions as it was for Descartes.

What distinguished the empiricists from the rationalists in classical modern philosophy was not a rejection of the intuition theory of knowledge, but rather a distinctive way of conceiving the basic operation by which, according to this general theory, knowledge is achieved, namely, intuition itself. For the empiricist, as for the rationalist, the basic validating procedure in knowledge is intuitive apprehension, and the development of knowledge is a matter of the progressive accretion of the results of these atomic, intuitive steps. But the empiricists very early exhibited misgivings about the extent of the knowledge that intuition of a certain kind, namely *rational intuition,* can achieve. The diffidence of Locke concerning the power of rational intuition to validate relations of ideas that he called "agreement or disagreement in coexistence," and the relations between ideas and their external supposed archetypes which, according to him, are expressed in "knowledge of real existence," flowered in Berkeley and Hume into a more general skepticism concerning the capacity of this procedure, either singly or in multiple application, to yield certain commonly regarded desiderata in the domain of human knowledge. The problem of induction refers to one of the most basic and disconcerting of these deficiencies.

7. The primary reason for this deficiency, as well as for other prominent difficulties in the empiricist program, thus lay in the permutation effected upon the conception of rational intuition by the empiricist followers of Descartes and given theoretical formulation and rationalization in their theory of ideas. It is not that the older, more orthodox versions of Cartesian philosophy were without difficulties, these being generated only by the modifications made in it by empiricist theory. It is rather that the difficulties attending these two versions of the philosophy were different, sometimes because the distinguishing features of the two versions led to really different difficulties, sometimes because they led the same basic difficulties to assume different forms. The problem of induction, as will be argued later, illustrates the latter type of effect. Peculiar as this problem is to empiricism, it is its form that makes it so. At the bottom there is a fundamental difficulty common to rationalism and empiricism, but which in empiricism assumes this particular, identifiable form. In this form it is a consequence, and one of the most important consequences, of the confluence of these two streams of thought, the basic Cartesian expansion-of-intuition theory of knowledge, and the empiricist theory of ideas.

8. The empiricist theory of ideas is not exclusively or even

primarily a theory of how ideas are developed. In spite of the emphasis by the classic authors upon the origin of our ideas, and the recurrent disputes about whether there are innate ideas, or only adventitious ones, the main burden of the theory has survived a variety of changes of view concerning how, as a matter of psychological fact, ideas are developed. The theory has always been, in a complex way, a broad epistemological theory. And in the passage through the changes of psychological view that have taken place in the past two centuries, emphasis upon these epistemological aspects has tended to dominate, though not altogether replace, consideration of psychological origins.

In its epistemological aspects the theory is a theory of meaning, and, in consequence, a theory concerning necessary truth, or, in the terminology of the preceding discussion, what it is possible to know by rational intuition and deduction. For the kind of intuition which knowledge consists in, according to the original Cartesian conception, is that which we are able to have by our ideas when, by proper care on our part, they have been rendered "clear and distinct." Knowledge, Locke said, continuing this tradition, is "nothing but the perception of the connexion and agreement, or disagreement and repugnancy of any of our ideas." [6] And Hume, further refining the conception, marked, in the seven kinds of philosophical relation he could discriminate, four which "depend entirely on the ideas, which we compare together" and which for this reason "can be the objects of knowledge and certainty." [7]

What we apprehend in intuition, what is grasped "so easily and distinctly that we are thereby freed from all doubt as to what it is we are apprehending," is what can be affirmed of some subject, either general or particular, necessarily and hence with certainty. That since I think I must exist; that 2 and 2 amount to 4, that the triangle is bounded by three lines only, and the sphere by a single surface—all these things are manifest because what is affirmed in them of the subject in question cannot be denied, because that denial would be repugnant to the

[6] *Essay Concerning Human Understanding*, Bk. IV, Ch. I, Sect. 2.
[7] *A Treatise of Human Nature*, Bk. I, Pt. III, Sect. I.

very idea of the subject in question.[8] It is in this way that the clarification and refinement of our ideas leads to knowledge. Just as in following Euclid we at one and the same time clarify our ideas and establish truths about planes, lines, figures, so the rationalists held that by clarifying our ideas of space, motion, rest, bodies, and so on, we could establish truths about the world of bodies, including our own.

9. On the empiricist view the supposition that knowledge could be secured in this way, by the clarification and development of our ideas, was a delusion.

How this view is dictated by the theory of ideas may be seen by considering Hume's encapsulation of the theory in the formula that all ideas are copies of impressions. This meant, in brief, that all our ideas are *of* impressions. That is what we can think of, about which we can significantly speak. This stipulation concerning the nature of ideas, of *genuine* ideas, represents a large concession on the part of the empiricist philosophers to the hyperbolic doubts raised by Descartes and given personal representation in his demon. The empiricist philosophers, vastly more impressed by Descartes's doubts than by his attempted theological resolution of them, moved, in the theory of ideas, to preserve rational intuition against the incursion of such doubt by excluding as deliverances of intuitions any claims to which such doubt might apply. If in the development and clarification of the idea of an object *A,* one comes to attribute to *A* a character *B* concerning which there can be, on the remotest philosophical grounds, any doubt whatever, then the connection between the characters *A* and *B* is not a really necessary one; and the attribution of *B* to *A* is consequently not the kind that can be established by rational intuition, in either its single or multiple form.

In intuitive knowledge, as Descartes said in the *Regulae,* we

8 "But the self-evident thing (*res per se nota*) which the mind apprehends, in a single and simple act [in *Cogito, ergo sum*], is the necessary and immediate coherence of two elements; that is to say, this self-evident datum, like all the objects of intellectual intuition, is then a simple proposition in which is contained the necessary but immediate coherence of two ideas" (L. J. Beck, *The Method of Descartes,* p. 76).

are "freed from all doubt as to what it is we are apprehending." But, as he recognized in later reflections, in any intuitions in which we extend our knowledge by the employment of clear and distinct ideas beyond the data of immediate consciousness, we can be freed of doubt in an ultimate degree only when the demon who represents these remote philosophical grounds for doubt has been exorcised and a good God installed in his place. The empiricist theory of ideas represented a reinstatement and undramatic codification of just the doubts about the efficacy of rational intuition that in Descartes's thought had been given dramatic representation in the person of the demon.

The doctrine that ideas are copies of impressions is thus a translation into epistemological terms of the empiricists' conclusion that God, if not dead, in any case cannot be trusted to guarantee the capacity of rational intuition, by exploring the relations of our ideas, to expand our knowledge beyond the immediate data of Cartesian self-consciousness. The empiricist caveat concerning the untrustworthiness of the relations that Descartes proposed to exploit in intuition and deduction is delivered in the material mode of speech. Instead of saying that relations of ideas are not to be trusted, it says there are *no* such relations, no real relations, no really necessary ones.[9] There are no such relations between impressions, because, as the demon hypothesis is taken to illustrate, given any single impression of the moment, any single apprehension of external or internal sense, we *could* conceivably be deceived or mistaken about all else. But that we could be deceived about all else, translated into this mode of speech, comes out as the doctrine that there are no necessary relations between this apprehension and anything else. Indeed that is just what an impression is. And since an idea is but a copy, a representation of an impression; since what we think of by means of our ideas *is* impressions; no thing, object, or phenomenon that we can think of has any necessary relations with anything else that could support thought in passing beyond it. The supposition that in intuition and deduction we could ex-

---

[9] What the empiricist theory did provide for, under the somewhat misleading title of relations between complex ideas, was relations of inclusion and exclusion between complexes or sets of ideas. Cf. Sect. 11 below.

pand knowledge by exploring the necessary relations obtaining between our ideas is a delusion because there are no necessary relations between ideas for thought to explore.

10. The force of the doctrine that ideas are copies of impressions is thus a product of two features of the doctrine: one, the claim that ideas, as copies, not only are derived from but, more importantly, stand for impressions; and second, the conception of what impressions are. Impressions are the deliverances of what is regarded as immediate present experience, the elements in a panorama of sensation and feeling that, begging some considerable epistemological questions, one may collectively refer to as the deliverances of outer and inner sense. Though we ordinarily take ourselves by means of sense to be apprehending far more than momentary impressions—but instead material objects, other persons, landscapes, heavenly bodies, and so on—all such things, as the conception of the demon is supposed to make clear, are, in contrast with these supposed pure apprehensions of sense, dubitable. Impressions, whatever they are, however far or near they extend, are not dubitable. They are the remainder left in the experience of the moment when one has winnowed out all elements concerning which, as Descartes would have said, it is possible under careful scrutiny to generate some degree of doubt. Or as a more recent writer, C. I. Lewis, has put it,

Subtract, in what we say that we see, or hear, or otherwise learn from direct experience, *all that conceivably could be mistaken;* the remainder is the given content of the experience. . . . If there were no such hard kernel of experience—e.g., what we *see* when we think we see a deer but there is no deer—then the word 'experience' would have nothing to refer to.[10]

These demonproof data of alleged immediate experience thus represent another kind of intuition, recognized by Descartes and his rationalist philosophers as well as by his empiricist ones, though accorded by these different groups a very different significance in the development of knowledge. Though Descartes seldom refers to our apprehension of sense contents as "intuition," the reason for his not dignifying this source of information

10 *An Analysis of Knowledge and Valuation,* Bk. II, Ch. VII, Sect. 5. Italics in orig.

with this title is not any judgment of its unreliability, but a judgment of the significance of its contribution in relation to that of rational or ideational intuition.[11] So little way does sensuous intuition take us by itself, that really significant questions of knowledge, of truth and error, arise only when we move beyond its deliverances, when the data furnished by it are employed together with, and as a means for, the development of clear and distinct ideas. But limited as are the deliverances of this source, so long as one restricts oneself to them—so long, that is, as one restricts oneself to the data furnished the mind by external and internal sense and does not pass beyond them—they are as certain as intuitions of the rational and more fruitful kind. Indeed they are more certain, since rational intuition depends for its certainty, as sensuous intuition does not, upon the benevolence of God. That is why, limited as it is in its deliverances, sensuous intuition may be termed literally demonproof. It is demonproof because, as Descartes said, "the understanding can never be deceived by anything experienced if it limits itself to intuiting the thing precisely as given."

This language may serve as a reasonably good definition of what an "impression," in the formula about impressions and ideas, is taken to be. An impression is an item of experience, intuited precisely as given, unclouded and undecorated by any judgments about its relations with anything beyond itself. Its maximum, demonproof certainty is a consequence of the fact that, ostensibly, nothing is claimed for the item but its own momentary limited existence. It is what it appears to be, this being what its existence consists in, as Berkeley said generally of all of what he called "ideas." Its existence is thus incapable of being affected by anything beyond itself. It is an isolated, utterly independent item of knowledge. This is the sort of thing that every one of our ideas, as distinguished from impressions, is a copy of, that every one of them stands for. And for this reason every idea is likewise, in its own realm of being, an atom. It

11 "And here we must note that the understanding can never be deceived by anything experienced if it limits itself to *intuiting* [italics mine] the thing presented to it precisely as given . . . and does not . . . proceed to judge . . . that external things are always as they appear to be" (*Regulae*, Rule XII; N. Kemp Smith, trans.). Cf. also *Meditations* II–III.

has no necessary relations with any other ideas that could be apprehended by rational intuition. This means that the rationalist portion of the program of accounting for knowledge as the progressive expansion of intuition must be given up, and hence, if the general program is to continue at all, it must be in the truncated form of expansion of sensuous intuition. If knowledge, in a word, is seeing; and if the only kind of trustworthy seeing is sensory seeing; then the expansion of knowledge must consist in the accumulation of this kind of sights.

From this conclusion, strong or weak as it may be, follows with the most remarkable ease and simplicity all those skeptical conclusions that William James referred to regretfully as the "sweeping negations" of Hume's philosophy, including therein the classic and notorious philosophical problem of induction. Repeating again and again the now fateful question, Hume runs through the catalogue of the items of the sort that we commonly take ourselves to know, and the knowing of which we look for a theory of knowledge to illuminate, correct, rationalize, and improve. Selves or minds? Causes or powers? Events of the unobserved present or past, and of the future? Goodness or beauty? It is altogether understandable how Hume could confidently challenge all those who suppose that we do have knowledge of any of these things to explain how this knowledge is possible, when a condition of solving the riddle posed for them is commitment to the proposition that whatever is known is sensorily seen. Descartes would have been among the first to agree that if that is what the program of the cultivation and expansion of intuition is reduced to, it is at the same time reduced to immediate and total ruin.

11. What is one philosopher's "ruin," however, may be another's "positive philosophy," waiting only for the nineteenth century to confer upon it this honorific name. If intuition is confined to the sensuous, aesthetic apprehension of the objects of outer and inner sense, then the expansion of intuition will have to be the expansion of just this kind of apprehension. If knowing is sensorily seeing, then the expansion of knowledge consists in seeing more. What seemed in the seventeenth and eighteenth

centuries—regretfully to some, rejoicingly to others—grounds for "skeptical doubts concerning the operations of the understanding," were for others, in the nineteenth century, the occasion for a new positive account incorporating a transvaluation of the capacities and contributions of the understanding itself. The failure of rational intuition to transcend the alleged data of experience, inferring and divining therefrom the truth of laws, principles, hypotheses, and the existence of novel entities, was regarded largely as an occasion for congratulation rather than regret. The disarming of reason of any pretense of capacity to transcend "positive fact" was a first step toward a better understanding of what its capacities and contributions actually are.

The dictum that all ideas are logically independent, that there are hence no necessary connections between them for reason to explore, while a faithful expression of one feature of this philosophy, neglects what is regarded in this same philosophy as our capacity in thought and speech somehow to treat sets or combinations of ideas as single totalities. This capacity has customarily been treated as the capacity of the mind to form "complex ideas," as if the difference between the logic of the phrases "a complex of ideas" and "a complex idea" could safely be ignored. The host of important errors to which this presumption leads cannot be explored here. But one consequence of this capacity to treat complexes directly concerns the contribution that reason is said to make in the development of knowledge. Nearly all the words that we commonly use to convey ideas signify them in complexes. We commonly deal with these intellectual commodities in wholesale lots. The compendious reference we are able to make to the data of sense by means of these complexes introduces a valuable, indeed indispensable, economy into our thought and speech. But to take advantage of this efficiency and economy, with a minimum of error, requires a clear understanding on our part of the contents of the complexes. And this is the function that reason performs in the exploration of our ideas. What we are able to do by reason alone, without presuming to add to the fundamental data of knowledge made available through sensuous intuition, is to make explicit and clear the contents of these complexes of ideas. Reason can and does, on this view, perform an invaluable service in making explicit, in rendering accounts of, these contents. The knowledge contributed by this intellectual bookkeeping, in intuition and demonstration, though valuable, is, however, as so viewed, knowledge of the contents of these complexes alone, and not of things beyond them.

Suppose, to take the simplest kind of example, that *A* is one kind of sensory apprehension and *B* is another. We may find it convenient sometimes to refer to both these together and may think of the totality of the two as an individual thing, a *C*. Having done so we may have occasion sometimes, in the clarification of our ideas, to render an explicit account of their components and in doing so may say, for example, that a *C* is necessarily a *B*, that it is repugnant to the idea of a *C* for it not to be a *B*. That a *C* is a *B*, on such a view, is a paradigm of a necessary truth. Like all others it gives no information whatever about the apprehensions to which it collectively refers. Learning that a *C* is necessarily a *B* we learn nothing about the behavior of *A*'s and *B*'s, collectively or apart. We do not learn whether *A*'s are always accompanied by *B*'s, usually accompanied by them, seldom, or never. What we do learn, in case it has hitherto escaped our attention, is something about the ideational complex *C*, or, in the idiom of more recent empiricism, something about our language. The information yielded by rational intuition, in its concern with our ideas, is restricted to this: to what sets of data are signified by the complex ideas we form and attach to various terms. That is why Hume said that knowledge acquired by intuition and deduction is knowledge of our ideas only. It does not depend, he said, "on what is anywhere existent in the universe," and consequently, however sure and true, does not inform us in any way concerning what the character of that universe may be.

12. Some natural ways in which the methodological consequences of such a view of the capacities and contributions of reason could be worked out were helpfully exposed in the work of various nineteenth-century empiricists with special interests in the philosophy of science. An aspect of the view that becomes of considerable interest under reflection is what explanation can be given of the accepted fact that we do commonly in thought

use words to signify rich totalities of ideas rather than single ideas, and, further, since there are a vast number of possible totalities available, what explains our operating with the particular ones we do. The general answer to these combined questions given wide currency by Ernst Mach, Karl Pearson, and others of the same period was that the compendious reference made possible by these totalities contributes vastly to the economy of thought and speech, and that it is from experience itself, from the vast panorama of sensation itself, that we learn what complexes, what sets and arrays of sensations it will be most valuable in the conduct of life and the development of science for us to be able to refer to in an abbreviated way, using this kind of intellectual shorthand.

However satisfactory in the end this kind of pragmatic phenomenalism would prove to be, the positive view it provided of what would customarily be called the "origin of our complex ideas" was a contribution to the general view of reason that constituted one of the main features of classical empiricism. It helped to make understandable how rational intuition, though itself incapable, according to this theory, of adding to the sum of sensuous intuitions in which our positive knowledge of things consists, might nevertheless, be conceived as capable, in rendering accounts of the complex totalities of such intuitions with which we commonly are concerned, of performing a valuable and by no means always simple service in the development and organization of our knowledge. Critics of the general empiricist program, on the other hand, might regard the explanations offered as less a contribution than a palliative, tending to obscure difficulties in the theory of reason by borrowing credibility from a theory of ideas that was in no position to support the loan.

For behind and expressing itself in the theory of ideas was the fundamental thesis of this revised Cartesianism that knowing consists in sensuous apprehension. But if knowing, to speak in the language of one sense modality, consists in "seeing," how can we account for our presumed though doubtless incomplete knowledge of all sorts of things that, at least on a first view of the matter, we cannot claim to see?

13. In the history of empiricist philosophy, as well as in con-

temporary discussions, the problem of the unseeable has tended to divide into two parts, the difference in the treatment of which may be suggested at once by the titles, "phenomenalism" and "induction." If what has been said up to this point concerning the basic character of this philosophy is correct, the difficulties about the unseeable dealt with under these two titles are but different aspects of a single, fundamental one, namely, the need to see what must also, by basic commitments of the philosophy, be designated as unseeable. The difference in the conceived problems is this: If we suppose ourselves to be provided by sensuous intuition with direct knowledge of the character and behavior of certain kinds of objects, and even if we suppose further that intuition is competent to give us adequate knowledge of objects of *these kinds,* when we compare this domain of putative knowledge, with what we ordinarily take ourselves to be competent to know in everyday life, in the sciences and the humanities, in the various practical and technical arts and in the learned professions, one prominent feature of our supposed knowledge in these latter domains is that, at first view at least, the objects we are concerned with, about which we confidently speak, are in the main, not the kinds that are accessible to sensory inspection.

To be more specific, in order to discriminate a kind of object that can be apprehended by demonproof sensuous intuition, it is considered necessary to confine the objects of such knowledge to the impressions of outer and inner sense. This does appear to entail a vast contraction in the domain of objects accessible to human knowledge, since by far most objects, or what we take to be objects, *are literally not impressions.* Though the pain that took us to the dentist's surgery may be such an impression, the tooth he treats, the instruments he uses, and he himself are not. Similarly, though the apparent line of red whose movements we report to the oculist examining our eye may possibly be such an impression, the eye he is examining is not; nor is the light he employs in the examination; nor is he. Nor, as Descartes had argued strongly in the *Meditations,* are tables and chairs, wax and stones, and the other common material objects that we intimately know in everyday life. Nor are causes and powers that in the development of our thought about these objects we are unavoidably led, as Hume conceded, to attribute to them. Nor are those more esoteric objects—molecules, atoms, particles, electric charges—that we learn about when we study the natural sciences, nor similarly human character, personality, or will, nor political sovereignty, public opinion, or national commitment, and other similar features of our world that we learn about as we increase our understanding of ourselves and of our fellow-men individually and in groups. Nor finally are these features of individual and social action and of social institutions—goodness and badness, rightness and wrongness, justice and injustice, etc. —that are the objects of our thought in ethical and aesthetic evaluation and in moral judgment.

14. The rejoinder of the empiricist philosophy to this apparently crushing objection, though it may be spelled out in a variety of ways, is essentially that the force of the objection is due to a misunderstanding. There are, so the matter may be put, "objects" and "objects"; one must not think simply that what we call material objects are objects of exactly the same kind as the objects of sensuous apprehension, that when we use the word properly to refer to items in these two different domains, we are using it in exactly the same sense. That is why, for example, it is proper to say that we eat apples but do not eat impressions, and that, on the other hand, we know impressions by intuition, and not apples. From the point of view of knowledge, impressions, what we are able to apprehend in sensuous intuition, are objects in what we might term a "primary" or "strict" sense, while all those others of which we constantly speak are objects in a derivative or analogical sense. As previously indicated, our language of material and other scientific objects, in its reference to primary objects, functions in a very compressed way. It conveys in a kind of intellectual shorthand that an apple exists, not as an object of sensuous intuition, but primarily as a complex of possibilities of intuition, only a minute portion of which can ever be realized, but in consequence of which it is an object in a very practical sense. Thus when I judge that there is an apple on the table, I am expressing, in affirming the existence of the apple, the possibility of a vast set of primary objects which might

be known if, to speak in the language of everyday life, I should pare the apple, eat it, slice it, cook it, plant its seeds in the ground, and so on.

This has been the general pattern of rejoinder in this philosophy to the problem of the knowledge of unseeable objects as it pertains to the existence of kinds of objects, kinds of abstract entities. Leaving aside the question whether this kind of rejoinder, can be successfully made—and the prevailing judgment is that it cannot—the program it involves has a consequence most important for understanding the philosophical problem of induction. In a word, it shifts the burden of the general problem of the unseeable from one kind of unseeable object to another. Though the reasons advanced for their inaccessibility to our sensuous intuition are different, yesterday's or tomorrow's impressions, as well as any day's merely possible impressions, are just as certainly and necessarily incapable of being sensed as today's apples, gamma rays, or electromagnetic fields of force. And one thing obvious to both partisans and critics of this way of attempting to account for unsensed objects is that any such account must appeal, and in a wholesale way, to past and future impressions as well as present ones, and to possible impressions, or the possibility of impressions, as well as to actual ones. A common place in which the need for such an appeal becomes prominent in a variety of versions of this philosophy is in the introduction of something corresponding to the idea of power in Locke's philosophy, in accounting for the idea of what he suggested might be referred to as "mediately perceivable" secondary qualities in this early anticipation of the logical construction of material objects.

15. As will be observed immediately in the next chapter, the manner in which the need for reference to unseeable entities emerges in this philosophy, as well as the fact that it does emerge, is of great importance for the problem of induction. All that needs to be emphasized at this point is that it does emerge. And since it does, it must be regarded as problematical how much has been achieved in this philosophy by the suppression of the need at one place, when the consequence is having it emerge, simply in a transmuted form, in another. For according to the

philosophical principles that have been described here as motivating and informing this philosophy, and leading in it to the transformation of the conception of cognitive intuition, any kind of entity or state that cannot be apprehended in sensuous intuition not only is incapable of being known, it is also incapable of being thought. For in order for us to be capable of thinking of any kind of entity or state, we must first know that kind in experience, have direct sensory knowledge of a specimen of it. And who is going to claim that he can sense the past or the future, or, after the brilliant exposition of the matter by Hume, that he can sense necessities, powers, or possibilities?

Often, when a difficulty of a certain sort, upon being treated in one way in a philosophical program emerges later in a transmuted form, calling for a somewhat different treatment, it is a signal that beneath both these forms lies a more fundamental difficulty that needs to be dealt with correspondingly in a more fundamental way. The original problem of seeing the unseeable and its treatment in phenomenalism, and its transmuted form in the problem of induction, constitute such a case. Both these problems, appearing in different versions of the Cartesian philosophy, are faces of a fundamental difficulty in that philosophy. That is the difficulty of "justifying" knowledge claims in the Cartesian philosophy, or, as it may be put, difficulty of comprehending how the "justification" of anything but possibly the most limited and trivial knowledge claims could be effected in this philosophy. But exposition of this matter must await further elucidation of the form this difficulty assumes in the familiar problem of induction.

CHAPTER 2

The Shaping of the Problem

1. The characterization of the problem of induction given in the preceding chapter is not the usual one. There the problem was described as one facet of a more general difficulty, that of seeing the unseeable, or, more exactly, of showing how, in a philosophy in which knowing is identified with sensuous apprehension, what cannot be sensed can nevertheless be known. This characterization, if sound, provides an explanation of the uniform failure of a variety of philosophers to devise any widely accepted solution for the problem, an explanation that should be helpful in relieving others of the constraint to expend still more effort in that cause. For if at bottom what one is setting out to do in attempting to solve this problem is to devise some way in which the unseeable may reasonably be held to be capable of being seen, then what one is attempting to do is as paradoxical, impossible, and, when it is understood, as senseless, as we now know was the project of squaring the circle, upon which many gifted men, including Hobbes, expended so much effort.

But in order for this characterization to have this effect it needs first to be established as a sound one. And as a first step toward this end it needs to be explained how a problem that normally is not conceived in these terms is nevertheless essentially of this character.

2. The problem of how to see the unseeable arises in the empiricist philosophy with the disarming of reason in that philosophy. Persuaded by, among other things, the difficulties encountered by the original Cartesian philosophy, that it is not possible

to succeed in the project of understanding knowledge as a systematic elaboration of *rational* intuition, the empiricist philosophers nevertheless remained dedicated to the general Cartesian project of understanding knowledge in personal intuitionist terms. They were thus led to restrict intuition, in its capacity to yield knowledge, to what were taken to be the direct revelations of sense. And therewith arose a problem. How, on the basis of the minute bits of information that could be plausibly held to be provided by this source, could we proceed to knowledge about matters clearly transcending it? Supposing such knowledge to be possible, it would presumably have to be validated by some procedure in which, beginning with what is known directly in sense, we reason or infer to what is not. But reason, rational intuition and demonstration, having been effectively disarmed, and the disarmament ratified in the doctrine about the nature of our ideas, how, as Hume asked, shall one go about providing a ground for this "inference," "argument," or "reasoning" from "experience"? Put in other terms, since knowledge is acquired by intuition, since expansion of knowledge entails expansion of intuition, what can be produced and validated as a means by which intuition can be expanded beyond the yield of sensuous apprehension? Quite clearly the answer in the end has got to be, "Nothing." But if, for the moment, one does not anticipate this conclusion and supposes that such means of expanding intuition may yet be possible, one thing that can be demonstrated is a fundamental need for means of a particular sort. If, proceeding along these lines, one is to be able to account for human knowledge, if one is to be able to illuminate and reconstruct the vast system of human belief, practice, presumption, and reasoned judgment that is the object of our philosophical study, we shall need for the purpose *general* intuition expanders, general inference warrants or licenses, general relations of the sort that Hume called "cause and effect." What has been taken, on the one hand, as the domain of sure knowledge, and what, on the other hand, is the general character of the system of knowledge which has to be accounted for—these determine in an important way the character that a fundamental class of these intuition expanders must have. For the sure base from which we must proceed, if such proceeding is possible, is what may plausibly be regarded as deliverances of sensuous intuition which in their pellucidity and certainty are secure against the most powerful and cunning demon; and these have been concluded to be, not the discernment of the existence and character of objects enduring in time and states of affairs extended in space, but the realization of certain sensory characters in the immediate forum of sense. Furthermore, as the matter is elaborated in the theory of ideas, since it is to the realization of such characters that our sensory knowledge is confined, so likewise confined to them is the vocabulary of our thought, so that it is in terms of this vocabulary that any intuition expanders that we can possibly understand and employ must speak. In order to develop on this basis anything that can be viewed as a rational reconstruction of our knowledge of things, the account of things—including pre-eminently the homely material things of everyday life—must be rendered in terms of such objects.

3. It is at this point, in a variety of ways, that the problem of seeing the unseeable begins to take on the more familiar aspect of generalization which we commonly associate with the terms "induction" and "inductive" in their application to reasoning and method. Speaking in the philosophical idiom of an earlier time, making its appearance is the question of universals in what is at heart a nominalist philosophy. One place at which the question arises, one place at which it becomes immediately apparent that means of intuition expansion must be provided of a general sort, is at what is commonly and naturally the first step in such a philosophy, namely, giving account of our common-sense knowledge of and capacity to deal with material objects. In a variety of ways, from Locke's recognition that "powers make a great part of our complex ideas of substances" to the elaborate discussion by Locke's contemporary descendants of "disposition terms," philosophers of this persuasion have shown their understanding that a rendering of an account of our knowledge of material objects in terms of a vocabulary borrowed from and apt for discriminable items of sensory experience will require the introduction of general means of expanding intuition, gen-

eral formulae of some kind expressing how one such apprehended item serves as reliable indication of the apprehension or accessibility to apprehension of another.

Given the need for intuition expanders, and given the determination, by the basic skepticism formulated in the theory of ideas, that these expanders must be expressed in terms of the impressions of inner and outer sense, including their sensible associations, nothing further is required to determine that the required expanders shall be assertions of, beliefs about, habits expressing presumptions concerning, general associations of these impressions. It would be too strong a statement that by these considerations it is determined in a strict logical way that the intuition expanders shall be of this sort. Rather what is logically determined by the theory of ideas, if it is taken seriously and strictly, is that there are no expanders and that hence the expansion of knowledge beyond the impressions of sense is quite impossible. The unseeable cannot be thought, and hence not asked about. There can be no problem of induction because one cannot understand what that is—the unseen—with which the problem is concerned. But this is not the way the game is played out in this philosophy, and in understanding the problem, as it finds expression in the philosophy, it is necessary to let the game take its course. Doing so, supposing that the expansion of intuition can be conceived and possibly effected, there are no remotely plausible candidates for the role except ones which do express associations of impressions, and, if these are to yield anything like our knowledge of objects and states in the world, beginning with the material objects of everyday life, again there are no remotely plausible candidates except those that express associations that are general.

4. What performed the role of general intuition expanders in the original philosophy of Descartes were ideas, purged by reflection of unclarity and indistinctness. The need remaining, but ideas having been rendered incapable of filling it, the resource appealed to, and the study of which consequently came to dominate the analysis of knowledge in this philosophy, was what Hume called the relation of cause and effect; in more modern terminology, laws and general rules of probability. What-

ever it is that can serve as an intuition expander, enabling us to pass from knowledge of some sensed item A to knowledge of some unsensed item B, will by that fact signify some kind of connection between A and B. But though B is as a matter of contingent fact unsensed, it cannot be so in principle, i.e., necessarily. Only items of a kind that *can* be sensed, even if they as a matter of fact are not, can be represented by our ideas, can, by the restrictions set by the theory of ideas, be the objects of our thought. Leaving aside the question how, on such a theory, there can be an idea of the "unsensed," since what is unsensed is, under that description, necessarily not sensed, we may note that whatever B is, it must, no less than A, be a possible impression or sensory apprehension, or a set of such apprehensions.

To be an intuition expander in this philosophy, then, the minimum requirement is that it signify a connection between some sensible A and some sensible B. But the resources of expansion that in a less severely positivistic philosophy, like that of Descartes, would have been referred to as our "ideas" of material objects, provide, not just a connection between a sensed A and something unsensed. Being general ideas, associated in language with common names, they signify *general* connections, general capacities to employ sensed A's as grounds in a variety of circumstances for conclusions about the unsensed. However it is represented, we do have such a capacity. In learning to employ our common-sense language, we are equipped with a variety of general responses to the stimuli of sense through which, as we would express it in that language, we are informed of the existence and character of material things, other living creatures and persons. If this resource of expansion is to be provided for in this philosophy, it is necessary, not only that there be intuition expanders signifying connections between sensory impressions, but also that the expanders at the very base of our knowledge, essential to our knowledge of such objects, signify connections that are general in character.[1]

[1] This point has been rediscovered and expressed in a variety of ways in recent philosophy, most prominently in the discovery that the conditional statements expressing the kind of relations necessary for giving an account of the possibilities of sensation in material objects cannot be understood apart from the lawlike universals and general probability rules that serve as their

5. It is thus that in the reconstruction of our knowledge from an empiricist point of view the question of the validity of phenomenal generals, generals associating impressions either in a strictly universal or in a probability way, becomes a matter of first-order business. Given the specific intuition-expanding function which these phenomenal generals were needed to perform in licensing actual and possible inferences between phenomenal grounds and phenomenal conclusions, they could be viewed in a variety of ways. The essential requirement was that the warrants or licenses they represented be general, and that the items connected by them be phenomenal. Consistently with this requirement they might be treated as habits or customs, as propositions or judgments, or simply as rules of inference.

It is not, of course, that it is solely in connection with our knowledge of material objects that the question of the validity of these generals arises in an important way. It is, rather, that in this connection, as the theory proceeds, the question is immediate, prominent, and pressing, presenting, as it were, an experiment that is crucial for the success of the program in two ways. First, a theory hardly can presume to explain our knowledge of such esoteric entities as alpha particles and gamma rays, or, in another domain, the public will or the common good, if it cannot rea-

---

grounds, that, as C. I. Lewis early formulated the matter, the conditional terminating judgments required in carrying out an analysis in expressive language of objective statements are "implicitly general" (*Analysis*, Bk. II, Ch. VIII, Sect. 8).

The general pattern of thought leading from sense data to phenomenal generals has been retraced by a variety of writers from the time of Berkeley and Hume, but nowhere in recent philosophy, in the judgment of this writer, with the excellence of Lewis. Lewis is notable both for the strength of grounds he offers for the philosophical view in question, and for the clarity and candor with which he faces and explores its difficulties. An oddity of the presentation of his views, to which no consideration may be given here, is the strong resistance he offers to the association of his position wth the name of phenomenalism (*Analysis*, Bk. II, Ch. VII, Sect. 6, n. 2 and Sect. 11). Among other notable contributions to the discussion of this matter were William Kneale's *Probability and Induction* and Rudolf Carnap's "Testability and Meaning" and "On Inductive Logic," *Philosophy of Science* (1936 and 1945). Readers not yet prepared for writing of this difficulty and technicality may find a useful introduction to it in the clear and sympathetic presentation of empiricist-analytic philosophy in the early chapters of John Hospers' *An Introduction to Philosophical Analysis*.

sonably explain the homely knowledge of material objects, and bodies generally, in dependence upon which the existence of these more elusive entities must be discerned. And second, it is in terms of exactly the same sort of general connections between phenomenal items that it is proposed, in this philosophical program, eventually to reconstruct what is valid in all our putative thought and knowledge of entities that are not impressions, not objects of direct sensuous intuition. The treatment of material objects in terms of the coherence and constancy of impressions (Hume) or the permanent possibility of sensations (Mill) is a model of the procedure to be followed with living creatures and persons, and with insensible entities generally, be they scientific, psychological, moral, or social. Like "apple" and "pear," expressions like "man," "dog," "goodness," "justice," "the popular will," and "positive charge" will have to turn out to be very complex and subtle *façons de parler;* and one important thing that they will be discovered to convey, sometimes in a most suppressed and deceptive way, are a vast number of phenomenal generals expressing the general possibilities of sensation and feelings in which, according to this philosophy, the significance of such expressions must consist.

6. This being so, a first crucial question for this philosophical program is whether these phenomenal generals, these general connections of probability or necessity can be depended upon to expand intuition in the desired way. To do so they must enable us in reasoning from experience to proceed from sensed A's to unsensed (though sensible) B's; and to do this and yet fit the requirements of this step-by-step theory of knowledge they must themselves be properly established; and this requires, in turn, that they be established independently of information about any B's that are to be the subject of conclusions drawn by means of them.

One may note here, for later reference, the remarkable similarity between this question about the trust in phenomenal generals arrived at by induction which arises as first-order business in the empiricist philosophy, and the question about trust in intuitions arrived at by clear and distinct ideas, which arises in the philosophy of Descartes. In effect, the empiricist proposes, beginning with certain immediate sensibles of experience, namely, those which are actually sensed, to show how our knowledge of external objects can be developed as an elaborate inference concerning the associations, and hence the accessibilities of these and like sensibles, provided the phenomenal generals conveying these associations can be established as a conclusion from the actually sensed sensibles, without dependence upon the phenomenal generals themselves. Similarly, Descartes proposed, beginning with immediate certainties of consciousness, which, except for the knowledge of the existence of self, were substantially those of the empiricist, to show how knowledge of external objects could be developed as intuitions made possible by clear and distinct ideas, provided that the truth-bearing character of such ideas could be established without dependence upon the ideas themselves.

7. Although at a first, casual view it may appear that the phenomenal generals can perform the function set for them in the empiricist philosophy, this appearance, as Hume showed, can easily be penetrated. The supposition that they can do this has to be mistaken, if the main elements of the philosophy, as described above, are accepted. If to know is to apprehend in sensory intuition, then what is not so apprehended is not known, and there is no procedure of reasoning or deduction, no method whatever, by means of which one can extend one's knowledge beyond these defined limits. Should one be inclined to suppose that it is possible by deduction from information about the character of sensed objects to establish conclusions concerning unsensed ones, one need only reflect that in order to establish a conclusion about the character of any object, the report of that character must be included in the premises, and in order for the premises to be known, as they must be, the character in question must have been apprehended by sensuous intuition in the first place.

This aspect of reasoning from empirical data employing relations of necessity or probability has been a disturbing yet necessary element in the empiricist account of such reasoning since it was elaborated by Hume in connection with his extensive analysis of the relation of cause and effect. An alleged causal connection between any sensed A and any unsensed B cannot serve to ground reasoning from *A* to *B,* said Hume, for the assertion that *A* causes *B,* or is caused by *B,* is really a statement to the effect that every *A* is followed by, or preceded by, a *B;* and this could itself be known only if *B* were itself apprehended in the case in question. Hume's analysis of causation thus serves to clinch his point that an attempt to establish by reasoning from experience that some *B* is of a certain character must first establish this fact in order to employ the premises of the reasoning, and hence must fail because of circularity. In the next century John Stuart Mill confronted the same difficulty in an even simpler form in his discussion of the alleged circularity of the syllogism.[2] Mill moved to absolve the syllogism of this charge by adopting an interpretation of general propositions employed as covering premises in the syllogism that takes them to be something other than summary statements concerning the conforming character of the individual instances covered by them. Here, as at other places in his philosophy, Mill demonstrated his capacity to react to the realities of a philosophical problem at the expense of the consistency with which he adhered to the basic empiricist principles upon which his philosophy rested. Since nothing but a radical revision of these principles would have been adequate to the magnitude of the problem, all that could be achieved by his move was a displacement of the difficulty, not a resolution. There was now the problem of how the generals, when viewed as formulae for effecting inferences from particulars to particulars, could be properly established, and the basic difficulty about the expansion of intuition that had taken one form in the study of deductive reasoning now emerged in a more familiar form, that usually identified as the problem of induction.

8. If the characterization of the problem of induction given here is a sound one, the negative result arrived at by Hume and many subsequent writers in their exploration of the justification of the phenomenal generals was a foregone conclusion. It is for this reason that, as was stated at the beginning of this chapter, it is of first importance in understanding the problem for one to see embedded in it the problem of seeing the unseeable. The

2 *A System of Logic,* Bk. II, Ch. III.

intractable difficulties exposed by Hume in attempts to account for our knowledge of the phenomenal generals all derive from the fact that within the philosophical matrix in which these attempts were considered, knowledge of these generals required that somehow the unseeable should be seen. The source of the problem thus lies in a certain basic philosophical position—itself a skeptical counterattack mounted within Cartesianism against Descartes's own attempts to dispel skepticism—which dictated that this impossible feat must be accomplished. From the time of Hume's discussion of our knowledge of causes, to the present day, when the same philosophical concerns are now expressed in the language of the "projectibility" of predicates, at the heart of these concerns, though obscured to most who express them by much intriguing logical embroidery, lies this elemental and obdurate paradox.

9. But if the arguments that take their start in an examination of our knowledge of laws, generalizations, and the rest, are circuitous routes to a conclusion already dictated in this philosophy by simpler considerations, the arguments nevertheless serve an important philosophical purpose. This is in making clear, in a way unmistakable and unforgettable to one who follows them seriously, how essential the aspect of generality is in our language, our thought, and our responses to sensory cues. As Hume saw it, our dependence upon items of knowledge, real or supposed, exhibiting this aspect of generality is revealed in the dependence of all "conclusions from experience" upon the relation of cause and effect. This assessment of the role of the relation of cause and effect, and the generality it represents, is an overstatement, even when the kind of general covering premise Hume had in mind under the title of this relation is construed very broadly so as to include general connections of a merely statistical or probability kind. Hume advances no ground sufficient to prevent some "conclusions from experience" being drawn without the employment of these general covering premises, for example, conclusions in which, to use syllogistic language, the middle term is a singular one.[3]

---

[3] Says Hume in his 1740 *Abstract of the Treatise:* " 'Tis evident, that all reasonings concerning *matter of fact* are founded on the relation of cause and

Viewed in the perspective of the large philosophical issues with which Hume was concerned, however, this exaggeration on his part represents a very minor error. If what one is concerned with is not what form a conclusion could conceivably take and still be a conclusion from experience, but rather what form must they in the main have if by means of them, starting from some alleged basic sensory intuitive truths, one is to be able to reconstruct and thus show the essential soundness of what we take, in everyday life and the sciences, to be knowledge of things, then it is clear that the general covering premises Hume concentrated upon are of overriding importance. They are important not only because the reasoning they are employed to validate represents a natural form, so essential to our knowledge that any theory of knowledge in which it did not occupy a major position would be hopelessly deficient. They are important also because, as has already been observed, given the category of beginnings in which Hume and fellow empiricists conceived the basis of our knowledge of the world to consist, and given the general structure of the knowledge which according to the theory must somehow emerge from this basis, the emergence could take place, and with it the phenomenalist reconstruction which this emergence entailed, only by means of a large-scale employment of such phenomenal-general principles and premises. One does not need to endorse the empiricist program to see in the requirement of generality in the intellectual instruments that are to effect the passage from primitive sensory intuitions to a knowledge of material things, living creatures, and persons a recognition that the common-sense conceptions with which we are equipped when we master the common-sense language dictate complex general connections

---

effect, and that we can never infer the existence of one object from another unless they be connected together, either mediately or immediately" (p. 11). Cf. also *Enquiry*, Sect. 22, pp. 22–23; *Treatise*, Bk. I, Pt. III, Sect. II, pp. 73–74.

But where is the causal connection—and that is what Hume means by "connected" in the above passage—in such "reasonings" from experience as the following? That house is 406 Elm Street; but 406 Elm Street is a pre-fab; therefore that house must be a pre-fab. Or, closer to the "data" of experience: A red datum has just now appeared in my visual field; promptly after the appearance of this red datum, a blue datum will appear; therefore a blue datum will promptly appear in my visual field.

among the sensory clues that stimulate and guide our employment of them. There is far more to apples and pears, desks and chairs, for example, than permanent possibilities of sensation, but an important part of our mastery of the language of these common names is an ability to use them in response to sensory cues and to derive from them expectations of further sensory responses. It is an altogether natural error, in a certain kind of theory of knowledge, for one to attempt to understand the information and mastery that is represented in this feature of our language by conceiving this response to sensory cues as a kind of direct knowledge of the cues, and our knowledge of further things as inferences from these to the possibility of others.

That this view involved a most serious misconception of the way this information and mastery is contained in and transmitted by our common-sense language is of less importance at this juncture than the recognition in the view that somehow in articulating the knowledge we convey in this language a place must be found for these important features. However it is best to conceive of the matter, however it might be thought to be in an "ideal language," in the actual languages we speak and employ in our commerce with homely material objects, other living creatures, and persons, a mastery of words is also in a most important intellectual way a mastery of the kind of entities or creatures represented by them; and *general* words represent a *general* mastery. Like any other inadequate theory, this theory, though obscuring certain features of its objects, serves also to call attention to these objects. In calling attention to the battery of general responses to sensory cues built into our common-sense language, the theory also helps to emphasize, as Descartes and the other rationalists emphasized in their own way, that, whatever may be the proper way to conceive of the significance of these cues in the development of knowledge, knowledge requires at the outset an advance from them. If the cues themselves be thought to represent knowledge of a kind, knowledge of things, creatures, and persons is never simply this kind, but something far transcending it. So that the question, as Kant would have said, in accounting for our knowledge of those further objects, supposing that we have such knowledge, is not whether in this respect we effect a transcendence of sense, but how we do. The skeptical argument emphasizing the combined necessity and impossibility of knowledge of the phenomenal generals thus helped to make plain in very immediate and specific terms—for example, in connection with simple perceptual knowledge—the far-reaching importance and extent of this transcendence.

10. On the other side of the ledger, the circuitous argument through laws, generalization, and so on which has become canonical in formulations of the problem of induction has had important deleterious effects. The first of these to be noted is the effect of the argument in promulgating a certain view of laws, probability judgments, and other similar epistemic judgments and general rules that are essential ingredients of knowledge. For convenience of discussion it will be well to concentrate here upon that version of the argument which treats phenomenal generals as statements or propositions, rather than as habits, customs, rules, etc. The view which the argument serves to promulgate is, then, that laws, general probability judgments, and other similar epistemic rules, are properly viewed as phenomenal generals, that it is in terms of statements conveying the phenomenal association of phenomenal entities that the aspect of generality in them that is so great a part of our knowledge is to be understood. The problem of establishing these statements arose in connection with the difficulties encountered in attempting to show that the observed associations of entities we are interested in could be taken as models for statements concerning unexamined cases of these entities. What stands between us and the establishment of laws and probability statements about the occurrence of B's with A's, for example, is taken to be the limitation of our powers of inspection, the shortness of our vision. We cannot establish in a direct, straightforward way that crows are uniformly black, or that the character "black" may be associated with "crow" with a probability of .95, because, not being gods, we cannot possibly see all the collection of crows, or crow-events, to which such general statements apply. For this reason we must have recourse to induction. What induction can then do, if it can somehow be justified, is to repair the lack in our knowledge by

providing assurances that the uninspected cases are like those "of which we have had experience" and thus that the associations that are accessible to inspection may be taken as models of what holds generally.

The justification of the general statements conveying these associations was a matter of crucial, first-order business in this philosophy because, for reasons already explained, it was essential to the phenomenalist program to which this philosophy was committed by its theory of ideas. The title "phenomenalist" is meant here to be construed widely, to apply to the kind of view of our language, discourse, and thought which holds that our discourse about all things whatsoever, to the extent that it is legitimate, can be translated without a remainder into discourse mentioning only items of a directly observable or sensuously apprehensible kind. The general intentions of the program permitted latitude in the determination of the domain of the directly observable, the currency in terms of which in the end all intellectual accounts were to be rendered; and the choice has varied widely, from the more traditional "ideas" or "impressions" of sense, through the "practical consequences" and "conceivable experimental phenomena" of Peirce, to the "operations," "operational results," and "observable thing-predicates" of more recent scientific and empiricist philosophy.

The common, traditional route to the problem of induction served to promulgate an extensional, phenomenalist view of laws, probability judgments, and other epistemic judgments and rules, for the same reason that the recognition of the aspect of generality in our knowledge and thought in this philosophy for the most part took this form. Both were expressions of a fundamentally phenomenalist philosophy, part of the program of reduction and translation represented by that philosophy. In the execution of the program of showing that apparent talk about insensibles can always be shown to be somehow, however disguised and indirect, talk about sensibles, it was necessary at once, in recognition of the general mastery represented by our terms referring to material things, living creatures, and persons, to provide some kind of general vehicle of reasoning or inference in which what is essential to this mastery might be reproduced. But these vehicles, unlike the clear and distinct ideas which performed a similar function for the rationalist, had themselves to be wholly accountable, wholly refundable, in terms of the basic sensory elements recognized in this philosophy. As general propositions they had to live up to the requirement which Russell expressed vividly, though with some untidiness, in *The Problems of Philosophy* in the dictum, "Every proposition which we can understand must be composed wholly of constituents with which we are acquainted." [4] The natural consequence of Hume's semantic analysis of the idea of cause, as generations of commentators have observed, is a "constancy" theory of laws, a view that scientific laws and other similar very strict epistemic rules express constant associations of objects, states, or events. And the natural accompaniment of this interpretation, applied to probability judgments and similar less strict general epistemic rules, is an attempt to construe these as expressing associations of a less constant kind, is, in short, an attempt to assimilate these to statistical statements in one or another version of the "frequency" theory of probability.

There is perhaps an air of paradox in the claim that a path of reasoning that led to a conclusion widely regarded as unacceptable, or at least an unhappy one, could serve to promulgate and win acceptance for some of the very views that were instrumental in reaching that conclusion. But the paradox is superficial. Often the repeated passage through certain steps in a series of frustratingly unsuccessful attempts to solve a problem confirms us in a disposition to continue making just those moves which prevent our reaching a solution. Our attention is so concentrated upon the frustrating outcome, upon the place where our progress is blocked, that we are led to give insufficient attention to some of the early steps which led us to this outcome. In consequence of this inattentiveness, more or less thoughtlessly we become more and more committed, more and more determined to make those perhaps fatal steps. It is in this fashion that the problem of induction, waiting sphinxlike at the end of the road of the skeptical argument, by its spectacular intractability contributed to the currency and acceptance of the extensional, phenomenalist

4 Ch. V, p. 91.

way of conceiving laws and judgments of probability. It has been the object of repeated exhibitions of this way of thinking about these subjects, accompanied almost uniformly by the presumption that this way is in no way responsible for the problem, being instead part of the logical background, neutral as the multiplication table, necessary only for disclosing what are independent philosophical difficulties.

11. The subjects of laws, probability judgments, and other more or less general epistemic rules are not the only ones the understanding of which has been seriously impaired by the phenomenalist, reductionist, and in the end skeptical cast of empiricist thought. They are just the topics most closely allied with induction. The philosophical machine, which applied to one set of materials produces the view of laws as statements of the regular association of events mentioned in the statement, needs very little adjustment, when applied to a different set, now ethical, to produce the view that general ethical statements about the good and the bad are statements describing, in wholly "naturalistic" terms, the kind of things people prefer, find satisfying. The analogy can easily be extended to apply to other important topics, in mathematics and the physical sciences, in individual and social psychology, in the social sciences generally, and in politics and jurisprudence. Over all of these applications of the positive philosophy to the project of understanding our knowledge and practice in such areas constantly hung like a specter the inductive problem, the problem of how in the end the general statements of association favored as means of explication in this philosophy were to be justified. But before meeting and dealing with the specter there was a prior question that it is now clear was very much in need of an answer. Even supposing that the statements of association upon which so much dependence was put could be justified, would they be adequate to the job assigned to them? Would the items explicated in terms of them, laws and general probability statements, for example, be capable, as so interpreted, of performing the essential roles they have in the system, or the various systems, of human knowledge?

12. With respect to the particular topics just mentioned there is now an abundance of evidence available, much of it deriving

from discussions of the past fifty years. It appears fairly clear that the understanding of laws by philosophers has suffered from a too exclusive concentration of attention upon laws themselves, upon general statements or epistemic rules of this very strict, apparently exceptionless kind, at the expense of the less strict sort exemplified by general judgments of probability and loose common-sense beliefs that we constantly rely on concerning what can "normally," "reasonably," or "for the most part" be expected as the outcome of a certain type of event or state of affairs. For with statements or rules of the less strict sort, the difficulties of the mode of interpretation inspired by this philosophy were more immediately obvious. Almost a century ago Peirce was alive to the serious problems generated by the attempt to treat these as judgments about associations of events that will display themselves in extended series of trials. Attracted to the frequency view of probability by his empiricist and scientific leanings, and repelled by the paradoxes and subjectivism to which the classical—what he called "conceptualist"—alternative seemed to lead, Peirce was nevertheless alert to the *prima facie* wide divergence between judgments of probability, as we make them and depend upon them, and statements of relative frequencies that will be approximated in some indefinitely extended long run. The difficulty represented by this divergence he attempted to resolve by discerning, in his social theory of logic, a fundamental though somewhat latent interest in all of us, when we make such judgments, in what the future will reveal in the way of realized frequencies, if not to us, to some race of sentient beings persisting without limits in time, and with whom in some Kantian fashion we may be conceived to form, as it were, a community of judgers. This way of elucidating what we are up to when we make judgments of probability, which Peirce's friend James might have seized upon as another "practical" consequence of theism, seems to have satisfied few except possibly Peirce himself.[5]

During much of the time from Peirce to the present the diffi-

5 C. S. Peirce, *Collected Papers,* 2.652–655; 5.341–357. For some critical comment upon the problem and upon Peirce's proposed solution see: W. Kneale, *Probability and Induction;* D. C. Williams, "On the Derivation of Probabilities from Frequencies," *Phil. and Phenom. Res.* (1945), and *The Ground of Induction;* and F. L. Will, "The Preferability of Probable Beliefs" (1965).

culties of the frequency theory of probability were not a matter of major concern, just as the theory itself was not a matter of major interest. With the resurgence of empiricist philosophy in the fourth decade of this century, however, came a resurgence of the theory and a quickening of concern with its problems.[6] Until recently the most influential response to these problems was the view, elaborated in detail by Rudolf Carnap, that these difficulties stemmed chiefly from the attempt to make do with one conception of probability where two radically different conceptions, one logical and one empirical, are called for.[7] The effects of this remedy for illnesses in the empiricist program can hardly be encouraging for the program. To the extent that the account of what was advanced as "logical" probability can be given in purely logical, semantical terms—and this is itself a controversial matter—the remedy appears to be an implantation into an intended empiricist philosophy of basically rationalist conceptions, from which operation the most serious rejection symptoms must be expected to ensue. And to the extent that the account of this probability is conceded to appeal, beyond purely formal, logical considerations, to broad, complex ones of the kind that Carnap called "pragmatic," its appearance of supporting the empiricist account of probability by providing a purely logical adjunct and complement to it is rapidly dissipated.[8] The reaction of disillusioned formalists now to the rediscovery that more is required in the intellectual funding of a probability judgment than counting the sides of a die or the possible state descriptions provided in a given universe of discourse has been to divest themselves as much as possible from a consideration of the vast complexity of factors to which probability, conceived as a measure of rational credibility or weight of evidence, must be conceived as relevant, and to concentrate upon the conditions which

[6] Some further important references are: R. von Mises, *Probability, Statistics, and Truth*; H. Reichenbach, *Experience and Prediction*; "Kausalität und Wahrscheinlichkeit," *Erkenntnis* (1930–1931); "Die Logischen Grundlagen des Wahrscheinlichkeitsbegriffs," *Erkenntnis* (1932–1933), trans. in H. Feigl and W. Sellars, eds., *Readings in Philosophical Analysis*; and *The Theory of Probability*; E. Nagel, *Principles of the Theory of Probability*.

[7] *Logical Foundations of Probability*.

[8] *The Continuum of Inductive Methods*.

a disposition of one's supply of confidence, in a given kind of situation, however subjective that disposition may be, must satisfy in order to be logically consistent. Though in some respects the limitation thus prescribed on the intellectual reach of probability theory is a valuable one, carrying with it in a pronounced way the recognition of the limitation of the kind of judgment which conventionally recognized formal considerations can validate, to the extent that it suggests that actual assessments of probability must be subjective in any pejorative sense, any sense beyond that of being not purely formal and mathematical, it must be regarded as a skeptical overreaction to the situation, one that however philosophically titillating, is no more exciting in this respect than Hume's pronouncements two hundred years ago, and, in relation to the broad facts of the case, no more justified.[9]

13. With respect to laws, the broad and deep grounds in this philosophy which argued for an extensional, quasi-statistical, "constancy" interpretation of these were strongly reinforced by the obvious and very deceptive analogy between laws and extensional universal statements, for which there were available well-developed formal deductive techniques in accepted extensional logic. The fact that a well-developed formalism for this latter type of statement was available provided a strong natural incentive for philosophers to follow the lead of this analogy and essay a treatment of laws along these lines. When the appeal of this available formalism was joined to the compelling motive for extensionality that derived directly from the theory of ideas, the joint attraction generated for some form of "constancy" theory of laws came to seem almost irresistible.

And up to a point the fit of the theory to its subject was remarkable.[10] Though from time to time difficulties in this way of

9 Because a more extended discussion of the issues that surfaced in the philosophical theory of probability is not essential to the development of the main themes of this book, and may even detract from it, further comment upon these issues is sequestered, for those who wish to peruse the topic a step further, in an Appendix at the end of the book.

10 In the case of ethical principles and moral and legal rules, the *prima facie* fit of the model was much less close and the dangers of corresponding

viewing laws forced themselves upon the attention of philosophers, it was natural for advocates of the view to attempt to minimize these, to consider that they must be difficulties of detail rather than of fundamental principle.[11] For one thing, the theory fit so well at some points, it provided so easy and simple an account of the way laws are employed to draw inferences from observed to unobserved facts, that, as in the case of the early geocentric astronomy, it was difficult to think that a relatively few discrepancies, like the aberrant motions of the planets, would, when properly understood, call, not for some ingenious emendation of the apparently successful theory, but for its rejection in favor of one radically different. And for another thing, so successful in the elaboration of an increasingly formal, mathematical logic had been the paradigm that was at the heart of this theory, that it seemed to many that the theory carried with it the authority of modern logic, so that defection from the view seemed to amount to a flouting of that authority itself. This, however, was a mistake, or at least a vast oversimplification of a complex matter. For the important question was not one of the internal adequacy of the systematic elaboration of certain logical forms that constituted the core of modern logic. It was a question of the applicability of some of these forms in the elucidation of certain kinds of expression, the employment of which in statement and reasoning is a fundamental feature of scientific knowledge. A recognition and admiration of the achievements of modern logic by no means committed one to the view that laws could or must be construed in terms of logical forms with which

---

deception (a species of naturalism) much reduced, though not completely obliterated. Cf. M. Schlick, *Problems of Ethics,* Ch. I; A. Edel, "Naturalism and Ethical Theory," in Y. H. Krikorian, ed., *Naturalism and the Human Spirit.*

11 In the face of the difficulties, the strong but specious attractions of the basic theory led to the question of the character of scientific laws and their differences between extensional universal statements being transformed (and distorted) into the question of what distinguishes those extensional universals which are laws, or lawlike, from those which are not. This was somewhat like the one-time puzzle that confronted astronomers when, viewing the planets as stars and hence implicated with them in the motion of the heavens, they were led to ask what accounts for the fact that circular motions of these particular stars persistently display aberrations.

they are in some respects similar, in spite of what many seem at one time to have thought. There was no more foundation for this supposition than for the corresponding one, to which many also were prone, that the celebrated truth-functional analysis in the logic of compound statements somehow committed one to the adequacy of this way of looking generally at conditional or hypothetical statements.

14. The discrepancy between theory and fact in the empiricist account of laws, though less immediately obvious than that in the account of probability, was no less serious and the consequence of the same basic features in the philosophy. In this case the discrepancy lay between laws, as they are understood and employed, particularly in scientific inquiry and technical practice, and the extensional analogues of these that this philosophy, by its theory of ideas, was led to advance in their place. It was a discrepancy between a law, for example, asserting, no doubt under the asumption of various loosely defined background conditions, that A's are uniformly B, and the statement that under these conditions all A's whatsoever are B, where the "are" is taken in its logical timeless sense, and "all" is taken in the common logical fashion as conveying exactly what is conveyed by the negation of "Some A's are not B" or, equivalently, "There is an A that is not a B." The term "collective judgment" was sometimes employed by logicians to refer to judgments or statements about limited and referentially definite collections of entities, such as, for example, all the Bourbon kings of France or all the present members of the United States Senate. Extending this phraseology somewhat, the view of laws that was taken in this philosophy may be expressed by saying that these were construed as being very extended collective judgments or statements referring to the collections of pendulums, gases, nitrogen molecules, and so on, wherever and whenever, and under whatever background conditions are implicit in the statement, these may be realized.

As in the case of probability judgments, the rise and fall of concern with the problems generated by this view of laws coincided with the rise and fall of the fortunes of empiricism in modern philosophy. Mill was dealing, though in different language, with one of these difficulties in his discussion of the alleged circularity of the syllogism. It was in response to a difficulty generated by construing universal premises as collective statements that he was led to argue, in accounting for the syllogistic conclusion that Socrates, or the Duke of Wellington is mortal, that "All inference is from particulars to particulars," and that general propositions, like that to the effect that all men are mortal, should be regarded as "merely registers of such inferences already made, and short formulae for making more." [12] Under the compulsion of a strict version of the verifiability theory of meaning, some of the early writers of logical positivism in this century advocated a similar view of laws, or "P-Rules," as they were sometimes called.[13] The more recent views of laws advocated by Gilbert Ryle and Stephen Toulmin, similarly emphasizing the aspects of these as general licenses for inference, explanation, or conclusions in argument, are more subtle and circumspect attempts to bridge the gap between the recognized functions of laws in the system of knowledge and the limitations of function that seem to be imposed upon them if in some more or less strict empiricist way they be construed as descriptive statements of fact.[14]

During the present century a variety of philosophers in England and America have made the rediscovery or sought to reemphasize the importance of the distinction between what a law or statement of general causal connection is and what, when they were construed on the model of collective judgments, they were taken to be. In his *Logic* W. E. Johnson made the distinction in terms of "universals of law" contrasted with "universals of fact." Two decades ago, in his influential *An Analysis of Knowledge and Valuation*, C. I. Lewis firmly proclaimed the difference between statements of formal implication, i.e., generalized material implications, on the one hand, and general statements conveying

[12] *A System of Logic*, Bk. II, Ch. III, Sect. 4.

[13] M. Schlick, "Die Kausalität in der gegenwärtigen Physik," *Die Naturwissenschaften* (1931; reprinted in *Gesammelte Aufsätze*); and "Causality in Everyday Life and in Recent Science," *University of California Publications in Philosophy* (1932); R. Carnap, *Philosophy and Logical Syntax*.

[14] G. Ryle, *The Concept of Mind*; S. Toulmin, *The Uses of Argument*.

what he called "real connections." This corresponded with the distinction made by William Kneale in his *Probability and Induction* between "constancy" statements or "unrestricted universals of fact" and "principles of necessitation." A generation of philosophers has just recently been introduced to the distinction, and much discussion of the topic has taken place, in the terminology of "accidental" and "nonaccidental" universals (R. M. Chisholm), and more recently and prevailingly, "lawlike" statements and other universals that do not have this distinctive character (N. Goodman).

15. The protracted and baffled discussion of the contrary-to-fact conditional that began around the year 1945 and has continued, with some abatement, to the present, may be understood as a particularly disconcerted reaction of a generation of philosophers to the discovery of this old truth, namely, that there is an inexpungible difference between laws and extended collective statements of fact. In the study of conditionals, of what is conveyed by them and what are their grounds, the difference appears in an especially prominent way. We do not call an expression a law, do not view it at all in this way, unless we are prepared to employ it as a formula or rule for the derivation of what, in the context of the conditional statement, turn out to be consequents relative to antecedents that may be, may even be known to be, contrary to fact. The gas in question may not be nitrogen; it may even be known not to be nitrogen. Nevertheless it is in conformity to the law governing this change of state in nitrogen to say that, should this gas be nitrogen, and given the proper conditions of temperature and pressure, it would liquefy.

It is essential to an expression that we take to convey a law, that it is proper to employ it in this fashion. A collective statement that all A's are B does not exclude the possibility that the uniformity it describes is a matter of law. But that there is such a uniformity is not conveyed in the statement, which, as indicated, is the equivalent of the denial of the existential statement that there is at least one member of the denotation of "A" that is not a B. All that the collective statement requires, therefore, is that there be no such exceptional A. This can easily be true, as the discussion of the conditionals amply showed, in a situation in which the allegation of a lawlike connection between *A* and *B* is altogether unjustified.

The decisive point here is essentially a very simple one. The protraction of the discussion of it, and the general bafflement exhibited in that discussion, are in part due to the fact that the lesson about laws came as a discovery to a generation of philosophers strongly indoctrinated in a philosophy that taught otherwise. According to this philosophy the logical analysis illustrated in the formalization of the collective judgment represented the model for construing laws in an ideal language, or a system of ideal languages, committed in a fundamental way to Humean principles of logical atomism, empiricism, and extensionality. According to these principles the only alternative models for understanding laws were "truths of reason" of the kind of which Kant's analytic judgments represented a species, a kind the denial of which was a patent self-contradiction. And the hope of construing laws in this way, which empiricists commonly mistook to be a goal of rationalism, was not difficult to discredit. On the other hand, if laws are to be conceived as collective statements, it is clear immediately that they constitute a quite particular species of these. There is then the task, in describing laws according to this mode of explication, of providing the differentia for this species, the specifications that account for its distinctive character. And now rearing its head, this time in a new dress, as a problem about conditional statements, was an old problem that in earlier versions of empiricism had been grappled with in the form of a problem about the "idea" of cause, power, or necessary connection. And the results achieved by the endeavors to solve the problem in its new form were remarkably like those achieved with its predecessor. Again and again the attempt to stipulate the differentia of lawlike statements among collective universals led bafflingly to the introduction of the very notions that the whole project of viewing them as collectives was designed to dispel. Given a basic philosophical position partial to the explication of the notion of natural laws through the model of the collective statement, it was natural for such philosophers that the partial success of their explication should stand in the way of their seeing that the route to fuller success required, not more industry and ingenuity devoted to the development of the old account, but a radical revision of point of view and the development of a new one. It was natural also that the vast amount of attention paid in this philosophy to the inductive aspects of the procedure of testing and accepting laws should likewise serve to emphasize those respects in which laws are most like collective judgments, and obscure or at least divert attention from those respects in which they are not.[15]

16. A second effect of the preoccupation of philosophers with the problem of induction in what has become its canonical form is no less serious and no less deleterious than the first. The elaboration of the problem as one about the justification of the pro-

[15] A volume could be written concerning the bearing of the matters just discussed, particularly the conception of the nature and role of laws that was a part of this philosophy, upon what was referred to during extensive debate in the past decade as the "covering law model" of explanation. The primary difficulty with the model to which both advocates and objectors directed attention was the apparent existence of large domains—e.g., history, fields of statistical exploration—in which laws of the kind the model called for are either scarce or apparently inutile.

The discussion of this matter suffered seriously from a lack of recognition that the alleged model, for all its supposed derivation from practice in the physical sciences, actually derived from and reflected empiricist preconceptions about the structure of knowledge more than it did the character of the sciences whose authority it seemed to convey. Obviously the kinds of intellectual assimilation and development which we refer to as explanation are essentially connected with the kinds of general principles, laws, rules, and conceptions that make up an important part of our cognitive resources. The empiricist philosophy was dedicated to taking a certain view of these resources, to viewing them as items having a basic sort of development, out of directly given empirical particulars. The conception of inductive generalization as the chief way in which the development of generals from particulars was thought to proceed led at one and the same time, and for essentially the same reasons, to the conception of laws as some kind of large-scale collective statement, to the conception of deduction as the expenditure of intellectual capital accumulated in these statements, and to the conception of explanation as an activity in which *explicanda* are revealed to be already part of the inventory of such accumulations. Basically the perplexities and deficiencies of the covering law model of explanation were not new ones, but the same as those already encountered by the corresponding views of laws and probability statements, and of deduction, though now making themselves known in a different intellectual context, and achieving in that context a distinctive and striking form of expression.

cedure of generalization or extrapolation in the establishment of phenomenal generals easily leads to a mistaken identification, as an essential feature of the problem, of what is peculiar to this way of developing it. What is essential in the problem of induction is the logical difficulty of conceiving knowledge of things unseen in a philosophy which identifies knowing with seeing. It is this difficulty which is represented by the common queries about generalizing from instances, about extrapolating, in the form of laws or probability rules, directly observed uniformities. The form of the queries is not the form of the basic problem, but the form that this problem takes in a context in which, for reasons already explained, the development of laws, probability judgments, and other general epistemic rules from alleged items of primitive information about particulars is a matter of first-order business.

The mistaken identification of this particular form of the problem as the problem itself has served to obscure in much philosophical discussion the deep philosophical character of the problem, has led many, in their response to the challenge it presents, to view it and try to treat it, not as a philosophical problem about a certain way of viewing knowledge, but as a technical problem that one might hope to solve by the exploitation of some technical means. These means might be some of the refined results achieved in mathematical statistics by the application of probability theory to questions about reliability and error in sampling techniques. Or they might lie in the attempted development, out of classical probability theory, of a calculus of "inductive logic" directly applicable to questions about the validity of simple generalization or extrapolation. Or they might possibly be the elaboration, as an appendix to the language in which inductions are made, of some hoped-for semantic theory capable of making the distinction, on noninductive grounds, of what are from what are not generalizable, extrapolable, projectible predicates.

17. One who is sensitive about the economic investment of our intellectual resources can hardly view with equanimity the enormous amount of ingenuity and effort that has been devoted to these lines of endeavor in this century. For though the explorations conducted along all these lines have not been without

some valuable side-effects, the results achieved in the assaults upon their main objectives have been, and have been widely recognized to be, negative. One cannot, to mention but one classical example, follow the careful elaboration of Bayesian principles in J. M. Keynes, and their application to questions about "pure induction," without deriving some illuminating insights of the way in which, in circumstances where we have reason to believe that there is some general connection between realized characters, eliminative induction may serve to increase the probability of a supposed connection between two characters, A and B, for which repeated instances of A have failed to produce negative instances.[16] But as Keynes's work showed, not least clearly to Keynes himself, while this inquiry may help us understand the character of some of the conditions which, if realized, may help us answer Hume's famous question about why the effect of a hundred seemingly identical instances should be greater than that of one, what it does not tell us is how we are to ascertain, as a foundation for inductive reasoning from such instances, when these conditions do and when they do not prevail. Whatever we may do with the principle of limited independent variety and the mathematics of probability, waiting for us at the end of our elaborate exercises, like the tortoise in Lewis Carroll's fable about Achilles, is the skeptic with his question about this principle, "And how do you go about establishing *that?*" One answer that Keynes proposed was that possibly in some cases this can be established by intuitive judgment. This fits well into his general view about the intuitive character of our apprehension of probability relations, and perhaps much can be said in favor of such an answer. But it does not fit well into the Humean context from which the problem of induction arises. For if it is possible to establish general probability judgments by intuition, what is to prevent us from establishing various other general principles by such means? The problem of induction stands as an enormous obstacle in the road to knowledge for the empiricist philosopher precisely because intuition of the type that Descartes celebrated is held in this philosophy to be incapable of establishing *any* of the general principles necessary for

16 *A Treatise on Probability*, Ch. XX.

constructing, on the bases of the deliverances of sensuous intuition, knowledge of objects beyond. In Keynes's theory of probability intuition is viewed as by no means so incapacitated, but
capable of the apprehension of such rich probability relations
that, while it may not by itself, in an extreme rationalist fashion,
be capable of establishing general laws and principles in science,
it should relieve us of any extreme dependence, in the foundations of our knowledge of objects, upon any procedure so infirm
as the procedure of supporting generalizations simply by the accumulation of positive instances that is represented by "Pure
Induction."

18. Like the work of C. D. Broad on probability and induction, which began to appear shortly before the publication of
Keynes's book, the work of Keynes, insofar as it was intended as
a response to the skeptical problem set by Hume, was the beginning of a long line of honorable but misconceived failures.
One of the most robust and sanguine of these attempts in recent
years was the direct line of argument mounted by D. C. Williams
in support of inductive procedures employing the Bernoulli
theorem, the chief effect of which, to judge by the critical comment aroused by Williams's book, was to confirm the supposition
that no such simple strategem for effecting a general justification
of inductive procedures will work.[17] The appearance of Williams's book was bracketed in time by the two editions of G. H.
von Wright's *The Logical Problem of Induction,* the work in
which that author made his most sustained and direct attack on
that traditional problem.[18] Valuable as many aspects of that book
were, and circumspect as were its claims, insofar as any attempt
was made in it to exploit elementary probability considerations
for the purposes of rationalizing simple inductive procedures, it
cannot be regarded as successful. The chief effort in this respect,
the attempt, following ideas of Keynes, to prove, as a "Principal
Theorem" of inductive logic, the realization of an increment of
probability for generalizations upon the information of pre-

[17] D. C. Williams, *The Ground of Induction.* Cf. critical reviews by E. Nagel
(*Journal of Philosophy,* 1947) and F. L. Will (*Philosophical Review,* 1948).
[18] Cf. F. L. Will, "Justification and Induction," *Philosophical Review*
(1959).

viously uncertain positive instances, itself has to be judged vitiated by a subtle, though serious and irremediable, logical mistake.[19] The results of two decades of discussion and elaboration of the ideas on inductive logic advanced by Rudolf Carnap fit well into this history of attempts to make mathematical ideas and judgments serve a purpose for which only philosophical ideas and judgments will suffice. Carnap's analysis and application of probability conceptions to questions about confirmation help to make plain, by the exemplary care he has devoted to the task and the candor with which he has evaluated the results, the enormous distance by which purely logical or mathematical considerations fail to provide a sufficient basis for the definition of an organon of human reason that we might, with some liberality, refer to as "inductive logic." Another line of inquiry at present, similarly proceeding in the hope of finding technical keys to riddles generated by the project of developing sound principles directly from crude observed fact, is that seeking to find, on semantic grounds alone, flaws in the ingenious predicates with which Nelson Goodman has constructed his own remarkable version of Hume's caveats about the perils of generalization. Unfortunately for this project, "green" and "blue," no less than "grue" and "bleen," though less immediately and spectacularly, may be made to generate paradoxes in the mode of "pure induction" or simple extrapolation, not necessarily because these are defective predicates but because, as in the mathematical case of "knowing how to go on," the injunctions to "go on," "do the same," "expect the same in the unobserved," are by themselves insufficiently definite statements of policy. Without specification, "same" and "like" are always sufficiently elastic to countenance, either in arithmetic or in inductive extrapolation, a variety of incompatible procedures and expectations. But fascinating as are these instances of the pathology of inductive policy, and worthy of study as they are in their own right, they are beside the main concern here. They merit mention only as examples of the frustration repeatedly and necessarily encountered when one is misled by the common form taken by the problem of induction

[19] G. H. von Wright, *Logical Problem*, Ch. VI; and F. L. Will, "Consequences and Confirmation," *Philosophical Review* (1966).

to conceive of it as a technical problem of the sort commonly met in sampling and extrapolation activities in everyday life, science, and statistical practice. Then one is encouraged to entertain the illusory hope that it, like them, can be solved by the application of new information, fresh ingenuity and technical skill, without altering the basic theory of the nature and development of knowledge the deficiencies of which are being revealed in the problem and upon which, inevitably, rude hands must be applied, before the problem can be adequately understood and resolved.

19. Since the problem of induction is most commonly thought of in terms of a procedure of generalizing from instances, extrapolating more or less strict uniformities exhibited by them, it should perhaps be made explicit here that what has been said about this particular philosophical problem should not be interpreted to imply that in the study and practice of generalization no serious problems, at least no serious philosophical problems, arise. The story of man's life and thought, from the beginning of recorded history, is replete with the record of genuine and difficult problems arising in a wide variety of areas concerning the justification of conclusions we draw when in specific ways we take associations of characters we have found in a more or less direct way in our experience to hold generally. How *do* we know that the way a sample of voters state they will vote, when solicited by questionnaire two weeks before a national election, is very likely the way they will actually vote? And how do we know that the way this sample will vote is a good guide to the behavior of that segment of the eligible population that will actually cast ballots? Why is it that, conceding all the impressive statistical evidence supporting a correlation between heavy smoking of tobacco cigarettes and the incidence of lung cancer in Western countries, respectable statisticians and physicians may still argue that a "positive link" or "connection" between smoking and cancer has yet to be established? Why is the link or connection less apparent here than in the cases of many diseases which we trace to the invasion of the body by microorganisms, in spite of the fact that the presence of these organisms in the bodies of persons *not* suffering from the disease is far from uncommon?

Part of the answer to the last question lies, of course, in what we take a cause to be when we are speaking of a disease, or diseased tissue; in how we conceive the effect in question, in this case the disease; and in what kind of theory we hope to illuminate and perhaps control the effect; and so on. The mention of these few aspects of the matter may suffice as a brief partial indication of the kinds of philosophical issue which on occasion emerge and require decision in the conduct and appraisal of inquiry directed to the establishment of general results in the practical arts and sciences. Corresponding topics equally rich in philosophical significance could be used to illustrate the point in connection with investigation in the physical sciences, or in the social sciences, including both the experimental domains of the latter and what are coming to be referred to more frequently as the "policy sciences." For as a variety of writers have maintained throughout the career of Western philosophy, including, very early, Plato and Aristotle, there are indeed as multiple and various things that may be called "causes" as there are multiple and various entities, events, conditions that may be properly cited in answer to the question why some object exists, some situation prevails, some event has occurred. And as in the various changes and developments which societies and civilizations undergo, different "why" questions come to be asked, and to take precedence over others, so differences are realized in the bodies of organized knowledge that constitute the science of these times.[20] The kinds of tension that changes of this sort both reflect and promote in the intellectual life of an age were well illustrated, at the time of the rise of modern physical science, in the theory of knowledge and metaphysics of many writers, including notably Galileo, Bacon, and Descartes.[21] Here and at

[20] Cf. F. M. Cornford, "Greek Natural Philosophy and Modern Science," in J. Needham and W. Pagel, *Background to Modern Science*; E. A. Burtt, *Types of Religious Philosophy*, rev. ed., Ch. VII, and "The Value Presuppositions of Science," *Bulletin of the Atomic Sciences* (1957).

[21] Galileo and Descartes are treated in detail by Burtt in *The Metaphysical Foundations of Modern Physical Science*. Of the presently unappreciated Bacon, Macaulay wrote in his elegant essay, "The chief peculiarity of Bacon's philosophy seems to us to have been this, that it aimed at things altogether different from those which his predecessors had proposed to themselves. This was his opinion. 'Finis scientiarum,' says he, 'a nemine adhuc bene positus

other places there is a superabundance of evidence of ways in which philosophical problems and reflection have direct relevance to the activities of inquiry of their time, including those inquiries in which an important feature is the construction, control, and establishment of general laws, principles, and theories by reference to, among other things, reports of particular observed fact.

20. In the complex web of philosophical and scientific questions, problems, and considerations the problem of induction, like the mind-body problem and the problem of determinism, has its place. As one does not expect (*pace* G. T. Fechner) the results of some new psychological or physiological experiment to provide the solution of the mind-body problem, nor (*pace* A. T. Compton) some new physical result, by itself, to answer the large philosophical questions about human nature and conduct generated by the application in the study of man of the principles of scientific determinism, so one should not expect the discovery of a new, clearer way of ordering our estimates of probability, or more powerful techniques of statistical estimation and testing, to solve the problem of induction. The problem of induction, though not altogether unrelated to the problem of what is the best test for a specific kind of statistical hypothesis, arises at a very different level and in a very different context from such a problem. Our immediate intuitive judgment of the insufficiency of solutions of the latter to serve for the former is grounded in our sense that what is presumed and what is the object of question or challenge in the one are far different in the other, and that hence what would be appropriate responses to the question or challenge in each case must be correspondingly different. The problem of induction is a difficulty encountered at a crucial point in the development of a certain theory of knowledge, a difficulty comparable in intractability, though even greater in extent, to that encountered by Plato's theory of forms in the considerations adduced by Plato himself in the *Parmenides,* or that encountered

---

est.' And again, 'Omnium gravisissimum error in deviatione ab ultimo doctrinarium fine consistit' " (*Francis Bacon,* New York, n.d., pp. 120–121; originally published in *The Edinburgh Review,* July, 1837, under the title, "Lord Bacon").

by Hobbes in attempting to account for all rational knowledge as a matter of exploring the consequences of definitions while at the same time maintaining an extremely nominalist view of the nature of definitions themselves. Just as these difficulties in theory call for remedies likewise in theory, no matter from what source of inspiration these may derive, so it is with the problem of induction. It is a deeply philosophical problem, generated by certain basic theses about knowledge that are the defining characters of a certain kind of philosophical theory. Loyalty and fortitude in defense of philosophical principles are admirable traits, essential in philosophical discussion for full understanding and evaluation of rival views. The uncovering of the problem of induction and the persistent response to its challenge by philosophers generally sympathetic to empiricist principles have been an important part of the philosophical trial of these principles, the results of which seem to warrant this conclusion: So long as these philosophers continue to embrace these theses, hugging them to their bosoms like the Spartan boy the fox, so long will the theses continue to have their destructive effect upon them.

CHAPTER 3

The Wider Problem
of Justification

1. The relation between the philosophical theses exposed in the examination of the problem of induction, and the problem itself, is not simply that the theses stand in the way of a solution of the problem, and hence that a change in them is necessary if the problem is to be solved. Closer than this, the relation is that the problem derives from the theses in such a way that, when the theses are relinquished, this particular problem disappears. But only *this particular problem,* not every important problem about the development of human knowledge, nor even every similar problem. For though it is only in the soil of empiricism that this particular problem grows, *this* soil gives rise to this problem, not by generating something altogether new, but by conferring novel features on something old, something that flourishes in different forms on other intellectual grounds.

For purposes of historical illumination, as well as ease of reference, the matrix of views about knowledge, ideas, thought, and objects in which the problem of induction arises has been identified as a species of Cartesianism, in particular a species differentiated from others by the radical changes effected in it by the installation of the empiricist theory of ideas. This suggests immediately that just as the empiricist program for the rationalization of our knowledge was a permutation of the basic Cartesian one, so the problem encountered in the empiricist version of the program may itself be a permutation of a fundamental difficulty in the original one. And this is certainly so. The problem of induction is a permutation of a very general and deep problem, which may be called the "justification problem," that is endemic in all forms of theory of knowledge which, beginning with the alleged certain deliverances of consciousness, attempt to reconstruct knowledge as an edifice built on these foundations, step by step, brick on brick, apprehension on apprehension.

2. Descartes did not have the problem of induction. Why he did not is a revealing question, the answer to which, if the preceding philosophical analysis of the problem is a sound one, has already been given. But Descartes did have a problem most remarkably like this, and the similarities between the two are for present purposes much more significant than their differences. Descartes proposed that the edifice of knowledge be constructed, beginning with the certainties of consciousness, including self-consciousness, by means of intuitions of a rational character, founded on the elaboration of those of our ideas which we are able to apprehend with both clearness and distinctness. Whether Descartes intended his hyperbolic doubt to apply to direct judgments flowing from the relations of clear and distinct ideas patent in the mind is a matter which has been extensively debated by commentators, the evidence in Descartes's own words on the matter being pretty clearly conflicting.[1] One of the grounds supporting the claim that he did intend the philosophical doubt to extend this far is that it is so very much in keeping with his intention to meet the attacks of skepticism that he should have wanted to invite and then endeavor to meet skeptical challenge at this particular point. Much more important here, however, than the historical question whether out of the extant evidence it is possible to construct a philosophical position to which Descartes was faithful at all times and which speaks unequivocally on this point, is the philosophical question whether the natural light, as Descartes in the main conceived it, was not open to this philosophical challenge, and, if so, what resource was available to him to meet it. If the skeptical challenge to our trust in our faculties, when we are employing these with a maximum of circumspection

---

[1] That is, the doubt apparently directed at intuition, at the natural light itself, in *Meditation I*, is restricted to deduction, insofar as that entails reliance upon memory, in Descartes's replies to the Second and Fourth Set of Objections.

and caution, is to be met by an appeal to Divine Providence, then that appeal has to be made without dependence upon the very faculties that are conceived to be under challenge. But how is this possible? How is it possible to establish the reality of Divine Providence without employing and thus trusting in advance the faculties which the reality of Divine Providence alone is regarded as rendering worthy of trust? There are theories of knowledge so constituted that in them knowledge of secular and divine matters may plausibly be conceived as developing together, in mutually dependent ways, the one reinforcing and illuminating the other. But these are not theories in which the development of knowledge is conceived as a procedure of achieving and building upon units of certain, incorrigible items of cognition, and not, correspondingly, ones in which the passage from thoughts about God to the affirmation of His existence is made in the simple, linear geometrical way illustrated in the metaphysics of Descartes.

3. The circularity in argument that threatens the Cartesian view of knowledge at this point is essentially the same whether the broader philosophy in which that view is worked out is basically rationalist or empiricist in character. In the classic empiricist version presented by Hume, the relation of cause and effect assumed the major role played by relations of ideas in Descartes's philosophy. Induction then replaced rational intuition as a way of apprehending the relations essential for the expansion of knowledge. And the problem of validating the inductive procedure without depending in a viciously circular way upon induction itself replaced the original problem of justifying the employment of clear and distinct ideas without arguing in a vicious circle in the process. From the point of view of the philosophy of knowledge it may thus be said of Hume—though the language is in some ways anachronistic and would have been repugnant to him—that he too had a powerful genius external to him upon whose goodness our capacity to have knowledge beyond the immediate certainties of present sense (and possibly memory) depends at every step. The language in which Hume presents his version of *la condition humaine* is secular, and the epistemic Providence appealed to an impersonal

one, but the thought expressed is in essentials remarkably similar to that which Peirce remarked in the Abbé Gratry, author of a nineteenth century book on logic, whom Peirce described as "a writer of subtlety and exactitude of thought as well as of elevation of reason." It was the Abbé's view, according to Peirce's report, "that the tendency toward the truth in induction is due to the miraculous intervention of Almighty God . . . every true induction being an immediate inspiration from on high . . . due to a direct inspiration of the Holy Spirit." [2] To such a pious mind any claim for inductive procedures, like that of Peirce's, that they are by their very nature, without any external support, truth-prone and truth-approaching, would have seemed a startling example of spiritual pride, the equivalent, in the philosophy of knowledge, of the denial of Original Sin. The difference between the thought of the Abbé and of Descartes at this point was more like the difference, on the relations between mind and body, between the views of the Occasionalists and those of Spinoza and Leibniz. In the broad outline of the Cartesian philosophy there was the need to show that the possibly malevolent all-powerful genius conjured up by Descartes was indeed benevolent, and that hence our cognitive faculties could in general be trusted. Hume, a true Cartesian in this respect, recognized the need expressed in this demonology. He conceded also the impossibility of avoiding the threatening circle in filling the need; hence his skepticism.

4. It is ironic, but not altogether unnatural, that in the theory of knowledge of one of the outstanding figures of the secular Enlightenment one should find this abstract logical expression of what in more explicitly theological views was a concern about grace and salvation. Speaking in the idiom of Comte one may appropriately describe it as a relic of theological thinking, albeit theological thinking of an eccentric kind, in a form of thought that was explicitly and intentionally scientific or positive. And while it may seem odd, at first view, that a philosophy that, on principle, provided no place for good demons should be so enervated by the thought of evil ones, some of this apparent oddity

2 *Collected Papers*, 2.749, 2.690, 2.21.

is dispelled, as the oddity of vestigial evolutionary features is generally dispelled, by an understanding of ancestry.

Viewed from the point of view of more orthodox theology, the original philosophy of Descartes is odd, odd in the way it conceives one to come to a philosophical knowledge of God. One does not know that He is, because the heavens declare His glory and the earth shows His handiwork, for the heavens and the earth are as yet unknown. What appears to be such may be illusions produced by an all-powerful genius who is evil, rather than good. In this state of extreme doubt, *de profundis scepticis*, Descartes set forth to dispel doubt, banish the evil genius by installing in his place a good God, and thus attain the salvation in the form of scientific knowledge that the existence of God will ensure.

Put in more prosaic terms than those of Descartes, the epistemological analogue of this progression in thought from supposed demon to demonstrated God is the adoption, provisionally, of a position of skepticism, the concession that the doubts raised, the questions asked, are legitimate ones (if only for purposes of philosophical clarification), and the attempt then, from these depths, to resolve the doubts, to answer the questions, and in this way to validate the enterprise of human knowledge. In both cases the project attempted is prodigious; in both, the most extreme concessions are made to the skeptical attack, as they must be if the legitimacy of that attack is granted and the attempt made directly to meet it. If the attempt is not to disarm the attack but to meet it directly and overcome it—in short to *answer* the challenging questions that the skeptic seeks to raise— then nothing must be taken for granted in the endeavor that is itself under skeptical challenge. This requires, in the first place, that one be able to begin the refutation with some steps that are in a special way so obvious, sure, and uncontroversial that they are not liable to objection by the skeptic. And, in the second place, one must be able, moving from these beginnings with equally doubt-free, demonproof steps, to rescue from the attack, to justify and re-establish, in perhaps a purged and reconstituted form, the essential features of what, prior to that attack, had been taken to be a corpus of human knowledge.

5. Obvious as are these requirements of a Cartesian program for providing a theory of knowledge capable of answering the attacks of skeptical philosophy against this corpus, it is far less obvious that such requirements can ever be met, the program ever succeed. Rather it appears that too much is conceded to skepticism in the program to permit success. So much is conceded, in fact, that those who engage in the program, whatever may be their intentions, must end up as skeptics at odds with themselves. In place of the triumph over skepticism to which they have aspired in their theories of knowledge, they have ended victims of the superior strategic position and intellectual armament which they have conceded to the skeptic before the engagement began. Or, somewhat more exactly, they have been overcome by the inexpugnable and essential elements of skepticism that are installed in their own position by these concessions, elements that transform each of these endeavors in skeptical refutation into an internal struggle, and the foreordained negative result into a kind of refined skeptical self-revelation.

It is not a question here of whether the attacks of skeptical philosophy upon our claims to have knowledge can be decisively met. It is a question of how they can be met, and, in particular, of whether this can be done in what appears to be a fair and direct way, namely, by conceding the propriety of the skeptic's challenges and then proceeding, using only materials not liable to these challenges, to meet them. It is a question whether, in attempting to meet the challenges in this way one has not already conceded so much of the skeptical contention that the attempt itself is subverted and transformed into a support of the challenges themselves. It is a question whether, from a position of skepticism, skepticism can be refuted; whether it is ever possible to win a victory over the advocates of that position while playing their own game.

6. The problem of induction is commonly conceived as a problem of justifying, justifying inductive procedures or conclusions. It represents a certain basic difficulty encountered in the project of effecting the justification, vindication, exculpation of inductive conclusions against a general charge of weakness brought against them from a certain philosophical position. The charge is

that they are all suffering from this weakness, not because they are poorly or carelessly drawn inductive conclusions, but simply because they are inductive. It is that all such conclusions, because of their nature as inductive, suffer from irremediable defect.

Charges of this kind can be met in a variety of ways. The charges may be dismissed, for example, and grounds given for this dismissal. Or they may be accepted and an attempt made to answer them. The latter procedure, illustrated in the projects of philosophers who set out to answer Hume and solve the problem of induction, admits by implication, in accepting the charge as one to be refuted, the existence of grounds upon which such a charge can be legitimately made. It admits, as it were, that a case can be made for the charge, and seeks to meet the case by preparing a superior case by which to oppose it.

This is a common, rational procedure in the world of charges, defenses, and countercharges. But there is significant difference in this particular case. If a charge is made against a man named "Smith" that he cannot be given security clearance to work for the Department of State, solely on the ground that no one by that name can merit such trust, no sensible lawyer, in setting out to defend Smith's claim to clearance, would admit the legitimacy of the charge as brought. Given the undeniable fact that his client's name is "Smith," the lawyer must make a case against the rule that no Smith is to be trusted, or at least a case for an exception to the rule in this instance. Given the acceptance of the rule by the court, or again, given the acceptance of what the rule apparently implies in this instance, namely that, being a Smith, this man is properly excluded from security clearance, there is now no case that the lawyer can make. To essay the "justification" of Smith, in these circumstances, is to essay a quite impossible task.

The induction case is essentially similar in this respect. The charge against induction derives from a theory of knowledge in which every inductive conclusion, like every Smith, is on principle deemed unworthy of trust. The problem of induction, like the problem of Smith, arises just because of the acceptance of this principle. It is in this principle that the case against induction, calling for its justification, resides. The only reason for there being a general problem of justifying inductive conclusions is the acceptance of this or some equivalent principle dictating a skeptical result concerning inductive conclusions as a species of cognitive claim, a principle dictating that when we run through the catalogue of the claims that we commonly make, there is very little that cannot, as Descartes said, be brought within the sphere of the doubtful, and that this includes the whole species that we should call "inductive." It is the acceptance of some such principles, at the outset, that both precipitates the need to justify inductive conclusions and ensures that this justification cannot be achieved. For it is manifest that the same principle that leads to the restriction of nondoubtful knowledge claims to a certain limited class, A, and the rendering of non-A's as doubtful, will also ensure that A cannot legitimately be expanded to include non-A's. The same angel who effects the expulsion of sinners from Eden prevents their return.

7. The situation portrayed is paradoxical, but the paradox seems genuinely to lie in the kind of theory of knowledge under examination, rather than in some misreading of it. What makes this situation of challenge and justification so markedly different from ordinary ones is the special grounds upon which the charge rests, namely, the principle in accordance with which anything that is not-A is, in contrast with things that are A, subject to doubt, the status of the A's being that they remain secure and indubitable even when the not-A's have been judged otherwise.

What is crucial here for the possibility of justification is not the bare fact that a partition has been made, separating the secure from the doubtful. It is rather the specific character of the partition, and the grounds upon which it is made. The partition in question is no simple, on-the-surface one, such as we commonly make in more or less restricted situations. In contrast, it is a partition based on philosophical, and, in particular, on methodological grounds, discriminating with respect to their liability to doubt what might be referred to as the respective yields or fruits of different alleged cognitive sources. Both Descartes and Hume, for example, though for somewhat different reasons, suppose that such a partition can be made, marking off the narrow preserve of things which can be known by recourse to one or a set of privileged and supremely trustworthy sources from the wider domain of those which cannot. Descartes's "Cogito" and his knowledge of his own existence as a thinking substance are familiar examples of items located within the preserve, according to the early portions of the *Meditations,* in contrast with judgments about the existence and character of bodies. Whatever be the principle on which such a discrimination between legitimate and illegitimate sources of knowledge is made, it is the adoption and employment of such a principle which is crucial in determining the insolubility of the kind of justification problem that is exemplified both in the original, rationalist version of the Cartesian philosophy and in the empiricist version articulated by Hume. Once one has conceded that any item, whatever it may be, that is a not-A, and hence depends for its rational credibility on some source outside the privileged ones, is, in contrast with items that are A, dubitable, one has in a very simple and direct way foreclosed the possibility of using A's in order to justify any not-A's, if by "justify" is meant some procedure in which the not-A's are redeemed from their state of dubitability by an appeal to the A's. The principle which dictates that A's can and not-A's cannot be known in certain canonical ways precludes the possibility of showing that not-A's can be so justified. It is this logical fact which is exploited in the skeptical counterattack represented in the celebrated Cartesian circle, and likewise in the threatening circle in which Hume proposed to enmesh anyone who tries, on the basis of present and past experience, to show that this experience could serve as a model for valid conclusions about the future, or the unexperienced generally.

For consider a certain item (or set of items), Y, stipulated to be not-A. The problem of justification, conceived in the customary way, is then that of devising some procedure for developing Y out of some other set of items X, stipulated to be exclusively A. But so long as one restricts himself exclusively to A's, and thus to the sources of knowledge represented in them, the project is doomed to founder on the logical fact that not-A's are determined by conception to be incapable of being known by these sources. It thus follows that any procedure devised for the purpose of eliciting Y from X must, if it succeeds in eliciting Y at all, do so at the price of violating its intention of restricting itself to X, or any other set of A's. It remains only for careful scrutiny to disclose the place where this transgression has occurred, the place where in effect some not-A is treated as if it had already been developed from A's, and, where, in consequence, this alleged procedure for justifying Y does not demonstrate that Y or any other not-A's can properly be elicited from A's alone but, rather, in relation to this specific issue, begs the question.

8. What is being urged here, then, is not that, in carrying out a critical examination of items of putative knowledge, or candidates for the status of knowledge, we cannot ever draw a line between what is secure and what is insecure in the domain under consideration, and then inquire, whether, on the grounds of the former some items in the latter can have security conferred upon them. This we do naturally and normally in all those cases of demonstrative reasoning in which, given premises we take to be certain, we inquire concerning their necessary or logical consequences. In such circumstances the question whether a proposed theorem or consequence is really such is also a question whether the candidate in question can be taken to be as secure as the premises from which it is proposed to be deduced. Our capacities to carry out this kind of examination and assessment is exemplified also in other reasoning in which the results or conclusions we come to, though not equally secure as their grounds or premises, can nevertheless be properly viewed as well-grounded, well-attested, even to the point, in some cases, of being beyond reasonable doubt. One may recognize all this, it should be remarked, without being thereby committed to what might be called the "lowest-level principle" with respect to the security of items involved in our reasoning. This principle, more commonly appealed to in reasoning about reasoning than followed in reasoning about more concrete matters, holds that the security of conclusions can rise no higher than that of the lowest of the items upon which it is based, and that hence no conclusion can be perfectly secure unless all of its grounds are similarly so. The facts of the matter are quite otherwise, as we recognize on occasion, when we are forced to face these facts. Often the degree of

sureness we properly confer upon results or conclusions is greater than that which we may attribute to some, or perhaps any, of the items upon which it is based. We may reasonably be more sure of the verdict than of any single item of the evidence which may be marshaled in its support.

9. So the issue is not whether it is possible for items of belief, judgment, acceptance to be brought into the realm of the doubtful and thereafter by proper intellectual means rescued and restored to good cognitive standing. The issue is whether this is possible under certain special circumstances, these being those exemplified in the Cartesian hyperbolic doubt, and the Cartesian and neo-Cartesian attempts to rescue brands from this supposed state of general intellectual conflagration.

In many ordinary cases, when we make a distinction between secure X's and doubtful Y's, we have particular reasons for putting Y's into question. We have reasons for not taking it as secure, as settled, that the accused Jones did commit the criminal act of which he is accused, and then we examine the secure evidence E and try to determine, among other things, whether this provides us with a sufficient basis for altering the status of the accusation against Jones and taking it as secure. Though at the start we hold Jones's guilt in question in a context containing the secure evidence E, we do this because we have positive grounds, which may be of various sorts, for taking up the question, and positive rules and principles to which we may appeal in the endeavor to determine, say, if the evidence does warrant a decision against Jones. The circumstances of our investigation are not ones in which we suppose ourselves deprived of all such rules and principles, not ones in which Jones's guilt is determined to be a matter of doubt because on general philosophical grounds we have suspended trust altogether in any procedure, any rules and principles, by means of which one might, on grounds of evidence like E, come to any conclusion on a question of this kind.

Returning to the language of X's and Y's, in the more ordinary case the grounds for the division we make between X and Y, leaving Y in question while X is secure, do not incorporate explicitly or implicitly the contention that X, however secure, is not the kind of item that *can* confer security upon the kind of item which is *Y*. If that contention were part of our basis for putting *Y* in question, there would be no point, having done so, in now asking whether, on the basis of *X*, security can be conferred upon *Y*. *That* question was answered when *Y* was assigned to the realm of the doubtful on the grounds that the security of such an item as *X* is no sufficient ground for conferring security upon such an item as *Y*. If we were right in the assignment on this basis, in the first place, we are equally right and logically committed to maintaining this when any question is raised concerning the capacity of *X* to justify *Y*, to validate it or make it secure.

The central reason why, after such a skeptical retreat to secure *X*'s as is under consideration here, one cannot advance to the achievement of security for the *Y*'s in question, is thus that the scorched-earth policy under which the retreat is carried out requires the destruction in principle of all possible bridges, all possible avenues, over which an intellectual counteradvance from the *X*'s could proceed. As a preliminary to later advance from *X*'s to *Y*'s, such a retreat must be self-defeating, since the elimination of the possibility of advance is a precondition of the execution of the retreat itself.

10. It is in this way that the manner in which skeptical doubts are developed in the beginning of the Cartesian program is crucial for the prospects of success of the program. The means used to generate these doubts preclude employment of the very means intended eventually to relieve them. Doubts about the existence of "external," material objects, as these are generated in Descartes's *Meditations,* illustrate the point. The possibility of doubt on this particular matter which is represented in the person of that possible evil genius, devoting all his powers to deceiving Descartes, when translated into less dramatic logical terms represents the logical independence of ideas, thoughts, judgments that frequent the mind of the thinking subject, in relation to any objects external to the mind which these ideas, thoughts, or judgments may represent. The grounds for doubt in the existence of external things, in the face of the ideas of perception which pow-

erfully urge upon us the conviction that various such things do exist, do not lie simply in ruminations about the fact that sometimes we have been deceived in such convictions. That I have been deceived in some such cases no more validates for me the conclusion that I may actually be deceived in all, than the true premise that I have been nonexistent at some times validates for me the conclusion that I may have actually been nonexistent at all times (may never have existed, and hence may not now exist). What the fact of sometime deception in perceptual cognition demonstrates, in the context of the metaphysical and epistemological presumptions within which Descartes is operating, is the sometime logical independence of "perceptual idea" from "perceived thing." But in order for Descartes to develop a universal doubt about the perceptual cognition of material things, this independence must be universalized, and this universalization, effected by Descartes with remarkably little supporting grounds, is personified in the demon. With respect to this particular philosophical matter the possibility that the demon exists is just the logical point that "idea" does not entail "thing." The generation of the universal doubt about material things is effected by utilizing this alleged independence. The universal philosophical doubt about perceptual cognition of material things thus does not rest, in any particular case, upon positive reasons that may be advanced concerning the way I have proceeded in arriving at this putative cognition. There is no allegation, and no grounds advanced to support a supposition, that in this particular case, say, of taking it that there is a robin before me, I have been precipitate, careless, overconfident in thinking that I can identify robins, or momentarily forgetful of the fact that I am in a museum, and not in an aviary. In place of this, and any similar ground, is the continued emphasis upon the utter independence of idea, whether of perception or conception, from thing, and hence the logical possibility, however persuasive the idea may be, that I am yet deceived.

11. But this procedure of erecting a universal provisional doubt concerning material things extracts a severe price in Descartes's philosophy. In order to maintain the universal dubitability of our putative cognition of material things, in contrast with that

of the mental things with which it is held that each of us is immediately and infallibly aware, including the so-called adventitious ideas of sense, Descartes is led to accept the doctrine of the universal independence of idea and thing, led to concede that the secure knowledge of the existence of idea, in the case of these ideas representing allegedly perceived objects, is not sufficient to ensure knowledge of the represented object. But having conceded so much, he is now in no position to retrace his steps to a secure knowledge of these objects. Having taken as foundations the knowledge of mental things, and having in the process of arguing for doubts about material ones, committed himself to the position that the certainty of our knowledge of the former is no sufficient reason for supposing certainty with respect to the latter, he has, in the process of marking off the difference between the intended foundational knowledge, of which we may entertain no doubt, and putative items or domains of knowledge to be erected upon it, rendered the former incapable of serving as a foundation for the latter. Integral to the success of the first step of the project, the discrimination of the materials, is the acceptance of a principle of logical independence which altogether precludes the success of the second step. The project as a whole is thus fundamentally misconceived.

12. The course of Descartes's own reflections on the matter illustrate immediately the philosophical perils and eventual frustrations of this way of proceeding, of trying to mark off a domain of putative knowledge which is so restricted in extent and modest in claim that it would not be disputed even by a skeptic, and then trying to establish to the satisfaction of such a diffident mind that this is a sufficient basis for conferring security from doubt upon much that had been provisionally, for philosophical purposes, considered doubtful. Descartes's secure bases were the alleged deliverances of immediate self-consciousness, the ideas in the mind. But now having generated a doubt about material things on the basis of an argued independence of thought and thing (where the thing is material) he was faced with the task of showing how this independence might be circumvented. If one's secure bases, one's "ultimate grounds" or "foundations," are known ideas, one will be able to obtain secure knowledge of

entities, beings that are not ideas, only if at some point the logical barrier between idea and represented entity can be breached. That there is such a breach, at one highly exalted and strategic place, Descartes attempted to show by his proofs for the existence of God. The idea of God is thus the pineal gland of Descartes's theory of knowledge. The strategic position of this idea in the development of knowledge and the refutation of skepticism, and the specific context of doubts and certainties in which the need for God's guarantee for clear and distinct ideas arises, dictates the peculiar importance for him of being able to establish God's existence by means of the kind of reasoning that is exemplified in the ontological argument.

13. Confronting from the point of view of skeptical philosophy the problem of establishing a connection between "the perceptions of the senses" and "external objects," Hume commented that to have recourse to the veracity of the Supreme Being for this purpose is "surely making a very unexpected circuit." But in view of the way in which the problem arises for Descartes, and, in particular, in view of the position that "the perceptions of the senses" together with other ideas occupy as modifications of mental substance which is "more easily known than the body," the circuit is easily understandable and hardly the occasion for astonishment. The celebrated Cartesian circle stands as a monumental example of the frustrations to be encountered by an attempt to meet in this particular way the challenges represented by the skeptical arguments against large domains of our putative knowledge. Likewise the prodigious breach which in the ontological argument Descartes attempted to make in the logical barrier he had erected between "idea" and "thing" stands as a striking monument of the extremity of the circumstances which are realized in such an attempt at dealing with the doubts easily aroused in serious, if unguarded, minds by skeptical arguments. One cannot hope to succeed in dispelling doubts raised concerning a domain D_1 by appealing as grounds for its security to the existence of another and secure domain D_2, if one has already accepted, as grounds for taking D_2 to be legitimately doubtful, that it cannot be rendered secure by the existence of any domain like D_1. That logical scaffold whose strength was maintained to be

insufficient to keep us from falling into the basement of ignorance in the first place, cannot consistently be expected to support our weight when we attempt to climb out. Or, to alter the metaphor, if it is conceded in the process of distinguishing the domain D_2 from that of D_1, that the constituents of D_2 are more resistant to the acids of skeptical doubt than the constituents of D_1, that they remain undissolved while the constituents of D_2 uniformly dissolve, then it is a paradoxical *volte-face,* having identified elements of D_2 in the mixture, to attempt to show that the presence of these will preserve from solubility some or all of the elements of D_1.

14. In closing the discussion of this particular aspect of justification theory some brief attention should be paid to a rejoinder which some advocates of the theory may wish to make to the general argument just advanced against it. Granted, such an advocate may say, that the argument has much force against *some* versions of justification theory, it does not have similar force against all. This is because, it may be urged, the argument seems to presume, in speaking of security, doubt, and the rest, that what is sought as justification is always some kind of demonstrable certainty. This need not be, nor is it always, the case. To be sure, there are compelling reasons in carrying out the philosophical examination of knowledge by means of a thoroughgoing skeptical doubt, for one to be able to end the doubt and initiate the reconstruction of the knowledge edifice in the discrimination of a domain or set of domains like D_2, the constituents of which are utterly sure. But as one does not require exactly the same strength in structures erected upon foundations which one requires in foundations themselves, so in the case of knowledge we now understand, what Hume willy-nilly has taught us, that it is not sensible generally to expect the conclusions, inferences, mediate claims we develop from the foundational domains of knowledge to be as certain as these domains, to expect that these conclusions generally will be logically deducible from these domains rather than rendered by them only in some substantial degree probable.

15. The skeptical position, to which Hume in the main ad-

hered on this point, is, in effect, that there is no hiding place in probability. And that position is right: right to this extent, that once the skeptical jinni of Descartes is released from his bottle, he is not going to be returned, or even mollified, by the kind of apparent concession that talk about probability and similar matters represents. This is a broad and perhaps even cryptic claim; and a moderately satisfactory elucidation and defense of it would require a forbiddingly detailed and extended excursion into topics which, though relevant, are not essential to the main theme of this work. What such an excursion would try to show, in the idiom of Hume's treatment of cause and effect, is that the same challenges which can be made to claims about what necessarily ensues from or accompanies a certain type of situation can be made to claims about what usually, for the most part, or probably, ensues from or accompanies it.

A brief hint of how and why this must be so may be had by considering the inductivist philosopher confronting the problem of how to show solely on the basis of the information that all of the known, and presumably numerous, A's are B, that probably all A's whatsoever are likewise B. Little reflection is required to disclose an apparently striking analogy between this philosophical predicament or conundrum and others generated by the application of Cartesian justificatory procedures to various large putative domains of the corpus of human knowledge. Extended penetrating examination will confirm the apparent analogy in the case of Descartes's attempt to show, on the basis of known "ideas" that there are material things more or less corresponding to them, in the case of Hume reflecting on the incapacity of attempts in this matter to validate an "opinion" which though "universal and primary . . . [in] all men, is soon destroyed by the slightest philosophy," in Hume's similar pronouncement that it is "not contrary to reason to prefer the destruction of the whole world to the scratching of my finger," and so on and on, one is tempted to say, into the philosophical night. In the case of the particular inductive conundrum traditionally put in terms of concluding from past to future, some to all, or observed to unobserved, a long line of careful endeavors in this century to refute Hume have failed to disclose that his reasoning was flawed by a lack of appreciation, necessary at his time, of the resources of probability theory and its applications in statistical method. It has disclosed rather that this philosopher was basically right in his presumption that on the fundamental philosophical points at issue, the translation of the venue of the judgment into the court of probability theory, though it may render the determination of justice in the matter more complex and complicated by stimulating a vast set of novel legal tangles, will not alter the final decision.

16. The long line of rebuffs suffered by ingenious, clever men in their attempts to solve the inductive conundrum constructed by Hume by using the resources of mathematical probability, testifies that one of the chief effects of the introduction of these resources has been to obscure what was otherwise obvious in a high degree, namely, that this conundrum, and others with which it is closely analogous, are, as they were designed to be, insoluble in the context in which they were proposed to be considered, and that the philosophical endeavor to handle and resolve them—and they need to be resolved—must be by less direct and ingenuous means. The rusting hulks of a priori inductive principles, theorems of inductive logic, and principles of inductive or statistical syllogisms which decorate the now extensive battlefield of inductive philosophy are memorials to the mistaken hope that somehow advance over the contested ground could be made by using the novel engines provided by probability theory. It would have been no further tribute to the value of this eminently successful body of theory, but rather a reason for suspecting it of some peculiar inner weakness, if its introduction into the predicament represented by the problem of induction could have been made to seem reasonably to transform it in the way required in order for the apparent problem to be solved. For the heart of this and other similar conundrums lies in supposing for the subject a situation of complete ignorance concerning some large area or domain, and then challenging him to make reasonable assertions about items or features of it. In such a situation, as scientific and statistical practice uniformly confirms, and as much philosophical controversy over "logical probability," the principle of indifference, and similar matters seemed

repeatedly to disclose, talk about probability is idle, ineffective, and incorrigibly prone to paradox. The project, therefore, of devising a means of extracting the desired kind of conclusions from the kind of situation supposed, even when the desired conclusions are qualified or mitigated with signals of probability, is as infeasible as when the conclusions are taken to be certain ones.

17. A principal theme of this work, as it bears upon the philosophical problem of induction, is that this celebrated problem is not what it seems, that it can only be understood as one form, taken in particular circumstances, of a much more general problem that is endemic in a certain broad kind of theory of knowledge. This latter problem has been called the justification problem. The problem of induction can only be understood when it is seen as one species of this latter problem, and when, further, the basic philosophical conceptions embedded in this latter problem have been brought to philosophical consciousness, subjected to critical scrutiny and assessment.

Preservation of the autonomy of this work in its development of this theme, and consistent adherence to the theme itself, would be sufficient reasons, if there were no other, for the terse treatment of probability in the body of the work and the spareness of the comment, reserved for the Appendix to the book, upon some of the main philosophical issues discussed in recent years in the philosophy of that subject. Before turning to more general issues concerning justification, however, a further brief word, relevant to both the general theme and to the character of considerable present and recent work on the joint topic of probability and induction, seems desirable.

18. The Appendix on Probability begins by commenting upon the philosophical search for definitions of probability, for formulae which will at the same time provide a short, noncircular expression of the meaning of this important term and an adequate operational guide or manual for its correct application.

Of course the people who were engaged in the quest for a definition of probability did not suppose that an adequate definition would obviate the need for a calculus of probability and a complex rule-governed practice for its application. They thought of the definition, rather, as an essential step in the completion and understanding of this practice. Viewed from the inside, what a probability calculus does is elucidate logical relations between assessments of probability, between probability premises and conclusions. It enables one to calculate, for example, given that the probability of getting heads or tails in the toss of a coin is each $\frac{1}{2}$, what is the probability of getting exactly three heads in a total of five tosses. But for this purpose probability may be treated substantially as an undefined term, leaving open the question what exactly we are saying when we say that the probability of a certain event like getting heads with the coin, is a certain number, and further, how we determine that this is so.

19. Granted that the formal specification of a calculus of something conveniently referred to as *Pr* is insufficient to specify what *Pr* is and how it is determined, there remains a large question of how one should consider that the definition and determination of *Pr* is to be made. Is legal justice something that can be conceived or determined apart from the vast legal institution by means of which it is constantly being inquired into, disputed, dispensed, defeated, and refined? One is missing something of great importance in the philosophy of probability if one does not understand that the strong interest, evident in much discussion of the matter, in definitions of probability that are syntactically, semantically, and operationally simple, cannot be accounted for merely on the grounds of a natural appetite for systematic simplicity. One is missing a major source of the interest which dictates, not just that our utterances, claims, judgments about probability must be controlled by, coordinated with, experience, but that the control or coordination must be effected in this particular way.

20. What needs to be explained is the widespread and strong attraction exerted by the kind of program that conceives of probability as something that can, in certain basic cases, be determined, apart from the successful employment of probability practices, in some directly intuitive or quasi-intuitive manner. What is it in the whole history of the joint subject of probability and induction that has so persuasively led work in the field to concentrate on certain cases in which our "natural light," so to

speak, guided in a simple way by some principle of indifference, or in a more complex way by the realization of indifference and equiprobability in a hypothetical language of independent predicates, is held to be sufficient to give us primitive assessments of probability? Here again, with other topics more essential to this work beckoning, only the suggestion of an answer can be given. One way of putting the question would be, why is it that as many philosophers who set out, apparently little preoccupied with Humean problems, to achieve a successful understanding of probability practices—and in particular those important species of these practices which are employed in inductive testing, extrapolation, and generalization—why is it that so many end up puzzling and disputing over primitive artificial situations in which simple probability assessments can be made, in detachment from all considerations of successful scientific, technical, or lay practice, on what are taken to be directly accessible syntactic, semantic, logical, or even psychological grounds? The best explanation of this peculiar phenomenon seems to be that in this case, as in others, appearances can be deceiving and intentions mistaken. We must often judge what a person is doing, not merely by his honest avowals, but also by the complex institutional means and practices in which his action is carried out and, in turn, by the role these means and practices play in larger society. So the activities of a person engaged in philosophizing about inductive knowledge and methods are partially determined in character by the resources at his disposal for this philosophizing and by his choice among these resources. If these resources have been in the main those which have been devised and employed for the purpose of providing direct answers to skeptical challenges of inductive knowledge and methods, there is at least a *prima facie* case that, even in the face of stout and sincere denials on the part of some of the participants in the activity, this is a just way of describing that activity. Furthermore, we do not need to be prepared to advance an accusation of duplicity in order to be on our guard with the reformed alcoholic who retains a fascination with glasses and decanters, or with the repentant master of the torture chamber who remains preoccupied with the ingenious efficiency of the rack and screw.

Men do not, as we are often reminded, gather grapes of thorns or figs of thistles. If a particular tree from which we expected to harvest apples, perennially yields crab apples instead, we may perhaps need to inquire whether the attempted graft of apple upon crab had succeeded, whether the tree that we had been cultivating was not a crab after all. The case is similar when the ostensible project of effecting philosophical understanding, criticism, and rectification of scientific, inductive, and statistical practice regularly issues in studies marked by scant attention to actual scientific and technical practice, in favor of a concentration upon primitive cases of probability assessment designed to provide "logical foundations" of that practice. Then one must be prepared to consider seriously whether the project is what it is intended to be, whether its execution by apparently Cartesian means has not in good part succeeded in frustrating its original intentions and subverting it to Cartesian ends.

21. It is thus not surprising that though Descartes, like his fellow rationalists, did not have the problem of induction, he had a problem that was remarkably similar, occupying a crucial place in the development of knowledge, as conceived in that philosophy, and presenting irreducible logical difficulty in its solution. The two problems are remarkably similar because they are, beneath their rationalist and empiricist garments, the same, namely, the justification problem. It is the problem of justifying certain basic items in the corpus of human knowledge, where justifying is taken to mean meeting a skeptical challenge against all knowledge claims of the kind in question, and where meeting the skeptical challenge itself has the following character: one first accepts the challenge as legitimate and then attempts to answer it without contravening the principle upon which the challenge rests. The problem is thus at bottom how it is possible, having accepted the skeptical questions, and with them the elements of skeptical philosophy from which they arise, to avoid the conclusions to which these elements inexorably lead. It is a problem of how, having accepted skeptical principles in order to raise certain questions about knowledge, it is possible consistently to give to these questions any but skeptical answers.

The skepticism residing in and constantly being elicited from philosophical problems concerning the justification of broad domains of our knowledge claims—inductive, psychological, ethical and social—derives primarily not from the character of these claims, but from the character of the procedure of justification, which is a central feature of these problems. It derives from the skeptical theory of knowledge which in the philosophy centering on this procdure is so effectively and seductively advanced. Elements of the Cartesian philosophy of knowledge which, if presented directly, might with their very obvious intimations of ensuing skeptical disaster have very reduced attraction, are made to seem irresistible when advanced as a mere elucidation of what is logically involved in the successful employment of this seemingly innocuous philosophical procedure. What is being urged here as a much needed corrective to this representation of the matter is that what is thus elucidated is, rather, the logical consequences of a conception that has its natural home in Cartesian philosophy, in which justification is conceived as a response to skeptical challenge within a framework of ideas itself sufficiently congenial to skepticism to render the challenge intelligible and sensible, and sufficiently also to ensure for it a skeptical response. This general justification theory, explicated in detail in a variety of theories of knowledge which follow Descartes in viewing the development of knowledge as linear progression or building from fixed foundations, is but that Cartesian view elucidated in the reverse order, regressing to, rather than proceeding from, the privileged body of fixed, incorrigible claims. It is thus not remarkable that the view commonly does issue in skepticism in the endeavor to expand our knowledge, inductively and otherwise, from this basis, since the original restriction of knowledge claims to this basis reveals it to be, root and branch, a skeptical view. Within such a view the constantly stimulated and much practiced exercise of answering skeptical challenge amounts in the end, as it did in Hume, to skepticism responding to, becoming aware of, knowing itself. Conceived in any other way, as, for example, a procedure for procuring relief from skeptical doubts, the exercise must issue in bafflement and renewed doubt. These are insured directly by the procedure of justification employed in the exercise, and indirectly by the broader theory of knowledge that dictates that it is in the form of this procedure that the philosophical examination and appraisal of knowledge claims shall be conceived and carried out.

CHAPTER 4

Justification and
Cognitive Practice

1. The preceding chapters have traced the philosophical diffi-culties expressed in the form of the problem of induction to their sources in a much deeper kind of difficulty or problem, which was called the "justification problem." This latter problem is endemic to a kind of theory of knowledge which, in considera-tion of the influence of Descartes in expounding and disseminat-ing such a view, has been called "Cartesian." Were one's frame of reference larger and one's interest more synoptic, the theory might with some, but not equal, justice also be called "Aristo-telian."

Whatever its more extended ancestry may be, Descartes is surely the father of this kind of theory in modern philosophy, just as Kant, though not with the same unmistakable clarity, is the father of an opposed tradition now beginning to take life again after some relative quiescence. At the hands of Descartes this theory was fashioned in part as a response to skeptical chal-lenges of our capacity to have knowledge, in this particular case of our capacity to have sure, systematic knowledge of the nature and behavior of physical things. Descartes sought to meet these challenges by means of a positive theory of knowledge designed to refute them. He set out to show concerning the skeptical phi-losophy that there was some mistake, not in the kind of question this philosophy seeks to pose concerning human knowledge, but in the answers it gives to these questions. The theory of knowl-edge designed to give positive answers to the skeptic's questions was one that would view all sound knowledge claims as beginning in certain simple, utterly transparent claims concerning the conscious states of the person making them, claims so very sure that no one, however skeptically inclined, could refuse to concede them, in their application to himself, without either paradox and self-stultification. From these beginnings, proceeding carefully by means of other steps, equally sure to all who recognize the benevolence of an existing God, Descartes hoped to demonstrate the possibility of a sound edifice of human knowledge, proof now against the demon's wiles and the skeptic's cavil.

2. But there is a great difference between the intentions of this philosophy and its achievement. Designed to oppose skepticism, it succeeds rather in supporting it. And this reversal in effect is apparently a necessary consequence of the means employed. What may seem only a matter of elementary fairness in arguing against the challenges of the skeptical philosophy— namely, making a start in argument that admits only what that philosophy itself concedes, and regarding all else as doubtful— accomplishes not fairness in argument but subversion, the transformation of what sets out as opposition to skepticism into a version of skepticism itself.

Generations of philosophers since Descartes have followed him in this path. Like him they have reasoned that the way to meet the skeptic's challenge was to retreat to a fortified position, consisting of impregnable claims, from which one could proceed to effect an ordered advance designed to drive the opposition eventually from the field. The establishment of the fundamental soundness of what we take to be the corpus of human knowledge is taken to require that this corpus, at least in its fundamentals, have a foundation or basis of this impregnable kind. It requires for this purpose, first, a proof that there is such a foundation or basis, and, second, a demonstration that by judicious and efficient employment this foundation or basis may be made to yield these fundamentals, either by exhibiting them as elements of itself or by exhibiting a capacity to generate them. It is readily granted that ordinarily when we adduce grounds in support of some challenged item of knowledge or belief we do not pursue the matter so far as to exhibit the derivation of the item in question from such foundations. But this, it is thought, merely reflects that ordinarily we are not faced with anything like a thorough challenge, contesting our claims at all possible points and calling for a thorough justification of them. For many practical purposes this may suffice; but for philosophical purposes, for exhibiting in full and defending against skeptical challenge what we take ourselves to know, or reasonably believe, it will not. The skeptical challenges, once accepted, must be answered at all points where they arise.

3. One way of characterizing this response in support of Cartesianism is to say that it exhibits a philosophically distorted and unsound view of what the justification of truth claims consists in. This way of reacting to skeptical challenges has been followed again and again by a variety of writers in dealing with a variety of philosophical problems, especially in recent British and American analytic philosophy. But though there is merit in this way of viewing the matter, there is one way in which it is seriously inadequate in the understanding it reveals of this and similar problems. To view the dispute, in this particular case, as one over different ways of viewing justification; to argue that what lies at the bottom of the perennially perplexing problem of justification is a misunderstanding of what justification is; and to attempt to correct this misunderstanding by advancing a conception of justification that is more in keeping with what is the practice of justification in science, the other intellectual disciplines, and in everyday life—to do this is to presume that in the domains referred to there is something that can appropriately be referred to as a practice of justification. There is without question a great discrepancy between, to use a very broad term of Peirce, the way "the fixation of belief" is carried out in the domains referred to above, and what is regarded as reasonable and ideal in this regard in the Cartesian view of the matter. Descartes himself would have admitted, indeed insisted, upon this. The question is not about this, but is rather whether it is accurate and philosophically illuminating to treat this discrepancy as a difference of view about *justification,* about the way this is and ought to be effected.

4. The danger here, and one common in philosophical discus-

sion, is that of entrapment in a problem by means of the language in which the problem is stated. While of course there is no magic in the sound of the word "justification," any more than in the sounds of the names "Montague" and "Capulet," there may indeed be great power in what such words or names suggest to us, in the view of things that these words and their natural employment tend to convey. The question whether the present King of France is bald implies, in some sense of this rich word, that there is a present king of that nation. Similarly the question about an item of knowledge, or supposed knowledge, "What justifies it?" implies that there is some other item or set of items, some circumstance, fact, or principle, or set of these, that stands in justifying relation to the first item and in whose existence in this relation to that item this justification consists.

What can easily be suggested by this language of justification, and what has been suggested to many philosophers, is a simple linear view of a nexus of considerations constituting the grounds of items of knowledge or belief, a view that has its counterpart in a simple linear view of causation that, like it, is often exhibited in abstract metaphysical discussion. This view of causation, which lends itself readily to reasoning about first and hence uncaused causes, is in very marked ways discrepant with our practice in ascribing responsibility for events in everyday life, in science, history, law, and other areas of investigation.[1] Similarly it appears that there is a great discrepancy between the simple linear view of the relation between items of knowledge or reasonable belief and their "justifiers," and the variety and complexity of consideration that we appeal to in actual practice when we investigate, adduce, and appraise grounds for such items, and when, on occasion, we determine that the grounds are sufficiently great that under critical inspection the items in question may maintain their right to be taken as matters of reasonable belief or knowledge.

The immediate question here is not about the existence of the discrepancy, but how it should be viewed. More particularly, it is a question whether it is philosophically felicitous to view

[1] Cf., for example, H. L. A. Hart and A. M. Honoré, *Causation in the Law*, Pt. I.

the discrepancy as one between two views, or two kinds, of justification, one Cartesian and the other not, one set forth in a philosophical theory, and the other exhibited in actual practice. It is a question whether the admitted discrepancy may then be used as a ground in arguing the rejection of the Cartesian view, since wide divergence between what that view claims justification to be, and the actual practice of justification, if such there be, leaves open the view to the charge that as a philosophical theory concerning a practice or institution, it is eccentric, aberrant, uninformed about the nature of the very institution or practice concerning which it is supposed to provide philosophical illumination. This is of course a serious charge. For while it is not expected of a philosophical theory, in the philosophy of morals or of law, for example, that it be faithful in every respect to the vast institution or complex of practices with which it is concerned, it is expected that it be firmly rooted in an understanding of the institution or practices in question, that it capture the essential features or nature of these as they exist in the world, and not simply as they might exist in some vastly different world populated by beings vastly different from ourselves. Plato's theories of justice and the state are offered as ideals for real people and real states, not merely as philosophical dreams.

5. A ready way of exposing the weakness of this way of dealing with the view of justification exhibited in Cartesian philosophy is to consider the response an advocate of that view may be expected to make to the kind of charge just mentioned. The regularity with which this kind of response has been given suggests that there is some reasonable basis for it. To adherents of the kind of philosophical views against which this charge has been made, the misunderstanding revealed in the charge is exactly of the same character, and exactly as great, as that of Samuel Johnson in answer to Berkeley, kicking a stone, or G. E. Moore exhibiting to philosophical audiences his hands or his watch. From the point of view of the philosophical issues under consideration these performances seem to many to be examples, not of thinking with the learned while speaking with the vulgar, but of thinking with the vulgar while addressing the learned. Appropriate as these performances may have been, had the question at issue

been one concerning the existence of objects external to us in some "vulgar" sense in which we speak of things being "in our minds" and others not, they seem somehow not appropriate when the issue concerns objects thought to be external in a somewhat different sense, a sense resulting when our ordinary views of the matter have been refined and altered by reflection upon certain aspects of perception, thought, knowledge, and science.

As a response to the justification problem, then, the argument that the view of justification taken in that problem is radically discrepant with what actually takes place in the adduction and appraisal of grounds is bound to seem much like kicking stones. And the primary reason for this is, of course, that what is in question in this problem is not, except in a very special way, a question about what takes place in this practice. The question raised about justification is not principally about what people do when they are seriously engaged in, and take themselves to be properly, effecting the fixation of belief. It is not a question like that of how cotton fibers are spun into thread or bourbon whiskey made from grain. Hence it will not be answered by one's securing a more and more full and accurate account of what actually takes place in the procedures in question. In the familiar story the naive man, when asked if he believes in infant baptism replies, "Believe in it? I've seen it done!" This inappropriate answer illustrates well the point in question. The man was not asked about what people did, whether they do practice the sacrament in question by applying water to the bodies of infants. He was asked whether he believed that these procedures, admittedly carried on, do succeed in doing what this sacrament is supposed to do, namely effect spiritual rebirth and bring salvation to sinful souls. So, correspondingly, in the justification problem, the question is not about what scientists, historians, courts of inquiry, etc., do when these are engaged in sifting evidence, developing and testing hypotheses, making judgments. It is a question of whether, in some further sense, the procedures engaged in and the results achieved can be *justified*. For as in the case of infant baptism, so here there is a disputed issue and an argument. For certain reasons, e.g., the description of certain practices, and certain other relevant texts, in the New Testament, some people question the propriety and effectiveness of infant baptism. They know what people do, but they doubt whether what is done can be defended against a certain criticism. Likewise there are some philosophers who, little disposed to dispute about the main characteristics of the practices of identifying knowledge and assaying the rationality of belief and judgment in various domains of life, including the sciences, nevertheless question whether the practices can be defended against a certain philosophical criticism. The question about justification, commonly the justification of inductive conclusions, but also conclusions, claims, judgments of a wider sort, is thus not a question about the character of various ongoing practices, but about the acceptability, judged by a certain philosophical standard, of the results of these practices. It is a question arising in a certain context of philosophical ideas and presumptions which generate a challenge concerning the efficacy of the practices, a challenge that can adequately be met only by dealing with the ideas and presumptions in which the challenge takes its rise, and not by a systematic description and codification of the practices themselves, no matter how accurate and elaborate this may be. To those who advance the challenge, the attempt to respond to it in this way must seem, if taken as an attempt to meet that challenge, to beg the main question at issue, and, if not taken as an attempt to meet it, simply to miss the philosophical point.

6. The general point here is of sufficient importance to justify repeating. It is that the justification problem is a problem within Cartesian philosophy, one which cannot be properly dealt with in isolation from the theses and preconceptions about knowledge which are at work in that philosophy. The problem represents a challenge arising out of difficulties encountered in the execution of the Cartesian program for the reconstruction of human knowledge, a challenge somehow to surmount these difficulties and make the program succeed. It is not a problem that will be either solved or satisfactorily resolved by a consideration, however careful, of the way, in actual practice, grounds are adduced, knowledge certified, belief fixed, because it is not in any direct way about that practice. It is a problem about justification in a dif-

ferent sense, a sense that has its home in the Cartesian philosophy; and it must be dealt with, therefore, by a kind of inquiry that pays attention to that philosophy, that is prepared to treat, though not necessarily agree with, the point of view about knowledge that is represented in that philosophy. In dealing critically with this and similar problems there is little more to be gained in present philosophy by continuing to kick stones.

7. Nevertheless the stones are there. And further, there is much to be learned by paying attention to what we do when we kick, or kick at, them: by taking note of the ways in which we can and do derive information about objects by means of such immediate action upon them. A cautious, exploratory kick is often a simple means of discriminating in poor light between real object and shadow, just as kicking, hefting, or pushing are often economical means of discriminating stones from contrived likenesses, and not always, as even the amateur gardener knows, to the disadvantage of copy in comparison with archetype. Might not a modern Democritus aptly characterize the various techniques we now have for exploring the finer structure of matter by applying to specimens of it different kinds of radiation, as refined procedures for kicking stones?

But what is to be learned by close attention to such procedures in the philosophical scrutiny of knowledge is not easily accessible to one whose thought about knowledge and knowing practices is preoccupied by the special kind of concern which is dominant in justification theory. Granted that what we take to be knowledge and proper knowing practices are in need of philosophical scrutiny, appraisal, and criticism, what distinguishes the advocate of such a theory from advocates of alternative ones is the particular manner in which according to him this scrutiny, etc., must proceed. His concern, the philosophical character of which will be explored in detail later, dictates a particular kind of program. In it detailed study of certain items, domains, and practices in question, and in turn the criticism and appraisal of them by means of the wide resources available in other items, domains, practices not in question—a way of procedure which issues naturally from accepted principles and practices themselves— is replaced by something very different, which might be called "trial by derivation." Items of putative knowledge are appraised and judged exclusively by determining whether or not they can be derived from, and thus validated by, certain ultimately basic premises in what might be regarded as *the* grand argument, *the* grand deduction of knowledge.

8. Some of those committed or inclined to this way of proceeding are well aware of the contrast between it and the methods of appraisal sanctioned by accepted practice in everyday life, in the intellectual disciplines, and in the various technical arts. Such readers may well dispense with further discussion of the contrast and proceed at once to the extended philosophical examination of justification theory which makes up Part II. For those to whom the contrast is not already sufficiently well marked, it seems desirable, before proceeding to that criticism, that an effort be made to portray the contrast in some detail, to render unmistakable the wide differences between the justification operation, as it is conceived and given a central position in this theory, and the multiform cognitive practices with which it is important that it not be confused.

It has already been conceded that the establishment of the contrast, however striking, does not constitute by itself a refutation of the theory. What counts most decisively against the kind of program in the philosophical examination of knowledge which the theory dictates is the broad fact that it is a kind which cannot be successfully begun, and, if begun, cannot be successfully completed. But before arguing the case for ascribing failure to the program, it is of first importance that it be very clear just exactly what the program is, what it is which is alleged to fail. This will be of assistance, not only in following and appraising the argument, but also, supposing the argument to succeed, in providing a first small step in the elucidation of an alternative approach in the theory of knowledge, one which, rather than proceeding on principle heedless of the character of actual cognitive practices, endeavors to learn from them and capitalize upon their settled capacities in designing a realistic program of philosophical appraisal and judgment.

9. For these purposes it is desirable that the discussion move at once to a more concrete level, to take under consideration a

few specific examples of the kinds of practice that are being referred to here. In treating these examples, in employing them to
emphasize the difference between the practices, on the one hand,
and the philosophical operation of justification, on the other, attention will be drawn repeatedly to the variety of consideration
and response provided for in the practices, in contrast with that
provided for in the philosophical operation. For the most prominent features of the practices are (1) a profusion of kinds of
grounds that according to them may properly be adduced in support of claims, judgments, hypotheses, suppositions, and so on; (2)
a similar profusion of means that may be employed to appraise
these grounds; and (3) a much greater variety also of cognitive
stance or attitude in response to this appraisal than can be accommodated in a few categories, such as the now highly regular-
ized philosophical ones of knowledge and belief. Though the
extent of the examination is slight in comparison with that of
the practices in question, this much elucidation of certain features of them, in contrast with the corresponding features of
the operation of justification, together with a brief notice of the
kind of appraisal of this contrast that the justification theory
provides, will help in making clearer the difference between
the question of justification, as it arises in that theory, and the
question of what people engaged in the predominantly nonphilosophical practices in question actually do.

10. There are clearly in these activities some aspects that at
first glance encourage a Cartesian view of what is effected in them.
Upon being challenged with respect to some claim I have advanced, say C_1, I respond by citing some further claim or set of
claims, C_2. If I take myself to be justified in advancing C_1, do I
not imply that my justification resides in C_2? If asked explicitly
about C_1, "What justifies you in holding *this?*" I respond by
citing C_2, am I not merely making explicit my supposition that
the justification, warrant, authority of C_1 lies in what I convey in
this further, backing claim or set of claims, C_2?

Suppose my friend Robert reports to me that he has been looking for a mutual acquaintance Martin, and is wondering where
he can find him, for there is some matter he needs to see him
about. And suppose I tell him, "Don't bother looking for Martin

now. You can see him tonight at the meeting." "Oh," Robert
may reply, "Do you think he'll be there?" or making his challenge more explicit, "What makes you think that Martin will be
at the meeting?"

Consider a few of the things I might say, a few of the grounds
I might adduce, if in response to this challenge I wish to maintain and support the implied prediction that Martin will be at the
meeting. "He'll be there," I might say, "he promised to come."
Or I might say, "He hasn't missed a meeting yet"; or somewhat
differently, "Martin never misses a meeting; he loves meetings."
Or, given the appropriate information, I might say, "Of course
he'll be there. He's the one who is going to submit the new resolution."

These possible *grounds,* and others that one could as easily
imagine, differ strikingly in the information they provide and in
the way this information serves as a ground for the prediction in
question. "He promised" conveys information concerning a past
action on the part of Martin. "He hasn't missed a meeting yet"
likewise conveys information concerning the past, namely, the
regularity exhibited in Martin's attendance at meetings. That
Martin never misses meetings, or that he loves meetings, is information of a different sort, information of a more timeless lawlike
character concerning Martin's disposition to act or react to certain types of situation and opportunity. The information that
Martin is the one who is going to submit the resolution to the
meeting may be taken most normally as information about Martin's present intentions or about a future event expected to occur
in conformity with that intention.

11. The grounds that we may have and employ in support of
a prediction like this are thus not limited in character in any
simple way. They are as various as the possible kinds of challenges to which on one occasion or another a statement of this
kind is liable. When one inquires concerning such possible
grounds, concerning the possible answers that might be proper to
the questions "How do you know?" "What makes you think so?"
etc., raised about any particular predictive statement, the difficulty is not in how to begin to answer but in how to stop. If
I warn you that traffic on the streets will be congested tomorrow,

I might, upon questioning, support the prediction conveyed with a reminder that tomorrow there will be a football game, or that tomorrow is Saturday, or that the state basketball tournament began this morning. Perhaps the most noteworthy feature of the first reply, which is unmistakably a statement about the future, is that, in contrast with the previous example, there is a clearer logical gap here between this statement about the future, mentioned as a possible ground, and the main prediction in question. The same holds for "Tomorrow is Saturday," but this, if construed as a statement about the future, must be considered as a special kind. In any case, that tomorrow is Saturday, or that there will be a football game tomorrow, does not by itself yield the consequence that traffic in the streets will be congested in as tight and ready a way as Martin's presenting a resolution to the meeting yields the consequence that he is present. The same point is illustrated in the case, to consider but one more, when I advise you, after we have finished mowing the lawn, to pick the sickle off the ground and stow it in the garage, since otherwise, I may add, it will be rusted by tomorrow. Among the possible grounds that I might adduce for this prediction is the further prediction that there is going to be a heavy dew tonight. This will serve as ground for the original prediction no less clearly than the observation that the sickle is cutting steel and has a high carbon content, or the reminder that it rusted overnight the last time we used it and forgot to put it away.

12. The considerations cited as grounds one might adduce in support of simple predictions like these are but beginning illustrations of the variety such grounds may on occasion exhibit. And just as there are a variety of grounds which may be adduced for such a prediction, so there are a variety of *means of appraisal* of the grounds, and also a variety of response to the appraisal. Variety in the means of appraisal of the grounds follows as a close consequence of the variety of these grounds. If called upon to assay the weight, as evidence that Martin will attend the meeting, of the information that he promised to do so, I should pay attention to, and rely upon, considerations of a very different sort from those that would come into play were the information rather that he never misses meetings or that he

loves meetings. In considering promises as grounds for expectations of performances, one relies, at a very general level, upon settled judgments and habits of thoughts concerning the social practice in question, and, at a more restricted level, upon consideration of the occasion on which the promise was made, the kind of performance promised, the character of the person who made the promise, and possibly various events that may have taken place in the interval between the time of the promise and that of its proposed redemption. In considering invariable attendance in the past as a ground for expectation of future attendance and in assaying its weight as a ground there are similarly a variety of considerations that one would appeal to. There has been no want of reminders from critical students of inductive extrapolation, classical as well as modern, that in some cases an invariable association of *A* with *B* in the past, or in known cases, has little or no weight as support for the judgment that the association is an exemplification of a law of nature, or even that this uniformity will be conformed to by the next *A* encountered. By his invention of the predicate "grue" Nelson Goodman made this basic fact of inductive life plain to even the slowest learner, who need not wait, like that chicken destined for the pot in Bertrand Russell's well-known example, to discover that, under certain circumstances, each additional example of the uniform association of *A* with *B* not only fails to increase the likelihood that these characters or events will be associated in the next case, but may positively decrease it.[2] Similarly, and in consequence, an additional example of the association of *A* with *B* may, in certain circumstances, serve, not to add to, but to decrease, the total strength of the grounds we have for the general association of these two characters.[3]

The now famous debacle suffered by public opinion polls in the presidential election of 1948, and the recent one in the British parliamentary elections of 1970, have served to freshen the sensitivity of students of the art of inductive extrapolation on such matters to the complexity of the considerations that must

---

[2] This was not exactly the lesson that Russell proposed to teach by this example in *The Problems of Philosophy*, Ch. VI.

[3] Cf. F. L. Will, "Consequences and Confirmation," *Philosophical Review* (1966).

be taken account of in employing the expressed preferences of an apparently representative sample of an electorate concerning candidates in an impending election, as a simple model for constructing a conclusion concerning what choices this group, as well as the whole electorate will make, when the time of the election arrives. Relevant considerations here range from those of individual and social psychology, and recent social and political history, to those of sampling theory and the abstract mathematical aspects of the theory of statistical estimation. The elaboration of these considerations, both the concrete and the abstract ones, which draw heavily, through the domain of mathematical statistics, upon the mathematical theory of probability, represents, in one particular domain, the materials for the answer to Mill's celebrated question about why, in some cases, a single instance is

sufficient for a complete induction, while in others myriads of concurring instances, without a single exception known or presumed, go such a very little way towards establishing an universal proposition.[4]

Though this question was propounded by Mill in tones of bafflement, considerations which he himself referred to in discussing the entire topic show that what prevented him from providing an answer to his question was not ignorance of the materials out of which the answer was to be constructed, but an inability, deriving from his philosophical preconceptions, to see how the answer could be formulated and advanced in a satisfactory way. As he said, in reflecting upon inductive generalizations about the position of organs in the human body or about the colors of birds, most people would say:

It was more credible that a bird should vary in its colour than that men should vary in the relative position of their principal organs. And there is no doubt that in saying so they would be right; but to say why they are right would be impossible, without entering more deeply than is usually done into the true theory of Induction.[5]

Neglecting for a moment the inaptness, partly anachronistic, of Mill's language, one can agree to a considerable extent that the heart of the matter lies in giving a philosophical answer to

4 *A System of Logic*, Bk. III, Ch. III, Sect. 3.   5 *Ibid.*

the question of "why they are right." This means showing philosophically that they are right: not by producing philosophical proofs about the positions of organs or the colors of birds, but by providing philosophical answers to philosophical questions about the grounds they may or do have in support of judgments of this kind, by developing sound philosophical responses to challenges that have been made to the ultimate worth, value, or cogency of the grounds themselves. The problem of induction, like the problem in its wider form, the justification problem, is a problem of how, in the philosophical examination, rationalization, and illumination of the practices in which we support claims that we take ourselves to know, or at least to have good reason to believe, these challenges can be met and the skeptical conclusions implicit in them avoided. It has been argued that this is a problem generated by deep and tenacious philosophical preconceptions about knowledge and reasonable belief, about the kind of rationality which, under the title of "justification" these must have and be able to exhibit on demand. To this problem, in both its narrower and wider form, and to the enlightenment which can be won by close scrutiny of the difficulties it manifests and the philosophical commitments it represents, the major efforts of this book are directed.

13. It will help in the process of clarification to pay some attention also to the variety of *response* that we make to the grounds we and others adduce in support of challenged claims. Some of this variety is recognized prominently in certain common distinctions made in the language of everyday life and epistemology; some of it, though recognized on occasion, receives much less prominence. The most familiar of these distinctions, to which reference has been made repeatedly in the immediately preceding sections, is that between knowledge and belief. One cannot begin to discuss the question of the propriety of our response to the advancement of some ground intending to support a certain claim, p, without recognizing the rough distinction between knowing p and having a reasonable, well-grounded belief in p. Yet a little reflection upon examples of the kind just considered is sufficient to reveal that, valuable as this distinction of response is, it is also, in relation to the subtlety of the variety of the responses possible, somewhat restrictive and insensitive.

Consider, for example, my assurance to my friend that Martin will be at the meeting, and the ground I offered in support, that Martin promised to attend. And suppose that there is no question that Martin did promise. There is no doubt in my mind about this; I was one of the persons to whom he made the promise. And my friend likewise has no doubts on this score. Does my friend then *know* that Martin will be at the meeting, or does he only *believe,* that this is the case? And if it is a case of belief, as contrasted with knowledge, is the belief justified?

Are these clear questions to which definite answers can be given? Or is it not rather the case that before we can determine whether it is appropriate to speak here of knowledge, belief, or something else, we need to understand more of the context in which the questions are asked. At the meeting, after Martin has made his appearance, my friend, if asked, "Did you know that Martin would be here?" might readily reply, "Yes. I was told that he would," or, "Yes, F. W. told me that he promised to come." But before the meeting, if challenged about whether he knows that Martin would be there, and fearful of the possibility of contravening events that might be hinted in the challenge, my friend *might* be reluctant to say that he knows that Martin will attend. Even recognizing Martin's definite intention and promise to come, my friend realizes that he is in no position to assure that Martin's intention will persist in the face of possible sudden sickness of his child, or given the persistence of the intention, that Martin will have a safe passage from his house to the place of meeting. On the other hand, if addressed with the same question, "Do you know whether Martin will be at the meeting?" as a request for information rather than a challenge, my friend might readily reply to another, much as I did to him, "Yes. He'll be there; he promised to come."

14. In the commonly employed distinction between knowledge and belief there is a recognition that not all truth claims that a person accepts in one way or other are claims that he can be said to know. That this is a useful distinction is obvious. But certain aspects of the distinction, and the exact domains of the terms distinguished, are far from obvious. If by an act of philosophical definition we divide the whole continent of what we may think of as positive responses to truth claims into knowledge and

belief, we do not thereby render the distinction between these simple and clear. And as just observed, in specific cases, whether it is proper to speak of a person knowing a certain claim will depend, not only upon the grounds he has for the claim, but the kind of claim it is and the kind of judgment, response, decision that is called for with respect to the claim in the broader context of his thought and action. What distinguishes claims that we may be said to know, among those that are true and that we do accept in one way or other, is not simply their greater strength of grounds. It is also the specific character of the grounds, and, further, the character and strength of those in relation to what is required in this kind of case in order for it to be proper for us to say, or to have said of us, that we do know the claim in question. There is, for example, to put the matter simply, but much too narrowly, no general point on the scale of probabilities at which we are justified in saying of claims we take to be true that we know them. Though it is the case that often the point in the use of the word "know," in contrast with "believe" and similar alternatives, is to call attention to the strength of grounds in support of the claim in question, this does not appear to be universally the case. And the investigation of the reasons why it is not, promises to be of service in illuminating the character of some of our most commonly employed epistemological categories.

However we draw the line, furthermore, between those claims we say we know and those we only "believe," we need to remember that having drawn the line marking off this vast area, the responses we have collected in it under this latter common name remain as various as before. The responses are as varied as the kinds of decision we make in accepting different kinds of truth claims, and as the kinds of attitude or stance we take in making this acceptance. We may accept a truth claim as a basis for action, or planning for action, as my friend may have done in planning to see Martin at the meeting. We may accept it, as a secure basis for action, judging the grounds for p to be adequate to warrant proceeding without further consideration of the chance that p does not hold. Or we may accept it with a large amount of insecurity, judging that though the chance of error is too substantial to be discounted, it is not too great to forbid *p* being taken as a basis for action, so long as the risks are recognized and in some degree perhaps provided for. The endeavor to ascertain the truth about matters, both in practical life and in theoretical inquiry, does not always provide us with unlimited time, resources, or ingenuity. Our decision can be forced in a variety of ways, and what is available as the best choice may be, in comparison with what we should prefer, a poor choice indeed. At other times acceptance of an insecure *p* may be indicated as desirable in much less straitened or pressing circumstances. In a case where acceptance of *p* threatens no great risk, but offers instead promise as a direct way to uncovering grounds for assigning this claim a more definite position in the spectrum of our commitments, the practical motives for decision have much more the character of attraction than compulsion. Not all such options are as desperate as that of Pascal.

15. When one looks away from the simple contexts of decision that have been illustrated so far to more complex ones, both in practical life and in theoretical inquiry, one sees also illustrated on a larger scale the variety of consideration and response that lies beneath the blanket terms of belief, establishment, justification, and so on, in which we sometimes speak of the positive response we make when, considering the grounds that can be adduced in support of some claim, we give to the claim some kind of nod or vote of approval. The difference that there may be in my friend's reaction to the grounds for expecting Martin to be at the meeting, depending upon the urgency of his need to encounter Martin there, has an elaborate institutional parallel in the difference in the evidence required for a decision against a defendant in a court of law in a criminal case, as contrasted with a civil one. The difference between a decision made in accordance with a balance of evidence, and a decision that requires no reasonable doubt of guilt, like a decision made by a split vote and one made by a unanimous vote of a jury, reflects a difference in the context in which the decision is made, a difference in the significance of the verdict, and, by virtue of these, a difference in the character of the acceptance or rejection of the charge, as the case may be. Having read, heard, and considered a great

amount of publicly available evidence, I may as a private citizen, be of the opinion that Lee Harvey Oswald shot President Kennedy. But however firm that opinion might be, it would be different in character from the judgment I might render, were I a juror passing on the same matter, supposing the case to have come to trial, just as it was different for the men who passed upon it in their capacity as members of the United States Investigating Commission presided over by Chief Justice Earl Warren.

16. It is in accordance with common usage to speak of a theory being killed by a fact. Recently a variety of writers in the philosophy of science have emphasized that in the practice of scientific inquiry the invalidation and rejection of theories are not as abrupt and decisive as this way of speaking suggests. Observed facts do lead to the abandonment of theories, but the neat and simple dispatch of a complex theory by a few irrefragable and discrepant facts is a rare and remarkable phenomenon. An analogy in legal and philosophical thought is the fact that the search for counterinstances of a rule or generalization leads more often to the refinement of the proposed rule or generalization than to its abandonment.

The complexity of the relationship between scientific theories and the observed facts that may support or count against them is widely recognized. It is not so widely recognized that what is illustrated in a prominent and elaborate way in the case of scientific theories is a complexity realized in a more modest, subdued form in the case of less expanded statements, reports, allegations, or descriptions. That this is so has been elucidated and emphasized by W. V. Quine in a variety of comments, among them the deft metaphor to the effect that "Our statements about external reality face the tribunal of sense experience not individually, but as a corporate body." [6] The understanding of the complex relationship that obtains between proposition and fact, or proposition and experience, when fact or experience is employed as a tribunal for proposition, involves a reference to the variety of responses or attitudes that can be taken toward propositions and correspondingly to the differential appropriateness, under varying circumstances, of specific responses or attitudes to

6 *Methods of Logic,* rev. ed., Intro., p. xii.

the propositions in question, given the experience or facts at hand. These attitudes or responses are as various as the kinds of acceptance or rejection that are exemplified in the widely various domains of practical life and theoretical inquiry. They encompass, among other responses, and in addition to belief and knowledge, idle surmises, suppositions, guesses, acceptance as a basis for practical action, acceptance for the purpose of further research and testing, assumption, presumption, judgment of fact such as is rendered in a court of law or in historical inquiry, and the kind of relative judgment that abounds both in practical life and scientific inquiry concerning, not the absolute merits of one or other of competing views or theories, but that one of these is clearly superior to the rest.

17. In the recently (1970) widely broadcast television documentary report of a criminal trial in Denver, the attorney for the defense advanced an argument that illustrates in a simple practical situation the need in certain circumstances to make the kind of discrimination in our responses to truth claims that are illustrated in the above catalogue. As part of his examination of a prospective juror, the defense attorney sought to establish that this man was incompetent to serve as a juror in this trial unless at this stage of the proceedings he already had "an opinion as to . . . [the defendant's] guilt or innocence," this opinion being required, according to the argument, by the legal requirement that the defendant in a trial be presumed innocent until proved guilty. That "you should already have an opinion" as to the defendant's guilt or innocence, "may come as some surprise to you," said the defense counsel, addressing this man and the other prospective jurors. He then proceeded to extract this logical rabbit out of his hat in the following way. It is a consequence of the required presumption of innocence, applied to this case, he argued, that if the jury were already empaneled and were required at once to render a verdict, without any argument or evidence being presented by either side, the verdict be, "Not guilty." From this it follows that each properly qualified juror is required by law already to have an opinion as to the guilt or innocence of the defendant, namely, the opinion that he is innocent.

So at this moment, without hearing anything more, you have the opinion that this man is innocent; he's not guilty. In fact, under our system of law you have to feel that way, don't you? So you have made up your mind about this man's guilt or innocence. You've made up your mind that he is innocent. And you are going to continue with that view until that person [presumably, the City Attorney], through his evidence, shows him to be guilty beyond a reasonable doubt.[7]

But surely the law no more requires such an antecedent opinion on the part of the juror as to the innocence of the defendant than it requires a similar opinion as to guilt. An opinion on the part of a juror to the effect that the defendant is guilty, and a decision, as a juror, that purely upon the basis of the evidence adduced at the trial the defendant may fairly, and without a reasonable doubt, be judged guilty, are two different things, though obviously they are related closely enough that a strong opinion one way or another may in certain circumstances seriously affect the capacity, including the will, of a juror to make the kind of decision required. This is what the legal presumption of innocence requires, viz., the capacity on the part of the juror, including the disposition of his will, to consider the question of guilt or innocence solely on the basis of the evidence presented, to require guilt to be proved in court, and to return a finding of not guilty if that is not done. It is surely not uncommon for men, acting as jurors or otherwise, to be firmly convinced of the guilt of a defendant, perhaps as a consequence of a trial, and yet to be as firmly convinced that the evidence produced in the trial does not, perhaps in consequence of the incompetence of the prosecution, sufficiently establish this to justify a verdict of guilty. But the chances of a significant effect of antecedent opinions on the matter one way or another are so great that jurors harboring them must normally be regarded as a hazard by counsel and the court.

---

[7] Later, in the examination of another juror, the attorney made the point even stronger, soliciting from the juror the avowal that at this point in the trial ("right now") he was "convinced" of the defendant's innocence. Transcript, NET Journal, "Trial—The City and County of Denver *vs.* Lauren R. Watson," The First Day, pp. 11-12, 34 (National Educational Television, 10 Columbus Circle, New York).

18. The institution of trial in criminal law exemplifies one set of accepted but constantly changing practices that determine in one particular area of our lives the kinds of consideration that are appropriately appealed to in responding to certain kinds of question of fact and the kind of response to which these responses are appropriate. It is this set of practices that students and apprentices of this art are indoctrinated in, which experts master, and which commissions, courts, and other agencies concerned with the improvement of courts of criminal law seek to codify, rationalize, and reform. Apprentices to the art of writing history, testing public opinion, or carrying on investigation in astrophysics, are indoctrinated into different sets of practices which exemplify in their own ways, and with highly various degrees of rigorousness and assurance, norms and regulations determining the kinds of decisions to be made in this line of investigation and the manner in which it is proper to make them. At the risk of seeming to elucidate the obvious, it needs to be emphasized now and then that determining the molecular structure of DNA and determining the social structure of the English Parliament in the reign of George III are very different kinds of tasks, properly done in very different ways.

It would be a travesty, but one not beyond the bounds of imagination, if one were to represent the activity of a natural philosopher like Galileo in achieving the result commonly referred to as the "law of free fall" primarily as an inductive extrapolation from observed data presumably attained from his experiments with the inclined plane. The basis for such a representation lies in the fact that, presuming that Galileo did perform the experiment he described in the *Dialogues Concerning Two New Sciences,* and recognizing that by 1604, as he indicated to Fra Paulo Sarpi, he had discovered this law, which he was now engaged in trying to derive from some indubitable, axiomatic principle, it is reasonable to suppose that in his discovery of the law he was influenced by the experiment, taking the exhibition of a certain relation exhibited between time elapsed and distance traveled by a ball rolling down a groove in an inclined plane as an appropriate model for a corresponding general conclusion about falling bodies, bodies in "natural motion." The law arrived at was the equivalently expressed "time-squared rule" or "odd-number rule" to the effect that "the spaces passed in natural motion . . . [are] in double proportion to the time, and as a consequence the spaces passed in equal times . . . [are] as the odd numbers *ab unitate."* [8]

One can understand Galileo's thought in coming to this important scientific conclusion in the foundation of modern dynamics, only if one takes into account the nature of the activity he was engaged in, namely, working on a theory of motion, and the wealth of consideration to which he was responding in this activity. If one thinks of Galileo as drawing this conclusion from the experimental data, unaided by the rich matrix of theoretical and practical knowledge that he brought to the experiments, one must be struck by the paucity of the apparent grounds in relation to the bold, broad claim advanced concerning falling bodies. One must indeed have a particular Providence guiding his thought who on the bases of a relatively few observations of a ball rolling down grooves in a wooden plane draws a sound conclusion about falling bodies generally. Such a person is presuming, first, that balls in all similar plane situations will duplicate the rough conformity exhibited in this experiment to the odd-number rule, and, second, that in respect to adherence to the rule, all bodies—not just metal balls, and not just balls performing on planes—will behave like this small "hard, smooth, and very round bronze ball" upon which Galileo said he had performed the experiment "a full hundred times."

19. Looked at from this point of view the passage of Galileo from his experimental data to the odd-number rule looks like

[8] Letter to Fra Paulo Sarpi, *Le Opere di Galileo Galilei: Edizione Nazionale,* Vol. X, No. 105 (Oct. 16, 1604). For this quotation and translation, as well as for much help in understanding the course of Galileo's thought on this matter, I am indebted to the unpublished M.A. thesis of Thomas B. Settle, "Galilean Science: An Empirical Source for the Odd Number Rule," Cornell University, 1963. A report of the experimental work done by Settle duplicating the Galilean experiment was published by him in "An Experiment in the History of Science," *Science,"* (1961). In a more recent article, "Galileo's Use of Experiment as a Tool of Investigation," published in E. McMullin, ed., *Galileo, Man of Science,* Settle has given a general account of his historical work and conclusions concerning this famous experiment.

magic, just the kind of mysterious serendipity that Hume and Mill and the Abbé Gratry, from their differing points of view, found exhibited in the procedure of inductive inference generally. But there is no magic, and no need of it to explain how Galileo could have arrived at his result, in spite of what Alexandre Koyré termed the "amazing and pitiful poverty of the experimental means at his disposal," and experiments which, as Galileo described them and with the perfection of result he reported from them, Koyré judged to be "completely worthless." [9] For although Koyré may have overestimated the rationalist and Platonic aspects of Galileo's work on this matter, and correspondingly underestimated the empirical, unquestionably a major portion of the considerations that led Galileo to this conclusion about falling bodies were of a highly theoretical, and, in this respect, a priori kind.

In his experiment Galileo was not just making trials with a ball rolling down a plane to see what could be observed. He was, in the first place, engaged, as he had been for some years, in highly theoretical work, in the development and perfection of a theory of motion. And in the second place he was by no means working upon such a theory *de novo*. If the early manuscripts collectively entitled *De Motu*, and expressing what have sometimes been referred to as Galileo's "Pisan dynamics," represent substantially his views on motion at the time of his discovery of the odd-number rule, his views then were markedly different from those expounded in the *Dialogues Concerning Two New Sciences*, just as they were different from the Averroist-Aristotelian views of some of his teachers and contemporaries. The Pisan dynamics were very similar to the dynamics of twelfth-century Arab writer Avempace.[10]

It is difficult to believe that, operating within this theory, Galileo would have designed an experiment to reveal something

[9] "An Experiment in Measurement," *Proceedings of the American Philosophical Society* (1953). Cf. A. Koyré, *Études Galileénes* (1939), p. 146 (*Étude II*, "La loi de la chute des corps: Descartes et Galilée," *Actualités Scientifique et Industrielles*, No. 853, p. 72): "Telle concordance *rigoureuse* est *rigoureusement impossible*" (italics in orig.).

[10] See E. A. Moody, "Galileo and Avempace: The Dynamics of the Leaning Tower Experiment," *Journal of the History of Ideas* (1951).

about acceleration, and proportional velocities consequent to this acceleration, since in this dynamics the emphasis was not upon acceleration, but upon velocities, and upon natural velocities, natural motions of bodies, which, though conceived somewhat differently from the conception in Aristotelian dynamics, was in agreement with it in being viewed as determined by some relation between the density of the body in question and that of the medium in which it moves. Galileo's view at this time, some years before reporting his observation of the odd-number rule, and many years before offering the demonstration of the rule from a very different "definition" of motion in the *Dialogues Concerning Two New Sciences,* was thus that there are specific velocities for bodies of different densities falling in media of differing densities, and that these specific velocities are determined in each case by the difference between the density of the body and that of the medium. There was a close analogy between this account of motion in a medium and the account given of position taken in a medium in the hydrostatics of Archimedes. The natural velocities in question were what were to be conceived in the later dynamics, in which acceleration had a more dominant position, as terminal velocities.

20. What is disclosed in a brief inspection of this example of the establishment of a general scientific uniformity is what many writers have emphasized in the study of sundry other examples, namely, that within the context of accepted judgment and presumption in which the work was conducted and must be understood, any *prima facie* aspect of bold extrapolation there may have been is dissipated by a fuller understanding of the work itself, including the aims of the inquiry, the nexus of thought from which it emerged, how the objects under investigation were being conceived, and the bearing of all this on what exactly the questions were, and what could be taken to be adequate answers to them. One cannot begin to understand what Robert Boyle thought he was doing with those tubes of air, mercury, and water, without taking into account that he was investigating some of the features, among them the "sprynge," of the "common air," a fluid substance whose various properties had been investigated by a long line of Boyle's predecessors, including Galileo himself. The

obvious anachronism of thinking of Boyle as puzzling over the "pressure of gases," construing that complex expression as we do now, is duplicated in a more subdued way if one thinks of Galileo as investigating acceleration in an experiment performed at a time at which his eye was focused upon "natural motion," which he then for the most part conceived as falling, and his inquiry directed to discovering the general characteristics of this kind of pervasive action.

Some features of natural motion Galileo had investigated with pendulums; and some evidently, although the evidence in this matter is not decisive, with balls thrown from towers. But the differences of specific velocities, and other consequences of the theory he then held, were difficult to observe, even in the protracted falls made possible by high towers. If the theory were sound, these velocities might be made more accessible to detection, if the falling could be uniformly retarded, as with a ball rolling down a plane, provided that the possible effects of the rotational inertia of the ball could be discounted. But reporting upon experiments with planes in *De Motu* Galileo writes that the prescribed ratios were not observed. Natural motion did not exhibit the properties expected of it. It did exhibit a different uniformity, one that at the time of *De Motu* he did not recognize, but which by 1604 he can report to Sarpi that he had observed. This uniformity was that described in the odd-number rule, and Galileo's gradual realization of the significance of it was apparently a key factor in his eventual development of a new and more satisfactory definition of natural fall.

21. The understanding of how this rule could have been adequately established by measurements of uniformly retarded falls of different duration made possible by the ball and plane, like the understanding of how Boyle's discovery about the spring of the air could have been established by the measurements Boyle could make with his tubes of water, mercury, and air, is to be found in the scientific situation in which these men were working, including therein the context of settled opinion, judgment, and conception that are a part of that situation. It is only by reference to this kind of background that one can provide an answer to Mill's question how sometimes a general law of nature

"can be inferred without hesitation from a single instance," while at others "myriads of concerning instances, without a single exception known or presumed" do not suffice. And should Mill be correct in supposing that whoever can answer this question has solved the problem of induction, then the solution of that problem lies in understanding the difference in situation between Galileo's investigations and conclusions about "natural motion," Boyle's about "the common air," and rough conclusions about the colors of birds such as ravens or swans.

When Galileo's work in progress to the odd-number rule is viewed in this fuller context, one sees that the difficulty he surmounted, by great genius and perhaps some favor of serendipity, was not so much in extrapolating a regularity exhibited by the ball but in detecting, discerning that regularity. So great was that difficulty, a difficulty both in knowing what to look for and in discerning it with his "amazing and pitiful poverty of experimental means," that Koyré was led to doubt that these experiments could have led Galileo to the discovery commonly attributed to them. Without agreeing with Koyré's skepticism on this point, one may note that to the extent that his case is strong, it reinforces the main point that has been urged here, since obviously the main difficulty in the discovery of the odd-number rule could not have been the extrapolation of the rule from conforming results, if these results were not as a matter of fact achieved. But supposing some results achieved in this way, supposing some kind of clear enough time-squared distance relation exhibited by the ball in its descent of the plane, for a man looking at this through Galileo's eyes there was no serious question about the pervasiveness of this uniformity, no question of whether it was restricted to planes or balls exactly like this, or to experiments performed at times and places like this. What was observed, what was exhibited in the behavior of the ball was a characteristic of falling bodies, of natural motion. Ingeniously interrogated by the retarding effects of the plane in the effort to expose specific velocities, Nature disclosed instead, to the perspicacity of a Galileo, the time-distance relation formulated in the rule. It disclosed it to a man who could be perspicacious about natural motion because he had a view of the world embracing this kind of motion, a view that had by theoretical and practical work been developed to such an extent that now a uniformity unmistakably exhibited by the ball in its descents of the plane could be taken, could be seen, as a feature of natural motion itself.

22. Contrasting examples of practices of coming to a decision concerning truth claims have now been briefly alluded to for the purpose of suggesting, in a minimum of space, the variety of activity which we engage in, and the significant ways in which, in these activities, the larger context and purposes of our activities, and the kinds of consideration we respond to, mutually affect each other. A jury pondering the guilt or innocence of a defendant accused of a crime responds to evidence of various sorts, as does a natural philosopher trying to perfect a theory of natural motion, but the kinds of consideration that each can properly respond to, and the kinds of response that each can properly make to these considerations are very different; and criticism is philosophically uninformed which persists in treating them as if they were the same. As the primary purpose in alluding to these examples is not to disseminate information concerning these differences, they must be briefly suggested here, in preparation for the discussion of a different, though related, point. In making the presumption of innocence of the defendant the juror divests himself of a variety of consideration that might bear on the question of guilt or innocence, or degree of guilt or innocence, or the seriousness of the alleged crime. Nevertheless these are excluded, for the purpose of carrying on this kind of adversary proceeding, in securing a verdict from a jury of one's peers, since, regardless of the relevance of some of these considerations to the question of guilt or innocence, wholesale exclusion of them, in so far as it can be achieved, is indispensable for securing a fair verdict. In the court of natural philosophy, however, Galileo was limited by no such intellectual restriction. Had he been, all that he might have learned from his experiments with the plane is certain curious features of the behavior of that very round bronze ball. Not limited, he was able to see, not simply features of the behavior of a bronze ball, but in these a characteristic of natural motion. To be sure, the more expansive the body of theory which one employs in making observa-

tions, the greater is the opportunity, not only for penetrating insight, but for error. In the case of the study of motion the opportunity for the former outweighs the risk of the latter, as it does not in the case of the jury. For one thing, the task of the jury is not to develop insightful theory; it is a mechanism for getting a restricted judgment of sober fact. And for another, there are other mechanisms in scientific research, including foremost the criticism of other investigators, the dialectical interchange of the responses of men with different points of view, which help to diminish the dangers and correct the errors of those in whom overambitious or imperfect theory, as an ingredient of observation, like an imperfect lens, distorts and deludes rather than clarifies and expands vision, disclosing features of the world that otherwise might escape discrimination. This liberality of response in the scientific case, in contrast with the legal one, is related to many of the differences in the whole institution or domain of activity in which these two responses have their home. For though we speak of a verdict in the scientific cases as well as in the legal one, what is referred to by the same word in the two cases is vastly different, as different as the purposes for which the verdict or decision is sought, the individuals who render the verdict, the items or individuals that are subject to the verdict, the procedure by which the verdict is rendered, and the consequences when it has been attained.[11]

11 Cf. A. Train, *My Day in Court*, p. 55: "Lawyers, being cautious as well as meticulous by nature and mentally adjusted to the technical rules of evidence, make the worst witnesses in the world. I had an excellent illustration of this while examining a member of the New York Bar, the complainant in an assault committed outside an election booth. It was a plain case but, as the latter took the stand, the defendant's attorney adroitly remarked: 'I do not wish to interrupt my learned brother while he is giving his testimony, and I shall not do so, provided he agrees to confine himself to strictly legal evidence.' The witness bowed gravely and began.

"'I was about to enter the polling booth, when some one bumped into me. I felt the bump, looked to see who was responsible, and saw the defendant standing close by. Of course I cannot swear positively that he was the one who bumped me, for I did not actually see him do it. He said loudly: "You idiot, why don't you look where you are going?" I answered: "Why don't you mind your own business?" He then made use of certain offensive words only the purport of which I now recall, and at the same time lifted his right arm. I felt a blow upon my nose. I cannot swear that the defendant struck me for I did not see his fist come in contact with my

23. At this point it is appropriate to return again to the question of the relevance of considerations such as these to the problem of induction, and to the more general problem of which this particular problem constitutes a permutation, namely, the justification problem. From the rudimentary beginnings just made one could proceed much further in discriminating, describing, criticizing, and evaluating examples of the variations of response to truth claims that are exhibited in the developing practices embraced in what may be called the institution of human knowledge, and the variation in the kinds of consideration that are appealed to in support of these responses in the various domains and subdomains of this institution. The project just described, the project of giving a sensitive, informed account and rational reconstruction of the various genera and species of practice that make up the institution of human knowledge, of discriminating the various forms, including the now extinct ones, that cognitive life has taken, is the project of a positive philosophy of knowledge. It is a project that has been carried on by a long line of philosophical writing extending from the *Theaetetus* of Plato to the most recent works in the philosophy of science, the theory of perception, or the nature and possibility of religious knowledge. Without meaning to impugn in any way the value of such positive philosophical accounts of the institution of human knowledge in its various forms—since rendering such an account is an integral part of the philosophy of knowledge— one may nevertheless question the extent to which such an account provides a solution to one or other of the above-mentioned problems.

One fundamental way in which such an account is not competent in relation to these problems is that in it one constantly employs considerations that the problems call into question. Philosophers like Descartes and Hume, who find a challenge in such problems, are not unaware of the richness and variety in the

nose, but I immediately lost my equilibrium and fell backward upon the sidewalk.'

"The judge discharged the prisoner on the theory, I feel sure, that any man who could talk that way ought to get punched on the nose and that the defendant deserved the thanks of the court."

taxonomy of human knowledge. Hume, a historian of experience and accomplishment, was very sensitive to the variations in the kind of consideration which one employs in determining whether an alleged historical event actually took place; some of this awareness he displayed, together with his own disposition to be provocative, in his essay on *Miracles*. But the Hume who presents himself, up to a point, in this essay, as critic and appraiser of evidence (frail human testimony opposed to established scientific impossibility), is not the Hume of the "Skeptical Doubts concerning the Operations of the Understanding," challenging us to show by what right, by what process of inference or argument, it is possible for one ever to arrive at "conclusions from experience," to produce the "foundation" of all such conclusions. This kind of challenge, and the problem to which it is alleged to lead, are not capable of being met by appeals to accepted practices by which truth claims are decided and responses to them appraised, for these practices are all, in a wholesale way, embraced in the challenge. Any such appeal, therefore, as a means of resolving the doubts implicit in the challenge will count only as a "skeptical resolution" of them, as an admission that in spite of lofty use by philosophers of such terms as "reason," "demonstration," and "experience," the edifice of knowledge is grounded in nothing more exalted than the principle of custom or habit.

24. In order to be able to deal adequately with the justification problem one needs to understand it. This problem, as it bears upon some particular item of information, say that Martin will be at the meeting, or that the acceleration of bodies in free fall at the surface of the earth is constant, is not a question of whether, in some fairly common-sense way of viewing the matter, there are good or adequate grounds for accepting the item as true. For this latter kind of question, which commonly we can answer with relative ease, is within our capacity to answer because in doing so we operate within a complex set of practices that enable us to discriminate what is involved in accepting the claims in question in the way that is appropriate to the question, and what may count as good or adequate reason for a response of this sort. But the question whether I am "justified"

in supposing that Martin will be at the meeting is not a question to be decided simply by the citation that he promised to attend. The question is, as that heavy word "justified" already indicates, no ordinary question about whether I have good reasons for expecting him to be there. It is a philosophical question, and further, one of a quite specific kind. It is a question whether the acceptance of the item, and the grounds of that acceptance, can be construed and rationalized in accordance with one specific model of reason, in which rational acceptance of any claim will consist in that claim being shown either to be a self-evident, utterly certain apprehension of some personal conscious state, or a certain or probable deduction from such an apprehension, or set of apprehensions, every step of which is equally self-evident and certain.

That is to say, what is at issue here is primarily a matter of philosophical theory. It is not a question of whether a necessary feature of the examined life is making a philosophical scrutiny of human knowledge in all its putative domains, and attempting to develop a systematic, illuminating view that will assist in the guidance of this aspect of our thought and conduct. It is rather a question of how this philosophical project should proceed, and, in particular, of the requirements that such a systematic view of the matter must have before the project can be judged to be successful. It is a question of whether, in the general winnowing of knowledge and superstition, truth and error, good and bad reasons, proof and fallacy that such a philosophical view effects, whatever is reasonable, acceptable in the way of knowledge, belief, and so on, shall be capable of being represented in Cartesian terms, capable of being shown as apprehensible in a Cartesian process.

This is the character of the justification problem as it appears in its various forms in philosophy, particularly in the theory of knowledge. This is what justification theory comes to. The problem in question is one that arises in the context of a certain philosophical theory, one encountered in the attempt to make that theory work. It is a problem, therefore, that will not be solved, though it may reasonably be avoided, while operating in another theory. Answers to analogous questions in another theory, will, as answers to the questions generated in this one, inevitably appear to be, and be, beside the point.

The question whether I am "justified" in supposing that Martin will be at the meeting, whether a full, adequate, philosophical justification can be provided for this supposition, is one that can be answered only by showing that, beginning with indubitable truths about my personal states of consciousness, this supposition can be arrived at in the way dictated by this theory. It is of great importance to see that this is the kind of question asked, and that without begging some philosophical questions of the first magnitude this question cannot be identified with the question whether in some less restricted sense such a supposition is a rational one, and whether any *prima facie* rationality it may seem to have endures when it is subject to careful philosophical scrutiny and assimilated into a carefully thought-out view of rational life and thought. Seeing this is of assistance in relieving one of the tendency to draw the conclusion that what cannot be "justified" cannot be philosophically defended, and of the corresponding impulse to view as catastrophic the conclusion that, as the results of much modern philosophical thought from the time of Descartes to the present now amply attest, very little, if any, of the corpus of human knowledge can be "justified" in this way.

PART II

JUSTIFICATION THEORY

CHAPTER 5

The Philosophical Temper
of Justification Theory

1. According to the view advanced in the preceding chapters, that broad genus of the philosophy of knowledge that has been called "justification theory" is an exemplification of philosophical skepticism. This may at first seem to be a wildly implausible contention concerning a kind of philosophy the most explicit motive of which has been, contrariwise, to dispel skeptical doubts raised concerning fundamental features of the corpus of human knowledge by answering the challenges that have led to the doubts. But a more particular examination of the theory in question dissipates this *prima facie* implausibility. It reveals that, in spite of its explicit motivation, there is in the theory a certain stance and attitude toward human knowledge, in particular toward the philosophical scrutiny of this knowledge, that is in a fundamental way oriented toward skepticism, so that the efforts on the part of the theory to answer skepticism turn out to be self-destructive expressions of skepticism at odds with itself.

2. It is important for it to be clear that what is to be objected to in justification theory is not its broaching philosophical questions about knowledge, but the way it construes these questions and conceives that they must be answered. Philosophical practice being what it has been now for over two millennia in the Western world, to repudiate the effort to accomplish some systematic and comprehensive rationalization of human knowledge that can serve as a platform for scrutinizing, criticizing, accepting, and rejecting knowledge claims advanced in various areas of life in a variety of ways—to repudiate this is to repudiate a good bit of

philosophy itself. Justification theory represents one view, highly prevalent but by no means universal in modern philosophy, of how the philosophical scrutiny of knowledge claims must proceed. Whenever there is dispute, or reason for dispute, over the status of any claim or set of claims, C_n, to be examples of knowledge or well-grounded judgment, opinion, belief, or whatever, this dispute is to be settled, if it is to be settled in a philosophically satisfactory way, by an investigation of the epistemological ancestry of the claim, or claims, in question. There is a class of claims, cognitions, that are known in a special direct, certain, incorrigible way; and all epistemic authority resides in these. The philosophical question of the epistemic status of any claim is always a question of the relation of that claim to this class of first cognitions. A claim can be established to be a genuine example of knowledge, or at least a claim worthy of some kind of reasonable adherence, only if it can be disclosed to be, if not a first cognition itself, in some degree authenticated by one or more of such cognitions. It must be possible somehow, beginning with such cognitions, by a finite set of steps in an acceptable procedure to arrive at the claim in question as a conclusion and, by virtue of this, as a justified result. It is this constraint put upon philosophical procedure in the philosophical scrutiny of knowledge that renders the scrutiny carried on in this way an exemplification of justification or Cartesian theory.

3. In the rationalist and empiricist versions of this theory the character of the cognitions in which knowledge takes its rise and by which it is expanded were conceived in very different ways. But in both kinds of philosophy the secondary, expanding cognitions were conceived to be essentially related to, to be essentially of the same kind as, the primary ones.[1] An expanding

---

[1] For the purpose of this general comparison of the rationalist and empiricist programs one may neglect the important role played by sensuous intuition at the primary level of knowledge in a rationalist program like that of Descartes. As Kemp Smith points out concerning Descartes's views on the matter, though "experience—here understood in its immediate, non-fallacious aspect—is the *sole* [italics in orig.] source of the data, the subject-matter, on which, as being indubitable, we can unreservedly rely," we must proceed from these limited data somehow using intuition and deduction, the natural light, with respect to essences, *principia*. For it is only by means of the apprehension of such objects, themselves not data of experience in the above

cognition in both represented an apprehension similar to that achieved in a first cognition except that it was one not capable of achievement by itself. It required the preparation, the impetus, the platform of a prior cognition; but given a proper prior cognition, given the benefit of that apprehension, a new apprehension could be had in the same way. The elements in the accretive process, the apprehensions, were conceived to be sensuous ones by the empiricist philosophers. There are a variety of reasons why, in a theory which views the growth of knowledge as a matter of expanding the apprehensions of the mind, it is more plausible to view these as apprehensions of the understanding than of the senses, if such a rude choice must be made. In this respect the rationalist program was far more promising than the empiricist one; but there was another respect in which it was far less promising. This was the requirement of fixity, certainty, incorrigibility in the first and succeeding cognitions. However restricted they may turn out to be—indeed, because of their restricted nature—the putative apprehensions of sense were much more plausible candidates for the fixed, certain, unrevisable elements out of which the structure of knowledge was intended to be built. The intuitions of the understanding exemplified in the highly rationalist development of early modern physical science demonstrated by their liability to criticism and change that they were indeed unsuited for the role of hard, imperishable items of knowledge that rational intuitions were called upon to play in this theory. This unsuitability, it now appears, reflected adversely less upon them than upon the role and the theory in which the role was conceived. In any case, the role having been written, it was easy for empiricist critics of rationalism to point out the fallibility and abstract dubitability of the various candidates for the role offered by the rationalists, and to urge the superiority for this purpose of their own candidates, the intuitions of sense. One thing this meant was that in order to be at all successful, a generally rationalist theory of knowledge would have to be designed along less severely Cartesian lines, a project

sense, that "a genuinely scientific understanding of ourselves and the world around us—so far as this is humanly possible" is to be achieved (*New Studies in the Philosophy of Descartes*, pp. 64–65).

for which the climate of thought was not propitious until after the message of the *Critique of Pure Reason* had been for some time digested in nineteenth-century Continental philosophy. Within the Cartesian tradition, it was the empiricist version which was the more viable and which as a consequence dominated work in this tradition from the time of classic empiricism through the resurgence of this philosophy in the various forms of positivism of the recent past and the present day.

4. So the search for first cognitions in modern philosophy has been predominantly a search for first cognitions of a certain kind, namely those of sense. Though the plausibility of these candidates, at least as roots for the validity of our ordinary knowledge of material objects and the physical sciences that have been developed from this, was superior to that of their rationalist alternatives, they too were not without their difficulties, as protracted philosophical inspection amply disclosed. So apparent had these difficulties become by the end of the nineteenth century that the dominant philosophy of that time, though deriving its inspiration and grounds from very different sources than Peirce, was in agreement with him that the search for first cognitions could be abandoned, that the very thought of such items of knowledge was radically misconceived. The sequel to this story is of a kind not unusual in the history of philosophy. Wide agreement that there were no first cognitions to be found was promptly followed by a shift in thought and a reinvigorated search to find them. And the debate between the prospectors claiming to have found at last, though in small traces, grains of this epistemological gold, and the opposition claiming in polite philosophical language to be able to identify the finds as an intellectual analogue of iron pyrites, persists to this day.

5. What mainly led to this reversal was not any new discovery of positive evidence pointing to the existence of first cognitions, sure items of original knowledge that could serve as the origins for other items because they themselves had no origins, and hence none that could possibly be mistaken. It was rather an increased sensitivity to the grounds that throughout the history of this kind of philosophy had constituted its main support. These were the grounds that bore on the existence of first cognitions

not so much by showing that they do exist, by uncovering and displaying them, but by seeming to show that they *must* exist. No matter how difficult their discovery may be, they must be there to be discovered, because of the serious, indeed philosophically disastrous, consequences which were thought to follow if they are not. These consequences assumed different guises and were accorded different names in the different contexts of thought in which they emerged. One broad term that encompasses them all is philosophical skepticism. Whether the consequences were conceived to be subjectivism, relativism, some kind of pragmatic disregard of the claims of truth, or the mistaking of the congruence of mere suppositions with each other for fidelity to external fact, what they pointed to was an apparent inadequacy of any theory of knowledge that did not provide for the kind of cognitions in question. Without them any theory would founder in the attempt to account for the validity of large domains of our putative knowledge of ourselves, our fellowmen, and the natural world. If such a theory is persisted in, therefore, the validity of this putative knowledge cannot be maintained; so that the choice that resolves for philosophical theories of knowledge is between first cognitions and irremediable large-scale skepticism.

6. But to pose a choice of this kind is to suppose that, at least for philosophical purposes, it is possible to put in question large domains of putative knowledge which, whatever they are, are clearly not to be viewed as complexes of first cognitions and for which, therefore, on this view, supporting relations in such cognitions need to be sought. What we take to be knowledge in everyday life, in the sciences and other intellectual disciplines, is neither a complex of first cognitions nor a complex of truth claims that have been demonstrated to be derivable from such complexes by acceptable means. Although it does not follow from this lack of demonstration that this putative knowledge is not knowledge, it does follow, on this view, that its claim to be knowledge is not yet philosophically accredited. In order to be philosophically accredited, putative knowledge must survive philosophical scrutiny that proceeds by exploring its relations with the indubitable first cognitions. Original historical parentage in these indubitables is not required of every item of putative

knowledge. What is required is that there be some complex of indubitables capable of adopting each item that is not itself an element in these first indubitables. In this adoptive relation the validity of each such item consists.

It is in this light that one must understand the claims of those Cartesian philosophers who, in contrast with their master, protest that their questions about the justification of our knowledge claims imply no doubt whatever concerning the correctness of these claims, being directed rather to elucidating the conditions in which this correctness consists.[2] When driving their motor cars, or testifying about what they saw when driving, these philosophers are no less confident about their knowledge of the existence of the car, and the traffic signal which signals them to stop or proceed, than other men. And it is disputable whether Hume, in spite of his professions, did not in fact know, *really* know, as well as we that the way to heat the teakettle was to put it on the fire and not to insert it in the snowbank outside the door. What is in question in the Cartesian exploration of the grounds of some item of putative knowledge is not the status of that item as it would be judged by accepted standards relevant to matters, where such standards exist. What is in question is whether the item, even if validated by such standards, qualifies as philosophically accredited knowledge.[3] And when the alternatives are set as *either* there are first cognitions in which these putative items, which are clearly not such cognitions, can have their grounds, *or* these items are not philosophically accredited knowledge, the clear logical implication is that as these items of knowledge are ordinarily taken and advanced, they are not such knowledge. While they may be knowledge in some sense or other, they are not philosophically accredited, and will become so only if proper philosophical parents, in the form of first cognitions, can be found for them.

7. As has already been observed, what is to be objected to in a view like this is not the supposition that there is a difference between philosophically examined knowledge and what has not been so examined, between knowledge which has the benefit

---

2 Cf. below, Ch. 6, Sect. 5.

3 In short, what is in question is the standards.

of philosophical illumination and refinement, and knowledge which has not. Nor is the supposition to be objected to that in the process of philosophical examination there is a natural effect of alteration of status both upon items of putative knowledge and other items that have not been so regarded. Promotions, demotions, accretions, and diminutions of various kinds naturally occur and are in order. What is to be objected to is the manner in which philosophical examination is conceived in philosophies of knowledge that are Cartesian in orientation, and the way its effects are thought to be realized. The presumption in these philosophies is that the effect of philosophical illumination and refinement upon items of putative knowledge are realized in a definite step of achievement that admits of no partway stages. It is an activity more like starting a car, or making the Dean's list, than like that of becoming educated or wise. A comparable contrast in certain branches of Christian theology is that between salvation viewed on the one hand as a definite occurrence, perhaps an almost instantaneous one, in a human life, and salvation conceived as a progressive achievement in a life more and more effectively guided by faith and more and more yielding the fruit of good works.

One who accepts the alternatives as being first cognitions *or* failure of philosophical accreditation is taking the former rather than the latter view of what might be called the "saving" effect of philosophical examination. He is supposing, with regard to all items and domains of putative knowledge that are clearly not first cognitions, that from the point of view of philosophical salvation they are lost. And from this point of view they will remain lost, unless and until they can be brought into relation with the redeeming force of the first cognitions. But this is to suppose, as Descartes took pains to make clear, both in profession and in practice, that from the point of view of one engaged in the philosophical scrutiny of these items or domains of putative knowledge, in themselves, apart from their relations with the sought-for foundations, they are not and cannot be philosophically acceptable.

Implicit thus in the posed alternatives of first cognitions *or* failure of philosophical accreditation is a presumption about the manner in which philosophical examination is carried out and illumination achieved. The contention that apart from its relation with first cognitions any item or domain of putative knowledge must remain unaccredited amounts in part to a contention that philosophically the source of the validity of this knowledge lies not in it but elsewhere. As it stands, in its unsaved state, before philosophical reconstruction, and abstracted from possible relations with first cognitions, it does not merit philosophical acceptance. This acceptance, to the extent that it is attainable by any item or domain, must be secured through the relation of that item or domain to the *fons et origo* of all accreditation, namely, the first cognitions. Until that relation has been established by philosophical examination, one's attitude in the examination must be that of suspension of belief, trust, acceptance, or favorable judgment. This, of course, applies only to one's attitude in the examination, one's attitude from a philosophical point of view, not to one's activities as a practical man. There an entirely different attitude may be called for and will prevail. That an item or domain of putative knowledge, when it is the subject of philosophical scrutiny, is regarded as a candidate for accreditation (justification), and that this accreditation is effected only with the establishment of appropriate first cognitions, means literally that until the accreditation has been effected by this establishment, the item or domain in question must severely remain in question, must not be employed in any way that would prejudice that delicate condition. The saving power of philosophical examination is conceived to reside solely in the establishment, for the item or domain, of avenues for the passage to it of the saving power of validity from the originals of all such power. As in religious analogues of such thought, the conception of oneself and one's fellowmen as totally depraved does not mean that in the conduct of daily life one cannot trust them to pay their bills, paint the house, or even to get to the church on time. It means that in the church, as it were, in the context of thought that supports the church as an institution, we are all utterly without merit, that in the words of one confession "the truth is not in us," and that thus we must remain, apart from the possibility, represented in the great Drama of Salvation, that truth and merit can be conferred upon us by a relation between us and the source of all redeeming power mediated by what is called the Holy Spirit.

8. The emphasis in the exploration here of the philosophy expressed in the alternative about first cognitions and accreditation has been upon the significance of the alternative rather than upon its grounds. The aim has been to expose in the methodological presuppositions of this theory of knowledge, a form of philosophical skepticism, and thus to explain and support the earlier advanced contention that this kind of philosophy may be fairly regarded as both an expression of and a reaction to such skepticism. It is an expression of skepticism, skepticism from a philosophical point of view, in the sense that it proceeds in the philosophical scrutiny of knowledge by consigning to *limbus dubitationum* vast domains of putative knowledge, every item in every domain that does not have complete, immediate certainty. It is a reaction to this skepticism in the sense that, having made this large-scale consignment of all items that do not have this prized character, it endeavors to effect large-scale redemption of them by effecting a relation between them and those that do.

In his discussion of skeptical philosophy in the first *Enquiry,* Hume emphasized a distinction between skepticism "antecedent to all study and philosophy," and skepticism "consequent" to such inquiry and deliberation. Without endorsing fully Hume's analysis of the character and significance of this distinction, or even its application to himself, one may employ the distinction to characterize the kind of skepticism expressed in the philosophy under examination as antecedent skepticism. It is not, as Hume described such skepticism, "an universal doubt," but it is doubt advanced on a grand scale; and though it is not antecedent to all philosophy, it is antecedent to the philosophical reconstruction and justification of items and domains of putative knowledge to which it has been directed. That it is a reaction to, as well as an expression of, such skepticism is indicated in the first branch of the alternative which it advances. The reaction is by means of the search for and intended exploitation of the first cognitions. And it is because centuries of philosophical experience have thoroughly demonstrated the attempted exploitation to be doomed to failure, resulting in "skepticism consequent to enquiry," that the career of such philosophy may be fairly characterized as skepticism at odds with itself.

9. The topic of the philosophical grounds for the alternative just discussed is a rich and fascinating one, but within the limits of this essay little may be said upon it. To embark upon a program of philosophical accreditation for certain domains of our knowledge implies at the very least that those domains are not accredited as they stand. This leaves, however, very much in question just how much transformation the translation from unaccredited to accredited will require, where the transformation is to be effected, and in what respects. In his 1924 essay "Logical Atomism," Russell related that his interest in philosophy was stimulated by "the wish to find some reason to believe in the truth of mathematics." [4] At the minimum this implies a judgment of some deficiency in the evidence at hand for this truth. Such a judgment, he related elsewhere, he had formed at the age of eleven concerning the geometry of Euclid, when, to his dismay, he learned that this geometry "began with axioms, which had to be accepted without proof." [5] Russell's delight in mathematics led him, as a similar delight had led Descartes, to an investigation of the philosophical foundations of that subject, and to an exploration of what in these foundations could be expanded and exploited for further progress, not only in mathematics itself, but in science and philosophy as well. One of Russell's most distinguished predecessors in British philosophy, Locke, set upon his critical essay on the powers of the understanding as a result of stubborn difficulties encountered by him and a small group of friends in discourses "on a subject very remote" from that essay, a subject that has been identified on

[4] J. H. Muirhead, ed., *Contemporary British Philosophy,* First Series, pp. 356–383.

[5] "My Mental Development," in P. A. Schilpp, ed., *The Philosophy of Bertrand Russell,* p. 7. Cf. also: "My brother began at the beginning with the definitions. These I accepted readily enough. But he came next to the axioms. 'These,' he said, 'can't be proved, but they have to be assumed before the rest can be proved.' At these words my hopes crumbled. . . . I never quite overcame my fundamental doubts as to the validity of mathematics" ("Why I Took to Philosophy," *Portraits From Memory,* pp. 14–15).

other evidence as the "principles of morality and revealed religion." [6] Little more than a generation later Hume would hardly have proposed in his *Treatise* "to introduce the experimental method of reasoning into moral subjects" if he had not taken this to be an end wanting advancement.[7]

10. What calls for explanation in the view of matters that is expressed in the alternative of first cognitions *or* failure of accreditation is not the presumption that certain domains of putative knowledge, which may be very extensive indeed, are not as well ordered as they might be, and that some improvement of this state of affairs might be effected by philosophical scrutiny, reordering and reconstitution. Granted that presumptions of this sort have been standard features of the philosophical scrutiny of knowledge, morals, politics, and so on, throughout its history in the Western world—granted that one of the features of the examined life is that it is not lived in exactly the same way as the unexamined one—there remains the question why it should be thought that the examination must proceed, and the effects of the examination produced, in the particular way specified by this alternative. The first, small step in answering the question, and the only one that can be made here, is a recognition that the severe character of the alternative posed, in relation to any domain of knowledge under examination, is itself a reflection of a profound disenchantment with that domain. The supposition that philosophical illumination, accreditation, reform in any domain of knowledge not constituted by first cognitions and their equally sure and intuitive consequences requires the stupendous effort to translate the domain into this state, reflects the judgment that from the philosophical point of view practically every domain of putative knowledge, even the delightful Euclid of Russell's youth, is deficient, and most of them sorely so. In such

[6] Locke, *An Essay Concerning Human Understanding.* "The Epistle to the Reader," A. C. Fraser, ed., Vol. I, p. 9.

[7] It should be remembered that Hume's view of what is a "moral subject" was much broader than what would be included under that term now. As the title *A Treatise of Human Nature* indicates, it embraced all those subjects for which an understanding of human nature is held to be essential; and that includes not only morals, strictly considered, and politics, but the theory of knowledge, including therein the philosophy of science.

a state is our common-sense knowledge of the world about us, including our knowledge of other living creatures. And, whatever may be the internal state of the special disciplines dealing with the natural world, both living and nonliving, and with human life, the thoroughgoing dependence of all these disciplines upon our common-sense knowledge is deficiency enough to call for their accreditation before any reliance can be put upon them, either in whole or in part, in the procedure of effecting philosophical accreditation of any portion of our putative knowledge.

11. For a variety of reasons, some of which are set forth eloquently in Descartes's *Discourse on Method,* the disillusionment on the part of some persons with what passes for knowledge in the domains in which they are interested is so extensive and profound that it appears to them that the only hope of securing an adequate structure of knowledge is to raze the present structure to the ground and begin anew. At any time, in the body of what is accepted as knowledge in any wide domain there are many discrepancies; and where the actual discrepancies are not prominent, there are always discrepancies *in posse.* For however static the domain may appear to an external observer, it is never finished, always open to further development. And one who is interested in that development will always be able to find in the system contrary clues as to how the development should proceed. Every wide domain of what is accepted as knowledge, and the collage of these domains, is always, in any moderately advanced stage of civilization, rich in complexity and sources of puzzlement. There are of course wide variations in this regard from time to time and from place to place. Athenian civilization in the fourth century B.C. was widely different in this respect from that of Massachusetts in 1640 A.D., and different, but not so widely, from civilization in that city and in the Peloponnesus in the second century B.C. (the time of Carneades) or in the second century A.D. (the time of Sextus Empiricus). And all these were vastly different in the aspect in question from the situation of the Polynesians in the eighteenth century or of the Iroquois in the seventeenth.

In any moderately advanced stage of civilization the composite domain of what is passed on as knowledge from one generation is a complex document, little exploration of which is needed for a sensitive mind to find in it not only many frustratingly blank pages but discrepant pages, and pages that in other ways generate under intense scrutiny increasing puzzlement. How one responds to these features of the document depends not only upon the state of the document, which varies from time to time in respect to these features, but also upon a variety of other circumstances in the society in which the document is read and in the individuals engaged in the reading of it. In consequence, the explanation of why, at a given time and in the life of a given individual or group, the reaction to the imperfections of the document turns out to be the extreme and negative one just described, is of necessity a long and complex story. It is long and complex in exactly the same way as the explanation why at times the reaction on the part of a rising generation to the inadequacies and imperfections of broad social institutions being transmitted to it should be one of large-scale alienation from these institutions; of despair in their capacity to reform; of total, or what is intended to be total, repudiation.

12. Translated into the domain of practical life the impulse that leads to Cartesianism in the theory of knowledge leads to utopianism as a means of political reform and reconstruction. Whatever may be the sources of epistemological utopianism, like its political analogue it seeks to satisfy its reformist ends by somehow wiping the slate clean, if only in imagination, and beginning again. The contrast intended to be drawn by the use of this term is that which Marxist-Hegelian political philosophy has intended to draw by it in its own domain. If one grants that reform, perhaps radical reform, is desirable or even imperative, is this reform more realistically pursued by attempting to proceed totally outside existing social institutions or by seeking to find somewhere within them the grounds and instruments for progressive political action? The Marxist answer to this question, as applied to capitalist society, was that although this society, in its pre-eminent capitalist features, is both morally and economically intolerable, it nevertheless carries within it, primarily in the labor movement, what are at one and the same time the weapons for its own destruction as capitalist, and the instruments of its rebirth as socialist and truly humane.

13. In the domain of knowledge the corresponding question for the philosopher of this phase of human life is that of how one proceeds in the philosophical illumination and rationalization of it. As in the political case, the question is how much it is possible for one to reject of the accepted institutions, in this case the items and domains of knowledge, or putative knowledge, and still retain the capacity of engaging in a realistic, credible program in this regard. Is it possible, is it necessary, in the pursuit of this philosophical end, to divorce oneself completely from the institutionalized forms of knowledge in science, in everyday life, in the humanities, in the technical arts, and so on, and then from the vantage point of this superior purity of mind, and hence objectivity, embark upon the construction of the New Order, the New Jerusalem in matters of cognition? One who regards this way of proceeding as possible, and perhaps necessary, requires special items of knowledge, special starting points, of the kind the first cognitions have been designed to be. He requires these because his reaction to the admittedly imperfect institutions of cognitive life, like the reaction of the social utopian to imperfect political and economic institutions, is to dissociate himself from these institutions. Taking the good, or the only partially good, to be the enemy of the better, he takes the road to the better to be, not in the acceptance and exploitation of the partially good, but in its wholesale rejection. It is in this rejection that the Cartesian-utopian in the theory of knowledge exhibits his skepticism, his skepticism before study, to use Hume's terminology, his skepticism for philosophical purposes.

One who thus seeks from outside an institution to find the means of its reform, who totally repudiates the authority of the institution, judging that there are no elements in it that can be accepted as bases for reform must appeal to extraordinary means and bases. The excommunicated and further alienated Luther, having rejected the institutionalized guides of faith and action offered by the Church, naturally appealed to what uninstitutionalized guide could be found in the Word of God speaking directly—or as directly as it could, when Luther had rendered its Scripture into a common language—to the individual soul. But to think of the Bible or the Holy Spirit as speaking in this way is to deprive each individual, in his interpretation of putative messages from these sources, of that instrument of criticism, correction, and authentication which in the Roman view is the Teaching Church. Of course Luther did not suppose that when the Holy Spirit did speak to him directly, rather than through the advertised channels of the ecclesiastical hierarchy, the message would be that indulgences were not as iniquitous as Luther had proclaimed them to be, and that in this matter, as generally, he should submit himself to the authority of Pope Leo and his agents. But apart from this substantive discrepancy, what is exhibited here on a restricted scale in Luther's challenge to a religious institution is exhibited on a very large scale in philosophical skepticism antecedent to inquiry in the theory of knowledge.

If one supposes that there is no item or domain in what passes as human knowledge that cannot be the subject of philosophical criticism, a natural but quite unwarranted step is to conclude that therefore they are all accessible to criticism together. The self-excommunicated epistemologist, now separated from all the bases and instruments of criticism contained in the corpus of human knowledge, needs to find a basis upon which his criticism can be made. Whatever this basis is taken to be, it must be of a character that can be employed without any appeal to the instruments of criticism embodied in one way or another in the ordinary institutions of knowledge, for the critic has, for the time being at least, separated himself from these institutions. Such a basis, whether it be the natural light of reason, or the direct messages of sense, must be such that it can be employed in the complete intellectual isolation that this separation entails. No facilities for interpretation, revision, criticism remaining, no correction being possible, it has got to be itself quite and literally incorrigible. And there being in this world room for incorrigible error as well as truth, the source of these affirmations must be one the deliverances of which can be plausibly regarded as also certainly true.

14. An often-advanced explanation of the appeal exerted by the Cartesian approach to philosophy is that this is due to an appetite for certainty in knowledge, and that hence, if it is an

approach that has turned out not to be a feasible one, this result indicates a necessity for a relaxation of requirements in this regard. The Cartesian program is an unfeasible and unrealistic one, but it is a mistake to attribute this lack of realism and feasibility entirely to the quest for sureness. Sureness is often a desirable and realizable characteristic of our knowledge. The avoidance of the frustrations of Cartesian theory does not require one to abandon the quest for certainty at all places in the pursuit of knowledge, but it does require some revision of our understanding of what certainty consists in, from what considerations it springs. For one thing the assurance that it is proper to accord to any complex view of matters is neither the mean sureness of the items that compose it, nor the minimum assurance that may be accorded to any individual item. These points are mentioned merely as one brief indication of the way in which the understanding of certainty in a non-Cartesian view of knowledge will diverge from that in a Cartesian view. This difference is but one aspect of a larger and more fundamental difference of view concerning what is proper procedure in the philosophical scrutiny and rationalization of knowledge. Is it the adoption of a general attitude of lack of credence in whatever domains of putative knowledge are under examination and a consequent inquiry to discover which items in these domains can win acceptance over that provisional withdrawal of confidence? Or is it desirable, and even necessary, that the "skepticism before study" which is an indispensable feature of the philosophical appraisal of any item or domain of knowledge be practiced in a more restricted and discriminating manner? And is the forced and severe alternative of first cognitions *or* failure of accreditation then not a false alternative: false, because accreditation need not be achieved through first cognitions, because one is never required by the momentum of skeptical rejection to navigate a strait so desperate? It is the desperate character of this apparent strait that contributes by far the major appeal of the philosophy of first cognitions. And as the strait itself, with its desperate alternative leading to a correspondingly desperate search for first cognitions, is a consequence of the large-scale skepticism before study, of the skeptical stance taken to a maximum extent toward the accepted domains and institutions of human knowledge, the alternative itself and the philosophical program to which it gives rise are correctly described as in this respect a reaction to and expression of philosophical skepticism.

15. And then there is skepticism *after* study. In this respect also it was pointed out earlier that Cartesian theory, the search for first cognitions and the endeavor to employ what seem to be such as bases for the criticism and reconstruction of human knowledge has been a story of repeated failure. These failures, so long as the theory and program are firmly adhered to, cannot but be regarded as skeptical in consequence, however delicate the announcement of the results may be, however decorated it is with well-meaning incantations about mitigated skepticism and the valuable mortifying effects of philosophical failure upon overweening claims on the part of human understanding. In any circumstances in which some premium is put upon economy of time and space, argument for the skeptical issue of this philosophical program may be omitted, for, as was remarked, this issue has been made plain in a variety of ways, and with great candor, by generations of modern philosophers whose allegiance has been attracted to the program and whose energies devoted, with great persistence and ingenuity, to making it succeed. For this reason, the primary effort here has not been expended upon calling attention to the various intellectual breakdowns that have signaled the failure of these efforts, and the skeptical consequences which ensue from them. Taking the occurrence of the breakdowns and the signaled failures as relatively unproblematical, and noting certain common familial traits that seem to signify a common genesis, the primary effort has been to discover and understand that genesis. These results have been traced to the view, taken in this philosophy and articulated in justification theory, of the way in which under philosophical scrutiny the warrant of truth claims is to be understood. One distinguishing feature of the view is that the procedure by which the validation of new claims is elicited from previously validated ones is taken to involve only accretion of the new to the already validated ones, and never transformation of these in the process. The

achieving of knowledge, its expansion at every stage, is conceived of as an operation of securing more and more items, more and more bits of maximally sure and hence logically incorrigible information. While this view can be attacked upon a variety of grounds, one economical way, illustrated in the writing of a variety of philosophers from the time of Hegel, has been to expose, using as paradigm cases the initial cognitions with which the accretive process is thought to begin, the basic untenability of the conception of knowing or establishing the rationality of truth claims by means of an act of either sensuous or rational intuition, the deliverances of which can and must be regarded as incapable of error, correction, or revision of any sort. Essential to this view of the justification or validation procedure is a certain asymmetry in the relation between justifying grounds and justified conclusions which renders the grounds both incapable of being validated by the conclusions and immune to revision by them. However difficult it is to maintain this incorrigibility in some phases of our knowledge, it is necessary to the hierarchical conception of the sources and transmission of validity that is represented in this view.[8] This necessity is at no place more appar-

---

8 It was argued earlier (Ch. 3, Sects. 14–16) that this contention does not mistakingly neglect those versions of the Cartesian philosophy in which the validating relations between grounds and supported truth claims are conceived to be not exclusively ones of demonstrative certainty, but also ones of probability as well. The effect of such a relaxation in the Cartesian philosophy can easily be exaggerated. Suppose such a probability relation holding between ground G and claim C. The justification of C by means of G will require, on this view, that the claim that this relation holds also be justified. And the response commonly given, that this relation is a logical one capable of being discerned by purely logical techniques (e.g., probability$_1$ as discriminated by Rudolf Carnap), represents merely an expansion in the theory of powers of logical intuition, which in the earlier versions had been identified with the logic of demonstration. Employing such intuition, suitably formalized, usually in some form of *Spielraum Theory*, the aspiration has been that one could establish, on purely logical grounds, and hence in a quite sure and incorrigible manner, the claim that G does confer a certain degree of probability upon C. Cf. W. Kneale's definition of "rational opinion" as the "knowledge that some proposition is probabilified to a certain degree by the available evidence" (*Probability and Induction*, Part I, Sect. 4).

Incorrigibility maintained in this way has somehow to be squared with the feature of probability assessments commonly expressed in the doctrine that probability is always relative to evidence. Kneale's definition, specifying that the probability in question be in relation to the available evidence, is typical

ent than at the stage of the alleged first grounds or cognitions. These cognitions thus may serve as fair test cases for determining the question, Are there such grounds in the reasoning by which the validity of our knowledge can be represented? Are there incorrigible grounds?

16. One whose reflections on this matter lead him to a more and more thorough rejection of the logical atomism implicit in the doctrine of ultimate incorrigible grounds naturally confronts the question of why, despite its by no means inconspicuous difficulties, the doctrine has exerted such wide attraction. The answer in good part seems to be that this attraction derived less from the positive promise of a theory of knowledge embodying this doctrine than from necessity. It has not been that during the years in which this theory has exerted its attractions it has been able to offer much in the way either of promise or achievement as a platform for illuminating the character of present knowledge and for directing its expansion and improvement. It has been rather that in the eyes of many, such a theory, in spite of its faltering performance, seemed inescapable; so that failures on its part had to be regarded as failures in the only possible kind of theory, and thus results that somehow had to be reversed, or, if irreversible, counted as failures in the philosophy of knowledge generally. Only a theory in which items of knowledge can be regarded as capable of being validated in independence of the tradition and practices that collectively make up the knowledge institution can serve as a basis for reconstructing knowledge once this institution has been wholly repudiated. Given this repudiation, given this destruction of the institution by an act of philosophical imagination, reconstruction must start somewhere. There

---

of the procedure followed at this point. Often for emphasis the full phrase "total available evidence" is employed. Leaving aside questions of how the development of knowledge constantly effects alterations on what we regard *as* evidence with respect to hypotheses—questions which bear on relevance of the incorrigible probability estimations whose possibility is sought in this way—one may observe that, on the incontestable assumption that provision must be made for changes in the total available evidence from time to time, the notion that these changes lead, not to a correction of probability assessments, but to a supercession of some incorrigible assessments by others that are somehow better grounded, does not so much preserve the theory of justification from the contingencies of corrigibility as admit them into the theory awkwardly, under an assumed name.

must be first steps, beginning items of knowledge; and, in the circumstances, these must be items whose philosophical validation as knowledge must be capable of being made out in complete independence of the institution and the instruments of criticism and evaluation that the institution provides. The items must be incorrigible because any possible means of correcting them have been determinedly forsworn; but if incorrigible, and yet first steps upon which all others depend, they must be such that they may plausibly be regarded as not simply incapable of correction or revision, but incapable because utterly without need.

The extreme character of the incorrigible grounds contemplated in this theory and exemplified with particular clarity in the idea of the first cognitions is a consequence and reflection of the extreme character of the reaction to the accepted traditions and practices of knowledge from which the theory springs. If the initial broad skepticism out of which the theory emerges is to be met by the production of secure items of knowledge, the security of these items has to be of a very special kind. It has to be a kind that was not the consequence of the items in question having passed test and criticism, but rather of their being beyond criticism. The first cognitions have to be attainable in a way that exempts them from all ordinary standards of criticism, for these standards, if they are to be reinstated in the corpus of reconstructed knowledge, have somehow first to be developed out of these cognitions. They cannot be employed in the validation of these cognitions, for if they were, the cognitions could not count as "first."

17. In his essay "Self-Evidence and Proof" Ch. Perelman comments aptly on the asocial and unhistorical character which is ascribed by Cartesian theory to what is known.

The Cartesian theory of knowledge is, in the end, a theory of knowledge which is not human, but divine; of knowledge as acquired by a unique and perfect Being, without initiation, training, tradition or need to learn.

Again:

What illusion, what presumption too, there is in the attitude of a Descartes, resolutely walking along the path of knowledge like a man walking completely alone, and in the dark (Descartes, *Discourse*). If we must think of the process of gaining knowledge in terms of the metaphor of following a path, I prefer the Leibnizian analogy, according to which it is a whole body of men, not a solitary wanderer, who do the walking.[9]

There is indeed something extremely odd and *prima facie* implausible in the idea that the proper way to proceed in understanding human knowledge is first to divest oneself of as much of this knowledge as one possibly can and then see how much of it, starting from new sure beginnings, and proceeding by new sure steps, can be regained. It is at least as odd and implausible as the supposition that the way in which to secure a philosophical understanding of any great social institution, like higher education, banking, or criminal or constitutional law, is for one first to extrude into some *limbus dubitationis* everything accepted as known or reasonably well established in the institution, and thus, having swept the board clean, in a state of pristine ignorance often mistaken for objectivity, to try to determine what can or cannot be reclaimed of the institution in question. If this were sound philosophical procedure, it would seem to follow that a desirable provision in the preparation for the study of jurisprudence is avoidance of that indoctrination in the institution which is an essential part of the study of law. Similarly philosophers of science might be encouraged to avoid the corrupting effect of an intimate acquaintance with the conduct of scientific inquiry; those interested in the philosophy of history might similarly preserve their objectivity with respect to historical research; and the philosophy of mathematics might best be entrusted to those whose capacity to judge fairly about such matters has not been impaired by immersion into the lore and practice of mathematics at a too early age.

The plausibility or implausibility of a basic philosophical approach or theory is relative to the conditions from which it arises and the purposes for which it is intended. One does not demolish one house and build a new one simply because the first has developed a clogged drain or a crack in the plaster. One does not commit works in large areas of human endeavor totally to the

[9] *The Idea of Justice and the Problem of Argument*, pp. 116–117, 120. Cf. also pp. 131–132.

flames unless, like Hume, one is convinced that they are totally without value, containing "nothing but sophistry and illusion." Conferring some plausibility upon the Cartesian approach to the philosophy of knowledge, apparently justifying the heroic measures it proposes for effecting improvement in the understanding and practice of human knowledge, has been a despairing appraisal of the condition of the knowledge institution, of the imperfections from which it suffers, and of the possibilities residing in it of reform. So complex and intricate is the institution, and so apparent in any age, in spite of great achievement, are the imperfections, that it is with little difficulty that succeeding generations of philosophically interested minds can be persuaded that the desperate attitude, for which some greater excuse might have been given in the early seventeenth century, or in post-Aristotelian Athens, is nevertheless a realistic one.

One response that can be made when a desperate remedy is proposed for a less than desperate predicament is to call for a reappraisal of the circumstances from which the proposal arose. Another effective response is to inquire whether the proposed remedy, desperate and heroic as may be the measures it calls for, can actually be put in practice. The question is not whether the measures can succeed in realizing the aims intended, but whether they can even be tried. A part of the question about the suitability of the means for achieving the aims intended concerns the ends themselves. There is reason to suppose that the means in question appear appropriate to the ends in view in good part because the ends in view are themselves ill-defined, and that, as so often happens in the deliberations of practical reason, progressive and mutual clarification of the character of both the means and the ends will reveal that what was first conceived as the willed product of the means would, if and as realized, fail in most important ways to satisfy the more or less indistinct aspirations which activitated the will in the first place. The exposure of the deficiencies of the Cartesian program in this respect requires an examination of much more extended and broader issues affecting the philosophy of knowledge than can be attempted here. Much more effective and practical as a first step in criticism of the program, and a step that requires much less transvaluation of values on the part of those attracted to it, is a demonstration, such as this second Part of the book is designed to provide, that whatever might be envisaged as the ends to be realized with the completion of the program, the program cannot be carried out. It cannot, because what it requires in the way of incorrigible grounds, and incorrigible steps linking conclusions with grounds, is precluded by the fundamental circumstance, well illustrated in the case of the supposed first cognitions of sense, that to require of any such cognition that it be logically incorrigible and at the same time a ground is to require what cannot logically be contrived. The impossibility of satisfying this requirement, and hence the impossibility of carrying out a program of philosophical reconstruction intended to implement the requirement, needs to be exposed to generations of utopian spirits upon whom the program exerts an appeal as a last desperate opportunity to escape from a glaringly imperfect world and a cognitive institution that fulsomely reflects these imperfections. A first step toward confronting and dealing with the imperfect real and trying to make it somewhat more perfect is the realization that there is no escape from it, that the apparent door of first cognitions leads to no asylum.

18. To the case advanced by justification theory that the philosophical scrutiny of knowledge *must* be carried out in a certain way, there is thus a directly opposed case that it *cannot*, that to be successful in such scrutiny one must proceed differently. So, as disputants over the role of first cognitions in the philosophical scrutiny of knowledge press their rival claims, each argues a certain necessity for his particular way of proceeding. To their adherents, first cognitions are necessary; necessary if the skeptical challenges to what we take to be genuine knowledge claims are to be capable of being met; necessary because, in consequence of the imperfections of that putative knowledge, whatever truth claims we may rightly be said to know after philosophical scrutiny are only those which can be salvaged after a thorough razing and complete reconstruction of our whole system of knowledge. To the opponents of this view, however, first cognitions are impossible, the very nature of truth claims being such as to elimi-

nate the possibility that any one of these can be the burden of a
first cognition. And this impossibility, if real, means that, for
better or worse—and it *is* indeed for better—the project of carrying on the philosophical scrutiny of knowledge, beginning with
the wholesale rejection of items and domains it comprises, must
be given up. It means that, recognizing the imperfections and
corrigibility of what we take to be knowledge, largely because
that is what we have been endowed with by virtue of being born
and brought up as human beings, there is no way to proceed
to take advantage of the corrigibility and reduce the imperfections but by proceeding on the basis of what we have, not giving
up the whole because we despair of its imperfections, for giving
up the whole, or at most trying to, is a way of ensuring that
whatever premonitions we have of inescapable failure and despair become self-fulfilling.

The "Book of Knowledge," like every other book in the library of tradition that each generation receives from its predecessors, is subject to change; and of course change is not necessarily
improvement. The book is not only subject to change, but, human life, being what it is, it is constantly *in* change. Philosophical scrutiny of knowledge is one way of affecting by deliberate
thought the character of this change. The alternative to the Cartesian program for affecting change proceeds on the presumption
that whatever insufficiencies, errors, distortions, blank pages,
smudged illustrations, etc., the book may contain, it is not the
kind of book that anyone or any group can utterly discard and
then proceed to write utterly anew. Speaking literally, there are,
as many an author has painfully discovered, unrevisable books,
books that in the interest of improving the doctrine they set out
to teach must be abandoned for a wholly new writing. But there
is no such alternative in what has been called figuratively the
"Great Book of Knowledge." There is, in this respect, as Otto
Neurath so eloquently said forty years ago, no *tabula rasa* to
which we can retreat and upon which then proceed to inscribe
"conclusively established pure protocol sentences as the starting
point of the sciences." Rather, as he said in a now-famous passage, "We are like sailors who must rebuild their ship on the
open sea, never able to dismantle it in dry-dock and to recon-

struct it there out of the best materials." [10] Indeed, when we think about the matter with penetration and care, we see that we have no clear idea of what returning with this ship to the dry dock, dismantling, and reconstructing it could be.

19. Neurath's figure of the mariners who must rebuild their ship on the open sea encapsulates neatly the main point to be made against justification theory. That point, whether made in connection with the first cognitions of sense and reason, or in connection with the construction difficulties encountered in the attempt to develop knowledge from such foundations, is that the program for effecting the philosophical scrutiny and rectification of knowledge dictated by this theory cannot be carried out. That it cannot is of the greatest importance for the philosophy of knowledge; and much effort has been expended by many gifted writers, wittingly and unwittingly, in making this plain. It is likewise of very great importance, for breaking the spell perennially exerted upon philosophers by this theory, that the innocuous cloak of pure investigative curiosity in which it sometimes presents itself be ripped away, disclosing the skeptical preconceptions beneath.

The justification program for the philosophical scrutiny of truth claims proceeds by repeatedly performing what may be called

---

10 "Protokollsätze," *Erkenntnis,* Vol. III (1932–1933). Republished in translation (by F. Schick) in A. J. Ayer, ed., *Logical Positivism.*

With the kind assistance of Robert S. Cohen of Boston University, who consulted Neurath's wife Marie on the matter, I have ascertained that Neurath's first use of the ship metaphor was in the monograph *Anti-Spengler* (Munich, 1921). The earlier statement of the metaphor is somewhat more elaborate and in some ways perhaps even more effective.

"That one always has to deal with a whole net of concepts, rather than with isolatable concepts, puts each thinker in the difficult position of having constantly to keep in mind the whole mass of concepts, which he is unable to survey all at once, in order to let the new emerge from the old. Duhem has demonstrated most forcefully that every assertion concerning any event whatsoever is steeped with hypotheses of all sorts which in the final analysis derive from our whole world view. We are like sailors who must rebuild their ship on the open sea, without ever being able to begin anew from the bottom. When a beam is removed, a new one must at once be put in its place, with the remaining ship being employed as a support. Thus, with the help of old beams and drifting timbers, the ship can be completely refashioned—but only through gradual reconstruction" (pp. 75–76; trans. mine).

the "justification operation" upon these claims and other claims that the operation progressively discloses. The asking of justification questions in this operation is no idle pastime. It proceeds upon a supposition of extreme philosophical importance, namely, that it is by means of this operation that the disclosure and philosophical appraisal of the rationality of truth claims is effected. Any such claim or domain of claims that we properly take ourselves to know or reasonably believe, conjecture, opine, presume, accept, and so on, must be capable of exhibiting its rationality in this operation. Since this is the method of appraisal, any item of putative knowledge that cannot survive this Cartesian sieve, any which is so situated that the operation cannot be carried out to completion with it, and with a positive result, must from a philosophical point of view be judged deficient, and hence cannot be trusted and employed in the appraisal of any other item or domain in the philosophical scrutiny of knowledge.

20. As was emphasized in Chapter 4 this is not at all the way we set about appraising items of putative knowledge, or reasonable belief, or other forms of reasonable acceptance, when we have occasion to appraise them in everyday life, in the practice of technology, in science, in research in the humanities, and so on. Nor is it the way we commonly proceed when the investigation of some item or set of items leads to the appraisal of some whole domain of putative knowledge, reasonable belief, or reasonable judgment, and when some comprehensive philosophical appraisal of that whole domain is called for. It is not the way we should be inclined to proceed in investigating the issues over determinism and indeterminacy in the study of subatomic particles. It is not the way Hume himself proceeded when investigating the claims of reports of miracles as evidences of religious belief, nor the way Descartes himself proceeded to deal with the issue of the validity of our perception of what we should call secondary qualities.

21. The supposition that this is the way one must proceed in the philosophical appraisal of items and domains of putative knowledge, and so on, the way to criticize the old and evaluate the new, represents skepticism antecedent to rather than consequent upon inquiry, skepticism in conception, as distinguished

from skepticism in result. In his early statement of his metaphor (above, n. 10) Neurath wrote of the mariners using the rest of the ship as a support while installing in it a new beam. This procedure—*das übrige Schiff als Stütze zu verwenden*—is what is in principle excluded from the philosophical program of justification theory. In the case of human knowledge *das übrige Schiff* comprises not only a vast and complex resource of accepted beliefs and presumptions about particular and general matters, matters of fact and matters of theory, but also a vast battery of accepted practices for dealing with questions and issues that arise concerning these. It is the supposition of justification theory that when one enters into the philosophical chamber and proceeds to deal with such questions and issues as a philosopher, he must for this purpose resolutely put aside all this, since philosophical appraisal is by nature *"von unten auf frisch [zu] anfangen."* Philosophical inspection and criticism should surely be *"von unten,"* if that means that it must deal with broad and basic issues, and must strive to do so in a way that is neither superficial nor narrow. But the antidotes for superficiality or narrowness are surely not innocence or ignorance, whether these are involuntary, or the voluntary, self-imposed kind that are exhibited in the practice of justification theory. A distinctive characteristic of this practice in the philosophical examination and criticism of items and domains of the corpus of human knowledge is its wholesale renunciation, for the purpose of effecting this examination and criticism, of dependence upon settled principles, practices, and items of acceptance that characterize these domains. The interesting question at this point concerning the skepticism in conception thus exhibited in justification theory is not whether, but why. What is it that perennially leads philosophers to choose this unlikely path in the examination of human knowledge? Now, after some considerable discussion of justification theory, the answer seems to emerge even more clearly than before. The primary source of the appeal of this kind of theory of knowledge does not lie simply in the recognition on the part of its adherents that one essential function of such a theory is to show how the challenges of skeptical philosophy can be met and disarmed. It lies rather in the combination of this recognition with an alto-

gether mistaken view of the way in which this meeting and disarming can and must be performed. That way is by accepting the
questions about knowledge that the skeptical challenges raise, or
seem to raise, by regarding as doubtful everything that these
challenges put in doubt, or seem to put in doubt, and then
proceeding to try to answer these questions, to dispel the doubts,
while yet proceeding upon a basis with which the skeptic would
himself agree, that would in no way transgress, on pain of
circularity, the abnegations from which his challenges began.

22. In an earlier discussion of justification and justification
theory (Chapter 4, Sect. 21) attention was directed to the fact
that when Hume, in consequence of his critical examination of
the relation of cause and effect and its bearing upon "skeptical
doubts concerning the operations of the understanding," came
to the conclusion that reliance upon custom could not be avoided
in these operations, he regarded this conclusion as a skeptical
one, and the resolution of the doubts which it provided a "skeptical resolution." The implication seems clear. The conclusion,
and the resolution of doubt, would be other than skeptical, only
if the analysis and grounding of the relation of cause and effect
and the operations of the understanding dependent upon it could
be effected without reliance upon custom. For "custom" itself,
in a wholesale way, and anything effected with reliance upon it,
is, or is intended to be, a primary object of skeptical challenge.

CHAPTER 6

The Justification
Argument

1. The primary purpose of the consideration in Chapter 4 of
a few concrete examples, actual and hypothetical, of cognitive
activity incorporating the appraisal of truth claims in relation to
grounds, was to draw a contrast between the modes of appraisal
illustrated by justification, on the one hand, and scientific or
cognitive practice, on the other. More specifically, the contrast is
between philosophical justification and cognitive practice, when
that justification is conceived in the way it is in a kind of classical argument designed to demonstrate that if it is possible for
anyone to show, in the face of philosophical challenge, that he
has good reasons for any truth claim whatever, it must be possible for him to show that the grounds of this claim lie in a special
class of such claims, claims that are absolutely certain and incorrigible. All truth claims that anyone has good grounds for advancing are either such claims themselves, which have good
grounds in a very special sense, or claims that can produce such
claims as grounds, from which whatever validity they have
issues.

In view of much that has been said and done on the subject
of justification in recent philosophy, it is important that the
contrast intended here be clearly understood. There are, on the
one hand, our practices and, on the other hand, our theory; on
the one hand the question of what we do, on the other the question whether what we do is justified. But this contrast is not a
simple matter of sheep and goats. Drawing such a contrast is not
intended to suggest that, to the extent that in the study of knowl-

edge one departs from a careful description of practice, and raises questions about the justification of these practices, questions of a kind that cannot be answered merely by a citation of the practices themselves—to this extent one is doing something intellectually or philosophically inappropriate.

One *is* doing something distinctively philosophical, to be sure, but the word here is not pejorative. Neither does the word imply incapacity of bad performance in the raising of the questions or in the attempt to provide answers. There is a sense of "justification" in which justification questions lie at the heart of philosophical inquiry, in which such questions are distinctly philosophical, and in which it is therefore no grounds for criticism of the activity of raising and seeking to answer such questions, that, in comparison with the cognitive practices we are ordinarily engaged in as scientists or laymen, this activity is deviant. If for purposes of brevity we say of the philosopher of knowledge that he is engaged with theory (leaving aside many large questions about what *kind* of theory this may be), one of the things he is concerned with as theoretician about knowledge is to achieve a general view of the spectrum of ongoing and proposed cognitive practices, on the basis of which the claims of each to give us reliable information of facets of ourselves and the world about us can be appraised and judged, issues between rival practices can be considered from a broad, nonparochial point of view, adjudicated, and the controversies possibly composed. A practice that has been subject to challenge, say that exemplified in the new mechanical philosophy of Galileo's time, or in the Freudian therapy or behaviorist linguistics of our own, and that succeeds or fails to meet that challenge and demonstrate its right to a place in such a broad view of the domain of cognitive life, may then be said to have succeeded or failed to attain justification. Viewed in this way the quest for justification, in ethics and politics, in science, and mathematics, in religion, in poetry and art, in history and psychology, in law and the social sciences, is a quest for a broad, coherently adequate view of practices in these domains in relation to each other individually and in concert. The questions raised by the incommensurability of the diagonal were too profound to be answered by the accepted practices of counting and measuring. They eventually required some recasting of the very notions rooted in these practices, and with it a reorientation in the philosophy of mathematics in which the discrepancies and problems arose. The questions raised by the Marxist view of history, or the Darwinian view of the origin of species, were not merely questions in history or biology. The views, attitudes, and practices represented by these theories constituted in two very different ways, and with greatly different degrees of success, challenges to a variety of views, attitudes, and practices deeply entrenched in our lives, our social institutions, and our world view.

2. To object to justification in this broad sense is to object to an openness to the consideration of philosophical challenges and the attempt to meet them. Such objection, though rarely expressed in so bold a form, is by no means unheard of in the treatment of these questions; it is the kind of response that was characterized in a preceding chapter as kicking stones.

A man considering sense perception as a means for securing knowledge of external objects, and perplexed by the obvious effects upon perceptual experience of physical, physiological, and psychological conditions, may easily be led to respond to frustrating skeptical exploitation of these perplexities by stoutly maintaining that he does see chairs and tables the presence of which is sufficient to make plain to others that he does. In so reacting he no doubt sometimes performs a useful service. For gray as a theory may be, and commonly insubstantial in confrontation with the realities and exigencies of life—even so subdued a portion of these as Hume's game of backgammon—its cumulative effect can be overpowering. And as a counterforce, helpful in resisting the temptation to escape the repeated frustration in one's attempt to understand how X occurs, by adopting the view that after all it doesn't, it is well to be reminded firmly that after all it does, and that consequently the denial that it does, though offering immediate relief from this frustration, cannot be maintained.

But stoutly maintaining that whatever difficulty may be encountered in giving a philosophical account of X, X nevertheless occurs, is no substitute for the account or for help in providing it, though, as much recent work in the philosophy of knowledge illustrates, there is a strong inclination among some to take it so. It is as if, to take a nonphilosophical analogy, in the face of the puzzlement and bafflement encountered by many men in accounting for the circulation of the blood in the human body, the concession that it does circulate could substitute for an explanation of the efficacy of the arteries, veins, capillaries, and chambers of the heart in conveying the blood in its rounds. What is to be criticized and rejected in Descartes's account of the circulation of the blood is not his attempt to give an account, but the account he gave, and the underlying physical view that indicated in general the kind of account that had to be given. His account is to be rejected and criticized, not because it is physiology, but because of its quality, as physiology, in comparison, say, with the account given by Harvey. Similarly what is to be criticized and rejected in that particular way of responding to questions about the philosophical soundness of certain knowledge claims which has been referred to summarily as Cartesian theory is not the sensitivity of the theory to such questions and attempts to answer them. It is to the way the questions are construed and treated in the theory, and the quality of the answers given. Corresponding criticisms hold for what has been called the "justification problem," arising in that theory, and to a common form of argument, which may be called the "justification argument," which expresses in its own way one central tenet of the theory. Carefully disclaiming any implications of artifice or deceit in the words employed, one may describe this argument as an insidious, and hence especially effective, vehicle for the propagation of the view taken in the theory of the way questions about the justification of knowledge claims must be answered in philosophy. That way is by discovering a starting place for our knowledge in immediately clear, certain incorrigible apprehensions, from which it is hoped that all other legitimate items of knowledge, can be shown to be derivable by a sequence of steps each one of which is immediately, and the end result thus mediately, equally clear, incorrigible, and, given proper qualifications about strength of grounds where necessary, equally indubitable.

3. Before proceeding to the statement and elucidation of the justification argument one further general point needs to be

made clear about the argument and the philosophical view it expresses. It was indicated earlier that so closely connected was the use of the word "justification" in philosophy with a certain kind of theory of knowledge, namely the kind expressing justification theory, that in general it contributes to clarity of discussion to follow that use, in effect conceding the word to that theory, rather than trying to extricate the word, redefine it, and reclaim it for other employment. But, as was also indicated, both by profession and practice, there are certain purposes which call for different proceeding. There are certain issues to be joined in the criticism of justification theory that are better clarified when put as issues over justification than as issues over things signified by other names.

This is particularly so when one is dealing with justification conceived as a philosophical operation, as something to be effected in the philosophical scrutiny of knowledge rather than as an operation engaged in ordinarily by scientists, scholars, and ordinary men but yet an object of interest to philosophers. If one takes the kind of justification which is the object of philosophical quest sufficiently broadly, if one conceives this justification as one of the things which is achieved in a critical, comprehensive, and systematic view of knowledge, then one may view the adherents and the critics of justification theory as joined in their quest for justification, but divided somewhat concerning the specific form this justification shall take, and very widely divided about the manner in which this more or less common end shall be pursued. We may think of partisans on both sides of the justification issue as devoted to achieving a philosophical view of knowledge which, like a logical theory or an ethical theory each in its particular domain, will not only illuminate the character of the items and practices of its domain, provide a broad understanding of what does and what should count as acceptable items and sound practices in it, and serve as a platform for rectification, reform, and development.

4. The Cartesian or justification program for the achievement of this broad end differs from alternative programs in a presumption that is not articulated, but rather put in practice, in the justification argument. The presumption is that the way to effect

the philosophical examination of any domain—settled or prob-lematic, accepted or disputed—of human knowledge is to pick out some typical example of a truth claim in that domain and perform what may be called the "justfication operation" upon it. This one does by asking justification questions about it, then about what grounds may be adduced in support of this claim, and then about the grounds in support of these, and so on.

A supposition is needed here to close the gap between the end in view and this particular way of proceeding to it. What in detail is implied in the supposition that by proceeding in this way one will reach the desired end? Something is supposed about the answers that will be forthcoming, about what are proper answers to the justification questions. It is supposed that such answers will contain, will make plain in the form of a sequence of statements or claims elicited by these questions, all that is relevant to the judgment whether, and to what extent, the original truth claims in question, and the domain of putative knowledge from which they have been extracted, live up to their cognitive pretensions. What is to be discovered by this operation is whether claims of the sort in question can be derived by some process of inference from a set of utterly sure first premises, and if so with what degree of certainty. Such a claim is justified if and only if it can be derived in this matter, and if (and only if) the degree of assurance attaching to its position in the corpus of knowledge is no greater than the degree of certainty of this derivation. This is a quite par-ticular conception of the way in which the philosophical scrutiny of items and domains of human knowledge can and should pro-ceed, of the way we can and should try to achieve the kind of un-derstanding of knowledge that will enable us to improve the quality of what we take to be knowledge, discriminating more efficiently and surely the mere pretenders to that status from those with a genuine warrant. Whenever questions arise concerning the status of individual claims (e.g., the existence of God, or of souls as substances) or of whole domains of claims (e.g., our apparent perception of the secondary qualities of things), this is the deci-sion process. The keys to the kingdom of fully accredited knowl-edge lie in the hands of those who practice this operation. The scrutiny of knowledge, the discrimination of what, under challenge, we may properly claim to know from what we may not, is effected by filtering items of putative knowledge and candidates for the status of knowledge through this Cartesian sieve.

5. It is a commonplace that to suppose that a certain method is appropriate for making decisions about a given subject matter is to suppose substantive things about the subject matter itself. Embedded in the doctrine under examination here of how the philosophical scrutiny of knowledge should proceed is a particular view of the nature of knowledge itself. Knowledge, as an endowment or achievement of individuals, or considered more impersonally as an entity having a more independent status, is conceived as consisting of a structure of truth claims ordered in relations of greater or less dependence; and the question of whether any claim or set of claims is properly accorded the status of knowledge is resolved by exploring the relation holding between the claim or claims in question and their justifiers.

Later in this book some attention will be paid to some of the more notable substantive features of knowledge that are neglected in such a view. At this point the primary task is not to criticize the view, but to understand it. The justification argument contributes to this understanding by setting forth one aspect of the view, namely the regressive aspect, the most signal feature of which is the thesis that there is and must be a level of foundation items in knowledge, items the status of which as knowledge is in a special way not subject to challenge and upon which the status of all other putative items of knowledge must depend. For the full elaboration of justification theory this regressive aspect must be complemented by a progressive one. Having established the hierarchical character of human knowledge, and fixed the nature of the top order in the hierarchy, from which all authority derives, it is necessary to make plain the route and procedure of the derivation. As the elaboration of this second, progressive phase repeatedly proved to be a source of frustration in the theory, from Descartes through Hume to their latter-day followers, it is evidence of the power of the justification argument that in the face of these frustrations in providing the progressive, constructive aspect of the theory, generations of philosophers persisted determinedly in holding that nevertheless this is the way in which the rationalization of knowledge claims must be pursued.[1]

6. The argument is seldom stated in any summary, explicit way. More usually it is adumbrated in philosophical activities that make sense in a context of supposition such as the argument translates into explicit pronouncements or claims, or in philosophical observations that signify for those alert to the clues what the suppositions are.[2] Fortunately for purposes of discussion here, there is a recent statement of the argument that can be appealed to. In his contribution to the cooperative volume on *Philosophy* in the Princeton Studies in the Humanities, R. M. Chisholm has advanced a version of the argument in support of "the doctrine of the given," including in that doctrine the thesis "that every justified statement, about what we think we know, is justified in part by some statement which justifies itself." [3] The argument presented in this work, which at some points can be helpfully construed in the light of Chisholm's fuller and systematic statement of his version of justification theory in *Theory of Knowledge,* will repay examination.

7. In *Theory of Knowledge,* setting out to explore our grounds for what we take ourselves to know, Chisholm discovers what he takes to be things that are directly evident. These items of knowledge are spoken of as directly evident "propositions" or "statements," and also as "self-presenting states of affairs." Directly evident propositions or statements are presumably about such

1 Part II of Lewis's *An Analysis of Knowledge and Valuation* is very instructive in this regard. The perceptive and scrupulously fair Lewis, like Canute, struggles against a mounting tide of difficulties, and by the end of this phase of the book, having discussed probability, induction, and memory, has made so many concessions that, though he may not be able to recognize it, the condition of his original impressive justification theory is one of thorough disarray.

2 E.g., Lewis, p. 171: "Empirical truth cannot be known except, finally, through presentations of sense. . . . Unless there should be some statements, or rather something apprehensible and statable, whose truth is determined by given experience and is not determinable in any other way, there would be no nonanalytic affirmation whose truth could be determined at all, and no such thing as empirical knowledge."

3 *Philosophy,* p. 263.

states of affairs, and are known by us when these states present themselves to us.

Earlier, in *Philosophy,* Chisholm had addressed himself to the question whether there are reasons in the philosophy of knowledge for supposing that there are such items of knowledge. The primary reasons he offered there for asserting that there are self-justifying statements, beliefs, claims, propositions, or hypotheses is not that instances of these can be discovered and produced, though alleged examples are cited; the reason is that the existence of such items is necessary, required in order for our claims to have knowledge to be justified. The argument setting forth and exploiting these reasons is more extended than what can be retailed here, for at certain points Chisholm advances his own position by considering it as one of a variety of alternatives open to or taken by rival philosophies. But the central line of argumentation is a fairly simple one, closely analogous to metaphysical ones concerning unmoved movers and uncaused causes.

Suppose we begin with some statement or claim, *C,* that we take ourselves to know, ask concerning the grounds of this, and receive as a citation of grounds in reply, a set of one or more further statements or claims. And let us suppose further that our original statement, or the statement that it is justified, is a necessary consequence of the grounds cited. Just citing them does not constitute justification. And so we may ask about the justification of these grounds, and then about the grounds of these grounds, and so on. Where do the questions stop?

The character of justification, as viewed in the argument, may now be defined a little more closely. Suppose we use *"C"* as an abbreviation for "claim" or "statement," the sort of thing whose justification is in question, and *"J"* as an abbreviation for "justified." And since the argument is about justification, and about the kind of grounds that effect justification, let *"G"* stand for "justifying ground." What is being employed at the outset of the argument is the supposition that every justified claim has some ground, "Every *JC* has a *G.*" And what is being employed in the step asking in turn for the grounds of the grounds, is the supposition that every ground, every ground that is not merely cited, but is capable of performing the justification for which it is cited, is itself a justified claim. "Every *G* is itself a *JC*." This situation with respect to justified claims and justifying grounds is taken to ensure that if any of these is justified at all, some must serve as their own grounds. The bare bones of the argument from which Chisholm derives the conclusion that there are statements, beliefs, claims, propositions, or hypotheses which justify themselves is thus:

     I Every *JC* has a *G*.
     II Every *G* is a *JC*.
∴ III Some *JC*'s must serve as their own grounds.

8. There is a variety of ways in which the first premise of this incomplete argument may be construed, and in some of these constructions it is very plausible. For example, "justified" in the phrase "justified claim" might be taken very broadly to mean a claim that we have a right to make, that we can properly or reasonably make; or it might be taken to mean, more narrowly, one for which the right, propriety, or reasonableness can be established by some justification procedure; or still more narrowly it might be taken to mean one for which this already has been established. In this last narrowest interpretation the premise is plausible, but the interpretation is too narrow for the intention of the argument. The argument is not designed to make clear something concerning just those claims which have been subjected to a justification procedure and *have* passed inspection, but about those claims that, if subjected to such a procedure, *will* pass inspection. And this can-pass-inspection sense is closely related to the first and broadest way of construing the premise, for it is presumed in the argument that there is a corresponding close connection between what is justified, in this particular can-pass sense of the word, and what is a reasonable, proper claim, one that we have a right ot make.[4] To be sure, in putting the question, "What

[4] Although the inquiry about justification in *Theory of Knowledge* is restricted to questions about claims we take ourselves to know, in contrast with those toward which we assume different attitudes, the target of the argument is justification, rather than the specific attitude assumed, and the considerations apply equally well or ill to those other attitudes, *mutatis mutandis*.

justification do I have for thinking that I know p?" I am engaged in a philosophical task. The question is a "Socratic [one] and therefore not at all of the type that one ordinarily asks." [5] Socratic questions are "not challenges and they do not imply or presuppose that there is any ground for doubting, or for suspecting that to which they pertain." They are "designed only to elicit information," in this case, truths about the rules of evidence. Presuming that we do have many and various claims which it is reasonable, proper for us to accept and advance in one way or other, we may put the question "What justifies us?" as a way of uncovering and formulating rules concerning what are reasonable, proper actions, dispositions, attitudes in such matters. These are philosophical questions because it is the business of the philosopher to seek and disseminate clarification in such matters. He does not invent justification, propriety, reasonableness, but inquires about them in a systematic, persistent way, and the putting and answering of Socratic questions is a procedure for the conduct of his inquiry.

Admittedly questions of this form have a curious sound: "What justifies you in X-ing?" "What justifies you in taking yourself to know p, or to be reasonable in accepting p?" This is not the way people ordinarily address themselves or others in the conduct of everyday or professional affairs. But that is primarily because for most people philosophical inquiry is not their profession or principal preoccupation. If we are interested in eliciting from our practice in dealing with truth claims, principles that can be supported by that practice and that can also be employed in the conduct, criticism, and guidance of that practice, we must investigate the practice, attempting to disclose what in it distinguishes reasonable and proper procedures from unreasonable, improper ones. The question, then, about claims we take ourselves to know, or to be reasonable in accepting in one way or another, is, "What justifies us in taking ourselves to know or reasonably accept these things?" And the argument for the conclusion that there are claims that justify themselves, has its basis in the answers we give to these questions. Philosophical scrutiny of our practice discloses that our reasonableness, in holding any claim that we indeed are reasonable in maintaining, resides at least in

[5] *Theory of Knowledge*, p. 25.

our having something specific in support of them in the way of grounds or evidence. These grounds or items of evidence are of the following character: they are themselves claims upon the reasonableness of which, as claims, the reasonableness of the items we take ourselves to know or reasonably accept depends. If we wish, as Chisholm does, to discriminate in the support that we can adduce for claims in response to Socratic questions, things offered as evidence which in the above formulation of the argument have been referred to simply as "grounds," and things offered as principles or rules connecting the reasonableness of this evidence with that for which it serves as grounds, we may leave room for the role of these principles or rules in justification in those occasions where they appear, by saying that every justified claim has grounds and its reasonableness depends in part on these grounds.[6]

9. The conclusion that there are self-grounding grounds, items of evidence that serve as evidence for other claims and that are the only things that can serve as evidence for themselves, is a central thesis in what Chisholm calls the "doctrine of the given." [7] This doctrine, as he rightly says, "is not merely the consequence of a metaphor," namely, the metaphor of an edifice and its foundations. "We are led to it," he says "when we attempt to answer certain questions about *justification*—our justification for supposing in connection with any one of the things we know to be true, that it is something we know to be true." [8] But this appears to be only part of the story. Whether we are led to this conclusion and other tenets of the doctrine of the given by our attempts to answer questions about justification depends upon what, in these attempts, we take justification to be. If we conceive of justification in the philosophy of knowledge as the achievement of a point of view, a broad, stable, coherent view of knowledge claims and other related matters, in which the items or procedures to be justified can find a place, can be assimilated, rationalized, guided, and expanded, then the supposition that justification questions must lead to a conclusion like this is a gaping *non sequitur*.

6 Cf. *Theory of Knowledge*, p. 26; *Philosophy*, p. 263.
7 *Theory of Knowledge*, p. 30; *Philosophy*, pp. 262–263.
8 *Philosophy*, pp. 262–263. Italics in orig.

The commonly accepted view of what is required for the philosophical justification of any alleged item of knowledge, any truth claim to which we profess some kind of reasonable adherence or acceptance, is a view of what is required when justification is conceived in a particular way, reflecting the ambitions and demands of a certain kind of theory of knowledge. Here, as often in philosophy, as well as other areas, what can be produced as the results of "conceptual analysis" is theory already implicit in the "concepts" under analysis. It is theory that can take this form, can be exposed by this kind of investigation, only because it has assumed such a settled position in our thought and language that it becomes a feature of the way we talk rather than of what, in an obvious sense, we say. What can be advanced or received as the results of an analysis of the concept of justification is thus a theory, or perhaps better, the congealed intellectual deposit of a theory or philosophy of justification. It is such a theory or philosophy encapsulated in a conception of justification having wide currency in philosophy, and not any necessity in the procedures by which truth claims are appraised and decided upon in science and in everyday life, nor any necessity in the development of a reasoned, comprehensive philosophy of these procedures, that leads, in much common reasoning about the justification of truth claims, to the conclusion that this justification, in the case of any item, must take its rise in certain fixed, self-supporting claims that a regress of questions about the backing of the item is bound to reveal.[9]

10. The main task at this point is not to appraise the philosophy expressed in the premises of this argument about justification, but to expose it. It is for this purpose that the two main premises, I and II, have been discriminated in the argument. The philosophy operative in the argument may be made more explicit by considering how one proceeds in it from these premises to the conclusion about self-justifying claims. In some respects the pro-

[9] In a word, what analysis reveals depends upon what is analyzed. And this may be (1) the broad spectrum of principles and practices present in the nonphilosophical domains of knowledge or putative knowledge; (2) the corresponding principles and practices in the domain of philosophy; or (3) the particular version of the philosophical principles and practices that is codified in justification theory.

cedure is very traditional. It consists of discriminating a set of alternative results that might ensue in the investigation of grounds for justified claims and making plain the ostensible incompatibility of these alternatives with the supposition that the claims are indeed justified.

Starting with the thesis of Premise I, that every justified claim has a ground, which is required by Premise II to be itself a claim, the immediate threat to the achievement of justification under these joint requirements lies in the possible generation of an infinite regress of grounds. One possibility of avoiding this regress, the possibility that some grounds need not be justified claims, has already been excluded by Premise II. Chisholm's comment on Reichenbach's proposal to avoid the regress in substantially this way, by the employment of "blind posits," is that this means "letting go of the concept of justification." [10] Premise II expresses this in a contrapositive way. [11]

[10] *Philosophy*, p. 268.

[11] Similar considerations account in most arguments like this for the elimination of one obvious abstract possibility, namely, a circular path of grounds which eventually leads to the citation, as a ground, of the very claim the justification of which one originally set out to investigate. The argument against this is, of course, not that there cannot be such a circular movement in the appeal to grounds, but that such movement will not yield *justification*. At this point the Cartesian aspects of the view of justification elaborated in such arguments as this are especially prominent. As the Aristotelian arguments about motion, in contending that no case of motion can be accounted for in such a way, reveal and depend upon a certain way of thinking of motion and causation—depend, to put the matter very plainly, upon a certain theory of motion and causation—so the present kind of argument depends upon a way of thinking of justification that is expressed in justification theory. If, in accordance with the theory, one thinks of the justification of a claim *C* as a procedure in which one effects the defense of *C* against a challenge to its presumed status as knowledge, or as at least a reasonable claim, then the justification of *C* will not tolerate the employment in it of *C* as a ground. Otherwise the original challenge to *C* may be reinstated at any point where *C* is so employed, and the effect of the challenge is not met, only postponed. A theory of justification permitting such a recurring regress would simply not do what such a theory is supposed to do, for reasons that are essentially the same as those in the case of the nonrecurring regress. As R. Garrigou-Lagrange wrote in his commentary on the nonrecurring regress in the argument on motion in Aristotle and St. Thomas, "You may conjure up an infinite number of intermediary causes, but by this process you merely complicate the series, yet do not establish a single cause. . . . To try to dispense with the necessity of a source is the same

The alternatives remaining open in the argument are now two. Either every justified claim has a ground in some other justified claim in a sequence of claims and grounds that reaches back endlessly, or some justified claims serve as their own grounds. It is instructive to observe why the first of these alternatives must, in argument like this, be rejected. The reason takes us back to a point that was made earlier in the discussion of the way the term "justified" should be construed in Premise I and in the argument generally.[12] A justified claim is one which under the philosophical scrutiny represented by Socratic questions can display its reasonableness, its propriety. This puts a special and clinching requirement upon justification. In order for any given claim, C, to count as a justified or reasonable one—a thoroughly, philosophically justified or reasonable one—it must be possible, in response to Socratic questions, to show its justification or rationale at every point where such questions can be put. The question can be put at every point at which a claim is advanced, beginning with C itself, and continuing with every ground advanced in support of C; for every justifying ground is itself a justified claim. Therefore, for every ground cited, justification requires that it be possible for us to cite an appropriate ground. It does not require that we do cite it, but that it be possible for us to cite it. Thus if in support of a claim C_1 I cite a ground or set of grounds G_1, it is required explicitly by the argument that G_1 be itself one or more justified claims. And it is required implicitly, since G_1 does consist, as it were, of claim material, that it must be possible for me to cite grounds for G_1, for G_2, and for any further ground that Socratic questioning may uncover.[13] No matter how long or short the sequence of grounds uncovered by these questions may be, it

---

as saying that a watch can run without a spring, provided it has an infinite number of wheels" (*God: His Existence and His Nature,* Vol. I, p. 265).

[12] This Chapter, Sect. 8.

[13] "In many instances the answers to our questions will take the following form: 'What justifies me in counting as evident (in thinking that I know) that a is F, is the fact that (1) it is evident that b is G and (2) if it is evident that b is G then it is evident that a is F. . . .' This type of answer shifts the burden of justification from one claim to another. For we now ask, 'What justifies me in counting it as evident that b is G?' " (*Theory of Knowledge,* p. 26).

must be possible to demonstrate the reasonableness of each ground in turn, employing only grounds that are justified claims, together with whatever rules of evidence need to be employed in deriving justified claims from these grounds. But this requires that the sequence of grounds must have an end, which in turn requires that some justified claims are self-justified, are justified by themselves.

11. It is worth observing that by themselves the two premises formally discriminated in the argument do not require this conclusion. It could be the case that every justified claim has grounds that can be cited in response to the question "What justifies?" and that these grounds are themselves justified claims, and yet that the sequence of grounds and questions has no end. The fact that all the grounds in the sequence cannot be cited does not exclude the possibility that grounds can be cited for any specified claim in the sequence. But the possibility that at any point in the sequence one can cite as grounds claims that are reasonable or justified is not sufficient for the purpose, which is philosophical justification, and which is supposed to be pursued and achieved by exhaustively putting and answering these justification questions. It is because the question about the justification of C is not yet answered, when one has cited grounds for C, even when those grounds are reasonable, justified ones; because such an answer, as Chisholm says, "shifts the burden of justification from one claim to another"; [14] and because, finally, the procedure of repetitively and exhaustively putting the question, "What justifies?" about C, and then about G_1, G_2, and so on, is viewed as a procedure for distinguishing philosophical justified claims from unjustified ones. A requirement for a philosophical justified truth claim is a certain determinable thoroughness in its grounding that can be exposed in this kind of scrutiny. It is required of such a claim, on this view, that under pressure of repetitive questioning, disclosing ground upon depending ground, as far as this may go, it be possible to show that all the grounds upon which the claim depends, mediately or immediately—*all* of them and not just *any* of them—be capable of being shown to be justified. But one can hope to descend to the bottom of such an epistemic

14 *Ibid.*

ladder only if there is a bottom, and not an endless sequence of descending steps.

12. It is difficult to employ the word "justification" in extended philosophical discussion without, in spite of determination to the contrary, being imposed upon by some of the ordinary associations and rules of usage of this word. One needs a reminder again and again that what is under consideration is not ordinary variety justification, whatever that may be, but extraordinary, philosophical justification. It was similarly with Luther when he proclaimed the doctrine that justification was by faith. His thesis was about a certain kind of justification, that had its home in Christian theology, not, say, in what could be said about a farmer, Hans, who entered the shed of Albrecht and walked off with a scythe that Albrecht had borrowed from him and persistently neglected to return. One cannot easily assume that the justification of Hans in this case is at every important point similar, though it surely is in some, with his justification as a creature by nature sinful in a situation in which the wages of sin is death and what hangs in the balance, accompanying justification, is the gift of eternal life.

What hangs in the balance with justification in the epistemological case under investigation is philosophical understanding and the intellectual and other benefits that such understanding yields. The philosopher seeking to "justify" some fundamental feature in the corpus of human knowledge, such as that there are other minds besides one's own, has not been caught, apparently *flagrante delicto*, emerging from someone else's shed with a scythe and hence needing to defend himself. What is called for in the case of this philosophical claim is not exculpation, but some effort to understand the claims in question, to assimilate them in a comprehensive view of human activity which, in finding some place for them, will also provide resources for criticizing, refining, revising them as, and to the extent that, the intellectual abrasion and friction generated by the attempt to assimilate them indicates that such critical operations must be considered. The species of justification represented in the kind of argument under examination here represents an attempt to perform this task in one particular way. That is by putting questions of a certain sort concerning individual truth claims which fall under examination, questions of a sort that require in answer the citation of other claims (for they are, in part at least, requests for such claims), and which must in turn be repeated and similarly answered for any claim cited. No claim is justified, no claim can be regarded as philosophically naturalized and assimilated, unless this procedure can be completed in its case. Therefore, if any claim is to be regarded as philosophically justified, some claims must be capable of serving as their own grounds, must be self-justifying ones.

13. A critic who has achieved this understanding of philosophical justification, as it is viewed in the theory and expressed in the argument under examination, and who recognizes the unhappy philosophical consequences to which such theory leads, has some choice in the form in which he may advance his criticism. One alternative open to him is to take justification, as it is viewed in this theory, as definitive of philosophical justification generally, and then to formulate his criticism as a criticism of justification procedures in philosophy. This way of proceeding has the merit of simplicity, and also that of providing a safeguard against the dangers of intellectual entrapment that attend the use of the word "justification." But it is not without its own dangers. One of these is that so sweeping a rejection of justification projects and procedures tends to obscure a distinction that needs to be made between the means employed in justification theory and certain deep philosophical ends that motivate the theory and to which the procedures are conceived to be instrumental. That the corpus of human knowledge neither needs nor can be provided with justification of the kind envisaged in Cartesian philosophy, does not mean that human knowledge is at all points immune to philosophical criticism; that philosophical scrutiny of knowledge, if conducted properly, ends up by leaving "everything as it is" (Wittgenstein); that the pursuit of knowledge in everyday life, in the sciences, the humanities, and the technical arts cannot only be altered, but improved, when that pursuit is understood and carried out in the framework of enlightened philosophical theory. Justification theory has been narrow, paro-

chial, misguided, in the means it has employed to reach these ends. It has proceeded as if the kind of justification achieved by Euclid for the geometry of his day was the model not only for justification in mathematics—an assumption parochial even in this field—but for philosophy, in which ethics, metaphysics, politics, logic, and the rest are to be, to use Spinoza's words, *"ordine geometrico demonstrata."* [15] But if, dissatisfied with the efficacy of these means for explicating, rationalizing, and criticizing the various members of the corpus of human knowledge, and having identified justification with these means, one expresses one's dissatisfaction by rejecting justification problems and procedures *simpliciter*, one tends, in the force of one's rejection, to reject the ends to which the means were directed. One then concludes, as Wittgenstein concluded on the relation between philosophy and language, that "philosophy may in no way interfere with the actual use of language; it can in the end only describe it." [16]

[15] "The Cartesian Regulae ad directionem ingenii essentially repeat these theses [of axiomatic method]—and thus the science of the seventeenth century aims mostly at setting up new axiomatic theories besides the traditional Euclidean geometry, first of all mechanics, but also with Spinoza and Hobbes, ethics and politics.

"It is interesting to note that Descartes's own geometry, the so-called analytic geometry, shows characteristics which do *not* fit in with this methodology. Analytic geometry reduced geometrical problems to algebraic ones, thus also to the Indian-Arabic art of algorithmic calculation." Paul Lorenzen, "Methodological Thinking," *Ratio* (1965–1966), p. 35.

[16] *Philosophical Investigations*, Pt. I, Sect. 124.

CHAPTER 7

Foundation Difficulties

1. What has been discussed in the preceding chapter under the title of "justification theory" or "Cartesian theory" is a philosophical view of a very general kind. The generic character of the view, sometimes discussed in contemporary writing as the "foundations" view, is a presumption about the source of the authority of those truth claims we take to represent human knowledge, and consequently also about the relation, in the development of knowledge, between consequent items or claims and those from which they can be developed or derived. The presumption, expressed in the metaphor of foundations and building, is from the point of view of cognitive authority hierarchical. It is that there are certain starting points in knowledge, certain items upon which other items depend but which themselves depend neither upon these or any other items. The flow of cognitive authority, warrant, rationality is in one direction, always from those starting points, so that what we learn by means of them always depends for its cognitive status altogether upon them. It never attains a position or status independent of these starting points and consequently cannot ever be employed in the criticism, correction, or even rejection of them. There is no logical room for an emerging reversal of roles of guidance between child and parent, let alone an occasional practice of merciful euthanasia, in the intellectual commonwealth envisaged in this theory.

Pains have been taken to explain how this general theory, or theory pattern, can be and has been filled out philosophically in a variety of ways, the two most prominent ways being the rationalist one, exemplified in Descartes himself, and the empiricist one, exemplified in classic British empiricism and its latter-day revivals. Closely related to this theory, but again a very general pattern, is the pattern of argument just discussed under the title of the "justification argument." The fact that this pattern can be filled out in a variety of ways, accommodated to a variety of philosophical persuasion, is sufficient indication that the argument expresses nothing like a full theory and commits its proponents to none. The key term in the argument, "justification," can within the restrictions of the argument be interpreted in a variety of ways, empiricist, rationalist, and otherwise, the former alternative being the one most favored by recent writers. The argument does constitute a kind of very partial, implicit definition of justification. It sets as a requirement upon justification that it be a relation holding between claims as terms, which in the most primitive case may be a claim and itself. It requires also that the relation also take its rise in such self-justifying claims, that the exploration of the justification of any genuine item of knowledge lead to, and the justification depend upon, such independent, or what is the same, entirely self-dependent items. Whatever else justification may be, it must consist in this kind of explorable and hence finite chain that comes to an end and finds its source of authority in such fixed, incorrigible, self-authorizing items of knowledge.

2. That there are great difficulties in carrying out the program of justification conceived in this theory is admitted on all sides in recent philosophy, by supporters of the program as well as those who reject it. A recognition of the difficulties is indicated, among its supporters explicitly in the energetic and persistent efforts of writers like C. I. Lewis to subdue them, and in the gradual relinquishment of main tenets of the theory during the last thirty years by some of the leading exponents of logical empiricism.[1] It is indicated less explicitly in the defensive measures taken by advocates of less robust versions of the theory, in

---

[1] A striking but by no means singular example of this is the thought of C. G. Hempel. See, for example, *Aspects of Scientific Explanation* (New York, 1965), especially "The Theoretician's Dilemma"; see also, when available, Hempel's Carus Lectures of May, 1970.

some of which the claims of the theory are made in so attenuated and guarded form, or accompanied by so many concessions, that what starts out as a defense of the theory ends more as a capitulation.[2]

Corresponding to the different ways in which the theory pattern can be filled out, taking a different coloration in differing philosophical contexts, there are different ways in which the difficulties emerge. These differences sometimes signify difficulties peculiar to a particular species of justification philosophy; more often they signify different forms taken by a common difficulty in response to differences in philosophical context. Two chief classes of difficulty may be discriminated: (1) those concerning the starting claims, the self-justifying certain and incorrigible cognitions in which the justification procedure must take its rise, on this theory; and (2) those concerning the procedure by which, beginning with these first claims, the justification of other claims is thought to be effected. Alluding to the metaphor of building commonly employed in discussions of justification theory, we may refer to these two kinds of difficulty as "foundation" difficulties and "construction" difficulties. Both difficulties concern the identification of items or procedures capable of doing what is required in the two phases of justification marked off in the theory. Foundation difficulties are thus encountered in discriminating a set of claims which can be established in utter independence from other claims; which can therefore serve as the bottom steps in the justification stairway; which are in consequence of their independence from other claims incorrigible by them; and which in consequence of their incorrigibility must be utterly certain, incapable of any error. Since incorrigibility without truth is a dubious merit for any set of truth claims to have, since incorrigible error is error of the worst kind, and since the aspiration to truth of any item in the corpus of human knowledge is taken to depend upon these alleged incorrigible claims, they must, in their splendid isolation, be incorrigibly true. Infallibility as a requirement derives in the theory from incorrigibility,

2 See A. J. Ayer, *The Problem of Knowledge* and *Philosophical Essays;* also A. Quinton, "The Foundations of Knowledge," in B. Williams and A. Montefiore, *British Analytic Philosophy.*

just as incorrigibility derives from the assignment of certain claims to the position of fixed and absolute beginnings in the justification process.

The construction difficulties are not simply those of developing further knowledge of some kind from these beginnings, though in view of the severity of the restrictions already put upon the beginnings, this may seem formidable enough. If what is to be developed is something like the corpus of human knowledge, this *justificandum* represents a fairly definite goal for the justification process. The construction difficulties are those encountered in attempting to proceed in a certain philosophical theory from beginnings of the kind specified, and by means congruent with them, to this relatively determined and philosophically desirable end.

3. The major difficulties encountered by Descartes and others in working out the rationalist version of justification theory are well known. Since in this version of the theory the laying of foundations and building upon these were effected by the same means, namely the clear and distinct apprehensions of the intellect, Descartes was faced immediately with the need for justifying the employment of this intuitive intellectual clarity and distinctness as a criterion of truth. This need precipitated him at once into the difficulties about circularity which, though much noted in his case, are not peculiar to his philosophy, but, as was argued earlier, are endemic in what may be more broadly referred to as the Cartesian theory of knowledge.

These internal problems were by no means the only difficulties encountered in the effort to reconstruct human knowledge in a concatenation of rational intuitions. If one supposes that the reconstruction is to be effected only by the making of sure, utterly certain, and incorrigible steps or additions, rational intuition, in spite of its proved value in the development of natural philosophy of the sixteenth and early seventeenth centuries, is not a very credible candidate as a means for making these steps. Hobbes, no less confident in the power of such intuition than Descartes, had radically different intuitions from Descartes concerning metaphysical matters; and on physical matters, on motion, for example, there were most serious discrepancies between the intuitions of Descartes and those of Galileo or Mersenne. That rational intuition was the single most valuable means at the disposal of men at this time for the development of a science of mechanics did not mean that it was an effective means for accomplishing the philosophical justification of this and other sciences when that justification was conceived to confer upon the items justified the lithic fixity then attributed to Euclidean geometry.

One possible response to difficulties like these would have been to give up the commitment to philosophical justification of this kind. Judged on the prospects of developing a reasonable, realistic theory of knowledge, capable of assimilating the procedures and attainments of modern physical science, this would have been a more favorable response. But the empiricists, Cartesians to the end, preferred fixity, and the illusory security which that fixity promised, to fruitfulness. And giving up the hope that basic fixities, first certainties, of any but a highly vacuous kind could be delivered by rational intuition (the promises of which, already in Locke, were being received at a sharp discount), they turned for these basic items to the deliverances of immediate self-consciousness, to what Locke called external and internal sense. In these deliverances, in our apprehension of what was conceived as being simply present to consciousness in our experience in these two domains, they sought to find intuitive cognitions that could more cogently be held to have the characteristics of fixity and certainty that the Cartesian program required.

On this point the empiricists were right, as the history of skepticism from ancient times amply testifies. They were right in supposing that in retreating from intuitively apprehended principles about the motion of bodies, or principles of causation (for example, the principle that something cannot proceed from nothing, or the more perfect from the less perfect) to reports of sense impressions and sensuous feelings, they were moving to a better fortified position, one from which it was easier to maintain the claims of incorrigible, certain cognition, because what was alleged to be known in this way was, in contrast with the large-scale claims of rational intuition, so very little. The price paid for this greater impregnability for the claims made on behalf of the "first impressions of sense" was a greater gap now to be bridged, a greater construction job to be performed in filling the gap, between the first, basic cognitions upon which all justified claims were taken to rest, and the full corpus of human knowledge that would now have to be jutsified on this basis. To confident adherents to the view this seemed at first a reasonable price; the gap appeared to be one that with diligent effort might be filled. Later, when the full magnitude of the price came to be realized, when the Zenonian character of the gap became more apparent in the obdurate problems associated with induction, other minds, the external world, and so on, the commitment of many to this view of what the philosophical rationalization of knowledge claims must be was sufficiently firm to lead them to find other kinds of response to these problems. One kind of response was to construct arguments designed to show that, precisely because there were no ways of solving these problems, they were not real problems. Another was to effect maximum logical refinement in certain subordinate aspects of the problems, and then, this cosmetic improvement achieved, to assign them permanent positions in the philosophic landscape where it was thought that they might serve, like whited sepulchres in a graveyard, decorously to curb pride and overambition in the claims of human reason.

4. Before narrowing the discussion specifically, in the present chapter, to the foundation difficulties, in contrast with the construction ones, a preliminary notice may be helpful concerning that aspect of the theory to which attention will be directed in the discussion of both kinds of difficulty in this and the following chapter.

The primary purpose of the discussion of justification theory in this book is not to establish that there are serious difficulties in the theory. Supposing this result to have been sufficiently achieved in the history of the theory, and not least by the efforts of advocates of it to devise means for meeting the difficulties, the primary purpose of the book, with respect to these difficulties, is to promote some philosophical understanding of them, to the end that this understanding may be employed in the development of a more adequate philosophy of knowledge.

One aspect of the theory, at both the level of foundation and ensuing construction, is particularly well suited to this purpose. This aspect is the incorrigibility at both the alleged foundation and higher levels of cognition which the theory requires.

5. The philosophical examination of various tenets and results of justification theory has persistently suffered from insufficient attention to the demand for incorrigibility made by the theory at the higher levels. The chief reason for this neglect has been the misjudgment that this demand was dissolved by the translation of the main questions of construction in the theory into questions of probability theory. It was supposed that if the construction steps in knowledge were conceived as effected by means of probability theory, if at the level of constructed conclusions the Cartesian search for certitude were replaced by a search for probability relations between the foundations and these conclusions, then the oppressive effects of the requirement of incorrigibility at this important place would be eliminated. What indeed are probability conclusions if not ones that are capable of being revised?

There is a very large question, however, whether the capacities for revision of judgment afforded by the mathematical theory of probability are adequate to the need, particularly when the resources of this theory are employed within the confines of justification theory. The main resource offered by probability theory for filling the need is the recognized relativity of probability to evidence, when the theory is construed as measuring the strength of a relation between the hypothesis and this evidence. To be sure, this relativity meant that in accordance with the theory there is a vast domain of cases in which for probability numbers in the open interval between 0 and 1, there is a possibility that an accretion in a body of evidence will alter the probability of a given hypothesis relative to its evidence. But there remains a very considerable question whether the assent to or assertion of a conclusion qualified by references to probability and evidence is adequately understood as a recognition or assertion simply that the conclusion has a certain probability relative to this evidence. Negative answers to this question were offered by Toulmin in his extended examination of Kneale's views on probability, and by Austin in his very brief comment on Keynes.[3] In an important respect, the doctrine that probability is a logical relation between statements effected a philosophical adjustment in which one kind of incorrigibility was preserved while relinquishing another. Probability judgments *per se,* being regarded as logical judgments, were apparently saved from the perils of revision. What had seemed to be a revision of a probability judgment was viewed as the substitution of one incorrigible judgment for another which, though incorrigible and thus uncorrected as an assessment of probability, was nevertheless rendered somehow epistemically obsolete by the accretion of further evidence. The disadvantages of attempting to save the incorrigibility of probability assessments in this way were philosophically serious in a variety of respects which cannot be treated here. From a broad philosophical point of view the corrigibility of probability assessments was not so much dispelled as suppressed, and also rendered less tractable to philosophical analysis by having to be dealt with indirectly and awkwardly by ill-adapted means, one of the most utilized of which is a principle of total available evidence which in its uncomfortably sweeping and uninformative character is comparable to the once popular principles of the uniformity of nature. (Cf. Chapter 5, Sect. 15, n. 8.)

6. A more serious inadequacy of the principle of the relativity of probability to evidence as a means of providing and accounting for corrigibility of items of knowledge at the supposed construction levels is the severe limitation in the kind of corrigibility to which it applies. It applies only to the kind of correction and revision which can be adequately treated as a matter of viewing an unaltered statement or proposition, *H,* in relation to different bases or grounds. It is not applicable to those cases in which new information, new developments, new ways of acting call for deep, sometimes extensive, and sometimes subtle changes

---

3 S. Toulmin, "Probability," *Aristotelian Society Supplementary Volume XXIV* (1950); J. L. Austin, "Ifs and Cans," *Proceedings of the British Academy,* Vol. XLII (1956).

in our ways of thinking which affect the very integrity of *H* and other would-be statements and propositions themselves. In many such cases the incorrigibility of *H* and statements concerning the relation of *H* with other statements cannot be preserved because it becomes more and more, and finally intolerably, difficult to preserve *H* itself. *H,* and its logical relations with other statements or propositions, are eroded by the kind of effect which it has now become customary to refer to, not very felicitously, as "conceptual change."

7. It is this aspect of the corrigibility of our knowledge which is emphasized in the following discussions. It is maintained, as against the demands of justification theory, that our knowledge is corrigible in a thoroughgoing way at both the supposed base level and at the higher levels which are discriminated in that theory. This corrigibility includes but is not restricted to the possibility of error, since error is but one of the ways in which our thoughts, opinions, beliefs, suppositions, presumptions, language, and so on, can fail to articulate properly with those features of ourselves and the world which we are exploring by these means. Error is a prominent kind of failure. In certain domains of cognitive practice it is both striking and important. But emphasis upon it in the philosophy of knowledge has led to an unfortunate, long-continued neglect of other kinds of failure which only in recent years has begun to be repaired. It is as if one tried to understand arithmetic as devoted exclusively to ensuring correct computation, not realizing what a vast achievement must already have been made, what an enormous machine must already be constructed, before "correct," "incorrect," and similar discriminations begin to be possible and make sense. It is as if one tried to understand the development of the automobile as exclusively directed to the problem of how to start the motor of such a contraption, not realizing how much one must have already progressed before one can think, as we do, of motors and what might be effective ways of initiating their operation.

8. The name "revision phenomena" is applied in Chapter 8 to a variety of concrete ways in which possibilities of correction of the kind just referred to are realized in cognitive practice, both in everyday life and in specialized disciplines, in those processes

which must be viewed, when reconstructed according to the requirements of justification theory, as incorrigible constructions, incorrigible derivations from premises. The name could easily have been applied more generally to include the phenomena of the realization of the same kind of corrigibility, the same kind of improvability of the articulation of our language and thought with its sometimes obscurely discerned intended objects that is realized at the supposed level of first cognitions, whether these be thought of as of sense or of reason. For the general doctrine maintained and elaborated concerning corrigibility, as applied both to alleged first cognitions and others, is basically the same. And it can be briefly stated.

9. Consider an avowal of belief, or a discrimination of a color quality at some very immediate level of sense experience such as is attained in a variety of psychophysical experiments or in tests of vision performed by an oculist. Cases of this sort may be regarded as crucial for the theory. They are advanced by the advocates of the theory as prime examples of incorrigible cognition; here, if ever, it occurs. Therefore in a Popperian way they may be regarded as test cases for the opposing view.

The doctrine advanced concerning these alleged first steps in cognition, like that concerning consequent ones, is that in having a belief (e.g., that the stepladder is in the garage) or in discriminating a quality of one's own visual experience (e.g., the redness of the after-image) one is participating in a practice that extends, and depends for its success upon conditions which extend, far beyond the subject as an individual human being. It is not just that without trees there would have been no wood and so no wooden stepladder, nor just that I would not know what a stepladder was if other human beings were not around to make stepladders, teach me about ladders, and so on. It's that I could not succeed in thinking about a stepladder, in having the thought of a stepladder, if there were not a vast set of ongoing practices of making things, climbing, storing, putting, finding. My thought or belief that the ladder is in the garage is possible only because there is this complex of practices. My saying to myself, "It's in the garage," can only have the significance it has because of these practices; its significance changes as these practices change. There is no preserve of thought objects, intensional objects, or meanings that is either safe from corruption by degenerating practices, or insulated from the improving effects of advancing, refined ones. Doctrines of incorrigible cognitions have depended upon the supposition that there is such a preserve. These doctrines are themselves corrected by the recognition that we are able to think the way we do because of the way we act, which in a way should not be surprising, since thinking is a form of acting. We are able to think in certain ways only because there are also certain ways in which we and our fellow human beings act, in which our ancestors and theirs have acted; and, of course, only because the world in which our actions and theirs have taken place is such as to support, to make possible, such actions.

10. All this has been put in the language of necessary conditions. In what sense are they necessary? In the sense, surely, that recognizing that language and thought are corrigible in the ways just maintained is part of understanding what language and thought are. This is not to be taken to mean that there is a "concept" of language and a "concept" of thought, which are our common properties, and which by some skillful logical strikes can be made to disclose inside them, like rocks under a geologist's hammer, thought deposits that are the philosophical propositions in question. These propositions should be thought of as necessary to the understanding of language and thought, to the understanding of what an avowal of a belief or a report of a sensory quality is, rather in the way that the denial of immutability is now necessary to our understanding of what biological species are, in the way in which recognition of the focal position of the sun is now necessary to our understanding of the solar system. There is no apparent general view possible of biological species or of the solar system which can successfully compose the denial of these cited elements with the wide areas of uncontroverted, accepted fact and doctrine in these respective fields. In a similar way the maintained corrigibility of items of knowledge, whether these be direct reports of our sensations or thoughts, or conclusions arrived at on the basis of these and other sources, is necessary to the philosophical understanding of our capacity to attain such items. When we try to achieve this understanding by

developing a view in which our admitted capacity in these respects will combine, fit, reinforce, and be reinforced by a large amount of uncontroverted fact and doctrine in the general areas in question, some of which has been alluded to—when we try to do this while retaining a commitment to incorrigibility, we apparently cannot succeed. Any possible tactic for achieving success requires too great a sacrifice of accumulated intellectual capital, either in the form of the ordinary stocks and bonds of accepted fact and doctrine concerning this and other areas, or in the select, blue-chip securities of general logical principles. A natural way of expressing the extremity and insupportability of such a sacrifice in the intellectual economy is by the formula that the doctrines requiring such sacrifices "cannot possibly" be accepted, "must necessarily" be rejected. In his comments upon skepticism at the end of Book I of the *Treatise,* Hume observed that, "If we believe, that fire warms, or water refreshes, 'tis only because it costs us too much pains to think otherwise." If it is possible to adopt Hume's language without being misled by the suggested discount of intellectual turbulence, the assimilation of fundamental intellectual discords to the more ordinary discomfort which is sometimes associated with intellectual surprise, one may say of corrigibility of the kind in question that it must be maintained at the places indicated, because it does indeed cost us too much pain to think otherwise.

11. It was observed above (Sect. 3) that in the empiricist version of the Cartesian philosophy a high price was extracted in exchange for the restrictions imposed upon basic propositions in the interest of their greater impregnability. This price was the expansion of the gap which in this philosophy had to be bridged between these propositions and the full corpus of human knowledge which somehow had to be shown to be derivable from them. The expansion of the gap did not create the justification problem, but did make it unmistakably obvious in a variety of forms. The greater the gap, the more obvious was that aspect of the problem of justification which was concerned specifically with means of filling the gap. But there was another, not so obvious aspect of the problem, more immediate and equally serious. This

derived from the fact that justification theory required that the conceived foundations of knowledge be impregnable, not merely in a high degree, but absolutely. This requirement too, it turned out in the end, could not be satisfied.

Why this is so is by now an oft-told story in the history of philosophy of the past two hundred years. It has been told in a variety of idioms, varying from the arcane ones of the *Critique of Pure Reason* to the latest attack upon a "foundations" theory of knowledge or exposé of the "myth of the given." Kant argued the case in terms of the necessity of concepts, with percepts, in the development of a knowledge of appearances, the concepts in question being the concepts of the understanding and the requirement basically deriving from the transcendental unity of apperception. Hegel, with good reason, took this advertised Copernican revolution in philosophy to be only partly secured and proceeded to complete the work of his distinguished predecessor by mounting a powerful argument against all fixed and immutable phases in the development of human knowledge, including both the alleged immediacies of sense and the eternally fixed battery of concepts of the understanding. A latter-day Hegelian, F. H. Bradley, spoke to the point in arguing the ineffability of immediate experience, while across the Atlantic a slightly older contemporary, C. S. Peirce, came to roughly parallel conclusions concerning the possibility of knowledge by sensory intuition as a consequence of different reflections concerning "certain faculties claimed for man," the doctrine that there are "first cognitions," and the bearing upon these of the theory of signs.

12. There is little to be gained by continuing this catalogue of voices, or rehearsing the variety of ways in which the case against basic propositions of sense, or of immediate experience generally, has been argued at intervals in the past, or in a swelling chorus of dissent in recent years. For the broad issues about knowledge that are posed by justification theory, the crucial aspect of the alleged first cognitions that are taken to be expressed in basic empirical propositions is their logical independence from every other possible cognition. This character of epistemic atoms is essential to them, essential to their role as self-justifying grounds for other claims. If they are not logically independent, other cog-

nitions may serve as grounds for them; and this is incompatible with their role as members of the justification sequence with which the sequence of questions must stop, because no more can possibly be asked. From this independence follows their incorrigibility. And given this incorrigibility, as was previously observed, they will have to be certain in a very strong sense that implies infallibility. Upon this, advocates and critics of the view can agree. Claims are said to be self-justifying ones only when they alone, and no other claims whatever, may be advanced in their support. Such claims may be equivalently said to justify themselves, or to be neither justified nor unjustified.[4] And such claims, whose only justification is themselves, must be true.[5]

Are there items in the repertory of human knowledge with the characteristics required in these "first cognitions," in particular this primary determinative character of utter independence from all other possible items?

13. On this subject there is one paramount point to be attended to. The point, briefly stated in Section 9, concerns the vast battery of equipment and resource that is employed by anyone in making discriminations of sense—to narrow the case to that, leaving aside such parallel and similarly vulnerable candidates for self-presenting states as beliefs, intentions, wants, wishes, and the rest. The argument here in essence is that in the discrimination of any sensation or datum of sense by an individual much more is involved than that individual and the alleged sensation or datum. In order for me here and now to determine that I am having the sensation X, I have in some way to employ or rely upon much that extends far beyond the domain of my sensations here and now, including X.

A second aspect of this battery of equipment and resource that needs to be emphasized, in addition to the vast extent to which it transcends the individual and involves real things beyond him, is that it is essentially social in character. Discrimina-

---

[4] R. M. Chisholm, *Philosophy*, p. 270; *Theory of Knowledge*, pp. 29-30.

[5] "In the case of what we have called the 'directly evident,' conditions of truth and criteria of evidence may be said to coincide. If it is evident to a man that he thinks he sees a horse, then he does think he sees a horse; and if he does think he sees a horse, then it is evident to him that he thinks he sees a horse" (*Theory of Knowledge*, p. 111; cf. also p. 49).

tions of sense are performances that we are able to engage in, and if we are clear-headed, can conceive of ourselves engaging in, only in a real world of objects and conditions that extend far beyond any human being. Similarly, we are able to engage in these performances, and conceive of ourselves as engaging in them, only because there is a real world of social practice, incorporating other human beings, both our contemporaries and predecessors, with whom, in a literal sense, we are cooperating when we make such discriminations, and without whose cooperation, the words we employ when we make these discriminations could not possibly have the significance they do.

14. These two aspects of the equipment and resource that we employ in making discriminations of sense are so closely related that it will be advantageous to discuss them together in the following pages. The bearing that these aspects have upon the traditional problems of the "external world" and of "other minds" should be fairly obvious. If we can make discrimination between red appearings only in a world of real objects and in reliance upon such objects, we cannot in our philosophy consistently suppose ourselves to be making such discriminations and at the same time holding in question whether there is a world of objects of whose features these discriminated colors may possibly be taken as signs. Similarly we cannot consistently discriminate our own mental states, our own sensations, memories, desires, and ambitions and at the same time consistently wonder whether this is as far as human life extends, whether what we have hitherto taken to be fellow human beings are mere mindless automata, or the phantasms of such.[6] But it is not the bearing of the considerations on these two traditional philosophical problems that is the major concern here, but rather the bearing of them on the question whether sensuous feeling or intuition con-

---

[6] Cf. E. Nagel's comment on the generation of the "problem of the external world" in his review of H. Reichenbach's *Experience and Prediction*, first publilshed in *Philosophy of Science* (1939) and reprinted in *Sovereign Reason*, pp. 225–265: "I have not been able to locate any account by him [Reichenbach] of impressions which does not employ such terms ['inside,' 'outside,' 'personal,' 'external,' etc.]. But if this language is taken seriously, the formulation of the problem of the external world involves the assumption of the existence of such a world" (*Sovereign Reason*, p. 252).

stitutes a sure, independent, though limited source of knowledge. Is there a kind of knowing or experiencing which lives up to Berkeley's dictum that to be is to be perceived? Do we have exemplified in sensations, sensa, or whatever, something that may be conceived as a personal event of this peculiar general kind: that its occurrence, with whom and when it occurs, is sufficient, quite independently of any other thing, to endow the subject with some knowledge of its specific character, with knowledge of some truth concerning this character, however limited that knowledge may be conceived to be? If so, there is a case to be made for sensation as a source of first cognitions.

On the other hand, if knowing any truth about a sensation, if indeed *having* a sensation of the kind that is specified in that truth, involves the employment and sound working of a vast array of equipment and resource extending far beyond any individual and what can be conceived to be private to him, then the possibility that this equipment and resource is not in place and working soundly cannot be discounted in the philosophical understanding of knowledge of such truth. If the sound discrimination of the sensation of X, in its character *as X*, can be made only by correctly utilizing something further, say, Y and if, in a case like this, discrimination of a sensation as X can be made while yet, for some reason, Y is not being used correctly, then a discrimination of X need not be a sound discrimination. If the discrimination of X is essentially related, both in respect to its significance and its soundness, to an extensive "external" resource of equipment and practice, then, just as malfunction in the resource can affect the correctness of the discrimination, so change in the resource can affect the very character, the very significance of the discrimination. Exposed in the light of such considerations, the supposition that knowledge of our sensuous feelings is an exemplification of our capacity to have infallible first cognitions rapidly loses whatever initial plausibility it may have had. We may or may not think it judicious to treat sensations as a peculiar kind of private object. And surely, if we do think of them in this way, we shall have to conceive of the determination of truth and falsity with respect to these objects in ways somewhat different from those followed with recognized public ones. In either case increasing understanding of what is involved in determining, describing, reporting, the character of our sensations increasingly excludes the possibility that the manner in which we achieve knowledge of statements concerning their specific character exemplifies a capacity on our part to attain knowledge by means of infallible sensuous intuition. It is a possibility that can hardly be thought, let alone thought plausible.

15. In exploring the close connection between the logical independence and the corrigibility of a first cognition like that to the effect that "I am being appeared to redly" (Chisholm) or, even more primitively, "Here-now red" applied to my visual field, there is some inclination for one to concentrate upon the question of the possibility of error in these putative cognitions. Is it conceivable that I might take myself to be appeared to redly and yet not be appeared to in this way, but orangely, perhaps, or even greenly? Questions like this are very proper. And the conceivability of this error, which is minimal when we think of ourselves operating in one set of circumstances, becomes considerable in others. Learning to make such discriminations is a practice which most of us begin to learn in early childhood and which in the case of many with aesthetic gifts continues long and can be exceedingly refined. And the central question about error is not whether a person could fail to learn this practice. Initial and permanent blindness is an insuperable obstacle. The question is whether it is possible for a person who has a mastery of such a practice still to make mistakes in the discriminations that he is the master of. The answer to this question is, Yes. Although there are some circumstances in which the chance of error is negligible, there are others in which it is substantial, depending for its magnitude upon such things as the fineness of the discriminations to be made (between red and green; or between vermilion and scarlet) and the physical, physiological, and psychological condition of the person making the discrimination (Is he sleepy or tired; in good health; under the influence of alcohol or drugs; disposed to be careful in doing what is asked; etc.?).

16. What is required by the Cartesian philosophy at this point in its development is an errorless practice, a practice that is

without error, not merely in the sense that errors are not made, but in the stronger sense that errors are not possible. At the level of these discriminations in sensory experience, there is posited a way of making discriminations and advancing claims conveying these discriminations, in which, as Descartes said in an understatement the qualification of which was challenged by Burman, there is "scarcely any material for error." [7]

This raises a question to which, in one way or another the whole tradition of idealist philosophy in the nineteenth century offered a negative answer, but which was pressed most effectively in recent philosophy by Wittgenstein. It is the question of how there can be such a practice, whether one can indeed consistently conceive a practice of advancing claims in which the claims themselves and our actions with regard to them are so simple and transparent that it is impossible for anyone engaged in the practice to make a mistake either about the claim itself or action with respect to it. If we take ourselves to be affirming a claim, then we *are* affirming one. There can be no mistake, furthermore, about the significance of the claim on our part. And, finally, the claim itself must be true. Something like this is implied in the illusory conceptions of "self-presenting states," "self-justifying statements," "the given," "basic propositions," and the rest, with which many philosophers have papered over the natural doubts that surround the theses that there are at the basis of knowledge infallibly certain intuitive truths of sense. Wittgenstein's most noted assault on the conception of a practice like this was made in the celebrated "private language argument," but his opposition to the conception is expressed powerfully in other places and in other ways. There is, he enables us to see, a fundamental opposition between that aspect of a practice in which certain ways of proceeding are determined to be right or wrong, proper and improper, and the feature which advocates of first cognitions seek to install in the practice of discriminating the data of sense, namely, that at this level of apprehension whatever *seems* right *is*

[7] "Vix mihi ullam errandi materiam dare possent" (*Meditations* III, A. T. vii, p. 37). Said Burman, referring to Descartes's own views in his conversations with Descartes, "Sed . . . videtur nulla esse errandi materia" (A. T. v, p. 152).

right. Essential to a practice is the difference between is and seems, because essential to a practice is a difference between right and wrong performance, and where there is no difference between is and seems, there likewise is no difference between right and wrong. Of such a curiously conceived practice, Wittgenstein writes, "One would like to say: whatever is going to seem right to me is right. And that only means that here we can't talk about 'right.'" And to the rhetorical question, "Are the rules of the private language *impressions* of rules?" he answers with an opposition reminiscent of one in Kant, "The balance on which the impressions are weighed is not the *impression* of a balance." [8]

In his well-known discussion of games Wittgenstein was engaged in advancing a different and in the end somewhat contrary point. Nevertheless it may be useful to think of the present matter in terms of games, and to consider the supposition of a game which, once mastered, is mastered so well that it is impossible for anyone to play the game wrong, since the game consists of doing what one wants to do at any given moment, and the definitive description of what one wants to do at any moment is just what one does at that moment. Clearly this putative game is one that one cannot misplay, for nothing that one can do can count as a misplay. But a game that cannot be misplayed is also a game that cannot be played; and a game that cannot be played, in which the impossibility is of this essential character, is also surely not a game.

17. While a digression into the subject is not desirable here, it may at least be observed that the point to be made is not that all sensory discriminations are in some degree uncertain. For clearly not all are. The issue is concerning a certain putative necessary property of the kind of discriminations that are expressed in basic propositions and that are advanced as candidates for the role of first cognitions of sense. It is an issue concerning whether, as identified in the philosophy that seeks to employ

[8] *Philosophical Investigations*, Sects. 258–259. Italics in orig. Cf. *Critique of Pure Reason*, Preface to the Second Edition, B xli, n. a, "This further remark may be added. The representation of something *permanent* in existence is not the same as a *permanent representation*" (Kemp Smith, trans.; italics in orig.)

them, these constitute a kind of discrimination which is logically preserved from the possibility, either in individual cases of its execution or in generic character, of being an erroneous, mistaken, misleading, inadequate, faulty performance.

The question of the logical possibility of mistake in such a discrimination is just the thin edge of the wedge in the larger question of the corrigibility and independence of the cognitions which these discriminations represent. We were reminded by Austin that there are more ways of "outraging speech than contradiction," and a variety of " 'infelicities'—that is disabilities which make an utterance unhappy without, however, making it true or false." [9] Similarly there are a variety of ways in which a discrimination may go wrong without being mistaken, without yielding anything sufficiently close to a good performance to be rightly called an error. And there are also a variety of ways in which a discrimination can exhibit its corrigibility other than by going wrong, by yielding somehow an unsuccessful individual performance. Just as mistakes and errors are more conspicuous ways in which the possibility of malfunction exhibits itself, so the possibility of malfunction is itself but one aspect of the general possibility that is represented in corrigibility. Not only individual performances can be improved, but also the practice, i.e., the general mode of response exemplified more or less well in the individual performance. Like every other mode of response, modes of sensory discrimination exhibit their liability to change, improvement, deterioration, and obsolescence in the dependence they exhibit at all points upon individual and social needs and the conditions under which these needs are filled.

All this would perhaps be obvious and little contested if it were not for the desperate need of a faltering theory of knowledge to make it seem otherwise. It is the most inexpugnable common sense, reinforced by expert information from psychologists, anthropologists, historians, and other students of the human scene, that the kind of discriminations that we are capable of making among objects of sense—both homely material objects and more abstract characters and qualities—is highly dependent upon the social context in which individuals develop and live,

[9] *How to Do Things with Words*, pp. 48, 134.

the various activities in which such discriminations are employed and in which individuals are brought up and trained, and the individual and social purposes which these activities serve.[10] The Eskimo needs to be able to make sensory discriminations concerning snow, ice, wind, and weather. The American Indian living by hunting in the Appalachian forests had sensitivity enlarged and sharpened in a different way, as did the nomad of the desert. All three could easily dispense with the kind of expertise in auditory discrimination that equips a Mozart, or the gustatory and olfactory sensitivity of a Brillat-Savarin. And none of the three, however much it would have profited him, could by any effort achieve the capacity to make distant visual discriminations that come relatively effortlessly as natural endowments to the eagle or hawk.[11]

18. Even among lower animals, whose modes of response to their environment are much more in order and much less plastic, when they emerge as separate organisms, than those of man, there is much more plasticity, a far greater range for the determination of behavior by the physical and social environment than the terms, "instinctive behavior" and "unlearned response" tend to suggest. While it is natural for the lion to kill and eat the antelope, rather than feeding on vegetation like a giraffe or rabbit, the development of this natural skill, as in the case of the famous lioness Elsa, depends upon much more than physical maturation. The difficulties encountered by Elsa's human foster parents, in attempting to return her to the wild, were striking evidence of the degree to which growing up a lion depends upon growing up in a certain physical and biological setting, in which trees, rocks, lions, and a variety of other large animals are more prominent features to learn to live with than human beings, tents, and motor cars. And an important part of growing up a lion, in this sense of the phrase, is learning to make kinds of discrimination that are necessary for successful lion behavior. The

[10] Leslie A. White's "The Locus of Mathematical Reality: An Anthropological Footnote" (*Philosophy of Science*, 1947) is an interesting essay on one aspect of this subject.

[11] A cautious introductory treatment of this and related matters is available in the chapter on "Linguistic Relativity and Determinism" in Roger Brown's *Words and Things*.

developing new science of ethology is rich with examples of an even more striking character, ranging over a vast variety of animals. Among these are birds which, in consequence of being deprived of association with their own kind at certain crucial stages of their development, have been rendered incapable of normal sexual discrimination and response to members of the opposite sex, and persistently strive to behave sexually with members of very different species with whom they have been associated at these stages, including men.

But it is of course in man that the effects of the environment, especially the social environment, in affecting sensitivity and molding response are most pronounced. One aspect of culture which in a pre-eminent way both exhibits and helps produce these effects is language. The language we use, the words we speak and write and hear and read, the ways we employ these words to form expressions, and the circumstances in which we learn to employ the expressions, are revelatory of many things, physical, physiological, and psychological, as well as social, in our environment as well as in ourselves. Language is not so much a social practice as a certain aspect of the vast spectrum of social practices. It is what it is by virtue of these practices. That there is a place in the linguistic practice of a certain community for such activities as counting, telling stories, or confessing faith, reveals something not only about the physical equipment members of this community have who participate in the practice, but also about features of the social life which serves as the medium for these practices, features that make these practices possible and that also, in some respects, are made possible by them.

It was this aspect of our discriminations of sensory characters that was intended above when reference was made to the vast battery of equipment and resource that is employed by anyone in making such discriminations. For whatever the discriminations may be, however varied they may be, in one respect they do not vary. That is in having their roots, from which they draw their essential sustenance, in social life and practice. And that means real human life, participated in by one's fellow men and common ancestors, in the real world populated by other living creatures and furnished with a variety of things, a world that is implicated at every step in that life and in the multiform practices that are essential features of it.

19. There is little temptation to deny this in the case of many of the discriminations we make and the terms we use to make and express them. We discriminate different styles of architecture, painting, or writing, and recognize intuitively when we do that we are engaged, whether as fumbling amateur or deft professional, with a very complex institution. One can discriminate Gothic perpendicular, one can use this term to refer rightly to Magdalen Tower and wrongly to the towers of All Souls, because of this institution and because of the physical and social environment in which this institution subsists, including in that environment, and not of least importance, actual buildings. Comparable comments may be readily seen to apply to other discriminations and terms, and though the application is more obvious when what we are discriminating is kinds of human artifacts, material or cultural, in the other cases it is no less real, applying as well to rocks, streams, trees, berries, clouds, heavenly bodies, and to whatever it is that we are able to make discriminations about in the domain of sense.

On the empiricist view the only important resources I require in order to mean red or green, mountain or hill, when I use these terms, think of these things, make discriminations among them, are, first, that I be a conscious being, capable of having, or being in, different states, and, second, that some of these states be relics of previous ones, be the relatively imperishable after-images left in the wake of earlier sensations. To have these after-images, to attend them in a certain way, and for convenience to associate them with certain expressible symbols—this is all that is necessary in order for me to be able to mean red or green, to intend red or green, when I make such discriminations, whether I make the discriminations correctly in each individual case or not. On the side of philosophical psychology the rationalist view was more subtle than this, discriminating sharply, as it did, between the concept or idea and the image, for example, in the case of space, matter, the chiliagon, or God. But in spite of the large-scale differences between these two philosophical schools on this and other points, they were in agreement in viewing the capacity to mean, to discriminate, as a kind of individual personal power. Regardless of disagreement about the way this power is developed in the individual, whether by preserving relics of sensation or developing and refining deposits of intellectual ore placed in the human soul by nature or nature's God, there was agreement that the power to mean, to intend, once developed, was a personal possession that did not require for its exercise any resource or support outside the individual exercising it. To be sure, when one moved to a different level, employing one's "meanings," "ideas," "concepts" to advance claims or make judgments, then one needed the cooperation of the objects of these judgments or claims, one needed correspondence on their part, in order for the judgments or claims to be true. The cat and the mat have the power to falsify my assertion that the cat is on the mat, but once given the development of my own intellectual resources, neither the cat or the mat, nor any other thing or combination of things, can, without operating upon my person directly, impair my power to think or mean what is the content of this claim.

20. The difference between this traditional view and that advanced in these pages is radical. What is being maintained here is, conceding the oversimplification that summary statement requires, that in so elementary an act as meaning red, and hence in discriminating red objects, red patches, or red appearings from orange, green, or blue ones, one is enabled to do what he does because he is acting within and drawing upon the resources of a complex social practice. This of course does not mean that in order for Swift to be able to speak of virtuous horses and discriminate these in thought from their inferior counterparts, there had to be a social practice of discriminating creatures of these sorts. It means that the power to speak and discriminate in this way is rooted logically in practices of speaking and discrimination from which the appropriate new practices can be elicited, in this case by inducing in the practices already in being a minor mutation.

The model in terms of which the empiricists sought to understand meaning was the same as that through which they sought also to understand knowing generally, namely that of seeing or feeling, where these are thought of in a primarily aesthetic way. Meaning red was like seeing red, except that the red seen in the mind's eye in meaning red was of course a pallid surrogate of the real thing. One sees or feels red in this attenuated way and this attenuated sight or feel enables him to mean red because of its genealogical relation to or similarity with actually felt red. To the question, "How is it possible for the sign 'red' or the sign 'apple' to mean red or apple?" the answer offered by the empiricist was, in highly bowdlerized form, "Because people can *see* red or apples." If the principal matter to be explained was how the words "red" and "apple" get associated with red and apple rather than with heliotrope and huckleberry, the answer does help in accounting for how the individual signs in question come to be signs for these particular things rather than others. But in moving to answer this question it leaves entirely unanswered the question of how these words come to be signs at all. It takes for granted that the machinery for meaning or signifying is all present and accounted for, leaving only the question of how, in its fine adjustments, it gets to be disposed in one way rather than another. But how did the machinery get there in the first place? How did it arise; how does it develop and change, and in response to what conditions? How, as Kant would ask if he were writing today, is signification possible?

21. On the view being advanced here, a much more appropriate model for understanding the act of meaning red by "red," of discriminating red as a color from green as another color, is participation in a complex social event. Meaning red is more like marching in a parade, or engaging in a transaction on the New York Stock Exchange, than it is like having a sensation; more like casting a vote for President, dancing the Virginia Reel, or participating in the Sun Dance of the Western American Indians. Of course in one prominent respect using "red" to mean red is not like any one of these things, since in the case of meaning there is no question of one's having to secure permission to participate in this activity, no questions of rules restricting the kinds or numbers of people who may participate. In this respect one's performance in meaning red, considered instantially or dis-

positionally, is more like joining a fiesta, celebrating Thanksgiving Day, or participating in Sunday morning worship. But for the purpose at hand this difference between parading, say, and meaning is less significant than the similarity of the two as social acts which require for one's success in accomplishing them the participation of other human beings and the cooperation of much stage setting in the world of things. In this respect both are markedly different from having a sensation, recalling a sensation, or rehearsing a schema of sensations in imagination, as these features of our mental life are conceived in the philosophical psychology that accompanies the empiricist theory of knowledge. This is a primary reason why a putative species of knowledge got by sensation has been chosen by these philosophers to serve as the sure foundations of our knowledge. Recalling a sensation or schema of them into the forum of consciousness appeared to be clearly within the power of an individual in the way that marching in a parade is not. I cannot by myself march in a parade. By myself I cannot *be* a parade. It is not altogether within my power to join a parade; there must be a parade to join or at least other people so disposed that when we join together in a certain way we form a parade.[12]

Attention to this aspect of the matter may serve to correct some of the aberrations to which one may be led by an uncritical reliance upon the principle that intentional acts like "intending," "thinking about," and so on are capable of creating their own objects. That this is so, that there need be no group of assassins posted with rifles on the grassy knoll in Dallas in order for James Garrison to be able to think about it, and that hence there can be no simple ontological proof of a conspiracy to kill John Kennedy, should not blind us to the further fact that there are conditions, and that philosophers have a need to understand the conditions, under which the creation of such intentional objects is possible.

In learning to use words to signify things and in learning to discriminate kinds of things signified, even so restricted things

---

12 Cf. Wittgenstein, *Philosophical Investigations*, Part I, Sect. 202, "To obey a rule, to make a report, to give an order, to play a game of chess, are *customs* (uses, institutions)" (italics in orig.).

as color qualities and sensations, we are being initiated into a social practice that involves men and things of various kinds, though not necessarily things of exactly the kind we learn to discriminate. In learning to discriminate a particular shade of blue, and in learning to think of that shade, it is not necessary, as Hume saw, that that shade be actualized in one's visual field, or for that matter anywhere, though certainly that actualization helps. But in learning to discriminate and think of that shade, I am learning to participate in a practice; and just as that participation depends upon the practice, so the practice depends itself upon both men and things. In meaning red by "red" I participate in a "dance" of a certain cultural sort, and as in the case of a more ordinary dance, my movements alone do not constitute a dance. There has to be a whole dance for my part to succeed, a whole dance for me to succeed in meaning red. It is the whole dance that gives the word its meaning. And of this particular dance, it should be noted that just as it is not a momentary event, but one that extends through time, so the dependence it exhibits upon social life is not merely upon life at the moment that any particular person makes particular use of this resource in meaning red or discriminating that color. The dependence is in a very real and extended way upon the social life of preceding generations who must have lived and acted in certain ways, in certain surroundings, in order for this practice to be what it is. Though it is in a less obvious way, when we discriminate colors and use words to signify colors, as well as when we declare a man guilty or innocent in a criminal trial, consecrate a bishop, or install a President in office, we are able to do what we do because we are the cultural beneficiaries, the residual legatees of many generations before us, marching in a parade in which these make up an indefinitely long vanguard, "treading where the saints [and sinners as well] have trod." The accumulation of capital resource, and its exploitation is a feature of successful activity in all domains of social life, domestic, scientific, religious, political, military, and aesthetic as well as economic.

22. As an answer to the question "How is signification possible?" the pronouncement that it is by participation in the

human dance, by means of the multiform activities that are features of that dance, takes one a very little way. But at least it takes him in the right direction. The story of signification, from the philosophical point of view, is a story as wide as human life and as complex as the social practices in which that life is lived and which are themselves both made possible by and expressed in human language. It is a story the main plot of which we can begin to discern, but the details of which largely remain to be determined. A hint of how, in certain simple, concrete situations the story will develop is given in Wittgenstein's discussion of primitive language games, such as that of the builder, in the early sections of the *Philosophical Investigations*. And some of the wide sweep of the story, with some of the emphasis that has been given here to the material conditions of life, was indicated over a century ago in the study of *The German Ideology* by Marx and Engels. These and other hints and previews which have appeared in the literature of philosophy have so far been singularly unsuccessful in weakening the hold that has been maintained widely by what may be called, with some unfairness, the Augustinian myth in the philosophy of language. This myth, concerning the nature of language, particularly concerning the function performed by language in human mental life, is comparable to the Hobbesian myth of the state. Both myths regard fundamental institutions, the functioning of which is constitutive of the character of those who live in them in their character as intellectual or political agents, as appurtenances of ready-made minds or individuals capable, in the one case, of independently signifying, and needing only sounds or marks to signify conveniently with, or, in the other case, capable of pursuing self-preservation and finding civil government an effective means to that end. In the linguistic, intellectual case it is as if the relation between the intellectual activities of man and the practices in which human life is largely conducted were so external that one could easily conceive of the former developing independently of the latter. So that one might have, on the one hand, an array of intellectual powers, activities, and procedures, existing independently of the ways in which objects are discriminated, produced, and employed in the conduct of life, and also of the ways in which men live and act together while engaging in these and manifold other activities. And on the other hand one might have, similarly independently, an already discriminated world of objects, men, and other living creatures with which these intellectual powers, activities, and procedures can be engaged. And then one has language, which serves as a convenient bridge for installing a connection between these two vast domains, a function it performs primarily through the agency of ostensive definition.[13]

On the contrary, the practice of signifying and discriminating itself, whether external objects or internal feelings, no less than the practice of giving warnings, issuing commands, or asking questions, arises out of the needs, activities, circumstances of social life. They can be understood only against the background of that life. Marx and Engels wrote:

> The production of ideas, of conceptions, of consciousness is at first directly interwoven with material activity and the material intercourse of men, the language of real life. Conceiving, thinking, the mental intercourse of men appear at this stage as the direct efflux of their material behavior. The same applies to mental production as expressed in the language of the politics, laws, morality, religion, metaphysics of a people.[14]

13 F. Waismann reports the following remark of Wittgenstein, July 1, 1932 (*Wittgenstein und der Wiener Kreis*): "Unklar im Traktat war mir die logiche Analyse und die hinweisende Erklärung. Ich dachte damals dass es eine 'Verbindung der Sprache mit der Wircklichkeit' gibt."

S. Toulmin translated "die hinweisende Erklärung" into "the clarification it [logical analysis] suggests" ("Ludwig Wittgenstein," *Encounter*, Vol. XXXII, No. 1, January, 1969, p. 62).

M. Lipton (*Encounter*, Vol. XXXII, No. 5, p. 97, May, 1969), took issue with Toulmin's translation, urging that the first sentence of Wittgenstein's comment should be rendered: "In the *Tractatus,* logical analysis and *ostensive definition* were not clear to me" (italics mine).

Toulmin replied that this suggestion introduces into the passage in question "epistemological implications foreign (in my opinion) to Wittgenstein's intention" (*Encounter*, Vol. XXXIII, No. 2, August, 1969, p. 97).

A later translation of the sentence in A. Janik and S. Toulmin, *Wittgenstein's Vienna* (1973), p. 222 is: "In the *Tractatus,* I was unclear about 'logical analysis' and ostensive demonstration."

14 K. Marx and F. Engels, *The German Ideology* (Parts I, III, R. Pascal, ed.), pp. 13–14.

The primary scope of the remarks of Wittgenstein that bear on the matter is much more restricted. Unlike Marx and Engels, in the development of his thought he was motivated to no great extent by reaction to the injustices of capitalist economy or the errors of idealist metaphysics. And his overriding purpose with respect to the human institution with which his thought was most concerned, namely language, was to understand the institution, not to change it. But in spite of this diversity, the implication of many of his comments, insofar as they bear upon the character of language as a social institution, reflecting the character and in part also helping to determine the character of intellectual and social life, is remarkably in agreement. "When one says," he wrote, " 'He gave a name to his sensation,' one forgets that a great deal of stage-setting in the language is presupposed if the mere act of naming is to make sense." Reading this remark one is apt to think that in it Wittgenstein wanted to remind the reader principally, or even solely, of the wider relations of a name in the purely linguistic structure of which it is a feature. And perhaps, at this point he did. But in appreciating the significance of the remark in Wittgenstein's later philosophy one must construe it in the light of the repeated observation, and other similar ones, to the effect that "to imagine a language means to imagine a form of life." [15]

[15] *Philosophical Investigations*, Pt. I, Sects. 257, 19.

CHAPTER 8

Construction and
Revision

1. Attention now needs to be given to the second kind of difficulty confronting justification theory, namely that of construction. Two considerations alluded to earlier help to determine how the discussion of these difficulties may and should proceed. The first is that, since many of these difficulties are and have long been prominent upon the philosophical landscape, no further time need be spent in establishing their existence, this having already been sufficiently done, chiefly by proponents of the theory engaged in outlining the steps to be followed in construction. The second consideration is that there is already revealed in the preceding discussion of the foundation difficulties an aspect of the justification program which shows it to be not so much a program beset by difficulties as one that is radically misconceived. The misconception consists in thinking of the acquisition of knowledge at both the foundation and higher levels as a matter of the accretion of items, bound together more or less tightly by relations of necessity or probability. It consists of thinking of the development of knowledge essentially as a matter of screening, adding elements to or subtracting them from this grand mosaic, and it consists of thinking of this process of adding or subtracting as one which, though it may radically affect the character of the whole, nevertheless does not similarly affect the character of the individual items. Whenever it is judged that an item, say X, may be included in the larger structure, on the grounds that already included items Y and Z call for or warrant it, since it is the logical attraction of Y and Z which leads X to

be included in the whole, *X*, as included, cannot subsequently be used as grounds for either questioning the position of *Y* and *Z* in the whole or for altering them in such a way as to affect fundamentally their nature and significance.

2. In the preceding chapter the criticism of this view of knowledge, of what knowledge must be in order to be capable of surviving philosophical inspection, centered on the incorrigibility required of certain features of this knowledge. Although the emphasis in that criticism was upon the failure of the supposed first cognitions to maintain the incorrigibility required of them, it was observed that the basic reasons for denying incorrigibility at this alleged foundation level hold equally well, are equally decisive against the higher levels discriminated in this view. It was argued that although there are certain resources in justification theory—particularly those of probability judgment—for providing some corrigibility in our knowledge, these resources are insufficient to provide the kind required. A view that affords us an adequate understanding of what are some of the conditions necessary for our performance when we make sensory discriminations and report them, and generally when we state, judge, infer, predict, suppose, and so on—such a view commits us to recognize that whatever items of knowledge we attain in these performances are susceptible to revision in a thoroughgoing way that cannot be accommodated to the requirements of justification theory. It is to the elaboration of some of the ways in which this susceptibility revision is realized in the development of knowledge, to some forms of what are called here "revision phenomena," that the present chapter is primarily addressed.

3. The reason for proceeding in this way is that the principal matter that needs to be made clear here is not that there is incompatibility between justification theory and thoroughgoing corrigibility, but rather that such corrigibility cannot be eliminated from our knowledge in the way that the theory proposes. For this purpose no simple argument will suffice. One cannot argue that the matter can be settled by attending in any simple, linguistic way to the "meaning" or "definition" of knowledge and other related terms. For a proper response from the advocates of the theory would then be that the meaning of the terms

in question, the definition in any significant sense in which these are relevant, is to be found in the theory itself. This tells us what knowledge is; this determines the kind of corrigibility that it will tolerate. The adequacy of the definition is the adequacy of the theory.

The case for the connection between corrigibility and knowledge, lies in knowledge itself. It lies in the relative responsiveness to this ongoing institution of a theory of knowledge which embraces corrigibility, in comparison with one which extrudes it. It lies in the relative success achieved by each of these kinds of theory in probing, discerning, and revealing the important features of the various species or forms of this institution. A variety of features to which justification theory fails to be responsive have already been dealt with, including, in the preceding chapter, our performances as human beings when we are engaged in discriminating perceptual objects and what, with some perhaps questionable generosity, might be called objects of sense. The case is continued in the present chapter by taking an extended view of the matter and calling attention, in the revision phenomena, to the profusion with which the susceptibility to revision abounds throughout our actual knowledge; not in something that might be called "knowledge" in some philosophical closet or some hardly conceivable dream-world, but in knowledge as we have it and might hope for it to become. The case, in so far as it can be made in this limited space, is that so deeply rooted and so pervasive is this feature of knowledge that the supposition that it can be eliminated in the manner in which justification theory requires is, as was observed earlier, one which can hardly be thought at all, let alone thought plausible.

4. From the end of the seventeenth century to the present, the most important exemplifications of justification theory have been the empiricist ones. And the history of these has been repeatedly one of confident beginnings followed by extended travail over certain enduring, insoluble "problems," construction difficulties encountered in trying to effect the reconstruction of human knowledge according to empiricist principles. The problem of induction, to which extended attention was given earlier, is, with

the possible exception of the "problem of the external world," the most significant of these, the two being closely related, not only in their logical genesis, but also in the fact that under close empiricist treatment the problem about external objects tends to dissolve into a phase of the inductive problem. In the philosophy of science, which in recent years has been dominated by empiricist preconceptions, all the essential logical features of the problem about external objects are duplicated in the problem about the significance and grounds of assertions of the existence of abstract or theoretic entities. Also closely allied with the problem of induction, as was discussed earlier, is a nest of problems about the significance of probability statements, allegations of causal efficacy and necessary connection, which are now treated in the idiom of lawlike statements and subjunctive conditionals. The logical features of these problems are again duplicated in the field of value theory, where the reductionist principles of the philosophy generate problems about construing judgments about right or wrong, good or bad, and where problems about the justification of value statements and moral claims exhibit a "naturalistic" gap that is the counterpart of the "inductive" gap in other areas. So great an effect of philosophical perplexity must have a cause. While the confidence of proponents of the empiricist philosophy naturally hindered them in their efforts to identify the basic causes of these problems, it just as naturally aided in their application of the fundamentals of the philosophy to various domains of human knowledge and in making plain the vast array of problems to which the application leads. Naturally too, since a strong motive for adherence to the philosophy was a deep trust that sensory experience serves as a ready source of absolutely sure, incorrigibile first cognitions, the emphasis in the development of the philosophy was on the procedures for constructing on these foundations, and the difficulties encountered in the development were principally construction difficulties. To those firmly convinced of the basic correctness of this philosophy the difficulties, however numerous and ready to proliferate, served as stimuli to efforts to produce corrected, more sophisticated strains of it that would prove to be progressively immune to the failings that had so far appeared. To those less committed, the resistance of the difficulties to solution, the ease with which they proliferated, and the common pattern which they for the most part exhibited, seemed rather to signify the need for a fundamental reassessment of the adequacy of the philosophical model or metaphor exemplified in this philosophy.

5. A very basic question posed by the construction difficulties generated in this philosophy is that of how to conceive of the development of knowledge and the logical relations between items of knowledge which that development entails. In appraising the acceptability of a truth claim, we commonly, if our appraisal is remotely reasonable, employ other truth claims that in one way or other have already achieved some kind of acceptance or entrenchment in our repertory of intellectual practice. And clearly the depth of the acceptance or entrenchment of claims is characteristically greater in some domains of this practice than in others, though of course there are wide variations of depth within domains. An adequate theory of knowledge needs to take account of these facts of intellectual life, but in a way different from the simple, hierarchical view of the matter that is taken in Cartesian theory. An adequate theory will make plain that the exploration of the logical relations of dependent truth claims does not require one to hold that there is no domain of claims that is more stable or more essential to the stability of other claims than any other. But it will recognize also that the stability of the keystone in the stone arch, as well as its contribution to the stability of the arch, is different from that of a foundation stone. And it will consequently make plain also that the exploration of the logical dependencies that are essential to the stability of truth claims no more leads to a problem about first cognitions than, as we now understand, the exploration of genealogical dependencies necessarily leads to a problem about the first man or the first conscious being. Characteristically, when we attain the stage of understanding at which conundrums like this are resolved, we attain likewise an understanding of what it was in our previous preconceptions that led to the conundrum, of what was wrong in the question asked. The question of which was first, the chicken or the egg, does not appear in the story of the evolution of the vertebrates; and it is not just because no one thinks to ask it.

6. The main contrasting model to that of building and building stones in the theory of knowledge has been that of an organism, literally as in the case of an animal or plant, or metaphorically, as in the case of some other complex of highly integrated and interdependent parts, like a strategic military plan, an architectural plan, an essay or work of art. There is a ready abundance of exemplifications of such a model of which we have a high degree of understanding and through our conceptual mastery of which we are able to render intelligibile to ourselves the kind of stability and growth that is realized in systematically interrelated congeries of knowledge claims. But what is in question here is not the general adequacy of these models. It is the adequacy of the explication given in the Cartesian one of the development of knowledge, of the employment of items that have already a place of acceptance in appraising, qualifying, or disqualifying other items proposed for a similar place. And the charge made against this model is that the large-scale dependencies exposed in the discussion of the corrigibility of first cognitions of sense count decisively against the model both at the foundation stage in the application of the theory and at every stage of construction.

The view of the dependency taken in this model is that of a logical scaffold, higher levels resting on lower ones and deriving from them whatever resistance they may exert against the pull of philosophically aroused doubt or disbelief. This dictates a view of the relation of logical dependency which is altogether asymmetrical, the consequences of which are elaborated in the argument for basic propositions. The independence of these basic propositions with respect to nonbasic ones in the structure of knowledge is just an extreme case—because basic propositions constitute the lowest level of the structure—of the independence that holds everywhere between lower and higher levels. In order to perform the service assigned to them in this theory of knowledge, these foundation items must be independent of items at every other level. They are to serve as ultimate premises from which other items at those levels can be validated by being derived from them by some kind of inference, necessary or probable. This service they cannot perform unless in the derivation procedure they can be counted upon to remain intact. They

must remain intact in two most important respects: with respect
to significance, which might with some stretching of terminology
be referred to as "semantic integrity," and with respect to their
cognitive status, which might be called "epistemic integrity." By
whatever procedure a secondary claim C_n is validated starting
from a set of primary claims C_1, the procedure must leave C_1 unaltered in both these respects. For the status of C_n as a truth
claim depends upon C_1; if the umbilical cord is cut it will die.
Its status depends upon it being possible to retrace the steps to
C_1, to justify C_n by beginning again and repeating the derivation
in which justification is taken to consist. If, in the procedure of
getting from C_1 to C_n, the secure status of C_1 could be altered,
or if, even more important, the claims that make up C_1 were sup-
planted by different claims, yielding a different set, C_{1a}, then this
whole scheme of justification would be impossible.

7. For basically the same reasons, this double inviolability in
the relation between C_1 and C_n is duplicated in the relation between C_n and any other claim C_k, or set of claims, which may
occur in the interval between C_1 and C_n and which may be disclosed in the multistep justification regress to C_1 from C_n. It is
perhaps worth mentioning that in the view under consideration
it is not necessary to maintain that this inviolability holds between any claim, C_x, and any other claim, say C_y, which *in
some way* supports it. It is not necessary to exclude the possibility
of there being sets of claims like this, and more complex sets,
which in some way do mutually support each other. Claims can
support each other and be mutually dependent, but the kind of
support relation exemplified in such cases, which one can trace
from one to another, and back again, is not the kind that fits the
logical requirements of the justification argument. It does not
necessarily lead to an ultimate term in the regress of "What
justifies?" questions. If C_a and C_b, say, have the kind of mutual
dependency supposed, the regress must somehow break through
this complex in order to terminate in C_1. This it may do by
directing the justification question to the whole complex that is
C_a and C_b in this relationship, inquiring for the ground upon
which the whole depends in a nonmutual way. What justification
theory requires is that between C_n, and some base claim or set of

base claims, which must of course be inviolable with respect to each other, there is a finite series of steps, each marked by a claim or set of claims which is inviolable with respect to any claims or sets of claims superior to it in the justification scaffold.

This relational incorrigibility which must hold universally between antecedent and consequent steps in the construction of the scaffold from C_1 to C_n is the analogue of absolute incorrigibility imputed to base items by the theory. This is the explanation and ground for the proposition already advanced that the kind of criticism directed in Chapter 7 at the foundation level of the justification operation can serve as a paradigm for the criticism of the operation at the construction levels. For the criticism is essentially a case against incorrigibility. If the case against incorrigibility holds, it holds at whatever level, and in whatever respect, incorrigibility is called for by the theory. The same general considerations that count against there being such incorrigible first cognitions—namely that our actions of discriminating, signifying, referring, predicating, etc., are ones that we can perform only in a context of practice and in the material, psychological, and social circumstances necessary for the existence of such a practice—these same considerations count equally strongly against the supposition that the development and expansion of knowledge can be viewed in such a way that new, derived items of knowledge are related to precedent ones solely by relations of dependency, so that the later, logically posterior items cannot by their emergence and derivation affect either the semantic or the epistemic integrity of their cognitive and logical ancestors.

8. As so far developed, the case against incorrigibility rests primarily upon considerations drawn from the philosophy of perception, the philosophy of mind, and the philosophy of language. The central principle of the case is that the more we understand what we are doing when we discriminate sensations, refer to them, and make predications concerning their characters and relations, the more we are led to reject incorrigibility in our achievements in these kinds of cognitive activities which are the focus of attention at the foundation level of empiricist versions of justification theory.

When the scope of the case is expanded to include the activities embraced at the higher levels of this theory, the catalogue of pertinent activities is enlarged enormously. It now includes perceiving—i.e., determining directly by means of the senses the existence and character of material things, living creatures, and other persons—inferring, deducing, predicting, calculating, making suppositions about hypothetical entities and states of affairs, and so on.

The range of consideration which in one way or another is relevant to the question of corrigibility is thus very wide indeed. And of course these considerations are by no means all on one side of the question. For example, a view which emphasizes the social roots and character of our cognitive activities—even so *prima facie* private ones as discerning our own "mental states"— is open to the natural and proper challenge about objectivity, about whether such a view does not commit one in the bitter end to some kind of social relativism, to the view that, put simply and somewhat crudely, cats and dogs are "here" because we have been conditioned to make discriminations in these terms, and further that, since this could be otherwise, for a different society, making different discriminations, there might be no such creatures.

What can be said in response to such a challenge within the limitations of this book is included in the outlines of a positive theory of knowledge presented in the final two chapters and epilogue. With respect to another challenge the response is necessarily even more constricted. This concerns the effect upon our understanding of the autonomy of reasoning and inference when the doctrine of thoroughgoing corrigibility is applied to these operations in connection with the construction difficulties. Corrigibility, mutual dependence, between premises and conclusions may seem bad enough. When the doctrine is further applied to the logical relations between these items, it may seem positively offensive, seeming to flout a most basic requirement of any theory of good or valid reasoning, namely, that the question of such goodness or validity be altogether decidable independently of a determination of the goodness, plausibility, or truth of the premises from which we start or the conclusions at which we arrive. Eventually is there not a fundamental circularity implied in any theory of reasoning in which the goodness of the reasoning is itself dependent upon the character of its conclusions, so that one cannot determine the goodness of the reasoning once and for all and then presume it without reservations in proceeding confidently to the conclusions?

9. As remarked earlier, the case for corrigibility in knowledge lies in knowledge itself. It lies in the adequacy of a theory of knowledge embracing thoroughgoing corrigibility to do what we have a right to expect it to do in relation to its subject matter, namely, to illuminate and render it more understandable, and provide a sound basis for the criticism and improvement of our activities in it or in relation to it. To show the relative adequacy of a theory of knowledge is to show its relative superiority in doing these things, and that means in the case of the particular theory outlined here, showing in detail that the above and other important challenges can be successfully met. In the case of the challenge about the goodness of reasoning, this means developing, as a correlate to a general theory of knowledge, a theory of inference which will reflect carefully not only the varieties of inferences and the variety of ways in which they are appraised, but also how the distinct contributions and limitations of purely formal techniques of appraisal can be understood without either depreciating these techniques or exalting them in a vision of some Leibnizian grand calculus. In this process a few venerated idols will have to be shattered and some prevailing simple categories transcended, among them those defining the insensitive and increasingly unserviceable distinction between necessary and contingent truth.

The multiplicity of issues and range of consideration relevant to this one topic are fair indications of the dimensions which will be attained by a broad and penetrating philosophical examination of all the important topics and issues relevant to the general topic of corrigibility as it bears upon the construction process in justification theory. So extensive an examination far exceeds the limitations of a study of this kind, which, on a topic like that of reasoning and inference, must be restricted to the suggestion of some key questions which the examination must consider and the general character of the answers which it can be expected to provide. One very important thing which can be managed, and which is offered in the present chapter, is a broad purview of the extent of the phenomena of corrigibility in actual knowledge, of the wide variety and depth of the ways in which corrigibility is realized in knowledge as we now have it, as it has expanded and developed and as it continues to expand and develop. A grasp of this is of first importance for understanding and appraising the radical alteration which the proposed excision or suppression of this feature would effect in knowledge as an actual social product and individual achievement, and as a living institution.

10. When we look at actual knowledge, or what at any particular time in history has been taken to be knowledge, from this point of view, whether that be in science, in common sense, or in other domains, one of its most striking features is its constant liability to change, not simply by accretion, but in a variety of subtle yet fundamental ways. The ways in which we deal with objects, things, living creatures, persons, both intellectually and practically, are not only constantly liable to change; they do change constantly. These changes take place at different points in the corpus of knowledge from time to time, and with great variations in rapidity. In one manner or another our ways of dealing with ourselves and other entities with which the world is populated, and with various features of ourselves and the world, become inapt and need to be revised. A most important section of our equipment in this matter is of course our language, and striking examples of this liability to inaptness are presented in the phenomena of the open texture of concepts in our language as well as in the topics of referring expressions, presupposition, indirect existential import, and ontological commitments of various sorts. What happens in these cases to our equipment and to our actions employing this equipment in making judgments, statements, predictions, and so on concerning putative objects of knowledge is much more interesting than the common event of having these objects falsify the claims we advance in our utterances, like nature sending showers on a day when clear skies have been predicted. The range of the phenomena in ques-

tion is considerably wider than that of the relations of our language to "objects"; and the adequate understanding of the phenomena requires eventually a more penetrating exploration than is possible within the limitations of this terminology. But restricting ourselves for present purposes to this very prominent aspect of the matter, we may say that in our commerce with nature and its objects, nature constantly affects us and our ways of dealing with it, not simply by verifying or falsifying what we say, but by indicating to us in a variety of subtle ways that what needs improvement on our part is our ability *to say*, to formulate claims, assertions, hypotheses that may be reasonably taken to be true or false. Our language gets out of joint with nature, but not in the more explicit way that by means of it we make false assertions. Prior to this there is a failure on the part of our language to be sufficiently well articulated with its objects, to be sufficiently apt with respect to them, to admit of any significant degree of truth or falsity in what we say. "True" and "false" are terms that apply well only to the products of very apt, extremely well-articulated linguistic dealings with reality. It is to such products, the results of highly skilled linguistic, intellectual work, for which the term "proposition" has traditionally been reserved.

11. The key point of relevance of the phenomena in question to the topic at hand is that they illustrate a variety of respects in which our ways of proceeding in making discriminations, formulating and considering claims, thinking about objects, and so on, are all dependent for their success upon objects, things, states in the world in which we engage in these activities. It is of this dependency that we are being reminded when in one or another of the respects signified by these phenomena our ways of proceeding show their disposition to get out of joint with the objects, and so on, upon which we depend while engaging in them. It is a consequence of this large-scale dependency that, to our good fortune, objects, and so forth, in our world have a vast variety of ways of making themselves known to us, of guiding and correcting us in our various pursuits; they are not restricted to the more obvious ways of verifying or falsifying, confirming or disconfirming, the hypotheses we construct concerning them. The recognition of this dependency is thus an occasion, not for con-

dolence, but for celebration, even though it is a direct consequence of this dependency that our thoughts, our activities, our pursuit of knowledge have been constantly, and presently remain, liable to perturbation and alteration through the effect of often as yet undisclosed aspects of objects, things, states, and hence liable to revision as these make their characters more plain to us.

12. The logical, linguistic phenomena embraced under this description are prominent and pervasive. The kind of corrigibility that they represent in our speech about objects, and hence in our knowledge of them, is present at all levels of inquiry, and represents a *prima facie* challenge to any philosophy that views the structure of knowledge in such a way that later discoveries can only add to, never lead to a modification of, the premises or bases from which they were logically developed. But a *prima facie* challenge is not a defeat. And what is the reaction of modern advocates of Cartesian philosophy to such important facts of the cognitive life as these?

By far the most typical, indeed the standard response is to admit the facts but to dispute their philosophical significance. Granted that all these "revision phenomena," indicating manifold ways in which later, consequent developments in knowledge lead to a recasting and reunderstanding of earlier, prior achievements, are facts, what are they facts *of?* Are they facts of life or facts of knowledge? And if facts of knowledge, of knowledge as it has been and normally is achieved, often by circuitous routes and faltering, stumbling steps? Or is it knowledge less as it is and more as it ought to be, knowledge of a thoroughly philosophically accredited kind?

Again concentrating upon the linguistic aspects of these phenomena, the general response has been to view the kind of revisions which the phenomena call for, not as essential aspects of the logical development of knowledge, but as signs of avoidable defects, in principle avoidable defects in knowledge as it has developed, in contrast with how it may develop. To be sure, knowledge as we have it, and have had it, and with it science and cognitive language, has been rich in these phenomena. But as these are signs of avoidable defects, measures need be taken to avoid them. If the language we inherit from our scientific and other ancestors is constantly liable to this defeasibility by nature, then it needs to be transformed or replaced so as to avoid this hazard; and the bold pronouncement of the distinction between "analytic" and "synthetic" represents the wishful anticipation of this longed-for achievement. A proper language would be an indefeasible language, one that would be apt for all possible worlds, hence proof against any untoward developments which would render it inapt for this one. We need not put up with a language that begins to creak and falter just because in the process of setting up a republic the French deprive the phrase "the present King of France" of its denotation, or just because John has failed to produce the male offspring required for the successful employment of accepted practices of predication with the subject phrase "all John's sons."

When introducing the topic of the open texture of concepts into philosophical discussion a quarter of a century ago, Friedrich Waismann judged that the phenomena signified by this expression represented a considerable stumbling block in the empiricist program that had been vigorously put into effect in philosophy and various of the sciences in the preceding two decades. A similar judgment is possible concerning similar phenomena investigated in connection with presupposition and referring expressions. A most important aspect of the theory of descriptions advanced by Russell in the early part of the century was the efficacy promised by the techniques of the theory for freeing logic and language from an apparent troublesome dependency for their smooth functioning upon certain apparently *de facto* features of the subject matter to which they applied, and the consequent liability to revision which this dependency entails. Other writers, for example Frege and, more recently Peter Strawson, endeavored to deal with these latter two topics along lines less in conformity with orthodox empiricist and Cartesian principles.

13. The assumption that the justification program can be carried out entails that somehow the revision phenomena can be eliminated. Implicit in the supposition that this can be done is a presupposition about the independence of thought, language,

claims, propositions, on the one side, and objects, things, states, and so on, on the other. Completion of the critical examination of justification theory will eventually require that some direct attention be given to this presupposition, to the deep preconceptions in the philosophy of thought and mind represented in it. This final step in the examination will not be made here, but is instead reserved for Chapter 9, which begins to draw the final contrast between justification theory, as an approach in the philosophy of knowledge, and an alternative, more realistic theory. In the present chapter attention will be restricted to the revision phenomena and the endeavor made in the justification program to eliminate such phenomena. This endeavor has been made through a variety of techniques of logical and linguistic construction, and a variety of theories of reference, of descriptions, and of naming, all more or less directed to this end.

Two questions deserve consideration concerning the collective program itself, in contrast with questions about its deep philosophical roots. The first is a question of achievement and practicability: How successful has the program been, and how successful does it promise to be? The second is a question of desirability: How desirable is that success? It will be seen immediately that under consideration these questions tend to merge. Certain difficulties disclosed in carrying out the program help to define certain conditions necessary to its success. These conditions may be thought to bear primarily on either one of these two questions, and to dictate a negative answer to either, depending upon how far one is prepared to consider the question of possibly satisfying the conditions. To one who is prepared to entertain the possibility of satisfying them, the conclusion that the program is infeasible because they may not be satisfied, may be expressed naturally as a conclusion that the execution of the program is undesirable. To one who refuses to entertain the possibility of the conditions being satisfied, the conclusion indicated by the disclosure that they are nevertheless necessary, may be more simply that the execution which requires them is then not possible.

14. The very pervasiveness of the revision phenomena in our intellectual and practical life, in our dealings with nature and

with ourselves and our fellowmen (e.g., in law and morals), suggests that the problems presented by these phenomena for the Cartesian way of thinking are not ordinary technical ones to the treatment of which terms like "success" or "failure" easily attach. What, for example, are we asking when we put the question whether it is possible to develop a view of knowledge from which these phenomena have been eliminated? What knowledge; what view; and for what purposes? Do we mean a view of knowledge of *some* sort, of *some* domain, however limited? The more restricted the domain, the less implausible, at first view, are the attempts at such a program. This is the story of the first cognitions of sense. They represent a formidable redoubt to which under attack the exponents of incorrigibility tend to retreat. Their dislodgment from it is comparable in difficulty with its importance. Unquestionably the less that is claimed as capable of validation through the Cartesian program, the more plausible the claims appear to be. Though in the end the answer is the same, whether the scope of the question be knowledge of present immediate sensations or of distant quasars, the significance of the claims of success and the *prima facie* plausibility of these claims are very different. To the extent that the domain of knowledge in which the program is thought to be put into effect extends beyond the putative level of first cognitions of sense, to the extent that it includes the world of material objects, living things, persons and other social objects, the breadth of the domain affects adversely whatever *prima facie* plausibility there may be in the claim that the program can succeed. Rather, the situation *prima facie* appears to be that a view of knowledge which adhered to a program for the elimination of the phenomena would at the very best be very restricted in scope and quite inapplicable to most of the domains of putative knowledge with which we began and in connection with which it was thought philosophical rationalization, reconstruction, and advancement could be furthered by means of the program.

15. That species of corrigibility and hence of revision phenomena that is represented by the broad term "open texture" well illustrates, in one segment of language and thought, the significance of the point about the pervasiveness of such phe-

nomena. In the next chapter some further consideration will be given to some views advanced by Waismann when he initiated the discussion of open texture in recent philosophy. As regards pervasiveness, Waismann's view was that open texture is a fundamental, indeed essential feature, of most of what he called "empirical concepts," and indeed integral in this way to all our concepts of material objects. In other words, though it may not be presumed that these are words that Waismann himself would have found acceptable, open texture and the liabilities to correction and revision that it represents are essential features of what knowledge we have of material objects. This, if true, represents an obstacle of a staggeringly formidable character to the success of any project of producing anything like a rectified, reconstructed version of knowledge, as we have it, purged of the revision phenomena and the conceptual open texture which makes this kind of phenomenon an ever-present logical possibility. The grounds seem strong for concluding that anything resembling a corpus of human knowledge surviving so drastic a purge would be so altered that it could not, with the remotest plausibility, be thought of as a philosophically improved version of knowledge as we have it, or as any kind of version of that knowledge, improved or not. It appears, for example, that what would be left as a residue of our present knowledge of material objects would not and could not be recognized as such by us. Material objects would have disappeared from our ken, to be replaced perhaps by entities or states as remote from our common-sense knowledge as the esoteric subatomic particles and states of present nuclear physics or the creations of some incredibly advanced science fiction, in a program which in the process of doing away with our world would have done the same with ourselves. In the remoteness of its possibility and difficulty in conception, success in this project is comparable to success in another of the grand projects of modern philosophy, particularly scientific philosophy, namely, that of establishing as a universal pattern of acceptable explanation that particular pattern that for a time seemed universally applicable to physical causal processes. Of this project it seems that one can say, at the very least, as Isaiah Berlin said of determinism generally in its application to human and specifically historical matters, that, though one may not wish to claim it to be "necessarily false . . . we neither speak nor think as if it could be true, and . . . it is difficult, and perhaps impossible, to conceive what our picture of the world would be if we seriously believed it." [1]

16. It was observed above that the question of the desirability of success in the project of eliminating the revision phenomena from the corpus of knowledge is closely related to the question of the possibility of success in the project, there being a close connection between the extent of the material which one is prepared to acquiesce in expelling from the corpus, and the prospects of carrying out the project. What is being put into effect in such a project, and needs to be given very explicit notice, is a severe limitation upon questions of rationality in the appraisal of items of putative knowledge, reasonable belief, and so on, and by this also a severe limitation upon our views about what would more traditionally have been referred to as our "definition" or "conception" of rationality itself.

Unquestionably what may be called collectively and loosely the "revision process" has been and continues to be a most important way—perhaps not so unquestionably *the* most important way—in which knowledge actually develops. For philosophical purposes, for the purpose of elucidating the rationality of our knowledge, this process is excluded from the purview of the justification program. But this is to suppose that the kind of expansion and development that proceeds by revision, emendation, correction of the old, rather than building upon or adding to it, is somehow not rational. Though a process of great interest from a historical, sociological, or psychological point of view, what takes place in it is thought to be not essential to the rational expansion of knowledge; hence it may be neglected in the philosopher's exploration of this process. This exploration may be directed to the goal of providing a purely logical analysis of the relations between ground*ed* claims and ground*ing* claims which together, according to the view taken, make up the system of knowledge. If, to use language commonly employed by advocates

[1] *Historical Inevitability*, p. 33.

of the view, the task of the philosopher of knowledge is to ex-
plicate the rationality of truth claims advanced either as knowledge or some kind of reasonable belief; and if that rationality
consists in these justifying relations between truth claims; then
the exploration of rationality is the exploration of these relations,
the principles governing them, and the claims between which
they hold. Revision phenomena need to occur only when and
because individuals and groups are lax in ordering their claims
in the ways determined by these relations. These lapses and
deviations are of interest in the pathology of knowledge; they
have no place in, and hence their occurrence is only indirectly
relevant to, the physiology or anatomy of the sound cognitive
body. Sound conduct in pursuit of knowledge, and hence its expansion from what are taken to be its logical beginnings, like
sound hygiene with respect to the physical body, consists in
ordering this pursuit so that the logical lesions that call for the
kind of revision and correction under examination here cannot
and hence will not occur. Rationality in the advancement and
acceptance of truth claims is achieved not because of, but in
spite of, the revision phenomena. Attention to them is important
for the theory of the rational development of knowledge, belief,
opinion, and so on, only to the extent that that theory needs to
be concerned with the remedial.

  17. This view of rationality is one of arresting implausibility.
The implausibility derives from the vast profusion of the revision
phenomena in knowledge as we have had, do have, and evidently
will continue to have it. So vast is the discrepancy between the
conception of rationality dictating the elimination or at least
philosophical disregard of the revision phenomena, and the actual
procedures by which in everyday life and a variety of professional disciplines we appraise the rationality of putative members
or suggested candidates for membership in the corpus of human
knowledge, that it suggests at once the question whether this
drastic philosophical conception of rationality, sometimes advanced as high-minded severity in philosophical appraisal, does
not represent rather, as a philosophical position, a certain per-
verse irresponsibility and disregard of fundamental features of

the social institutions, the aspects of human culture, it is intended to explore and illuminate.

Reference was just made to the profusion of the revision phenomena in past and present human knowledge as well as that which we may expect in the foreseeable future. The phenomena abound, not only in our everyday view of the world, our views of ourselves and our relations with our fellows, other living creatures, and objects in the world; and not only in the moral, political, legal, economic theories, hypotheses, ways of conception with which we seek to understand these relations. The phenomena abound also in such highly developed disciplines as mathematics and the physical sciences, which to some have seemed the most promising domains for the development of justification theory and hence for the demonstration in practice of the conception of rationality which that theory represents. In mathematics, for example, the theory of numbers is not what it was at the time of Pythagoras, not just because we have additional information about those entities that people at that time referred to as numbers, but also because, as a consequence of many developments since that time, we think of numbers differently. The word "number" has now a different reference. So great is the difference that many of the claims made at that early time are hard to construe, to assimilate in the language and thought in which we advance claims about numbers today. Unless we are willing, by an effort of historical learning and imagination, to recreate the intellectual situation of that time, and speak and think in a way appropriate to it, we are forced to make do with the rough approximations of thoughts that we are able to achieve by means of our own familiar linguistic and conceptual instruments, however anachronistic these may be. In the thought and knowledge that we have been able to develop about numbers, based upon that of our Babylonian, Greek, or Arabic ancestors, their thought does not remain, fixed and unchanged, as a part of ours, even as foundation. A similar comment could be made of many of the central elements of Western physical science, say the view of matter and extension taken by Descartes and by scientists today, or of combustion and of physical element before and after the revolutionary work of Lavoisier. Lavoisier did far more than make inductive discoveries about something, the physical element that had the same stable place in the intellectual landscape, before and after his work; he changed the intellectual landscape by revealing something about the physical landscape, namely, certain respects in which the view of that landscape was distorted, in need of fundamental reorientation. So too, finally, if we compare our own view of the earth, our home, with that taken in medieval geography, we see that what distinguishes our view from what was known, or taken to be known, at that early time is not simply a matter of enormous addition of information, but also a matter of great transformation. If, using the words, and making the normal presumptions implicated in the use of these words now, we say of a man in the thirteenth century that he believed that the earth is the center of the universe, how far are we from beginning to express his thought! In one respect it is right to say that this man believed that the planet earth is the center of the universe, and in another respect it is very wrong, since his belief was not about anything that he would think of as the planet earth, and *a fortiori* was not about what we would think about under the name "the universe." Copernicus, Galileo, and other astronomers did not simply set in motion what men like Dante thought of under the name of "mondo." They also so radically transformed the intellectual landscape, by revealing so much about the physical landscape, that we cannot now, without effort and study, begin to understand what Dante thought of under that name.

18. A theory of knowledge that by design neglects the manifold ways in which revision and correction of this kind take place in knowledge, that so narrowly defines the domain of the rational that all these ways are excluded from it, renders itself by this design incompetent to provide understanding, and, by understanding, assistance in the conduct of one of the most important ways in which knowledge actually is achieved and developed. From the point of view of the philosophical enterprise this narrowness is intolerably expensive, the expense being in terms of what could be learned about and possibly improved in our cognitive activities, individual and collective. And if it should be

urged in justification of this expense that it, and the narrowness from which it proceeds, are dictated by a scrupulous regard for the "logical" in the study of knowledge and the rationality of claims, in contrast with the "psychological," there are two brief related comments that may be made in response. One is that an extreme and impoverishingly narrow conception of what is rational is naturally associated with a similar conception of what is logical. The second is that when the choice is put in this way between "logical" and "psychological," the narrow way of viewing the logical is the key factor in the generation of this harsh, and in the end, false alternative. Illustrated immediately here is the kind of inaptness of our linguistic and other cognitive ways of grasping matters that continually leads to the revision phenomena. For what is the consequence of taking seriously these phenomena in the theory of knowledge is not a descent into some kind of crude "psychologism" that cannot distinguish questions about the actual course of thought from questions of its soundness or validity. It is rather a recognition that questions of logical propriety, of validity, though surely at some remove and commonly and correctly considered in abstraction from questions about the kinds of discriminations we make in the world, and hence necessarily also about the kind of objects, entities, states, relations that form the substance of that world, cannot in the end, for some purposes, be cut off from these questions. Some questions that arise in the expansion of knowledge and in the appraisal of various features of what is taken to be knowledge are generated by indications of various kinds that features of our cognitive apparatus, including sometimes the logical features of that apparatus, are in subtle but deep ways not well adapted to the domain or subject matter which they are being employed to explore. Questions arise about numbers which are not questions of what can be ascertained about these entities and predicated of them within the confines of ordinary number theory, but of how we should think of these entities which in the ordinary procedures of number theory are the objects of investigation and predication. Similar questions arise in physics about particles, about density, position, motion, and so on; about cause, intention, and action in philosophical psychology; about property or freedom of religion in politics; about freedom of speech *vis-à-vis* freedom of action in constitutional law.

19. Questions of this kind—questions not so much of how to think truly or deal surely with objects of our concern, but of how to think sufficiently well enough about them that terms like "true" and "false" will apply; of how to conduct ourselves and arrange matters so that we have an opportunity to deal surely with these objects, well or ill, rather than grope and fumble in their vicinity—questions of this kind arise much too frequently and commonly in the conduct of our logical enterprises to be regarded as less than integral to these enterprises. Questions about how to formulate clear claims, to construct propositions, are as central to these enterprises as questions concerning what connections there may be between these propositions when we have constructed them, and how we may determine which of them are true. These questions are integral to our cognitive activities in ascertaining the character of the world in which our activities take place, not only in the respect that these questions cannot be avoided in the progressive ascertainment of this character, but also in that this character itself helps to determine what sound answers to such questions must be. One thing that the revision phenomena demonstrate—and in view of the significance of the phenomena the verb does not seem too strong— is not only that questions of this sort have to be faced, but that the facing of them is a continuing process in the development of knowledge. These are not questions that can be answered, once for all, in some broad prolegomenon to epistemology and metaphysics, by the determination of one correct-for-all-time set of procedures, by the devising of a similarly immune-from-change-and-revision "ideal" language, a similarly philosophically congealed "system of concepts." As life changes, as the forms of cognitive life extending from common sense to the most advanced intellectual disciplines change, our procedures, language, forms of discrimination and thought undergo revision and change. The topic of presupposition, to consider one aspect of our cognitive practice which is integrally related with the phenomena, will not yield to adequate treatment by the attempt to devise logical techniques that will expunge it from our claim-

making and claim-appraising activities, nor by an attempt to determine once for all the presuppositions to be made, then make them and have done. Satisfactory treatment of the phenomena requires that our view of claim-making and claim-appraising be broad enough to include this aspect as an enduring feature of our activities, and that hence a theory of inquiry, scientific and otherwise, include responses to those phenomena as an integral part of our cognitive activity.

20. It is a mistake, then, to suppose that questions of this sort do not qualify as logical ones and hence can be neglected in philosophical inquiries seeking to illuminate the rationality of putative items of knowledge, belief, opinion, and the rest. And to the extent that this supposition is made and adhered to in the philosophical scrutiny of knowledge, that scrutiny will be rendered incompetent by design to embrace in its scope and cast illumination upon some of the most important of the processes and activities which are involved in the acquiring and development of knowledge. The cost of this incompetence and deprivation of illumination has already been judged to be intolerably high. Whenever questions of the kind that are generated by the revision phenomena are excluded like poor relations from the domain of the logical or the rational, when because they are not tractable to the procedures countenanced in justification theory they are relegated to the realm of the pragmatic, to the inescapably subjective or conventional; then they lose what assistance can be derived in their consideration by the kind of persistent, careful, broad, and responsible examination that has been the mark of philosophical reflection at its best. And when other students of the history of thought, including the history of science, follow philosophers in this mistaken assumption and way of proceeding, their work too suffers from this narrowness. They too are led to view the kind of progress in knowledge, if progress it is, that occurs through the processes of correction and revision represented by those phenomena, as somehow nonrational. To be sure they are nonrational, if what determines the domain of reason is "logic and experiment," reason and sense, viewed in accordance with the narrowed interpretation of these that has been disseminated widely through modern versions of Cartesian phi-

losophy. This untoward result constitutes one more reason, though more are surely not needed, for facing the question whether the philosophy that leads to this result is greatly in need of critical inspection, whether the fault in this case—the extreme aspects of nonrational development that seem to appear in all cases of scientific revolutions—does not lie less in the processes by which revolutions are effected than in the theory of rationality to which the endeavor has been to assimilate them.[2]

21. If the disadvantages of the view of rationality with respect to truth claims that is incorporated in Cartesian theories are so great, the question suggested by the notice of each new disadvantage is naturally, Why have philosophers in large numbers been attracted to this view? At this stage in the inquiry into justification theory the principal answer to this question should now have been made very plain. The support for the justification program in the philosophical scrutiny of knowledge obviously does not lie in any convincing demonstration of how the program can be put into effect. All the foundation difficulties, and all the construction difficulties encountered by the program stand as obstacles to any such attempted demonstration. The principal philosophical answer to the question of why one should engage in this program is not prospect of success in the attempt but an imperative that, despite past failures, devotion to it must not falter. It must not falter because, problematic as success in the program may be, that success is a necessary condition for achieving one goal to which the program is directed. The goal is constructing a theory of knowledge capable of meeting the skeptical challenges that have arisen in certain kinds of theory, and doing so in the very direct way of accepting the questions through which the challenges are advanced as legitimate, treating the mistake of those who advance these challenges as being not that of putting ill-considered questions, but of underestimating our resources for answering the questions as asked. It is not disputable that one of the functions of a sound theory of knowledge is to make plain the mistakes of less sound theories, including the

[2] Some further attention to this matter will be given in connection with the positive view of the philosophical scrutiny of knowledge advanced in Part III.

mistakes of those theories that purport to show the hollowness of any claims of reasonableness we may make on behalf of practically anything which in our cognitive and other pursuits we take ourselves to know. Again, the question in the theory of knowledge is not of *whether* the challenges of skeptical theories are to be met but *how*. At the root of the inadequacies of justification theory is a misconception of how this task of philosophical theory is to be performed. It is this mistake, and the enduring preoccupation with the baffling task of attempting to perform the task in a mistaken way, that leads to the correlative search for incorrigible cognitions upon which to begin the reconstruction of knowledge and the endeavor to find a way of construing the procedure by which knowledge is developed from these phenomena in such a way as to eliminate from it the kind of corrigibilities that are represented by the revision phenomena.

22. The main contention advanced in criticism of the philosophy of knowledge expressed in justification theory and the corresponding justification argument has been that careful attention to the character of certain operations which it is recognized by all sides that we must perform in securing knowledge, discloses that, no matter how privately these operations are performed, they are profoundly dependent for their success upon social and material conditions that extend far beyond any person engaged in performing them. For this important reason, the truth claims that we formulate and seek to appraise cannot pretend to have either the kind of epistemic integrity or, even more important, the kind of semantic integrity, that they are required to have if this philosophy holds. The seriousness of the criticism advanced deserves emphasis. The criticism is not simply that, in comparison with the claims we do make and seek to appraise in our normal activity as cognitive beings, these integrity requirements are unrealistic. It is not merely that, in contrast with the way in which in everyday life and even in the scientific disciplines we perform a variety of activities implicated in making and appraising such claims, there is another, purer, more demanding way in which we might perform these activities and yet satisfy the integrity requirements. The implication of the considerations adduced is quite otherwise. It is that the more one seeks to

satisfy these requirements in the performance of these activities, the more these activities lose their character, become intellectually etiolated versions of themselves. The more we understand the activities the more we see that essential to the functions they are designed to perform are aspects which render their performance impossible in the way that justification theory demands. The reason that one cannot succeed in the project of reconstructing human knowledge generally, or his own individual share of such knowledge, according to the requirements of the theory is not that the standards the theory sets are beyond frail human adherence. They are beyond logical adherence. The project itself founders, a victim of fundamental, internal logical difficulty.

23. The considerations advanced as grounds for giving up the foundation model in the theory of knowledge, and the corresponding decision to give it up, have many important philosophical consequences. Some consequences which have not already been discussed, and some consequences of an unhappy nature which have been alleged by critics to follow from such a crucial philosophical decision, will be discussed at some length immediately in the following two chapters. In advance of that discussion there are two points about the consequences of the view advanced here which, since they are closely related to the foundation view and cannot be treated later, deserve a brief comment at once.

First, to give up the model of sensing and inferring as the one with which the philosophical clarification of knowledge is to be pursued is not to deny that we do sense and do infer, any more than denying that the model for all mechanical explanation is pushing entails that pushing does not occur. Nevertheless what has been urged here concerning the corrigibility of the supposed ultimate first premises of knowledge has consequences upon how we view inferences from premises generally. The prevailing view of inference, in which young philosophers are commonly indoctrinated from their earliest instruction in logic, is distorted by a fixation upon a certain kind of standard case. In this respect it is very like the prevailing view of scientific laws. The standard case is one in which the context of the inference is such that the steplike pattern, *A, B,* . . . *N;* therefore *Q,* fits very well. But this pattern fits very well because the context of the inference is so stable that there is no question about the identity and significance of the proposed premises and conclusion, so that the only question of substance remaining is whether from the fixed premises the fixed conclusion can be derived by fairly fixed means.

Without doubt the preoccupation of many philosophers with this kind of standard case has been strengthened by the intense interest in formal patterns of demonstration aroused in many by the vast strides in the mathematicization of logical forms taken in this century. The achievements of formalization have been a heady subject for philosophers, many of whom might not have so easily misconstrued the significance of these achievements if they had come to them with a sounder view of the role of formalized techniques in mathematics itself. The misuse of these valuable intellectual instruments by philosophers endeavoring to extract goods from them that they are ill-designed to deliver may be a provocation, but is no excuse, for Luddite hostility to the instruments themselves. The energy of the reaction can much better be directed to the development of a more adequate view of inference which will hinder, rather than encourage, the misunderstanding out of which some of these misuses have sprung. The well-worn, well-tamed standard forms of inference will be understood, in such a view, in a new way; not as intellectual ideals, the realization in thought of eternally perfect logical forms, but as valuably developed and systematically understood intellectual habits, capable, like habits, of valuable, confident exercise in appropriate circumstance, and capable of being rendered inappropriate and being superseded in others. The mathematicization to which these forms are susceptible will not be extruded from such a view, but assimilated in a different manner. And when considerations from these sources are combined with others available in what have been until recently the more traditional and orthodox domains of mathematical study, they will lead to a more realistic and, especially to philosophers, a more helpful philosophy of logic and mathematics.

24. Finally, after all that has been said about the discriminations of sense not serving as the absolutely fixed first premises of

our knowledge, about there being in this sense no foundations of knowledge, something needs to be said to redress the balance. In the minds of some, the view that is conjured up by the thought of giving up faith in such foundations, is a view of intellectual disaster. And one supposed primary source of disaster is the loss of authority of certain ruling truth claims, in the absence of which the polity of truth claims is seemingly reduced to a kind of leveling anarchy, each claim seeking to maintain itself by means of alliances, and the strength of the successful alliances receiving philosophical sanction under the aegis of the coherence theory of truth.

The one thing needing to be said on the topic at this point is in opposition to such a Hobbesian presumption concerning what the sources of authority must be. Authority, intellectual or political, does not have to be absolute. In the whole body of what at any moment we regard as human knowledge, there are clearly some domains that are more stable, in which the claims made are more fundamental, more essential than those other domains and less susceptible to revision. The pre-eminent example of such a domain is the common-sense knowledge that we have of material objects, other living creatures, and other persons in our world, a knowledge that rests in a very important way upon the discriminations that we are able to make by means of sense.

One aspect of the foundation theory that is right is its recognition that this is so: that there are, in brief, foundations in our knowledge, and that these foundations are closely dependent upon sense experience and observation. But the form that this recognition took has been extreme and seriously in error. An unmistakable segment of the foundation stratum of our knowledge, a segment that is fundamental in a psychological-historical way as well as from an epistemic point of view, is the common-sense knowledge of material objects that we develop growing up in a human community and in being indoctrinated in the practices of that community. This knowledge by no means consists of a collection of appraised truth claims about particular objects or particular sense appearings. It is a rich mixture of lore and tradition, as well as these; a good part consists of accepted practices, techniques, skills; it always contains not only a good share of imperfection, but also positive error; and in certain important respects it differs from community to community. It is therefore a mistake to think of this domain of our knowledge, however essential it is to the rest, as consisting of a collection of particular, absolutely certain statements or propositions. And it is a mistake also to think of that portion of it that can be rendered in propositions, particular or otherwise, as axioms from which all else must somehow be inferred, but which, in their splendid logical isolation, are incapable themselves of being inferred from, invalidated by, or corrected by any other source. The recognition that there is this foundation stratum of common-sense knowledge is compatible with and needs to be combined with a recognition that the relation between this stratum and the uncommon knowledge that develops from it is one of mutual, though not equal, dependence. An adequate account of the relations between these two strata of our knowledge has to provide for much more complex relations than are contemplated in traditional justification theory. There has to be an account of how the higher strata of knowledge can be developed from the lower, not merely as a matter of psychological or historical fact, but in such a way that in the development the authority or warrant of the developed species of knowledge is made plain. And there must similarly be an account of the effects of the higher upon the lower, how in giving rise to the higher species the lower is itself altered, sometimes in subtle and sometimes in very noticeable ways, one of the most prominent of these being that in which items of higher strata eventually displace items in the lower and themselves are eventually assimilated to the level of common sense.

When the foundation stratum of our knowledge is identified thus roughly with the common-sense knowledge that is our endowment as men in civilized society, these mutual relations of dependence between foundation and superstructure must be conceded and the complexities of philosophical theory that the dependencies entail must be faced. The traditional view of foundations avoided the complexity by denying the dependence. But this meant identifying the foundation stratum in another way, with a kind of superior common sense (cf., "*le bons sens*" of

Descartes) which, though conceived differently by rationalist and empiricist practitioners of the theory, was conceived in unison as one which, in conflict with claims from any other sort, must always win. According to the view that has been advanced here in making a criticism of the justification argument, the search for such an uncommon common sense, necessarily victorious against all opponents, must now be given up. And this is not merely because the search has been unsuccessful. It is also, in a very practical sense, misconceived. For if, *per impossibile,* what was sought could be found, it is hard to see what advantage to the philosophy of knowledge it would be. What could be erected on this curious foundation, in the curious way that was intended, would have so little relation with human knowledge as it is attained in this world that it would be of little assistance for the understanding of that knowledge.

The philosophical search for an all-conquering common sense is one that can be given up without lament. The object sought is not one that is too good for this world. Rather, considering the purposes for which it was intended, it is not good enough.

PART III

THE PHILOSOPHICAL SCRUTINY OF KNOWLEDGE

CHAPTER 9

Conditions and
Dimensions of Scrutiny

1. Agreement upon the need for philosophical scrutiny of the traditions and accepted practices that at any time form the settled definable portions, the continents as it were, of the institution of human knowledge, leads immediately to questions about how this scrutiny should proceed. The theory of knowledge that embodies justification theory and a regress to first cognitions represents one answer, or, more exactly, the broad framework of an answer to these questions, which can be filled out in practice in alternative ways. In the process of giving its answer to the *question*—to speak thus, simply for the purpose of brevity—this theory construes the question in a particular manner, one that has very deep and important philosophical consequences. For to construe the question as that of how to proceed to answer the challenge of large-scale skepticism concerning the knowledge institution is to accept the legitimacy of such a challenge; it is to presume that it is possible for us in a large-scale way to abstract ourselves in thought from this institution and the world that is represented to us in this institution. Then, fortified by this deprivation, it is presumed that it will be possible for us, not only to think, but to think clearly and objectively about the possibility of knowledge of this world. This way of construing the question leads to the erection, or the attempted erection, in our philosophical thought, of a curtain between our thoughts, our views about the world and its contents, and the world itself.

To suppose like Descartes that it is possible for one, in utter independence of such a world, its objects and creatures, and of one's fellowmen, past and present, and the vast social and intellectual tradition they embody—to suppose that it is possible for one in this state to muse about problems of knowledge and error, is to suppose that for philosophical purposes the position of the skeptic is a position that at least can be occupied, if not permanently maintained. The supposition that a skeptical view of these matters is a possible view, even a false possible view, is a supposition that without what Berkeley called "the vast choir of Heaven and furniture of the Earth," we would still be able to think of them. This is exactly what Descartes held for all thought representing objects beyond itself, with one exception, namely thought of God, which according to the ontological argument could not be the thought it is without God's own being. But to view matters in this way is thus to erect a curtain between thoughts and things which, in order for knowledge of things by thought to be possible, would have to be breached at some location, by some thought of an extraordinary kind. This thought, in the case of Descartes, was the exalted thought of God; in the empiricists it was the much less exalted thought realized in the form of the sensory states which provide us with the first cognitions of sense, both inner and outer. This curtain, and the philosophical skepticism that it represented was given constitutional status in this philosophy in the form of the celebrated mind-body dualism. To say this is not to suggest that this metaphysical view was solely an expression of the epistemological interest just noted, that it derived its claims of support exclusively from the way it provided metaphysical rationalization and sanction for what the hyperbolic doubt set out to do in the theory of knowledge. There were a variety of interests, scientific, religious, ethical, humanistic, and psychological which this dualistic theory served in its career in modern philosophy, and indeed served well; hence its most remarkable pervasiveness and durability. It represented a kind of intellectual demarcation line, far exceeding in importance the Line of 1493 drawn by Pope Alexander in the Western hemisphere, but designed like it to mark off territorial claims on the part of rival claimants that would enable both sides—in this case the established humanist, religious traditional view of man, and the expansionist mechanical view of the new physical science—to preserve a position and cultivate certain domains behind metaphysical borders protected from encroachment from the other side. Among the various philosophical ends served by the dualism, by no means the least in long-run philosophical significance, was the metaphysical rationale, support and sanction that it provided for the skeptical stance toward the traditions and accepted practices of the knowledge from which Cartesian theory proposed to engage in its scrutiny of this institution.

2. To give up the Cartesian answer to the question of how to proceed in this scrutiny is not to give up the question. But, free of the confines of the Cartesian view, one can look upon the question in a different way. And just as the Cartesian view was supported by what has just been referred to as a metaphysical constitutional provision designed to assure that the scrutiny could proceed in a particular manner, so the opposed arguments show, if they are sound, the need for constitutional revision in this regard. The recognition, which is the fruit of the arguments about the first cognitions of sense, that even in proceeding in such a limited act as that of discriminating among sensations one is already employing, relying upon, in a deep and complex way, features of the knowledge institution, destroys the prospect that such discriminations can serve as first steps, taken in utter independence of the institution, in a proceeding that will provide a kind of independent audit of the institution, using figures and computational means that do not depend at any point upon the institution for their own validity. The consequences of this recognition are immense, for the philosophy of mind and human action as well as for the theory of knowledge. For if it is true that in making simple sensory discriminations, in "accepting" the so-called "given" of much recent theory of knowledge, one is already engaging in a practice that integrally and deeply involves fellow human beings and a world of things which one cohabits with them, how much more deeply involved with these must he also be when he thinks of objects, other human beings, and other living creatures; when he thinks of Albuquerque, New Mexico, or of the rings of Saturn; when he intends to vote a certain way

in an election; when he desires, hopes, wonders, wishes, loves, hates, and so on?

3. The first cognitions of sense thus represent a thread in the fabric of the Cartesian philosophy of mind, as that is represented in the empiricist versions of this philosophy, which, when subjected to persistent tension, initiates the disintegration of the whole. And the lessons to be learned from this disintegration are by no means restricted to empiricism, but apply to the Cartesian philosophies in general. To say that in making discriminations of sense one is engaged in a practice that integrally involves one with his fellowmen and a world of things, is to say that these fellowmen and things are essential to the practice. To discriminate red in one's sensory experience, to take oneself to be confronted by a red datum rather than an orange or green one, is to do something that could not be done except in the matrix of practice that extends far beyond the limits of the individual and his sensation at the moment the discrimination is made. What further is involved is a long and complex story that cannot be begun here. The keynote of the story, however limited its backing necessarily has been, needs to be clear. It is that without a certain subsistence level of support in the form of the activities of men engaged together in a common world of things, there would be no practice of discriminating sensations, and that without that practice, neither you or I, nor even Descartes or Hume, could be doing what we know very well we are doing when we discriminate red from orange, or sweet from sour. It is not a matter of making bricks without straw; it is a matter of making bricks without clay or earth of any kind, without kilns and fire, merely in the supposed privacy of the mind. One can no more discriminate sensations in the supposed private way divorced in imagination from men and things, than he can so make bricks, fly a kite, or split atoms. And *a fortiori* one cannot, in this utter metaphysical privacy, hunt the Northwest Passage, intend to hunt it, desire or hope to find it, wonder if it exists, love the prospect of success in finding it, or fear the prospect of failure. This being so, it is no longer possible to maintain the supposition that such acts or states as these constitute modes of a private, utterly self-sufficient mind which, in engaging in such acts,

in apprehending its own states, is quite independent of any external things. It is no longer possible to think of a human intention, desire, or aspiration as something so well sealed in the personal consciousness of whoever entertains it, so independent of anything beyond this consciousness, that nothing beyond it, by existing, altering, or ceasing to exist, can add or detract from the capacity of this consciousness to have whatever intentions, desires, or aspirations it has.

4. To discriminate a datum or appearance as red, to distinguish a dull ache from a sharp pain in one's tooth, is something that one does, and can do, only by utilizing a vast apparatus, including features in himself, in a world he never made. In doing so one draws upon and exploits a vast supply of mental capital of which he is the legatee; sometimes beneficiary and sometimes victim, but always and necessarily a legatee. Some of this inheritance comes to him in his physiological make-up. Passed on to him by his parents are structural features and capacities to react, some highly adaptive, some not, and some largely vestigial, which are the residue of millions of years of evolutionary selection. Passed on to him through a variety of agents and institutions is likewise the residue, including a great deal of dross mixed with the useful metal, of an indefinitely long span of human experience ramified and particularized in many ways by the effects of tribal, national, and religious identification, familial connections, schooling, occupational training, apprenticeship, and service, and so on. In all these ways is the mind of man formed and constituted. If following Leibniz we think of each mind as a monad, we must also think of that monad as necessarily reflecting, if not every other monad, a vast array of present and historical existence; of being what it is because of this reflection, and consequently because there are these aspects of existence to be reflected. To think of the human mind in this way requires a considerable alteration in philosophical perspective. It is only with a considerable philosophical wrench that one can come to recognize that although there need not have been any Fountain of Youth in order for Ponce de León to think of it and search for it, there did need to be a rich framework of things involving, not only time and aging, but also, say, something of elementary hy-

draulics and the practice of ablution, or possibly potation, in order for Ponce to have these aspirations, in order for him to think about these matters, in order for his essays toward such thought to succeed in making minimal sense.

5. It is important that the thesis advanced here be made very plain. For if it is sound, there are valuable lessons to be learned from it, and if it is not it is important that its unsoundness be promptly exposed. According to the thesis, the activity of Ponce in thinking about the Fountain of Youth is derivative from activities and practices dealing with real objects. It is derivative not only historically but logically; so that apart from the practices of dealing with, referring to, and speaking about real objects, and without the objects which must exist in order for these practices themselves to exist, Ponce could not engage in the activity of thinking about this unreal one. In much of Western philosophy in this century the exploration of questions of knowledge has been strongly oriented toward questions about the language used in developing and expressing this knowledge. During this period some of the most interesting and novel phenomena relevant to these theses have been disclosed and treated in the discussion of such topics as meaning, the definition of terms or concepts, the reference of linguistic expressions, and the presuppositions that seem to be involved in the use of expressions for certain purposes, for example, making statements or assertions.

Of these topics, one whose bearing on the matter at hand has been insufficiently noted, though it has been well remarked and much discussed in other connections, has been the phenomenon to which Waismann, apparently following the lead of Wittgenstein, called attention in his paper on "Verifiability." [1] Waismann spoke of this under the title of the "open texture of concepts." Some aspects of open texture were touched upon in Chapter 8, since the revisions in our procedures, thought, and language which at times are occasioned by the incidence of open texture represent an important class of what were discussed there under the title of "revision phenomena." This open texture

[1] *Aristotelian Society Supplementary Volume XIX* (1945), pp. 119–150. Reprinted in A. Flew, ed., *Logic and Language*, pp. 117–144.

quality, or "porosity," is a pervasive feature of those components of our thought and linguistic practice to which, in terms of dominant rubrics at the time of his essay, Waismann referred to as *empirical* concepts. It is exhibited in relation to each concept in the circumstance that it is always possible to imagine border-line situations in which the question of whether the associated term applies or does not apply is indeterminate in a peculiar way. It is not just that there are many terms like this. That contention would be excruciatingly banal. What Waismann and Wittgenstein, and also Austin in his discussion of essentially the same matter, offer for consideration are examples of a type that are more easily noticed than captured in a formula. There is the creature that seems for all the world like a cat, yet grows to be gigantic (Waismann).[2] There is that object that looks for all the world like a chair, yet unlike ordinary chairs trifles with our vision by repeatedly disappearing from sight, vanishing into thin air (Wittgenstein).[3] And there is that creature in Austin's garden which we have surely identified as a goldfinch, and which then confounds us by doing what Austin describes as "something out-rageous (explodes, quotes Mrs. Woolf, or what not)." In such circumstances, Austin observes, "we don't say we were wrong to say it was a goldfinch, *we don't know what to say*. Words literally fail us." [4]

6. If we are going to speak in these matters in the traditional idiom of "concepts" and "ideas," it appears that Austin's description of the phenomenon in question gives one a better clue to its character and derivation than the descriptions of Waismann and Wittgenstein. Austin says that following the outrageous behavior of this goldfinchlike object or creature, *"we don't know what to say,"* that in the supposed circumstances, "words literally fail us," and, as he adds in further comment upon the matter, the future can always "make us *revise our ideas* about goldfinches or real goldfinches or anything else." [5] Waismann and Wittgenstein speak of the phenomenon in terms of the in-

2 *Ibid.*, paragraph 4.   3 *Philosophical Investigations*, Pt. I, Sect. 80.
4 "Other Minds," *Aristotelian Society Supplementary Volume XX* (1946), Sect. I. Reprinted in A. Flew, ed., *Logic and Language*, Second Series.
5 *Ibid.* Italics in orig.

completeness of definition of the terms or concepts in question (Waismann), or of our not being equipped with rules covering every possible application of the words in question (Wittgenstein). It is not so much that these latter characterizations are disputable, so far as they go, as that they do not go far enough, and that as they stand the emphasis and hints toward further development are somehow misdirected. There is a rich supply of words that in application leave open a large domain of borderline cases, and often the domain of such cases is richly populated; and we complacently contemplate this situation without turning a philosophical hair. An important feature of the kind of case that constitutes this phenomenon is that they are capable of troubling us. They take us by surprise, and in doing so reveal that there is something about our practice in using such words that is not to be accounted for by our capacity to devise rules of application for the words. They, and an indefinite domain of words like them, are such that we cannot, as Waismann says, construct for them a "complete definition," cannot provide for them "rules ready for all imaginable possibilities." [6]

7. The words have the capacity to surprise us in the way they do, because, as we see in our reflections, the world has the capacity to surprise us in our use of them. The world would surprise us if it presented to us prodigies of the kind imagined, the thoughts of which Leibniz, in his comments on the discussion of similar possibilities in Locke's *Essay*, characterized as "bizarre fictions." [7] Confronted in imagination by such bizarre entities, we don't know what to say, because also we don't know what to think; and our not knowing what to think is of a particular kind, deriving more from an incapacity to think than from indecision about what thoughts to follow or credit. By means of such an experiment in imagination there is revealed, in a sudden, spectacular, and concentrated effect, some of the influence over our thought that the world outside us constantly exerts, though ordinarily in a much slower, more subdued and extensive way. The gigantic "cat," the literary "goldfinch," and so on, affect our ability to think, by creating conditions for which our habits

---

[6] "Verifiability," paragraphs 11, 4.
[7] *New Essays Concerning Human Understanding*, Bk. III, Ch. VI, Sect. 22.

of talking and thinking about cats, of making cat and not-cat discriminations, and so on, were not designed, and in which our attempt to continue these operations leads to contrary responses and frustration. The "cat" and "goldfinch" of the examples, by misbehaving and through this misbehavior adversely affecting our power to think clearly in this limited situation, indirectly show us how dependent we are, when we think well of cats and goldfinches, upon the "good" behavior of what it is we are talking about, directly and indirectly, and that includes not only cats and goldfinches, but also other small fur-bearing animals, feral and domestic, and other birds and related creatures.

8. It is because of the existence, the character and the "good behavior" of certain things, though not necessarily goldfinches, that we are able to think well, when we do, of goldfinches. This does not mean that if birds were radically different from what they are now—or perhaps more properly put, if instead of what we comfortably think of under the title of "birds," we had similar though in some respects radically different feathered, flying creatures, we should not be able to think well about these. It does mean that our present practices of discriminating, referring to, dealing with, reasoning about birds would not equip us to think well about them. We should falter on a large scale, as in imagination we falter on a small scale in confronting Austin's hypothetical specimen, and as we do falter again and again in practice, particularly in scientific practice, when unexpected phenomena require us to make important changes not only in our thoughts *about* objects that we are investigating, but also in our thoughts *of* the objects themselves. And it is of course out of the revision in our thoughts to which this faltering in performance leads, that some of the most interesting and revolutionary features of scientific progress ensue. One of the very fundamental ways in which objects and creatures in the world around us make their characters known to us is by affecting our capacity to think of them and the ways we think of them. And although there are a vast number of questions to be answered about the way this effect is produced in detail, some of the gross features of this process are unmistakably clear. Objects and creatures affect us, for example, by affecting our behavior in dealing with them, by

affecting various complex practices of our lives out of which our ability to think of them derives and upon which this ability is essentially dependent. They affect us also by having affected our ancestors in a variety of ways, not least importantly by having affected the very character of our ancestors through the evolutionary process and thus affecting the physical constitution and capacities of the bodies we have and with which we are prepared to deal with these and similar features of our environment.

9. But this aspect of the matter, though fascinating, is not what is of primary relevance here. Rather it is the intimate and essential dependence of our thoughts about things upon things themselves, in view of which the formulation of Section 7, that our thoughts are subject to influence by objects in the world about us, must count as an extreme understatement. Objects, things, other living things, our fellow men, all influence our thoughts because they are all implicated in complex social practices in which these thoughts have their roots. These thoughts are what they are partly because the practices are what they are; and the practices are what they are partly because of those with whom we participate in the practices, and the objects or other entities with which the practices are concerned, are what they are. It is quite impossible therefore to carry out any project for the philosophical construction of human knowledge that calls for one first to divest himself of the influence of men, living creatures, and things in the world around him as a preparation for beginning to think clearly and achieve fully accredited, objective knowledge of that world. A corollary conclusion with the one to the effect that when things fail us our thoughts fail us, is that, could we divorce ourselves from commerce with and the influence of things and fellow creatures we would not then think surely and objectively; we would not think at all. The reason that we must not try to wipe the slate clean in order to begin philosophizing about knowledge is not only that we cannot succeed, but that it is fatuous to try. It is fatuous because it is fatuous to suppose that in such metaphysical isolation it is possible for one to apprehend incorrigibly and surely the character of sensory appearances or appearings, the character of one's acts of will, of one's thoughts of possible objects or beings, of

one's aspirations, undertakings, desires, fears, loves, or aversions. It is fatuous, as it is generally fatuous to confuse innocence on any subject, including therein anything relevant to the character of what is open to observation by us, with the capacity to determine fairly and objectively, by observational means or otherwise, what that character is. Had Descartes understood sufficiently what he was saying when he affirmed that he was a thinking being he would have understood that it was indeed impossible for him to make this affirmation and yet consistently entertain the possibility of there being no world of objects, other living creatures and men, in which this thinking was taking place.[8]

10. During the past two centuries in Western philosophy it has been principally among philosophers oriented in the idealist philosophy of the Kantian-Hegelian tradition that the aspects of mind and thought emphasized here have been most frequently recognized. The large metaphysical questions in the philosophy of man and nature that recognition of this association naturally arouses cannot be treated here. The idealist philosophers, recognizing that in our very thought of objects we are engaged with both objects and other human beings, judged that the best way to make all this understandable was to assimilate what we are engaged with to thought, and to account for the striking difference between these two kinds of assimilated entities in terms of grades of thought, hence differences of degrees of reality. But there are other ways of trying to understand this engagement, for example that of Marx who, in attempting to rectify what he regarded as the inverted position of Hegelian dialectic, urged that the way to do this was to assimilate thought to the material

---

[8] It is possible, by selecting certain portions of Descartes's thought and construing them in a certain way, to interpret his proofs of the existence of God and of material objects as an exposure of this impossibility. An advantage of this subtle move in the interpretation of Descartes's theory of knowledge is that it is the only one that, if acceptable, plausibly succeeds in exculpating Descartes from the famous charge of circularity.

A most serious disadvantage is that the position of the *Cogito* in Descartes's philosophy, and the certainty attributed by him to our apprehension of the character of our own ideas, have to be reinterpreted in a manner that departs widely from the *prima facie* significance they seem to have as Descartes presents them and that they seem necessarily to have if they are to be composed with the major tenets of the theory of knowledge set forth in the *Discourse on Method* and the *Rules*.

and social. In recognizing some features of the implication of our thought with features of the world in which this thinking occurs, it is not necessary to make a choice between these two large-scale modes of assimilation. It is indeed not clear that both programs, and other similar ones, do not rest equally upon a philosophical mistake, that the pressure for assimilation itself derives from an antique and progressively obsolescent way of thinking about such things as minds, bodies, thoughts, and actions. In any case it seems worth emphasizing that the arguments offered here in support of what seems to be a more realistic view of our mental activity in apprehending those items that various philosophers have advocated as candidates for the position of the given, the first cognitions of reconstructed knowledge, are not intended to carry any subliminal stimuli for viewing the whole world as a congeries of spirits, or one all-encompassing spirit, or viewing the mental activities and thoughts as merely a way of speaking of facets of the interactions of purely mechanical systems that we as yet do not understand.

11. The view advanced here concerning the implication of objects and creatures in the world around us in our thoughts, in the activities, states, and achievements that have traditionally been regarded as the preserve of a private, internal, independent mind—which then, by some herculean effort of philosophical genius, such as that of Spinoza or Leibniz, must be brought, if not into interaction, at least into correspondence with things beyond it—is the correlate in the philosophy of mind of the epistemological doctrine that in the philosophical scrutiny of the cognitive status of any truth claims, taken individually or in wholesale lots, there is no possibility of wiping the slate clean and beginning anew the inscription of our cognitive accounts. It is an expression, in another mode, of Neurath's thesis that no *tabula rasa* exists on which, in carrying out such a project, we can begin to write. This view, like any other living philosophical view, is not without its own difficulties, confusions and (it is hoped) minor inconsistencies. But one particular difficulty that it does not have to face is the grand difficulty just alluded to in the Cartesian metaphysic. It does not need to devise means to join together what it never has put asunder. Thinking, to use

the broad term in which Descartes sought to capture the essence of mental substance, is an activity which we engage in, not only in a rich world of objects, men, and other living creatures, but also, and necessarily, by means of all these things, supported and sustained by them. In our capacity to think the way we do, in the very thoughts we have, all these things are at present at work. Our task in securing and improving knowledge is not that of establishing contact of thought with them, but that of utilizing that contact, of doing what we can to see that the effect they have, have had, and can have in the determination of our thoughts is used more and more as clues in discerning their existence and character. The power of an intellectual Hercules is not required to relate thinking with objects and creatures in the world about us, but to succeed even partially in severing these relations. To the extent that such an effort at severance succeeds, thinking weakens, and in any case where, *per impossibile,* it succeeds completely, there thinking, separated from the sustaining power of its Mother Earth like the giant Antaeus of ancient myth, quickly dies.[9]

12. According to the view being advanced here, one projected program in the philosophical scrutiny of knowledge is irreparably unworkable. It is so, because it misconceived. The steps by which it proposes to carry out this scrutiny cannot be taken, because at certain points there is a fundamental contrariety between what the program dictates must be done and the conditions under which it proposes to do it. To be successful, scrutiny must be carried out in a different way. But in what way? If it cannot proceed by means of a regress to sure islets of certainty left from a deluge of skeptical doubt, from which, like philosophical Noahs, we can proceed to repopulate the intellectual firmament with those cognitive species that have survived, then how can and should it proceed?

13. In the course of elaborating a positive answer to this question some further deficiencies in the program advanced by justifi-

9 For a more extensive, detailed, and historically oriented discussion of this topic see F. L. Will, "Thoughts and Things," *Proceedings and Addresses of the American Philosophical Association,* Vol. XLII (1968–1969), pp. 51–69.

cation theory will by contrast be rendered prominent. One of these, a direct consequence of the preoccupation of the theory with one philosophical concern, is a neglect of other concerns to which a program of philosophical scrutiny needs to be responsive. The character of this neglect and the intellectual deprivation to which it leads are strikingly evident in the inaptness of the procedures provided by the program in relation to the needs represented in these concerns, as illustrated by some typical problems, questions, and issues concerning knowledge which arise in the conduct of life and inquiry and call for broad philosophical illumination and, if possible, resolution.

Some examples have already been mentioned: questions about the existence of God, or souls as substances, or about our apparent perception of secondary qualities. The list may easily be extended. When a philosopher poses a question of *what* he really sees when he sees a tomato, and *whether* what he really sees is a tomato at all, the question of what this philosopher sees in this particular case is of little significance except as it bears on the general question of how we come to know material objects like this by means of perception. How, taking account of what we take ourselves to know about ourselves, such objects, and the conditions of perception, and supposing that perception is a way in which we do attain such knowledge, can we construct a comprehensive, adequate view of how we effect this attainment, a view that will not only account for the visual experiences associated with partially submerged apparently bent sticks and apparently converging railroad tracks, the auditory experiences of sounds that persist after the bell has ceased to turn, and so on, but also will provide an adequate understanding of the fundamental role of observation in what is called empirical science?

For centuries philosophers have been grappling with issues about the nature of man and of human action that were posed for them with increasing sharpness by striking successes of mechanical explanation in the physical sciences. In the present century new elements have been added to the problem. For example, from the scientists word came, with increasing insistence, that successful advance in understanding the character and behavior of ultraminute entities required giving up, in their application to these entities, of certain features of the determinism that had flourished with classical mechanics. And from the side of medicine, neurology, and psychology came hints of a different sort that, however determined certain aspects of our mental life may be, the kind of determination to which they were subject needed to be thought of differently both from the determination of physical mechanics and from what had seemed to introspective psychology up to that time to be the principles of psychic determination.

14. In the examination of issues generated by such developments how much inclination do we or should we have to proceed in the manner prescribed by justification theory? Was this a likely, plausible procedure, for example, in the case of the Freudian challenge in the early part of this century to the accepted introspective psychology, itself the outgrowth of previous challenges, some of them from developments in physiology in the preceding century? In following this procedure one might choose some crucial or sample claims from the new theory for examination. Such a claim might be the general allegation that there is a realm of unconscious mind needing to be recognized. Or it might be some more restricted claim made in the elaboration or application of the theory, such as the diagnosis (Freud) that the troubling dream of a woman that she was attending the funeral of a small nephew, of whom she was fond, was generated by a wish for the return of a man with whom she was in love and whom she first met at the funeral of a nephew. Then presumably one might evaluate the rationality of such claims by means of justification questions, determining whether the grounds for them could be traced back and laid out in the prescribed way.

What may at first view seem to be a striking advantage of this way of conducting the philosophical scrutiny of claims such as these, and of the complex domains of putative knowledge that they represent, upon further reflection is revealed as a serious limitation, and ultimately a disadvantage. Attractive as may be the prospect of a simple decision procedure requiring a minimum understanding of Freudian psychological principles and their development, and none whatever of their alternatives in the field, this attractiveness is surely but specious when the task to be performed is that of making a serious philosophical examination of what were originally and still remain to some extent radical and far-reaching proposals concerning the kind of views to be taken and the kind of techniques to be followed in investigation of basic questions concerning human nature and conduct. Surely the philosophical appraisal of the rationality of such claims and principles as these; surely the large task of contributing to the refinement, definition, and rectification of the large domains of human knowledge of which such claims as these are regarded by some, and discounted by others, as putative members; surely this kind of philosophical work in the appraisal, judgment, refinement, and development of human knowledge can effectively be carried on only in circumstances and by procedures that are not so intellectually deprived and disadvantaged. One needs enlightened judgment in this matter. And this is not furthered when, misled by the demands of some skeptical asceticism, one cuts himself off from a broad consideration of such matters as the neurotic phenomena which Freud and Breuer were treating when this vein of psychological theory was developed, how the theory was begun and developed through a consideration of these phenomena, and how it was applied in therapy and with what actual success; this together with the elaboration of the general theory in the study of dreams, of literary and other artistic masterpieces, of wit, of minor errors in speaking, writing, and executing simple acts in everyday life, and so on. One is hindered, not helped, by prescriptions of method which dictate some simple regressive uncovering and exposition of empirical, justifying grounds for individual claims, at the expense of a broader, more synoptic consideration of aspects like these. A consequence of the narrow method prescribed for the philosophical appraisal of such proposed scientific developments as these is a considered neglect of the broader views of man, society, and civilization that are associated with them, the implications these views in turn have for ethical, moral, legal, and political philosophy and the practices which these branches of philosophy reflect and seek to inform, and the alternatives, scientific, practical, and philosophical, that at each stage in the proceeding must be weighed in making an informed judgment of present worth and future possibilities.

15. The general character manifest in these examples should serve as a reminder of a fairly obvious point stressed earlier, which it is most important to keep clearly in mind in exploring the topic of philosophical scrutiny. It is that not all scrutiny and appraisal of putative items of knowledge is philosophical. Though different domains and times show great variations in this respect, there is always a vast range of questions at any time for which fairly settled means of ascertaining the answers exist. This is true of the conduct of inquiry in both the most highly theoretical as well as the most severely practical domains. In his study of scientific revolutions, T. S. Kuhn gives the name "normal science" to the kind of scientific activity which is mainly devoted to answering questions that arise within a broad and settled intellectual framework in certain fields of study at certain times as a result of certain past achievements that are accepted by particular scientific communities as models or paradigms for further practice. Such paradigms, comprising characteristic components of "law, theory, application, and instrumentation together, provide models from which spring [such] particular coherent traditions of scientific research" as those we refer to under the titles of Ptolemaic (or Copernican) astronomy, Aristotelian (or Newtonian) dynamics, or corpuscular (or wave) optics.[10] In normal science the means of conception of topics, the orientation of questions, and the methods of dealing with these questions follow settled ways of thinking and doing which themselves flow from certain dominating intellectual achievements.

16. It is easy to exaggerate and distort the difference between normal science and revolutionary science, as it is easy with similar differences in the areas of political, economic, religious, or artistic activity. It would be a gross exaggeration, for example, to think of revolutionary science as the work of one or a few intellectual geniuses who purely by personal intellectual force break old intellectual molds and fashion new ones, and normal science as the work of uncounted numbers of workers in the

[10] *The Structure of Scientific Revolutions*, p. 10.

scientific hive routinely filling in the details in the comb provided by the masters. Revolutionary steps in knowledge as elsewhere have their antecedents and preparatory conditions; the
American Civil War was not "caused" by a few cannonballs
lobbed at Fort Sumter. And normal science, normal religion,
normal art, is never just the point-perfect following of previously
established norms of thought and action. The differences between
normal and revolutionary are differences of degree, albeit often
differences of great degree, so that a time of revolution is not
in every respect in motion or change, nor a normal time in every
respect settled and at rest.

At any time, in the collective institution that is human knowledge, there is a vast reservoir of settled theory and practice to
which appeal can be made when questions arise concerning the
acceptability of and grounds for truth claims on a great variety
of topics. The effect of a broad, identifiable intellectual framework of the kind that Kuhn calls a "paradigm" is a striking example of an effect that in less striking ways is exerted and felt
throughout knowledge. The investigation of the grounds for any
truth claim and the formation of a judgment on the acceptability
of that claim is never restricted in its effect to just this claim.
Every successful claim, every successful inquiry leading to the
fixation of a claim somewhere in the constellation of facts, beliefs, opinions, and so on, is always to some extent a pattern
for further inquiries about other claims. Every successful claim,
however modest its scope, is to some extent striving to be a paradigm in its own world, a leader in its family. But ordinarily in
the body of accepted knowledge the positions of dominance and
subservience between these rival models for emulation are fairly
well fixed. That is to say, the collective institution of human
knowledge at any time is not merely a catalogue of accepted and
more or less closely related truth claims. It is also a reservoir of
practices, and, with this, a reservoir of lore, judgment, and evaluation concerning the domains of appropriateness and the character of the results to be expected from the application of these
practices.

17. Does this mean that all we have to do to answer questions
about methods and results in the appraisal of truth claims in the

institution of human knowledge is to follow accepted judgment and lore in that institution? It means that this is all we have to do some of the time, fortunately much of the time. And before we go on to consider what we do when the appeal to accepted opinion and practice does not suffice, and as a preparation for that consideration, we need to consider this kind of appeal a little further. In the many and varied lines of activity, both lay and professional, in which we have need to make judgments concerning truth claims, we are guided by a code of judgment and practice that is much like what in political life we call a "constitution." These constitutions differ from area to area, just as history differs from horticulture and architecture from aviation. With all their differences and discrepancies these constitutions are not unrelated. Collectively they form a huge sprawling entity that represents what may be thought of as the constitution for the institutionalized activity of human knowledge.

18. So far, what has been emphasized is the role that this collective constitution and its several parts play at any given time in guiding activity in the appraisal of truth claims. Most questions that arise concerning the appraisal of such claims, and concerning other matters integral to the development of human knowledge in its varied domains, are questions that can be answered to a considerable extent, and often quite adequately, given sufficient time, effort, and resource, by constitutional means. They are not in any significant degree constitutional questions. The whole constitution which performs this regulative function, like the individual constitutions that perform thus in their several domains, is exceedingly rich and complex in its provisions. Any attempt to encapsulate these provisions, or to find substitutes for them, in some simple prescription like that to the effect that the future should be supposed to resemble the past, or unobserved entities to resemble observed entities, is bound to founder upon the prominent reefs that it must try to steer between: namely prescribing no more than can be guaranteed against exception, which means prescribing nothing, or making a definite prescription that can soon be reduced to absurdity. The history of the exposure of these absurdities extends in Anglo-Saxon philosophy back to Peirce's criticism of Mill on

the subject of the uniformity of nature.[11] And the cumulative effect of exposure is now fairly impressive. In recent years the flurry of excitement over conditional statements, and over the related topic of the judgment about general connections that is implicitly expressed in such statements, has signified again, this time speaking in the language of linguistic and logical problems, the kinds of difficulties that are to be encountered when simple formulae are substituted for the complexities of the cognitive tradition. If we take as a methodological principle in the pursuit of laws of nature that we should "generalize on the basis of the broadest background of available evidence, with a minimum of arbitrariness," [12] we can only avoid a paralysis of indecision about how to proceed in any given case if we are prepared to make some judgments about what is evidence, when this is broad rather than narrow, and what is the arbitrariness in generalization that we are supposed to minimize. If we think of scientific induction as a matter of projecting predicates, we are brought up short by striking demonstrations like those of Goodman, that not all predicates are or can be projectible. And when we then proceed to investigate the projectibility of predicates and its connections with the "entrenchment" of certain terms in our language, thought, and practice, we begin to surmise at once that while there is much more to science and knowledge than projection, the elucidation of the practice of projection cannot be carried out apart from a consideration of the theories and the practices, and the philosophy of these theories and practices, scientific and otherwise, in which projection is carried on and has its effects.[13]

11 *Collected Papers*, 1.92; 6.98–100.

12 H. Feigl, "De Principiis Non Disputandum. . . ?" in M. Black, ed., *Philosophical Analysis*, p. 134.

13 The fact that paradoxes of projection can be precipitated in a striking way by the introduction of predicates designed for the purpose should not be permitted to obscure the rich possibilities of paradox constantly present in very natural, common-sense predicates. In their discussion of the difficulties of "tide watching," in comparison with "ripple watching" in the study of elections, R. M. Scammon and B. J. Wattenberg illustrate the point in a very direct and concrete way. On election day, November 5, 1968, in support of the prevailing view that America had been living through a Democratic era, begun with the election of Franklin Roosevelt in 1932 and continued

19. In the various domains of human life our ways of thinking and acting are given form and guidance by complexes of habits, rules, and principles that form what has been referred to as the constitution of the domain of life in question. In the political domain from which the analogy is drawn, in the conduct of the government of the United States, for example, legislation is enacted and enforced, disputes about action according to law are brought to trial and adjudicated, and public affairs are administered by and large according to agreed-upon provisions in the Constitution, and according to practices and regulations for the establishment of which the Constitution provides. Of course in the conduct of normal affairs, political or scientific, things are not as routine as this description may suggest. The difference between the routine and the anomalous is always a matter of degree. Routine decisions always have an aspect of anomie, an aspect that is exaggerated in neurotic behavior, while the extraordinary original decisions always partake to some extent of the settled and principled, otherwise they cannot count as decisions, or even as human acts. In his own way the most subordinate clerk contributes his mite to both the maintenance and the construction of the constitution of the institution in which he serves. On the other hand, he and his fellows are always the repositories of a great amount of social inertia that limits severely the amount of change the minister, the holder of the secretarial portfolio, the dictator, the revolutionary party, can effect. The innovative ambitions of these personages are always limited by what may seem to them to be *la trahison des clercs*.

20. While for many philosophical purposes it is important to delineate in detail the nature of what here has been described as serving as a constitution for human thought and action in the

---

through the Johnson landslide of 1964, was the fact that the Democrats had won the presidency in six of the last eight elections, and that the two losses were to the extremely popular war hero, Dwight Eisenhower. But next morning, November 6, the following were also true: (1) Three of the last five elections were won by Republicans; (2) the Democratic presidential candidate had received a majority of the popular vote only once in the last six elections; and (3) the total sums of Democratic and of Republican votes cast for President since World War II was just about even (roughly in millions, 186 to 185). (*The Real Majority*, pp. 25–26).

various institutions of human life, including the institutions of human knowledge, what is here important is to recognize the existence of the entities so far identified and their essential function in the guidance of our cognitive activities. The existence of such entities and their controlling function in the development of knowledge have been recognized by many widely divergent figures in the history of philosophy, among whom there has been a corresponding divergence of emphasis upon features of their character. In his Theory of Forms, Plato, like Kant in his teaching about the Categories of Understanding and the Ideas of Reason, emphasized features of the institution that seem to be determined for us by our nature as cognitive beings. In his own reaction to the repulses of Cartesian philosophy which in much of his own writing about knowledge is both exemplified and celebrated, Hume emphasized the role in the guidance of custom or habit in the development of something called "belief," the necessary but illegitimate pretender to the throne of knowledge that his own criticism had declared vacant. When the inflammatory and pejorative overtones of the language conveying his insights on this matter are disregarded, Hume may be fairly construed as recognizing and emphasizing a somewhat different aspect of the constitutional features of human knowledge, an aspect that he consistently and valuably emphasized also in his ethical and political writings, and in his work as a historian. This aspect, the cumulative effect of life, experience, and achievement, is likewise emphasized in the history of science by Kuhn in his portrayal of the controlling effect of paradigm achievements in the guidance of research in "normal science." It is an aspect that was likewise emphasized in the theory of knowledge of Dewey, whose liberal hopes for the achievement of human intelligence naturally led to an overemphasis upon the extent to which the constitution of inquiry at any time is the consequence of past cognitive achievement. That effect nevertheless is real, and Dewey was justified in assigning to it the fundamental importance he does in saying that

attained knowledge produces *meanings* and . . . these meanings are capable of being separated from the special cases of knowledge in which they originally appear and of being incorporated and funded cumulatively in habits so as to constitute *mind,* and to constitute *intelligence* when actually applied in new experiences. . . .[14]

This recognition of the effect of "attained knowledge," the deposit of preceding inquiry, in the determination of mind or intelligence is compatible with a recognition, also sometimes clear in Dewey's writing, though not so much emphasized, of the wider effect of human experience, life, and custom. As he wrote, speaking of his own philosophical development,

Hegel's idea of cultural institutions as "objective mind" upon which individuals were dependent in the formation of their mental life fell in with the influence of Comte and of Condorcet and Bacon. The metaphysical idea that an absolute mind is manifested in social institutions dropped out; the idea, upon an empirical basis, of the power exercised by cultural environment in shaping the ideas, beliefs, and intellectual attitudes of individuals remained.[15]

To the effect of the "cultural environment" in shaping the minds of individuals must be added, in rounding out a picture of the constitutional aspects of human knowledge, the effect of the noncultural, the physical environment, which, during millions of years before there was man and human culture, nevertheless was having its own cumulative effect in producing men, with their physical features and capacities to respond. For in producing man, as he is, with these features and capacities, the material world exerted in its own way, and in an essential way, an effect upon the constitution of human intelligence, and with it of human knowledge.

21. By virtue of being born and brought up in human society, each human being is inculcated with a variety of constitutions which, in the social group or groups in which he is acculturated, control a variety of more or less settled, institutionalized activities. And when he is trained for an occupation or profession in a civilized society in which such activities have been brought to a high state of development, this constitutional indoctrination is extended in most important ways. This holds for the scientist

14 "Experience, Knowledge and Value: A Rejoinder," in *The Philosophy of John Dewey*, P. A. Schilpp, ed., p. 564.
15 Jane M. Dewey, ed., "Biography of John Dewey," in *The Philosophy of John Dewey*, p. 17.

and the historian, the lawyer and the physician, for the mechanic and the farmer. That each knows how to proceed, by and large, in normal situations, knows what to do and how to go about doing it, is what is implied in saying that each knows his craft. In the conduct of his affairs, in doing his job, all sorts of questions arise which the constitution of that kind of work does not provide ready answers to. It does not tell the farmer what to plant or when to plant it, or what medicine to give the ailing calf. It does provide a framework of presumption about the procedure for answering such questions, when and if they arise. In science the kind of regular, orthodox inquiry that is carried out in accordance with the more or less implicit constitutional regulations, the kind that is concerned to answer questions that arise within paradigms rather than questions about the suitability of the paradigms themselves, is characterized by Kuhn as "puzzle-solving."

Questions of this sort are not to any considerable extent philosophical; they do not in any considerable way pose constitutional issues, issues of broad principle concerning how to think and act. But when one views the conduct of human affairs, including that of securing knowledge, in this way, one puts enormous weight upon the accepted principles, and with it upon settled practices and traditional lore transmitted from generation to generation, from teacher to student, from master to apprentice, from leader to follower, and even upon elements in our make-up determinative of our ways of proceeding, the result of extended teaching of living creatures by Mother Nature, which are now a part of our biological inheritance. It is by virtue of all these things that we know, when we know; but of all of them the most important for the kind of questions about philosophy and justification that have been treated here are the broad questions about principles of thought and action in the various cognitive institutions in which we participate that may be characterized as constitutional. If we suppose ourselves, as creatures engaged in the attainment of knowledge, to be guided by broad principles with which we are endowed, indeed indoctrinated, both by precept and practice by our fellowmen in making—with, to be sure, widely varying degrees of success—civilized human beings out of us; if we suppose that normally it is by means of these principles that we know how to proceed in answering questions to which we, as knowers, are called upon to respond; then, by this philosophical emphasis upon the importance of such constitutions in guiding our thought and action, we precipitate the question of how then do we think and act about the constitutions themselves.

22. A judgment on the necessity of revolution as a means of installing a new constitution is at the same time a judgment on the efficacy of other possible means. Of course, if the definition of a revolution in any institution is large-scale constitutional change, then that such change requires revolution becomes incontestable, but also deceptively uninformative. The question of substance is that of how constitutional change may be brought about: whether, if the constitution itself dictates the primary principles of thought and action, the supposition that one constitution may give place to another by constitutional means is not a basically inconsistent one, deserving all the disdain with which Hobbes would have treated it.

From the time of Parmenides there have been philosophers capable of pointing out certain inconsistencies in what we easily suppose takes place under the broad title of change. How can Constitution *A* change, become Constitution *B*, remain *A* and yet become *B*, become what it is not? "E pur si muove." In the case of those political institutions whose anatomy and physiology are definitely prescribed by written and ratified provisions, constitutional change by constitutional means is normally one of the provisions; and this includes change even in the provisions *for* change. But as the American experience and the experience of other institutions with less definite and formal constitutional regulations illustrate, constitutional change is not restricted to such means. On matters of this kind the loose and untidy views of Locke were more realistic than these of the strict and tidy Hobbes.

23. Just as promises and a dominating sovereign to enforce them do not create a community out of what, till then, have been totally alien individuals, each sovereign to himself, so, without a basis of fundamental agreement in ways of thinking and

acting, little can be effected by the draft of constitutional regulations, however skillfully this drafting may be carried out, whether these regulations are for individuals or for nations. In the domain of politics the fact that explicit constitutional regulations do not so much create agreement—though they certainly do this to some extent—as formalize and ratify it, is of great significance, as is also the fact that the basic agreements in thought and action that find their expression in this way are constantly undergoing some change. This change, as we are all much aware in the case of the Constitution of the United States, has its effects upon the Constitution; and it is one of the functions performed by the Supreme Court, the supreme agency for interpreting the law in the United States, to discern and help make plain these effects and their complex implications. These elementary facts about constitutions, viz., their social basis and their consequent disposition to change, are of great significance in other domains of life, including that of our cognitive institutions. One reason why revolutions—periods in which changes are effected in constitutions rapidly and with considerable intellectual violence—are not more frequent is that constitutional changes are constantly being effected at a more moderate pace, which often suffices. One reason why such revolutionary periods, and such violence, appear to some to be necessary for effecting any consequential constitutional change is surely that they underestimate the significance and cumulative effect of the changes that are constantly being effected in constitutions in the normal course of events, in their normal employment. Creeping mechanism, creeping behaviorism, or creeping Keynesianism in cognitive institutions may be as real, and significant, as creeping socialism or clericalism in political ones. The young snakes in the garden shed their skins entirely to grow new ones to accommodate the changes in size that the old coverings will not accommodate, and the young crabs in the bay do the same with their shells, their very skeletons. Other growing animals, including human beings, change their coverings or coats in a much less wholesale and dramatic fashion.

24. The effect upon some philosophers of views like those advanced here, emphasizing the determinative power of cognitive

constitutions upon our ways of thinking and acting, is to produce in them a feeling of intellectual claustrophobia. Caught always in the web of some constitution or other, able to think only in the ways made possible by that constitution, such a person feels condemned to some kind of relativism or subjectivism, some inescapable lack of objectivity, in what he takes to be knowledge or reasonable belief, assurance, commitment and the rest.[16] If the constitution itself dictates what is reasonable in the assessment of knowledge claims, will it not follow that reasonable assessment of constitutional provisions, reasonable proposals for constitutional change are out of the question, so that "in the last analysis"—whenever that is—one is never able to give any reasonable defense for the view he takes upon such a matter when it is challenged by someone who takes another? The doctrine that relativism and subjectivism are the inescapable fates awaiting a philosophy of knowledge which insists upon the recognition of the role of the cognitive constitution in the generation and validation of knowledge claims seems to derive much of its plausibility from the same sources as a doctrine to which it is superficially opposed, namely, the doctrine that substantial changes in such constitutions require revolutionary means. Both doctrines tend to exaggerate both the fixity and the monolithic, totalitarian character of the constitutions in question, as if, on the one hand, cognitive constitutions, once established and ratified, were not subject in use to fundamental changes, however glacial may be their speed; and as if, on the other, in the sciences, as in cognitive life generally, our life were guided by one dominant set of regulations, an intellectual imperium that exerts such effective thought control in all areas that changes in the regulations must come from without.

25. A choice between paradigms, which are surely important features of constitutional control and change, is, as Kuhn observes, "like a choice between competing political institutions,

16 An example of this philosophical reaction is neatly captured by I. Scheffler in considering the appeal to observation, as a correction to subjectivity in science, and the "paradox of categorization," as he calls it, to which this appeal seems to lead: "If my categories of thought determine what I observe, then what I observe provides no independent control over my thought" (*Science and Subjectivity*, p. 13).

. . . a choice between incompatible modes of community life." [17] These latter choices are of course made in a great variety of ways, and with a great variety of degrees of significance. Not all political choices are as fateful as that between Comrade Breshnev and Prime Minister Heath, nor all philosophical choices like that which faced the young Leibniz, not yet fifteen years of age, walking in the woods of the Rosenthal, pondering the choice between Aristotle or Democritus.[18] For nearly three centuries the political constitution of the British monarchy has been undergoing change, sometimes change of a most fundamental sort, yet change that can be construed as being change in, as well as change of, that constitution. And with one notable exception, the same may be said of the Constitution of the American republic during the nearly two centuries of its career. In his reasoning on the political analogy, Kuhn remarks that "As in political revolutions, so in paradigm choice—there is no standard higher than the assent of the relevant community." [19] But in political communities, scientific communities, cognitive communities generally, the flavor of assent is always more or less highly seasoned with the spices of dissent. There are always in any civilized community, despite great variation in this regard from time to time, place to place, tradition to tradition, contrary tendencies and contrary parties arrayed behind these tendencies in development. A neglect of the omnipresent possibilities of criticism, evaluation, and change already thus resident within the constitutional agreement leads easily, from one point of view, to the supposition that this agreement can act only as a bond, inhibiting, never generating, change (as if friction could only retard, never make motion possible), and that thus individuals and groups operating under such a constitution are by that fact somehow bereft of any means of making a nonpartisan, fair, objective appraisal of any feature of that constitution. From another point of view the neglect leads to an exaggeration of the difference, and an unrealistic

17 *The Structure of Scientific Revolutions*, p. 93.

18 "Je n'avais pas encore 15 ans que je me promenais des journées entières dans un bois pour prendre parti entre Aristote et Démocrite" (Letter of May 8 [18], 1697, quoted by Friedrich Ueberweg, *History of Philosophy* [1909], Vol. II, p. 102).

19 Kuhn, *Structure*, p. 93.

sharpness in the distinction drawn between, questions decidable within the confines of the constitution, questions for which "logic and experiment" suffice, and constitutional questions, ones for which, in addition to these, there is a necessary appeal to the "techniques of persuasion," the effect of which is bolstered by the slow but sure effect of Nature practicing her own form of euthanasia upon those too old or inflexible of mind to make the "conversion" that adoption of a fundamentally different constitution seems to require.[20]

26. The doctrine of the necessary effect, implicit or explicit, of constitutional agreement in the assessment of knowledge claims is one of great illuminating power. It is hard to overestimate the extent of this effect, but easy to misjudge the consequences of that effect both for the objectivity of knowledge claims made according to the constitution and for the possibilities of constitutional change. One is easily dazzled and misled by the extent of the effect, and the manifold changes which its recognition obviously requires in what in the past half-century has been the orthodoxy in theory of knowledge and philosophy of science, and in the relatively naive views concerning objectivity and the development of knowledge which those views represented. Giving up the simple view of objectivity as what is seen with an "innocent eye" or logically construed by a naked mind, or calculus, and the view of the growth of knowledge as exclusively accumulation, is not giving up either objectivity or growth. But it may easily seem so. The force of the new views may easily lead one to think that, to the extent that he is necessarily tractable to the constitutional system, he is also the necessarily, the irremediably misled victim of any weakness, imperfections, distortions, lacunae that our experience tells us such a system must be expected to have, and that any considerable release from the bondage of this system must be accomplished by a forceful destruction and repudiation of it and a translation to another system, a higher, improved system it is hoped, but one, alas, with a bondage of its own. Persuasive as these views may be, the arguments for the necessary bondage are no better, and no worse than the Hobbesian arguments that there can be no legal constraint upon the

[20] Cf. Kuhn, *Structure*, pp. 92–93, 147–51.

sovereign, since he is the source of all legality. And to the extent that the necessary bondage is fictitious, the necessity of the unconstitutional means advanced for securing periodic release from that bondage, and hence for securing fundamental constitutional reform, is likewise fictitious. The means are not fictitious, and the doctrine that they are sometimes employed and are of extreme importance is not fictitious; nor is the view that in certain conditions they are required. But it is a mistake to suppose that in every case of substantial constitutional change, by virtue of the fact that it is such change, means of this character are required.

27. But just as it is a mistake to suppose that such means are always required, so it would be a mistake to suppose that they are never. For in the practice of knowledge, in the conduct of affairs in the various domains of the knowledge institution, and in the philosophical scrutiny of these domains, constitutional problems constantly arise, or are uncovered. Constantly our ways of thinking and acting in the various domains of knowledge are subject to change and development, both internally as a result of inquiries within a certain domain, and externally as a result of changes and developments in other domains of inquiry, and in the conduct of life. And there is apparently no unseen hand that can be depended upon to ensure that only those incipient developments which represent improvements will in the end prevail.

More important for present purposes is the fact that some of the constitutional problems that arise in these ways are acute and baffling in an extreme degree. They represent fundamental dissidences, cleavages, contrarieties in the development of the constitution and of the practices of thought and action of which it is literally constitutive. Just as in disputes between nations, and between factions within nations, there is no guarantee that for every dispute there is a possible peaceful settlement, so in the case of constitutional problems in the institution of knowledge, there is no guarantee that for every constitutional dispute there is a means of adjudication capable of bringing the dispute to some kind of rational settlement. The name which has been traditionally given to that part of the domain of the knowledge institution to which problems in this adjudication have been assigned as a primary concern, has been of course, "philosophy."

This is not to say that these problems are the only concern of philosophy, nor that they are the concern of philosophers only. Nor is it to imply that it is the function of philosophers to judge and settle such disputes, in the fashion of the arbiter in a labor dispute. In his role in promoting a rational settlement of disputes within the institution of knowledge the philosopher acts less as a judge and more as a constitutional lawyer. An expert in the particular constitution the development of which is in dispute, he is no more called on than his legal counterpart, to advance his personal preferences, disguised by persuasive definitions, as dictates of constitutional law. Supposing that there is a rational, objective answer to many questions arising in this area, he seeks to help his fellowmen find them. This he may do by preparing detailed briefs in support of one party in the dispute when his philosophical judgment is that in that particular dispute this one party is clearly or predominantly in the right. Or, more typically, he may try to devise a solution that will set the dispute in a new light and enable the just claims of each of the rival parties to the dispute to be maintained and composed. A response of the first kind is illustrated in Hobbes's spirited advocacy, in his metaphysics, of the claims of the new mechanical philosophy. Descartes's response to the same concerns was more of the second kind, as were also those of Spinoza and Leibniz. A similar contrast, in issues in the theory of knowledge, is that between the strong defense of empiricist principles advanced by Hume in the *Treatise* and first *Enquiry,* and the proposed resolution of the apparent issue of experience versus reason that was advanced in the *Critique of Pure Reason.* The outbreak of war between nations is commonly regarded as marking a failure of diplomacy, though viewed purely as a matter of means and ends, it sometimes marks success, since peace was not the end which the means were intended to achieve. Similarly the role of philosophical enterprise in the resolution of constitutional disputes in the institution of human knowledge is to promote and if possible assist in the achievement of rational solutions, ones that can be defended as proper by fair, objective means. There is no reason to assume that in the case of every dispute such solutions are possible. The philosophical enterprise is based on the assumption that they are eminently desirable.

The Judiciability of
Constitutional Issues

1. But the question persists of what, in circumstances of great constitutional dispute, a rational decision, defensible by fair, objective means, can be. If what is rational, fair, objective, not partisan, and so on, is defined by the constitution, how can one manage to be reasonable, fair, objective when it is the constitution itself that is in question? What could "fair," "reasonable," "objective" in such cases possibly mean?

Kuhn has vividly painted the picture of the severity of the problem of communication, argument, and decision that besets partisans trying to make a case for rival scientific paradigms. Some degree of severity in the problem is a mark generally of dispute over substantial constitutional issues. The defenders of classical physics tended to react to the challenge of quantum theory just as one would expect if Kant's doctrine of the categories were right. Since the category of causation, conceived along the lines of classical mechanics, was constitutive of science, how could there be science that was not classical in this respect; and how indeed particles which could not be thought of as having determinate position and velocity? About the same time as these matters were being disputed in one wing of the scientific edifice, in another wing the defenders of what had already become orthodoxy in the new science of psychology were fending off the baffling and seemingly wrong-headed attacks of the gestalt theorists who seemed to be advocating a science of mind bereft of fundamental analytic principles, the Freudians who perplexingly wanted to combine the notion of mind with that of the unconscious, and the behaviorists whose iconoclasm extended as far as the notion of mind itself. Skipping rapidly over two generations, one now finds in the social sciences the barely achieved orthodoxy of behavioral science challenged by a movement that sees this orthodoxy not as liberative, as Comte might have thought, but as repressive as Marx would have judged it, considering its severe abstention from questions of value and policy to mean the relinquishing of decisions about such matters to repressive elements in society who were little disturbed by such "scientific" qualms. The list of instances can easily be extended with examples from the historical, the social, the biological, the physical, and the mathematical sciences. What does it mean to be reasonable about issues of such magnitude? Or in *Kulturkämpfe* is not reason necessarily one of the first casualties? Freud, trained as a physician, with a specialty in diseases of the nervous system, considered the theory of neuroses, with its broader implications about mental life, to represent the application of scientific method, guided strictly by the principle of determinism, to a certain field of phenomena. Such a claim to the mantle of scientist in this field is strictly rejected by others who pursue a behavioral study of mental disorder, confident that their approach, rather than the appeal to the highly speculative entities appealed to by Freud, is more on the path that the constitution of scientific practice dictates for the study of such subjects. Similarly, in 1861, the partisans of both the Confederacy and the Union in the threatening dissolution of the United States appealed to the Constitution to argue the justice of their respective causes. The Confederates and their sympathizers argued that succession was a right inherent in individual states by virtue of the federal system, and that they were driven to the exercise of this right by the unconstitutional tyranny practiced increasingly by the central government over the preceding decades. Unionists denied both the right and the tyranny, urging further, as did Lincoln progressively in the conduct of the war, that the Constitution represented a deep commitment to certain ideals which had to be considered in construing the rights and duties of citizens under the Constitution, and the rights of states in respect to the central government, including the right to tolerate and preserve slavery. A similarly fundamental, though not so disruptive dispute was generated in the tradition of American liberal thought by the actions and political legacies of President Franklin D. Roosevelt. Roosevelt, acting in the name of liberalism, advanced a program of government activity which subjected the economic activities of individuals and corporations to much greater regulation than had been traditional. This program was vigorously opposed both by elements in the opposition party and elements in his own party as well who argued that economic liberties could only be so severely abridged at the expense of a severe threat to political liberty as well. In appraising this program, writers like Arthur Schlesinger, Jr., and John K. Galbraith would argue that the program in question was fundamentally a sound one, that it represented much better the essentials of liberal philosophy in modern industrial society than the New Liberalism of President Woodrow Wilson, or the philosophy of Justice Louis D. Brandeis. This judgment would be disputed by exponents of what may be called "classical" (to its opponents "fossilized") liberalism, both here and abroad, including among the latter such eminent writers as Friedrich A. Hayek and Karl R. Popper.[1]

2. Not all constitutional problems are of this magnitude, in the political as well as the cognitive institutions. But it is these whose consideration is most important here, since it is with them that the threat of philosophical subjectivism and relativism is greatest, and the feeling of philosophical claustrophobia most realistically entertained. Problems of this magnitude are encountered more freqeuntly in progressive—or at least changing—societies and institutions; disputes over them are a common

1 Cf. the following illuminating comment on Marx's labor theory of value by G. H. Sabine, *A History of Political Theory*, 2nd rev. ed., p. 789: "In spite of Marx's disclaimer of any moral presuppositions, his argument is more powerful when it is regarded as ethical than when it is taken as purely economic. It really sought to accomplish two purposes: first to bring to light the ethical bias implied in the bourgeois defense of a competitive economy and to show that this bias is incompatible with the moral professions of individualist liberalism, and second, to pose the question of the nature of social justice in a highly organized society where individualism has ceased to be a tenable moral position."

occasion for philosophical scrutiny. Embarking upon scrutiny in areas of such deep concern and baffling controversy in the institution of human knowledge, one is offered by the Cartesian program a decision procedure of startling simplicity. Somehow all the issues can be resolved, the proper decisions made, by a recursive procedure that will trace all putative claims back to first cognitions, that will accept as claims only those that can be validated as first cognitions or as the product of the same kind of apprehensions of which the first cognitions consist. The simplicity of the proposed procedure might be attractive, if there were any reason to suppose that it could be made to work in such a way as to lead to a plausible result. But it is hard to view a method as a promising way of dealing with difficult problems in the understanding of subatomic particles, or claims made about the supernatural, if after centuries of trial it has been unable to give a remotely plausible answer to the question whether there are dogs and cats. It is hard to be confident of the capacity of a method to yield an acceptable answer to the question of the reality of unconscious mind which after much effort has yet to be shown capable of yielding a plausible answer to the question whether there is or ever has been in the universe any mind except one's own. But Cartesian theory is not so much a theory that fails as a means for solving constitutional problems as one that ignores these problems. Its striking simplicity is a sign of the fact that it was not designed to solve them. The presumption of the theory was that there were in reality no such problems to solve; or at least there would be none, once the philosophical approach to knowledge had been purified of the gratuitous errors of tradition and superstition, and reliance put solely upon clear and distinct perceptions of the mind, whether these were taken to be the intuitive apprehensions of sense or those of the understanding. The requirement that the development of knowledge shall proceed always by means of such sure, indefeasible steps was designed to free those engaged in this enterprise from the need to make constitutional choices, by excluding the possibility of constitutional change. The sure intuitions of unclouded reason and sense were at the same time intuitions sufficient for all constitutional direction. For Descartes, for example, all this had been settled for us by God when he endowed us with the natural light and the incipient ideas with which, once these ideas had been stimulated by sense and suitably refined, and so long as the impetuous will could be kept tractable, we could proceed upon a journey of truth in which no missteps could be made, nor any path, once traversed, need to be resurveyed or altered.

3. As was observed before, recognition of the importance of the constitutional aspects of thought and action in the knowledge institution generally, and in the various subinstitutions and practices that collectively make up this institution, entails a recognition of the importance of constitutional questions and problems. Essential to an appropriate response to these questions and problems is an appreciation of their constitutional character, their character as questions and problems about what is, or should be, constitutional procedure, rather than ones that can be dealt with in a fairly routine, agreed-upon way by an appeal to constitutional provisions themselves. One who has an appreciation of this character need not have progressed very far in understanding the way these questions and problems are to be dealt with, but he knows in general in what direction to face, in what directions not to look for answers and solutions.

Questions of the kind just referred to may be called "extrainstitutional" or "extraconstitutional." They are "extra-" or external in the sense that, and to the degree that, answers to them require an appeal to considerations beyond the institution or constitution itself. The importance of drawing a distinction between external and internal questions arising in the conduct of affairs of an institution is not diminished by the fact that a sharp line cannot be drawn between the two kinds of question, that the difference between them is one of degree, albeit sometimes of extreme degree. A question that is routine to the extent that its extrainstitutional implications and dependencies are negligible may for most purposes be treated as intrainstitutional *simpliciter*. The foundations of arithmetic need not be referred to in adding up the bill at the food store. The calculator in the cash register is an embodiment of the institution; the man who designs calculators can and sometimes does investigate features of institutional practice that he is building into the gears and circuitry of the machines he is engaged in producing.

In the lives of all of us the first questions we learn to answer are intrainstitutional ones, as are similarly the ones which predominantly engage most of us, both in our education and in our occupational pursuits. A natural consequence of this is that we have both a natural grasp of such questions and a natural inclination to view any question that arises as being of this kind. Like a devout believer brought up to believe that God in His prevision has provided in revelation all the answers to the questions we need to answer, we are inclined to suppose that somewhere in the institution, if we just look in the right places and construe properly what we find, we shall have the answers to questions, the solution to problems, that at first view seem to baffle institutional practice, to transcend institutional resource. And of course commonly we are right. As we learned early in solving difficult problems assigned to us in mathematical instruction, and as the teacher again and again demonstrated, the fault in our bafflement lies commonly not in the poverty of the resources of the institution, but in our lack of ingenuity in exploiting what is already there. But this is not necessarily nor always the case in mathematics, as the history of the subject amply shows as it is not in other institutions, cognitive and otherwise. Even in so flexible an embodiment of the religious institution as the Roman Catholic Church, with its doctrine of revelation through Tradition supplementing Holy Scripture, there are times in which the bringing to collective consciousness of an item of revelation involves great institutional stress and transformation. There are times in the lives of all enduring institutions such as that of religion, and knowledge and science, when, to speak in an exaggeratedly simple way, rules, regulations, and recipes do fail. It is important, then, for the rational conduct of affairs to recognize the failure for what it is. And it is important also to keep in mind that in such circumstances the persistent search for rules, regulations, and recipes, together with the superstition that they must exist somewhere in the institution, by diverting the search for answers to questions from where they may be found to where they may not, is a positive hindrance in that search.

4. The distinction between internal and external questions is relevant to the topic of truth. It appears that some of the issues debated in the exploration of this topic would be illuminated if more recognition were given to the kinds of differences in our cognitive activities that are represented in a rough way in this distinction.

The elementary contention that the truth of a statement, proposition, or judgment lies somehow in its conformity with its object is not contestable. Disagreement begins, as William James observed in his essay "Pragmatism's Conception of Truth," when we consider how to go on from there.[2] The dictum that the statement that the cat is on the mat is true, if and only if the cat is on the mat, does not take one very far, but it is a good beginning. What is commonly debated under the title of the "correspondence theory of truth" is a doctrine that extends far beyond this elementary insight and implicates in the end a whole view of knowledge, a view not only of what truth consists in but how true statements are ascertained to be so in the knowledge process. Implicit in this doctrine, or at least in the common versions of it, is a supposition that there is a phase of the knowledge process in which the determination of the truth of statements is made by means of a nonstatemental apprehension of objects, states, or states of affairs, be they appearance or reality. In this phase things of some sort are known to us, and the truth about them made evident, because they visit our minds, our perception, rational or sensuous, and as direct visitants provide us with standards or archetypes by which the conformities of statements with objects may be judged.

Some of the attraction this epistemological model has for many of us is apparently due to a preoccupation with internal questions and an inclination to assimilate all others to this form. Whether the cat is on the mat, whether he did eat the canary, whether the bird-feeder is now empty, are questions that can be

2 *Pragmatism*, p. 198.

answered in a highly routine way. They are internal questions in an extreme degree, questions which can be so easily answered by looking that whatever of the institution that is implicated in telling-by-looking becomes invisible through familiarity, has become second nature, generating the thought that all that verification requires in such cases is the recognition on the part of the mind of the visitations to it by some entities.

5. Under the spell of such a metaphor we are disposed to neglect some of the illuminating associations that truth has with other characters that we commonly ascribe to our statements, views, judgments, and so on. In his essay on *Truth* Austin called attention to some of the "numerous other adjectives which," he said,

> are in the same class as "true" and "false," which are concerned, that is, with the relations between the words (as uttered with reference to an historical situation) and the world. . . . We say, for example, that a certain statement is exaggerated or vague or bold, a description somewhat rough or misleading or not very good, an account rather general or too concise. In cases like these it is pointless to insist on deciding in simple terms whether the statement is "true or false." Is it true or false that Belfast is North of London? That the galaxy is the shape of a fried egg? That Beethoven was a drunkard? That Wellington won the battle of Waterloo? These are various *degrees and dimensions* of success in making statements: the statements fit the facts always more or less loosely, in different ways on different occasions for different intents and purposes.[3]

Austin thought correctly, not only that our preoccupation with but one set of these words was philosophically narrow, but also that the restriction of scope of study greatly increased, rather than decreased, the difficulties of philosophical analysis.

We become obsessed with "truth" when discussing statements, just as we become obsessed with "freedom" when discussing conduct. So long as we think that what has always and alone to be decided is whether a certain action was done freely or was not, we get nowhere: but so soon as we turn instead to numerous other adverbs used in the same connexion ("accidentally," "unwillingly," "inadvertently," &c.), things become easier, and we come to see that no concluding inference of the form "Ergo, it was done freely (or not freely)" is required. Like free-

[3] *Aristotelian Society Supplementary Volume XXIV* (1950), Sect. 5 (italics in orig.). Reprinted in *Philosophical Papers*.

dom, truth is a bare minimum or an illusory ideal (the truth, the whole truth and nothing but the truth about, say, the battle of Waterloo or the *Primavera*).[4]

6. Ascriptions of truth or falsity are thus one among many ways by which we characterize the relations between what we say, when the force of our utterance is to identify or specify some feature of our world, and the feature, however minute or grand, which is the object of the identification or specification. "That truth is a matter of the relation between words and the world," Austin said, is a "trite but central point" which coherence and pragmatist theories of truth failed to appreciate.[5] What advocates of these theories, however, did appreciate more than their opponents, and what they can help us to appreciate, without losing sight of the "trite but central point," is that the ways in which words, statements, thoughts, and practices incorporating these, relate to the world and make their identifications and specifications of features in it, are both fantastically complex and varied. The truth of the statement that the cat is on the mat is determined by the position of the cat with reference to the mat, whatever this may be; and something similar may be said, if it is useful, about the theory of the double-helical structure of the DNA molecule. But one must not be misled by this similarity between the homely statement and the scientific theory into supposing that both of these claims, thoughts, utterances, in their aspect as true, correspond with the facts they represent in exactly the same manner. James, for example, emphasized this aspect of truth, and surely at the expense of others. "To agree in the widest sense with reality," he said, "can only mean to be guided either straight up to it or into its surroundings, or to be put into such working touch with it as to handle either it or something connected with it better than if we disagreed." [6] From an appreciation of this aspect of the matter James proceeded to the conclusion, for which he promptly received much due remonstrance and correction, that " 'The true' . . . is only the expedient in the way of our thinking, just as 'the right' is only the expedient in the way of our behaving." [7]

4 *Ibid.*   5 *Ibid.*, n. 24.   6 *Pragmatism*, p. 212.
7 *Pragmatism*, p. 222.

7. Of course truth is not "only the expedient in the way of thinking." This incautious doctrine was too great a price to pay for a release from what James regarded as intellectual narrowness in traditional and opposed views. After following James's elaboration of what he regarded as an improved liberal view, one begins to have some greater appreciation of some of the very restrictions against which James struggled. But on one point we can surely learn from his reaction and struggle. The distinction between internal and external questions is a first step toward recognizing the constitutional aspects of thought and action in the refinement and development of human knowledge, and this in turn leads to a recognition of the possibility of varieties, and of change, in constitutions. The Kantian effort to demonstrate that there is but one such valid constitution for scientific knowledge, and that this was forever fixed by transcendental necessities in the knowing process, now seems to have been mistaken. If it was; if, on the contrary, just as there is more to physics than is dreamed of in Newtonian mechanics, and more to science than physics, and more to knowledge than science, then the philosophical scrutiny of knowledge needs to face, for it can learn much from, the possibility that there are very substantial differences in constitutions of the various subinstitutions that make up the collective institution of human knowledge. That there are these differences, and that it is right that there are, are both instructive. These differences need not be regarded as contrarieties, unless one supposes that all institutions in the collective must in constitution be exactly alike, a supposition that is about as reasonable as the supposition that in its constitutional features the government of Cook County, Illinois, embracing Chicago, must be the duplicate of that of Hinsdale County, Colorado, which recently reported a permanent population of two hundred and eight inhabitants.

As it is a mistake to suppose that truth is "only the expedient in the way of thinking," so it is a mistake, the shade of Oscar Wilde, turned philosopher, might tell us, to suppose that truth is *only*, or *simply*, anything, whether that be expedience in thought, rational coherence in judgment, or correspondence with fact. Too many philosophers have derived too much righteous satisfaction out of this last phrase, a kind of satisfaction that has tended to make the end of inquiry into the matter out of what is only a beginning. Truth is by no means all that one seeks in investigation, nor is it always what one prizes most, any more than is accuracy, penetration, or the cautious avoidance of error. It is one of the things that one prizes, though in varying degrees (compare cosmology or archeology with chronology), in highly disciplined investigations in the sciences, the humanities, and in certain domains of practical affairs. Prized under the title of fidelity to fact, to the objects of question or inquiry, is an intellectual grasp of these objects that is secure, though not because the beliefs, assumptions, and so on, embodying this grasp are adhered to by what Peirce called the "method of tenacity," but rather because they enduringly provide intellectual and, where appropriate, practical mastery of the object that is progressive, cumulative, and combines with these a minimum chance, so far as such matters can be foreseen, of future reversal.

8. But more important than these generalities, for the purposes here, are certain particularities. While these general qualities in our answers are sought in the search for truth, they are sought in vastly different ways in different constitutional domains because the grasp or mastery of objects sought in them is different; the variations of essentially interrelated ways in which we engage in knowledge with the world are expressed in, and in important ways determined by, constitutional provisions in the various branches of the collective knowledge institution. In internal questions the manner of engagement is in major respects settled, and consequently the determination of truth in the operations of verification is rendered a fairly definite decision process. The net of language and thought is in them closely textured with respect to the quarries sought, and a reflection of this determinacy is that procedures are designed and employed in a way that in abstract logic is called the "law of excluded middle." In external questions the character of the net is itself more undecided, and the quarry consequently less determinant. While the fishing is going on, the practice itself is liable to considerable revision. The quarries may be altered, and in consequence of these two alterations the character of the net under-

goes great change as well. In contrast with internal ones, external questions are definitely not ones yielding table-thumping answers. It is pure superstition, an egregious idol of the theatre, to suppose that because we have a common comfortable way of referring to a certain character of the answers we seek in all the various and more or less alterable domains—that because in all of them in a persistent way we are eager to achieve something we call correspondence with reality, fidelity to fact—therefore we have a clear idea of what actually in the actual operations in the knowledge institution, in specific cases, this correspondence or fidelity consists in, or how it is achieved. One of the lessons Wittgenstein seems to have succeeded in teaching philosophers of our day is that words like "same" can easily be intellectually inflated and illusory. "Do the same as I" is never, entirely by itself, a sufficient indication of what I am instructing you to do. A similiar lesson needs to be learned now, just as much as when James wrote, concerning some of the beguiling phrases that frequent discussions of truth. When one says that the cat is on the mat, or that the chemical atoms in the DNA molecule are arrayed in a double-helical structure, one may indeed in both cases be saying something that conforms to the facts, to the realities in the case. But how in each case our utterance and thought reach out and lay hold on these realities, and what this conformity consists in, both in the case of the cat and the theory with all those intervening X-rays, genetic experiments, calculations, and physical models, remains an untold story. Austin said of truth that it is "a bare minimum or an illusory ideal." Whether this is so or not, the idea of correspondence, in the philosophical account of truth, does seem to approximate the value of a bare minimum, needing to be filled in and expanded enormously and in varied ways before we understand better what truth is and what role the pursuit of it plays and ought to play in the conduct of affairs in the various theatres of the knowledge institution. In the debates between the advocates of the coherence and the correspondence theories of truth, advocates of the latter repeatedly advanced the criticism that their opponents did not succeed in making clear just what coherence consists in. Though in a somewhat different and perhaps even more serious way, the advocates of correspondence were liable to similar criticism. This, as well as the failings of the opponents, may help to explain why at crucial places the advocates of ostensibly contrary views seemed to be saying almost identical things, using ostensibly contrary words, and why the debate, in spite of the vigor of the contest and the excellence of the contestants, subsided in such an indecisive result. For a better understanding of the philosophical questions that were at issue in the debate we need to penetrate the glassy exterior of some of the shining phrases in terms of which the debate was conducted. A valuable step in that penetration is a recognition of the constitutional aspects of knowledge, and with it the liability to change and criticism of cognitive constitutions, and the importance of constitutional questions in the elucidation of the significance, in the cognitive institution, of the pursuit of truth.

9. With internal questions the emphasis is within the institution, because to a considerable extent the constitutional resources of the institution provide a sufficient framework for the thought and action, including therewith the resort to observation and experiment required to secure adequate answers to the questions. To the extent that a question is an external one, assistance in dealing with it must be found elsewhere. The chief resource available to this appeal outside a given institution is other institutions and the societies in which these institutions exist, in which they represent one dimension of human life. The intellectual discipline and practice of philosophy is one of the institutions for which an important role is provided in this connection.

In the modern world the knowledge institution is an enormous collective of subinstitutions, all more or less interrelated, all more or less jostling each other for intellectual *Lebensraum,* all more or less representing distinctive ways of proceeding, some elements of which are offered for export to other subinstitutions and some of which display clearly their own marks of foreign importation. Work in one field of science is always a subject of comparison and contrast with work done in closely related fields. And when intractable difficulties arise in a given field, these related practices are always a possible source for the importation of new ideas and practices which may lead to solution. A mathematician encountering impasse in a certain area in his own subject may see promise in certain features of research in other areas of the same field. He may find, for example, that the systematization of principles in the theory of probability will profit from a large infusion of ideas from set-theory, and the exploitation of these ideas in the exploration of the mathematics of probability; and the application of these in statistical practice, may in turn suggest some revisions and developments in the theory of sets from which the original importation began. More serious, more enduring difficulties may lead to more far-reaching appeals, as in the case of Frege and Russell, who found themselves impelled by problems in the philosophy of mathematics to make independent investigations in logic, in the philosophy of that subject, and more widely in the philosophy of language.

10. But this kind of interinstitutional criticism and reenforcement is now a familiar fact that does not require demonstration here. It is helpful to be reminded of this pervasive phenomenon whenever the effect of institutional provisions in guiding our thought and action impresses us to the degree that we begin to think of ourselves as the prisoners of theories, thought-systems, *Lebensformen*, paradigms, which we are never capable of criticizing vigorously and objectively, because the institutions themselves provide the only instruments of criticism that we have; hence it is only reasonable to expect that the criticisms that result will be safe, "constructive," sympathetic ones, never in any fundamental way searching and unsettling. The facts of the matter, in the knowledge institution in the Western world, are quite different. The knowledge institution is by no means a totalitarian one, but rather a federation of powers as disparate in character and influence at any one time, and as subject to change, as that organization of powers in the political world that bears the plaintively wishful title of the United Nations. It is the case that all of us, to the extent that we participate in the practices of human knowledge, are to some extent members of a multiplicity of powers or subinstitutions. And we live in the company of others who represent different participations and allegiances; so that the occasions for criticism, rejection, revision, and reform

are always with us, and similarly always at least some resources upon which these activities can draw.

Psychologists need neither the direction nor the permission of philosophers to explore the relation of their work with that of the sociologists, and vice versa. And the same holds of their relations with anthropologists, linguists, physiologists, electrical engineers, psychiatrists, and so on. To the extent that such relations are exploited for the purpose of effecting constitutional change in a discipline, to the extent that importation from one discipline into another requires such change, the exploitation and the change are philosophical. What makes questions philosophical, and answers philosophically illuminating, is of course not that the questions have been asked and the answers given by people who have been commissioned by society to be philosophers. The philosophical work in the scrutiny, criticism, rectification, reform, revivifying of the institutions of human knowledge is not restricted to, and indeed has little in common with, the practice of pursuing "justification" questions to their apparently abstruse and esoteric end.

11. This is a final nail to be hammered into what it is no doubt too optimistic to refer to as the coffin of justification theory. There is a task to be performed in the philosophical scrutiny of knowledge, in the understanding and criticism, in the care, feeding, cultivation and refinement, of the various institutions in which knowledge consists. These institutions are constantly liable in some degree, sometimes more and sometimes less, to change in their basic constitutional structure. As with political institutions, the question is not whether but how such change shall proceed. The invocation of philosophy at this point represents the presumption that there is a way of being reasonable about such changes, that the possibilities of change also represent to some extent possibilities of choice, and that though by taking thought man may not add a cubit to his stature, he may be able to have some appreciable effect upon the careers of these institutions and on the character of life lived in them. Whether an effective preparation for discerning what effects are desirable, and how one should proceed to make them, is first to try to divest oneself in thought of all features of the institu-

tions under examination, is a question that easily answers itself. The kind of "objectivity" concerning questions of institutional arrangement that is the consequence of involuntary ignorance of or voluntary dissociation from the provisions of the institution is not a feasible or desirable platform upon which to make institutional judgments, even though certain popular practices suggest an opinion on the part of some that this is so. An informed judgment, made by one who has immersed himself in institutional provisions, principles, and lore is not necessarily a fair one, but there are resources for guarding against the dangers of prejudice, bias, and partisanship. A judgment that is fair in the sense that, by design or otherwise the relevant practices and principles have been ignored, is literally an ignorant judgment. The implication in Descartes's metaphysics that only a benevolent God could rescue a man from such philosophical perversity is an expression in the rich language of theology of what, from the point of view of the philosophy of knowledge, has to be regarded as a sober truth. In appraising a view of the philosophical scrutiny of knowledge as a kind of institutional self-examination, the residual Descartes in us keeps prompting us to ask how we are to proceed when the institutional means of examination are themselves the subject of examination. If by this question is meant, How do we proceed when *all* such means are under examination? the answer is of course that such a predicament never does and never can confront us. Problems of institutional change always arise, can only be problems, in a situation of some institutional stability, either in the institution under examination or in related and relevant ones. Only in circumstances where some institutional provisions are not in question can some be in question. As Neurath said, the problem of building the ship entirely anew, after it has been dismantled in the dry dock, is one we never face.

12. Hard and at the same time inescapable problems in the scrutiny and cultivation of institutions derive not so much from the poverty as from the richness of resource available for making the judgments that this scrutiny and cultivation require. The position of any subinstitution in a congeries of others, and the position of the whole in a congeries of other institutions, and

the disposition of all these in the life of the community, including the roles they have played, do now play, and tend to play in the future—all these circumstances in the life of an institution or practice offer alternatives of future development incorporating more or less change. There are manifold possible alternatives; and at least some of these are feasible enough to represent choices in the development of the institution, developments in political, economic, and other institutions, and of course developments in human knowledge. The problems and the choices are especially difficult, baffling, and divisive when some of the alternatives in the deliberation mark sharp departures from accepted, traditional modes of thought and practice, when what is being debated is the launching of an institution upon bold new pathways of development, entailing new methods of investigation, new ways of reaching decisions, and new roles for the institution or subinstitution to play in the cognitive commonwealth and in society as a whole.

When recipes fail one does not search for recipes for recipes. When what is up for judgment are definite accepted decision procedures, the derivation of some of these from the principles of some metascience amounts to an elaborate way of begging the question at issue. The Leibnizian dream of achieving a state of logical clarification in which argument and dispute over judgment might yield completely to calculation is not just a dream, but a nightmare.[8] This is precisely because calculation as a decision procedure presupposes constitutional agreement; hence such hegemony for calculatory procedures can only be achieved at the

[8] The hope of Leibniz was that in the refinement of the art of reasoning which the *Characteristica Universalis* would make possible, all disputes, in philosophy, science, medicine, history, government, and so on, *in so far as they are amenable to reasoning* (the emphasis is his), would be reduced to matters of calculation. Then, "If someone would doubt my results, I should say to him: 'Let us calculate, Sir,' and thus by taking pen and ink, we should soon settle the question" ("Preface to the General Science," *Leibniz: Selections*, P. P. Wiener, ed., p. 15; *Opuscules et fragments inédits de Leibniz*, L. Couterat, ed., p. 156).

The more famous "Let us calculate" remark is in Section 14 of Leibniz, *On the Universal Science: Characteristic*. See Leibniz, *Monadology and Other Philosophical Essays*, ed. and trans. by P. Schrecker and A. M. Schrecker, p. 14; *Die Philosophischen Schriften von G. W. Leibniz*, C. I. Gerhardt, ed. (1875–1890), Vol. 7, p. 200.

price of the suppression of constitutional questions, of sanction-ing in the maximum degree the *status quo* in such matters, and helping to ensure that constitutional changes, when they come, will be effected by less reflective means.

To be sure, not all constitutional problems are of the same dimension. Though relatively few of them represent issues over the fundamental character of the institution, or subinstitution, in question, it is worth emphasizing problems of this magnitude, since after all they do occur and their occurrence seems to some to represent the severest test of a theory of knowledge that emphasizes in the present manner the importance of constitu-tional provisions in the conduct of affairs in the institution of knowledge. It is important to realize, in considering the question of the tractability of such problems, that to the extent that they concern the validity and retention of traditional procedures they cannot be resolved by an appeal to the same procedures that are in question. Since not all traditional procedures in any domain will be in question at any time, it is not excluded, and yet not implied, that they will be amenable to some traditional pro-cedures, including those of common sense, the stability and cultural inertia of which are great, and including those of dis-ciplines sufficiently remote from the core of the dispute that their validity is not in any substantial question. It is important to be aware also that completeness in this regard is a character-istic of highly refined logical and mathematical systems, and there is no reason to suppose, and good reason to doubt, that there is a general logical providence that ensures for man that for every problem he comes to face there are resources available sufficient for its solution.

13. The considerations that are effective in producing a col-lective change of mind about constitutional arrangements are many and various, much too various to permit any brief survey or citation. One kind of consideration that is of great importance in science has been elucidated and emphasized by Kuhn. This is the example of a striking, unprecedented achievement, a success that serves as an enduring model or paradigm of investigation in one or more lines of scientific research. Another kind of con-sideration that the history of philosophy makes one alert to is

the social and intellectual background of science which is implicated in the judgment of success in scientific achievement because
it affects the standards by which success is judged. This is a
matter of importance in present science, and hence of importance
to the philosophy of science, including the philosophy of social
science and of closely related, though perhaps not so obviously
scientific, social studies.

As we sail these institutional ships we are forced, as Neurath
said, to rebuild them on the open sea. This is not just because
equipment fails and needs to be replaced, but also because as the
voyage proceeds inadequacies emerge in the design of the ship.
Some of these inadequacies are aspects of the design that only
progressive sailing could reveal but which would have been
recognized as inadequacies earlier in the voyage had they been detected. Other disparities between the capacity of the ship to perform and what the mariners look for in the way of performance
are due to the fact that the latter has changed. On the open sea
not only ships but voyagers change. Their demands, their hopes,
their aspirations for the voyage change. And in consequence of
this the voyagers are called upon to engage not only in ship car-
pentry and repair, but in ship design. That old prow, those old
sails, may have served well, for the kind of sailing that was satisfactory in the past. But the ship is called to do things now that it
did not need to before, and preserving its capacity to do certain
things that are now less and less essential is a handicap to adapt-
ing it to new demands. The prow will have to be redesigned,
different masts installed and perhaps fitted with a new type of
sail.

For a variety of reasons we are now more sensitive to the kind
of consideration in the development of the institutions of human
knowledge that have just been alluded to metaphorically. We
are in a better position to appreciate what some perceptive
scholars have emphasized in the past concerning the social and
evaluative determinants of scientific development, and how
certain important changes in the sciences in the Western world
were in part due to changes in views about what kind of science,
what kind of refined, disciplined, systematic knowledge it is desirable to have. One might guess that valuable as was its religious

sources of inspiration, Greek mathematics would not have developed as it did if it had not been possible to free itself progressively from this framework. Scholars like F. M. Cornford and E. A. Burtt have called attention to the contrast between the aims of science or natural philosophy in the ancient world and in the modern era.[9] In elaborating this contrast Cornford cited some of Macaulay's eloquent praise of Francis Bacon's clarity of vision concerning the "fruits" to be garnered in the study of nature. Whatever may have been Bacon's misunderstanding about the proper method of proceeding to reap these fruits, his grasp of the kind of fruits there were to be harvested and of the appetite of men for these fruits was marvelously prescient.

14. Sometimes problems in the development of knowledge are chiefly about effective means to achieve certain broad ends concerning which there is general agreement. Disputes over these matters not uncommonly achieve constitutional dimensions. At the beginning of this century both the defenders of the psychophysical "establishment" and the advocates of behaviorist "revolution" seemed to each other to be violating fundamental provisions of the scientific study of certain aspects of human life and action, though it seemed that they both could agree that in this respect the apparent transgressions of the new depth psychology were even greater. To what extent the disputes about method derived from deep, much less explicit disagreements about ends is very difficult to judge, though some derivation is undeniable. As psychological investigation, as the study of man and society enters the eighth decade of this century, some of the social, evaluative issues in the disputes over the conduct of investigation are much more explicit. One of the reasons why the title of "behavioral science" is less regarded as a sign of merit now than ten years ago, why explorations in "human engineering" are less frequently heard of, is that there is an increased sensitivity about the aims of social inquiry and about the way in which a commitment to disputable aims can be deceptively embedded in a commitment to canonical methods.

[9] F. M. Cornford, "Greek Natural Philosophy and Modern Science"; E. A. Burtt, "The Value Presuppositions of Science"; *loc. cit.* above, Ch. 2, Sect. 19, n. 20.

15. In certain essential respects a philosophical judgment about this aspect of the development of the sciences, the other intellectual disciplines, and of knowledge generally is like the judgment of the moralist and the political philosopher, like a judgment of constitutional law itself. That there are interstices and indeterminacies of greater magnitude in the accepted fabric of the law does not mean that there is no basis for filling the gaps, reducing the indeterminacies, when occasions call for this to be done. Cognitive institutions live, develop, improve, retrogress in the medium of human life. Not everything in human life is ours to change as we wish, but some things are, including features of our cognitive institutions. Where revision is possible it is the most elementary kind of sense to keep in mind the role of the institution in the communal life which supports it and which in turn is constituted and given form by it. A society expresses itself by its cognitive institutions as well as by its religious, political, legal, and aesthetic ones. A philosophical judgment concerning constitutional issues on such a matter is but an informed judgment, one that is responsive to the society in which the institution has its home, one that helps that society become aware of and express its own will about what that institution should be. A society like an individual is always to some degree in the process of both losing and finding its own identity, always in the process of trying to get clear just what it is, just what it wants to be, just where lies its true self. In the *Republic* Plato addressed Athenian society in an effort to assist his fellow citizens in this process. Whether correctly or not, he told them that if they knew themselves better they would realize that they were really more Spartan than they were aware of, that many constitutional features of their society were at odds with this character, were frustrating its development, and perhaps now, under the stimulation of defeat in the Peloponnesian War, were ripe for change. Of course the *Republic* does not put the matter this way. But it is not presumptuous for us to suppose that our point of view enables us to understand better some aspects of what Plato was doing than he did in his own often mythically enshrouded pronouncements.

16. The view of knowledge advanced in this essay emphasizes its social and existential components. In a realistic view of the matter we must think of knowledge as a social institution, and individual knowledge as something we attain as we participate in this institution. Knowledge embraces in an essential way a vast and not very orderly system of practices; it can only be misconceived if we try to think of it as systems of propositions encapsulated in individual minds and preferably arranged in geometric order. Because knowledge is a social institution, like all such institutions it has its existential matrix. Institutions are not just human bodies or minds, in spite of what the frontispiece of the *Leviathan* may suggest. They are human beings acting and reacting in a world which makes these actions and reactions possible and which constantly imposes its character upon these modes of human response, as it has upon human responses and the responses of other living creatures from the time, hundreds of millions of years ago, when life began.

The tiny bit of knowledge about the brightness of the day and the state of the street that I can acquire by looking up from my desk and through the window on my left is in its way a product of all these components, physical, physiological, biological, psychological, and social. My seeing that cars are traveling west on the brick pavement is not the divine far-off event which the universe set out to produce. It is nevertheless one of the things which it did produce, something that could not occur without the cooperative action in the present and the past of all sorts of things in the world, both external and internal to my own body, without which there could not be the kind of settled practices that a capacity to discern objects generally and to discriminate them by vision logically requires. The discussion of some philosophers of the topic of knowledge by means of vision read as if they regarded all these things less as means by which genuine knowledge is attained than as obstacles to that knowledge. It is as if, for example, what it is necessary to explain is how we can see *in spite of* eyes, light and shadow, brains, the whole store of bodily equipment and acquired response; as if ideal sight, which we unfortunately cannot aspire to, were a kind unmediated by any of these things, pure consciousness enveloping objects, the innocent eye giving way, since it too is a contaminating organ, to the innocent mind.

17. The famous, much discussed and much disputed "private language argument," brilliant and provocative as it was in the *Philosophical Investigations,* is one facet of a larger argument, which may be called the "private knowledge argument," some features of which have been outlined in the preceding pages. This argument is squarely in the tradition begun by Kant in asking in a variety of forms and in a variety of domains the question of how knowledge is possible. And, as in the case of Kant, the question is not the question of how anything that one with some justice *might* call "knowledge" is possible. The primary intention is to give an answer to the possibility question as it bears upon certain domains of putative knowledge whose claims to be accepted as knowledge are so strong that they must be regarded as paradigms of knowledge, if there is knowledge at all, and which therefore can be regarded as test cases for determining whether a certain philosophy of knowledge can adequately account for the contours of what may be thought of as the main features of the cognitive landscape. The result of this argument is not so much to discredit Cartesian attempts to give a philosophical account of our actual knowledge, since this result has already been achieved by the career of this philosophy itself, as to expose some of the essential reasons in this philosophy for its frustrations, and thus to indicate some of the respects in which a satisfactory theory of knowledge must be different. A fatal weakness in the Cartesian program is its endeavor, for reasons already sufficiently explained, to account for our knowledge of material objects, living creatures, and other human beings, as a theoretical or inferential derivative of a more basic form of knowledge which, in spite of the initial presumptions to the contrary in this program, is itself, not just historically and psychologically, but also logically dependent upon the very "theoretical" or "inferred" entities that in the program were supposed to appear only in the conclusion. If, as a variety of philosophers inspired by Kant's teaching kept saying during the nineteenth century, knowledge of the "I" is essentially connected

with knowledge of the "not-I," it is a mistake to suppose that there is a natural preserve of self-knowledge with which we can begin our philosophical ruminations about knowledge, including ruminations on the question whether there are things other than ourselves, of how knowledge of them can be philosophically "justified."

18. A philosophy of knowledge that emphasizes the social and existential components of our knowledge offers a release from the justification problems that are the bitter fruits of Cartesian theory. The enduring resistance of many philosophers to this mode of release is not due so much to a lack of appreciation of this benefit as to a judgment that in the philosophy in question the benefit is purchased at an exorbitant price. A principal component of this price is a haunting suspicion that the price of the admission of social dependence in the institutions of human knowledge is a degree of social relativity in knowledge that seriously prejudices the capacity of anyone to render fair judgments about, make fair criticisms of, the beliefs, practices, presumptions, principles, and so on, of which knowledge at any time consists. If we think of ourselves, when we take ourselves to be having knowledge of anything whatever, as operating with, as utilizing a vast material and social mechanism in which each individual operates as a knower because his responses are coordinated with the rest of the mechanism, how is it possible for someone, in the criticism of knowledge, to achieve sufficient independence of the mechanism ever to make an independent judgment or criticism of any part of it? Must there not be some basis of individual knowledge, altogether without social components, upon which criticism of the admittedly social can be advanced? Is not a judgment made from a position within the system one predetermined to be favorable, and is it not only judgments of this kind, on this view of knowledge, that can ever be made?

19. It is to fearful suspicions of this kind that the discussion of the present chapter has been primarily addressed. The discussion in general, and the employment of the political analogy of constitutional action and questions in particular, have been designed to show that these suspicions are generated by a misunderstanding of the situation. In the main these suspicions derive from an

exaggerated judgment of the degree to which all of us in our engagement with social institutions are reduced to being mere embodiments of these institutions, determined in act and thought by their structure. When social institutions are regarded merely as sources of bondage, the natural response is for one to seek preserves of noninstitutional thought and action. This response, and the one-sided view of institutions which it represents, have been much discussed in the past in treatments of determinism and freedom of the will.

Philosophers who are both impressed and depressed by the extent to which in practical thought and action we are creatures of our physical and social environment, of our native endowments as well as acquired characteristics, often write, when they turn to the topics of cognition, like the most extreme libertarians. The view of the social determinists about knowledge, in spite of its exaggerations, is more realistic than this. As in politics, economics, education and religion, so in science and in our cognitive life generally we are, on the social side, the inheritors of and initiates into complex institutions of vast inertia; institutions that tend to move in certain directions in response to all kinds of forces and which in most respects, though not all, determine the major features of the kind of knowledge that is accessible to any individual. In order to carry on economic activity as we know it there must be available as constitutive features of that activity such subinstitutions as money, banks, corporations, markets, and exchanges of all sorts. The character of most of these institutions is very little in the power of most of us to change, and we constantly are liable to exaggerate the power that other selected individuals whom we think of as individuals "in power" have over them. Though power they have, frequently much more is expected of them in the way of alterations of the institution than one or a few men in it can possibly deliver. Part of the intractability of institutions is due, as many reformers have emphasized, to the effect of social habit or custom; part is due to the character of the world in which these institutions have their home; and part is certainly due to certain relatively fixed and determined characters of the human species.

20. One of the reasons why it is so easy for us to learn to

discriminate dogs, cats, apples, and pears is that vicariously through our ancestors, human and otherwise, we have been practicing this for millions of years. We come into the world already endowed physiologically and psychologically with the results of this practice. There is much in human knowledge that we do not have to learn because it has already been learned for us. Part of this comes to us, as a common inheritance, passed on from parents to offspring through physical inheritance. And part of this, built directly upon our physical inheritance, comes to us in the common social inheritance, the common social intelligence that helps to bind us all together in the common cognitive world: Maoists and Stalinists, Democrats and Republicans, Protestants and Catholics, Keynesians and Friedmanians, behaviorists and Freudians, and idealists and realists in philosophy.

Instincts, habits, practices, customs are all real though, like the rest, fallible components of the knowledge institutions; and in the disputes that arise in the criticism and evaluation of portions of the institution, the remaining components constitute a vast common background against which the disputes take place, a kind of intellectual ballast without which navigation of the cognitive ship is impossible and disputes about alternative courses meaningless. Of course instincts and the rest do fail, but they do not all fail simultaneously and completely, and the ideal of objectivity does not require that we treat them as if they had. When the jury or investigating commission is called upon to determine whether individual A did or did not fire the gun which killed B, it is not required for an objective, fair decision on this matter that the jury investigate also the existence of guns, the kind of chemical processes in gun powder that makes it explosive, why gun barrels are made of metal rather than wood, or whether lead bullets emerging from gun barrels do not dissolve like emissions of steam in the exhaust of an engine. A reason for doubting, investigating whether A shot B, is not by itself a reason for doubting, investigating the existence of firearms, explosives, or projectiles. It is in terms of a settled background of practice, belief, opinion, and presumption about such things that an investigation can be launched and conducted in such a way that partisans of different judgments on the matter can agree that the matter at issue was dealt with by a procedure that did not itself in any way favor or prejudge the rightness of the claims or counter-claims that were involved.

Objectivity is not the only characteristic that is prized in cognitive decisions; but it is one. And in the context of the questions here discussed concerning the philosophical scrutiny of knowledge, it needs to be emphasized that what makes the procedure for answering a question prejudiced, one-sided, unobjective, is not the taking of things for granted—matters of fact, principle, or procedure—since *every* question itself does that. What makes a question tendentious or unfair, what makes procedure for answering it prejudiced is *the kind of thing* that is taken for granted: in the above case not that weapons fire and bullets pierce flesh, but whether the bullet that pierced the flesh was fired in such a way that *A* can be identified as a responsible agent.

21. The essential component of a rational decision on cognitive matters, as on others, has been identified in this book as the practice which this decision exemplifies. This being so, when there is a question about practices themselves, if a rational decision is to be made about this, it must be made in part by reference to some further practice. Whatever may be the weakness of such a view, there is implicit in it no potentially endless regress of appeals to practices that must somehow be accomplished by an Achilles step in order for a decision to be effected. A decision does not precipitate the regress, because we all make our beginning in the process of making cognitive decisions equipped with practices. We do not need to "justify" them in order to employ them. We do need on occasion to evaluate and judge them, and when this need arises, in the employment of these practices or in the philosophical scrutiny of them, it is a need to evaluate and judge *them,* not every practice hitherto followed, not even every practice that might in some way be relevant to it. This kind of wholesale doubt and quest for security, as Descartes and Hume both conceded, is not really appropriate in the practical conduct of affairs, and Hume observed that large-scale indulgence in it is very little to be dreaded, since "Nature is always too strong for principle." Where Nature so easily overcomes principle, where "the first and most trivial event in life" is sufficient to put to

flight the doubts and scruples that principle has generated, there must have all along been something wrong with principle itself, something very wrong in the view it represents of how the philosophical scrutiny of knowledge can and should proceed.

22. A feature of the contrast that has been drawn here between two ways of engaging in the philosophical scrutiny of items or procedures of knowledge is that in one the direction of inquiry is regressive or inward, in the other expansive or outward. In the face of challenge, say, to some element of accepted cognitive practice, the impulse of the Cartesian philosopher is to retreat from challenged practice to further and automatically challenged practices until a point is arrived at from which a counterattack can be mounted by beginning with some practice that can itself be rationalized without reliance upon any other. The contrasting impulse is to look abroad, to investigate what resources there are, beginning close at home and ranging farther and farther afield, in practices not now in question, reliance upon which in one way or another may help in the evaluation of the practice which is the object of examination. When it is viewed in this way the analogy between questions of law, in particular when these are questions largely of common law rather than of statute, and questions of what is acceptable practice in the knowledge institution, is very close. Controverted questions about what is the law, as it applies to a particular case, are decided reasonably, not in ignorance of tradition and practice, nor in slavish obedience to some elements of these that are regarded as having some special sanction, but by a judgment on the case that tries to reflect the wisdom of the institution on the matter. Such wisdom is achieved, not by a narrower and narrower scrutiny, excluding more and more of the institution, but by a broader and more inclusive scrutiny, that takes into account relevant practices and procedures, their origins, careers, and present position in the institution. An intention to render a just decision cannot substitute for what is an indispensable means for determining what justice is in particular cases, namely, a knowledge of the law, as the features of that institution bear directly or indirectly on the questions at issue. Similarly in science, and in the pursuit of knowledge generally,

the intention to discover the truth, however laudable, is a poor substitute for the indispensable means for that discovery that reside in the resources of principles, practices, and ideals that make up the collective cognitive institution.[10]

23. To the philosophical question of how reasonable judgments on such matters are possible, then, part of the answer is that they are made possible by the institution, and that a capacity to make such judgments is part of what one develops by being trained in the institution. In the first instance the task of the philosopher with respect to the institution, like that of its vocational apprentices, is, to reverse Marx's formula, to understand the institution, not to change it. It is to master its lore, its technique, its rules and principles; and to acquire its habits of mind. But understanding an institution is not merely a matter of being indoctrinated in settled ways of proceeding. It is learning the unsettled as well as the settled, the dissonances as well as the harmonies, the questions and issues about future development as well as the answers and decisions on such matters that are included in the institutional legacy. The kind of question about the future career of an institution that raises deep and fundamental issues about its character, about its ways of proceeding and the validity of the results, have been called here, still following the legal analogy, constitutional questions. Here the analogy is helpful in calling attention to a fact about institutional examination which is of the greatest importance for a theory of this kind, namely, that questions do arise in the development of institutions for which intrainstitutional procedures do not suffice as means for criticizing and judging alternative proposed answers.

---

[10] The literature available to a reader wishing to explore further the analogy between legal and philosophical judgment is vast, embracing as it does a good deal of jurisprudence. For an approach from the philosophical side, one may begin with Essays IV–VI, in Ch. Perelman's *The Idea of Justice* and his book, *Justice*, including the Appendix entitled "What the Philosopher May Learn from the Study of Law." The two central chapters, IV and V, of B. Bosanquet's *Implication and Linear Inference* will repay study if one will make the effort to master what has now become a somewhat outdated philosophical idiom. Abundant material for philosophical lessons is available in E. H. Levi's short but valuable *An Introduction to Legal Reasoning*, but the reader must himself work at extracting these lessons, since Levi's philosophical comments on the material are spare.

To the extent that questions are of this kind, they are answerable by reasonable means only if such means exist. They may not. But if they do, again, to the extent that intrainstitutional means are not sufficient, there will need to be appeal to extrainstitutional resources.

24. It is not as if institutions exist like islands in society, each, to use Donne's phrase, "entire of itself," from which expeditions may be mounted abroad in times of need. As Donne said about men, each institution and subinstitution "is a piece of the continent, a part of the main." Each lives in matrix of thought and action that is informed by many other institutions, the character of each helping to determine and being mutually determined by the character of the others. So that what is done explicitly when constitutional issues arise and are faced is, as it were, a continuation at the level of higher social consciousness of a process that goes on at lower levels all the time. Here again the political analogy is apt. In the United States we have a highly developed institution of judicial review on constitutional questions, it being primarily through judicial decision that constitutional issues in this country are explicitly resolved. When a judge is called upon to decide whether a certain enacted law or administrative act violates the Constitution of the United States, and when he considers the item in question broadly, not only in terms of the original words of the Constitution, but also in terms of what those words have come to mean in almost two centuries of life in an explosively expanding nation—when he does this, he is not for the first time opening the Constitution to change. He is to a considerable extent inquiring what that change has been. By a combination of circumstances he has been entrusted by a populous nation which takes itself to be committed to a way of handling political affairs originally outlined in the document of 1787, with the task of progressively redefining what that way is. He is called upon to determine as a matter of practical reason what commitment to the intention and ideals broadly expressed in the language of the enacted provisions and amendments, and subjected to centuries of successive interpretation, now means.

25. But, of course, the judges who ruled in 1954 that the employment of state agencies to effect racial segregation in the

schools was a violation of the equal protection clause of the Fourteenth Amendment (in this case reversing a decision by their predecessors over half a century earlier) were not simply ratifying a public judgment. There was scarcely a public judgment on the matter then, and if there had been it is by no means clear that it would have coincided closely with the decision of the court. Nevertheless there was a basis for this decision; and for the philosophical scrutiny of institutions this is a matter of the very first importance. However opposed a judge personally may be to racial segregation in the schools, to prayers or religious instruction in them, to laws restricting the abortion of pregnancies, or to laws exacting a fee for the privilege of voting, when he is called upon to rule upon the constitutional aspects of such matters what he is not asked to make is the kind of personal moral or political judgment that an ordinary citizen might make. Whether a poll tax is a stupid or unfair way to determine an electorate is not the point; it bears only upon the point if the stupidity or unfairness in question, if stupidity and unfairness it is, does contravene fundamental principles of American constitutional government, as these have been developed and been altered from time to time through the years of national and constitutional growth. The set of principles that at any moment may be regarded as constitutional in any institution is not a seamless web of decision patterns perfectly harmonious and competent for any occasion. An institution is always more or less the product of diverse and to some extent contrary influences that in the highly settled practices have found some more or less coherent resolution, but which, as new occasions arise (for example the admission of new states into the American union), are always liable to break out afresh and require further adjustment. In this respect there is a close analogy between the determination of what might be called the collective will of an institution at any time, and a determination of will in the life of an individual. Our determinations, our decisions, our wills in both cases are always subject to revisions, refinements, and even greater alterations as action consequent to them further clarifies the significance of the decisions in ways that may not otherwise have been possible. In any complex venture we never do exactly what we set out to do, for one thing because in setting out to do what we wish to do in such cases we always learn more than we did before about what our wishes and determinations are.

26. At first view the connection between such topics as Descartes's meditations on first philosophy and Hume's inquiries concerning the foundations of all conclusions from experience, and the topic of the scrutiny, evaluation, and reform of the constitutional aspects of institutions may seem very indirect. The effort here has been to reveal it as being, rather, direct. For if, on the kind of grounds that have been adduced here, one rejects the possibility of there being the kind of first cognitions that have been sought in the Cartesian philosophies, one rejects at the same time the possibility that the philosophical scrutiny of knowledge can be carried out in a certain way, namely, independently of accepted items and other features of the knowledge institution. That means that in order to understand how the philosophical scrutiny can proceed, how the critical function which is essential to the philosophical vocation can be maintained, it is necessary to begin to understand how it is possible, while relying to some extent upon this and other institutions, yet to be able to evaluate features of it in a way that is not thereby rendered distorted and partial.

27. In the portrait of philosophical scrutiny drawn here with the intention of revealing its character in this regard, only a few broad strokes have been possible. When the hope is abandoned of securing objectivity and fairness in critical judgment by first repudiating all accepted standards in such matters; when the program of pursuing wisdom through ignorance is recognized as being as unpromising as it sounds; then one is in a position to see philosophical scrutiny more as it is, less as it was thought it had to be in the confines of mistaken theory of knowledge. Seeing it this way does not easily foster hopes of easy answers to questions, or great consequences readily to be achieved. One does not look for algorithms when what is in question is principles of computation themselves, nor for sure procedures for elucidating answers when one of the things that may be most in doubt is whether the resources for answering the questions, at least at

the time they are asked, and in the form in which they are put, do exist. Just as the putting of questions is but one of the ways we have of responding to difficulties of one sort or another, so giving something as definite and neat as an answer is but one way of responding to questions. If in the case of a carefully drawn and explicitly ratified political constitution we have no temptation to suppose that its provisions contain answers to all questions that may arise concerning basic political procedure, why should we suppose the situation to be otherwise in the case of institutions in which constitutional provisions are more drawn by precedent action and ratified by successive practice? What general logical providence are we relying upon when we suppose that for every constitutional difficulty that arises we are always prepared with constitutional means sufficient for its resolution?

28. But the point to be emphasized here is not that our resources in this regard are sometimes insufficient, but that they are sometimes sufficient. As in the case of international diplomacy, the case for philosophical scrutiny as a means of relief in constitutional difficulties is not that there is reason to believe that this means will always be successful. It sometimes is; and when it is, the resources that make success possible are the very elements in the situation, i.e., the richness, power, and variety of the institutions in which we always act, that in some philosophies are regarded as the chief obstacles to success. It is no new comment that institutions can serve not only to repress but also to stimulate, support, facilitate, and, on occasion, even demand critical examination of fundamental features of our lives. It is essential for the understanding of human cognition, as well as of political and social life generally, to recognize that institutions can do all these things.

29. One aspect, alluded to earlier, of the analogy between constitutional issues in political affairs and certain broad issues in cognitive ones deserves a final word of emphasis. If we think of institutions as agencies through which individuals not only pursue more or less settled goals but also from time to time reassess and alter the goals, we can be prepared to recognize that constitutional issues can arise concerning either one or both of

these aspects of institutional activity. As the history of the physical sciences since the time of its origins in the West seems to testify, and as a comparison of the various sciences and other cognitive disciplines which have a place in the collective cognitive institution at any time seems to confirm, different ways of conducting scientific inquiry result, not merely from there being different subjects about which questions are asked, but also from different kinds of questions being asked. And one important reason that different kinds of questions come to be asked is that in certain important respects the broader life in which the practices of asking and answering questions are carried on undergoes some change.

At any point in the life of an institution broad agreement about practices is a sign of agreement, or, in some cases, of what had better be described as a lack of disagreement, concerning the ends toward which in a very broad way the institution is directed. In cognitive disciplines, when there are radical disagreements about methods of inquiry, as there have been in recent years, for example, in psychology, economics, and political science, an important source of the disagreement, though typically not well recognized, is often a disagreement about the ends which the discipline, as a social agency, should serve. When there is this disagreement about the ends of an institution or subinstitution, about the role it should play, together with other institutions, in the broader life of society, the resources for any resolution of the disagreement that philosophical scrutiny can discover or devise must reside in that common life and in the institutions that collectively determine its main characteristics. But in the investigation of this disagreement the search for resources for its resolution is not restricted to anything so simple as that of uncovering, in the welter of disagreement, fundamental agreements that have been obscured and overlooked. As in individual lives, so in the lives of social agencies, a program of action that provides a resolution to conflict is often not so much discovered as devised. So to say that the resources for a decision about ends reside, as they sometimes do, in the institutional life of a society, is not to say that the solution itself lies there, waiting to be discerned by some refined instrument for taking the public pulse and revealing something like public opinion or social agreement on the matter at issue.

The pursuit of any end in individual lives and by societies is always dependent upon and affected by the means available for the realization of the end and by the existence of other ends likewise pursued or inviting pursuit. For the resolution of conflicts about ends, the elements of indeterminacy thus introduced into the ends themselves, and the flexibility thus made possible in our pursuit of them, are of crucial importance. Because of them, in the process of utilizing the resources that are available for resolving disputes about constitutional issues there is an important role, once intellectual understanding of the issues has been achieved, for intellectual ingenuity in devising, out of the materials that understanding has laid bare, a program for activity in the institution in which the original conflict of ends can be to some extent composed or resolved. Serious disputes about ends, and about appropriate means for the pursuit of these ends, about fundamental principles, cognitive or otherwise, do not always defy resolution that, when once devised, can happily be agreed upon by all parties in the dispute as assimilating and accomodating, fairly and without distortion, the claims originally advanced.

30. That disputes concerning the conduct of cognitive institutions, even so well-established ones as scientific disciplines, can be in an important respect disputes about social ends, as well as about means, is a feature of the philosophy of knowledge that has become more apparent in recent years with the mass infusion of both scientific practices and consequences into our lives. The recognition that this is so is a natural step in the development of a theory of knowledge that grasps the essentially social character of its subject. To some, this may seem, rather than an advantage, a further difficulty in a theory now shown to be prone to degenerate into some kind of "pragmatic" theory of knowledge in which the satisfactory working of social institutions, like bad money driving out good, replaces the more severe claims of reality and that correspondence with it that constitutes truth.

The practices of the knowledge institution are like the practices of other institutions in being practices, unlike them in being practices of this particular institution. To recognize the institutional, social character of knowledge does not commit one to the assimilation of this one institution, and its practices, to others—to business, for example, to politics, athletics, or family life. Nor does the recognition that the character of this institution changes in response to changes in other institutions and in social life generally (just as also this institution itself produces such changes), and the recognition that the character of the institution is always in some respects determined by larger goals of social life that the institution may be used to achieve, commit one to holding that within the institution every decision—of fact, theory, hypothesis, historical interpretation, and so on—is explicable as a response to some kind of wide social motivation. The kind of distinction that has recently been drawn in ethical theory between act-utilitarianism and rule-utilitarianism has some application here. Furthermore it is important to remember that the kind of virtue in our utterances, hypotheses, theories that we refer to under the rubric of "truth" is by no means the only virtue we seek in them. The supposition that it is, makes the adventuresome and arduous way in which the pursuit is carried on in the sciences and other intellectual disciplines thoroughly inexplicable. In short, it is possible, and necessary for a philosophical understanding of our knowledge institutions, to recognize the practical, moral, and social determinants of various features of them without losing sight of the ways in which they are, as institutions, distinctive. And it is possible and necessary to recognize the essential position occupied in these institutions by facilities for the disinterested pursuit of truth, without supposing that so broad and abstract a formula takes one far in comprehending in any one of them the character of the activities by means of which this pursuit is carried on.

31. Until recent times versions of the theory of knowledge which emphasized the resources in our institutions, cognitive and otherwise, to provide resolutions to the difficulties encountered in their development were largely advanced from a metaphysical point of view that seemed to its advocates to provide large-scale assurance, in the brooding presence of the World Spirit, of the

possibility of eventual solutions to every problem, of resolutions to every dispute. Reacting against what appeared to him to be unrealistic idealism in this view, Marx modified this beneficent metaphysics by installing, in the place of a dialectic of thought, one of material processes, in which the main determining motive power of institutional change derived from these basic features of economic life that he called the "powers of production." Then, in view of the vast inertia of institutions, and the difficulty with which, so he thought, in the absence of socialist social arrangements, social institutions are kept in correlation with economic developments, he concluded that, until the time when these arrangements could be installed, the rectification of institutions in society would be destined to take place in the main, not by means of social criticism carried on in them and effected by means of resources in them, but sharply, and without, by revolutionary force.

It may be comforting for some, as they engage in the philosophical scrutiny of our cognitive institutions, and investigate the possibilities in them of development and reform, to presume that, however we may falter, the everlasting arms of some vast historical process, ideal or material in nature, will see to it in the end that the job is done. The comfort to be derived from this source may suffer diminution with reflection upon the character of the grounds that can be marshaled in support of such a presumption and the notorious indefiniteness of the promise conveyed. Furthermore, whatever is destined to happen in the end, if anything is—whether this be socialist society, the realization of large-scale reason, or to use the language of one of Russell's early apocalyptic visions, "a universe in ruins"—it seems clear that what will be achieved in the preservation and improvement of the institutions of human life in the immediate future depends partly upon us. And however modest our capacity may be, by taking philosophical thought, to contribute to this process, it is hard to think that a better understanding than we have generally had of what we are doing when we engage in this activity would not strengthen our capacity to do it well.

Knowledge and
Revelation

1. A primary aim of our cognitive enterprises is to secure reliable information concerning ourselves and our world: concerning what entities, states, and processes can be discriminated in ourselves and the world, concerning the character of these and their interrelations. The question is not whether we do this, but how. And the "how" question, as it is a concern of philosophers, is a very special one. It is not a question about the particular techniques employed by expert investigators in various fields, e.g., those of the archeologist, the physiologist, the organic chemist, the expert in solid state physics or in Arabic history. It is not so much a question of exposing epistemic or methodological lore as developing a theory about this lore, recognizing, of course, that theory about the lore cannot be developed successfully apart from some accurate, concrete information about what the lore actually is.

2. One important reason for developing a theory of knowledge that fits this lore is that, as in other cases, this is a most important way of increasing our information about the lore, securing a kind of illumination and intellectual mastery of it that can be won in no other way. Philosophic understanding of these matters is an end in itself. And there are, in addition, rewards to be gained from this understanding. Problems do constantly arise in the cultivation and application of the lore which require, if intellectual resolution of them is to be possible, a broader and more penetrating view of the cognitive enterprise than those who specialize in one or another of its particular facets can be ex-

pected to develop automatically with the attainment of their particular expertise.

3. There is a wide division of view among philosophers about the broad outlines of the answer that should be given to this "how" question. What has been referred to as the Cartesian view is dedicated generally to the proposition that the roots of knowledge, especially of what it is now the fashion to speak of as "empirical knowledge," lie in some kind of direct revelation of matters of fact. Some things are known to us simply by our being us and having certain entities or states thrust upon us. At this level of knowledge we need do nothing. Remaining passive, our consciousness is ravished by certain entities and states, in consequence of which ravishment, this pure intercourse between us and them, we are possessed of fundamental first truths concerning them. The logical beginnings or foundations of all our knowledge lying in these truths, whenever questions arise concerning items and domains of putative knowledge, or concerning the procedures upon which the items depend or which the domains exemplify, the proper mode of thorough philosophical examination is to determine whether the items, domains, procedures, can be justified, can be made to expose their legitimacy by demonstrating their sources in those roots.

The nineteenth-century algebraist Leopold Kronecker held that God made the natural numbers, other numbers, e.g., fractions and real numbers, being the work of man. Similarly on the Cartesian view of knowledge, though there is much in the development of knowledge that depends upon us, is to some extent our handiwork, there are some items which do not depend upon us, are known to us simply because certain entities, states visit us and by this visitation reveal to us truths about their existence and character. There are wide variations of view among versions of Cartesian philosophy concerning the extent to which our knowledge is directly revelatory. For Descartes himself the vast bulk of our knowledge is, rather, indirectly revelatory, depending upon the employment of our ideas and thus indirectly upon a beneficent Creator who in fashioning us endowed us with ideas which, treated properly, truthfully inform us concerning the world beyond them. But among the variations of view concerning the nature and extent of directly revelatory knowledge, an element of constancy is the thesis that however much or little of the edifice of knowledge is our handiwork, the validity of the edifice, of its claims to truth in all its parts, depends altogether upon the directly revelatory stage. It is through recourse to this that ultimately we must determine whether what we take to be knowledge *is* knowledge, whether the plausible opinions with which we are endowed by teaching and custom, or which we develop on our own, do reflect, beyond their plausibility to us, real features of an obdurate world which we are concerned to know, and not dream, conjecture, or imagine. This is the explanation of the otherwise curious fact that discussions by philosophers of the "foundations" of empirical knowledge turn out regularly to be discussions of sensation and sense-data.

4. That is one kind of answer to the "how" question. The answer derives from a philosophical view according to which knowledge is a structure of truth claims the warrant of which ultimately depends upon revelation. It depends upon there being a state of life, a kind of experience, in which some kinds of entities, if only phenomenal ones, are known and known about because in that state, in that experience, they and we are as one. What else we know, about other entities, objects, states, we know because of what we can divine concerning them on the bases of the first, primitive, yet utterly sure clues.

Another kind of answer to the question is offered in a variety of forms by the tradition in the theory of knowledge associated with the names of Kant and Hegel. In drawing the contrast between this tradition, and that which has been referred to in this book as "Cartesian," in speaking thus of philosophical positions and emphasizing the difference between them, one unavoidably does some historical injustice to the great figures whose names are thus employed. And when the person suffering the injustice is a philosopher of the dazzling brilliance and subtlety of Descartes, the unavoidability of this kind of fall-out from philosophical debate is especially regrettable. These words in homage to Descartes, from whom this writer in company with many others has learned much, are written, not to mitigate in any degree the criticism made of what it is now convenient to refer to as "Cartesianism" in the theory of knowledge, but rather, without sparing the criticism of the position, to redress in some degree the intellectual balance with respect to the man. The philosophy of Descartes, like that of any great and continually reflective thinker, is not all of a piece, and not at every point thoroughly Cartesian. The Cartesian elements in it are pronounced and in some respects powerfully persuasive. They are especially prominent when Descartes is engaged in "first philosophy." But at some other times, when his interests are more methodological and reflect his experience, both directly in his own work and indirectly in that of others, in research in the sciences, he seems to express a somewhat different and not altogether compatible view. He then seems too alert to the complexities in the task of adjudicating the sometimes competing claims of observed fact and interpretative principle to remain content with the somewhat rigid program of cognitive development that is strongly prescribed in the *Rules for the Direction of the Mind* and in much of the *Discourse*. Without committing oneself to the general adequacy of his treatment of the main point he is concerned with in his discussion of his knowledge of the wax in *Meditation II*, one may observe that this discussion well exemplifies such a view, as at a more general level does the often remarked passage concerning "principles" and "experiments" in the early part of *Discourse VI*.[1] In the flexibility and breadth of consideration which are indicated to be characteristic of a well-developing understanding, the teaching of these passages is more in keeping with that of Descartes's great rationalist successors than the narrow view of the operation of reason which his empiricist successors took from him and which according to some commentators

[1] "But I must also confess that the power of nature is so ample and so vast, and these principles are so simple and general, that I observed hardly any particular effect as to which I could not at once recognize that it might be deduced from the principles in many different ways; and my greatest difficulty is usually to discover in which of these ways the effect does depend upon them. As to that, I do not know any other plan but again to try to find experiments of such a nature that their result is not the same if it has to be explained by one of the methods, as it would be if explained by the other" (*Philosophical Works*, Vol. I, Haldane and Ross, trans., p. 121).

PT. 6.

was the main source of the skepticism to which the empiricist movement eventually led.[2]

5. The alternative answer to the how question, proposed by the non-Cartesian tradition, proceeds on the proposition that the idea of knowledge—propositional knowledge, knowledge of possible truths—by revelation must be given up, whether that knowledge is exalted knowledge of fundamental features of the world, or the relation of the world to some transcendental being, or is the very restricted alleged knowledge by acquaintance of the characters of the ephemeral visitors of external or internal sense. In the contrasting theory of knowledge of this tradition the emphasis was upon the activity of the knower at every level at which knowledge is achieved. The fundamental unit of this theory of knowledge was "judgment," in contrast with the "presentations," "concepts," "propositions" of the other tradition. The "root-metaphor," to borrow a phrase from S. C. Pepper, was that of divining, employing a vast variety of physical, physiological, psychological, and social means in the process, rather than that of being "appeared to," coupled with a theory of how further knowledge could be developed, composed, constructed, from the original information deposited by the apparitions.

Among the difficulties which critics seemed to see in such a theory, an apparently prominent and seemingly enduring one, was that to which attention was directed in the just completed discussion of the philosophical scrutiny of knowledge. If—to put the matter again in a simple metaphorical way—if at all levels of knowledge we are active and hence implicated; if what we take ourselves to know is always to some extent dependent upon the whole physical, psychological, social machinery which we as aspiring knowers bring to the cognitive situation; how do we ever manage, on such a view, to appraise, criticize, and correct

2 "It is abundantly evident that the theory of knowledge . . . formulated by Descartes corresponds in a very real way to the most fruitful scientific procedure of the time. . . . It is equally clear, however, that his statement of the theory hovers always upon the verge of falsifying the method which gave it life. . . . In the hands of Descartes the epistemologist . . . [the mathematical method] too frequently suggests the evolution of experience from the mere logical manipulation of concepts" (G. H. Sabine, "Rationalism in Hume's Philosophy," in Sabine, ed., *Philosophical Essays in Honor of James Edwin Creighton*, pp. 47–48). Cf. also p. 44.

the machinery? If an essential part of the role of the philosopher in relation to knowledge is to perform the kind of criticism just referred to, is it not necessary for him to be able to extricate himself, to however limited an extent, from this machinery, to achieve thereby a kind of knowledge that is independent of the machinery and which then can be used as a basis for criticism of the machinery itself?

If no test can be performed on any of the results of the collective machinery without employing and thus depending upon the results of the machinery itself, does not this mean that a test of the machinery as a whole is impossible? And supposing that the answer to this question is indeed, Yes, does this not mean that all we can effect, when we endeavor to test the validity of the machinery as an instrument for divining independent truth, is, instead of a test for this, a test of the congruity of the results of one part of the machine with the rest—in a word "coherence" —or its capacity to minister to some kind of ulterior personal or social need under the broad heading of "satisfaction"?

6. The situation here is a generalized form of that explained in Chapter 7 in discussing the first cognitions of sense. The primary ground and need for these is not that they can be found and shown to be capable of discharging a certain desired function; it is rather that the needs of a certain kind of philosophy are such that it seems that they *must* be found. The alternative that seems to confront the protagonists of such philosophy is: either revelation or disaster. Unless there is a revelatory stage of knowledge, it is possible to criticize some parts of the machinery only while employing and trusting other parts, like testing the credibility of one of a set of witnesses by comparing his testimony with others, so that what we can achieve is at best a congruent story, leaving the possibility that all the witnesses were wrong, and that what we may accept is plausible but false. It may not be false, and it may have all the assurance that for ordinary cognitive purposes is required; but for extraordinary purposes, for meeting the kind of extraordinarily searching challenges to which our accepted judgments and practices are liable under philosophical scrutiny, we may have no ground to advance

in support of what is the object of this challenge, namely our accepted judgments and ordinary assurance.

To be sure, it is the nature of philosophical challenges to be searching in a way that ordinary challenges are not. And, as has been emphasized in the preceding discussions, genuine philosphical challenges require genuine philosophical responses. Implicit in the above alternative of revelation or disaster is a supposition that there is a certain kind of philosophical challenge to be met, the general features of which are now very familiar. It is easily possible in the terms of the metaphor employed to speak of the possibility of our being deceived by the whole aggregate of machinery we employ in utilizing and developing the knowledge institution. This is of course but a less dramatic way of speaking of what Descartes spoke about in his fable of the evil genius. But is it as easily possible, or possible at all, to think clearly and consistently of such a possibility, of deception on so grand a scale? For, as the reference to Descartes indicates, the hard philosophical alternative, with its supposed disastrous consequences following upon the impossibility of revelation, is not a new predicament, but a very old one in new dress. The rejoinder expressed in the supposed predicament is that of the Cartesian philosopher, the advocate of justification theory, the victim of the philosophical skepticism which finds its deceptive, inverted expression in this theory.

7. As was beginning to become apparent in the preceding remarks on Descartes, the use of the unqualified term "revelation" in the posed alternative "revelation or disaster" is in some degree ambiguous and can be seriously misleading. For there is a sense in which revelation is indeed essential to knowledge, and hence to genuinely cognitive procedures. One thing we want most imperatively in these procedures is a capacity to reveal to us the existence and character of entities, states, and processes, as they are, not as somehow produced or affected in character by the procedures themselves. This was a point argued sharply and effectively by A. E. Murphy some years ago against some pronouncements otherwise by Dewey in *The Quest for Certainty*.

For reasons that are understandably persuasive but in the end not valid, Dewey was led in this book to express himself to the effect that "scientific conceptions are not a revelation of prior and independent reality." Rejecting the implicit agnosticism or idealism in such a pronouncement, Murphy protested vigorously, "that antecedent being, as it existed prior to the operations of inquiry, can . . . be a true and legitimate object of knowledge. . . ." And further,

that some scientific conceptions *are* [ital. orig.] revelations of prior and independent reality in that by the use of them, true and warranted statements can be made about events and objects that existed before cognitive situations ever occurred and [that are] independent of such situations.[3]

It is at least arguable that in the above and other offending remarks Dewey was not so much advancing an unsound philosophy as expressing himself badly. His response to Murphy was not to defend the object of Murphy's criticism but rather to express astonishment, mixed with some annoyance, that the object should be taken to be himself. In the sense in which "antecedent reality" was viewed by Murphy as a genuine object of knowledge Dewey seemed as unwilling as any common-sense realist to dispute Murphy's contention.

8. But the central point here is not a historical one concerning Dewey's philosophy. It is rather, irrespective of what Dewey may have held at some time, that there is a very fundamental way in which revelation is essential to knowledge. The issue raised, posed by the Cartesian philosophy with respect to this point particularly in its empiricist forms, is not whether reality, objects, or whatever are disclosed or revealed to us in knowledge. It is, rather, how this disclosure or revelation can be conceived when we recognize the thorough dependence of what we ordinarily take to be knowledge upon what we as physical, psychological, and social creatures bring to and contribute to our apprehension of the objects of knowledge. This dependence generates a philosophical problem, namely, of how it is possible that an appre-

[3] "Dewey's Epistemology and Metaphysics," in P. A. Schilpp, ed., *The Philosophy of John Dewey*, p. 205. For Dewey's response to this critical comment see *ibid.*, pp. 556–568.

hension of objects so thoroughly conditioned by the physical, psychological, and social apparatus of apprehending can yet be maintained to be, at least under favorable conditions, disclosure of the true character of these objects. Viewed in a certain way the machinery of apprehension seems to interpose itself between us and the objects, giving grounds for the general philosophical suspicion that what is disclosed by it is, as Scrooge said about the apparition of Marley, less grave than gravy, less the character of the objects themselves and more of the character of the machinery of apprehension, including therewith ourselves. If one is going to maintain that the machinery has the capacity to reveal the existence and character of objects, must it not be possible to show that its employment can be founded upon objects? And given the apparent inutility of Descartes's beneficent Creator for this purpose, what better way is there than the discrimination of a special stage of revelation in the knowledge of objects in which objects are apprehended without the employment of the machinery and which thus can serve as the philosophical foundations for that employment? At such a stage of knowledge some entities, states, or processes can make themselves known to us in utter independence of ourselves, independently of any intellectual machinery we might employ, independently of any activity or cooperation on our part. At this stage, as a foundation for the valid employment of the machine, a direct purchase upon some limited segment of reality can be effected. This purchase is indefeasible, not open to any suspicion that in it we are possibly misled by anything we do in, or contribute to, the cognitive proceedings. For at this stage we do and contribute nothing.

The question of the possibility of revelation that is at issue is a question about revelation of this specific kind. It is a kind of revelation in which, in a quite unusual way, with respect to certain entities, states, or processes, their existence and their coming to be known are conceived to be exactly the same things. Knowledge of the existence and character of a certain object A, for example, at this putative stage of cognition, is dependent exclusively on its existence and character as A. To be A is to be known to be A. *Esse est percipi et nosci.*

9. Behind the posed alternative of revelation or disaster is the supposition that if there is no revelation of this kind, if the revelation of objects is always indirect in the sense that there is always activity, work, efficacy on our part in achieving whatever revelation there is, then thorough philosophical scrutiny of what at any time we take to be revelation, and the discrimination in it of the sound from the unsound, is impossible. If we view the world exclusively through such intellectual eyes and spectacles that our vision of that world clearly depends upon the efficacy with which these perform, then we have no independent way of testing what these organs or instruments tell us. Is it not conceivable that what they effect is some kind of systematic distortion or delusion which, so long as it is sufficiently consistent, could impose upon us completely? We should be unable to penetrate the deception because any instrument that we might employ would be likewise implicated in and would consequently corroborate the very deception we were trying to penetrate.

This is a form of intellectual paranoia, and for that reason not less, but more difficult to combat in those who find its anxieties real and oppressive. Such persons are often not relieved, but rather subtly disturbed by the reminder that just as in the office of the oculist, so at home reading the newspaper or inspecting the edge of the knife, we test the efficacy of the eyes or spectacles in revealing the print or the edge of the blade by using them. Such, in the large, is the story of the development of optical instruments: of magnifying glasses, microscopes, telescopes, and the rest. And of course the reason that we trust the spectacles or the microscope is not just that we like what we see, that it provides a satisfying picture. For some purposes we prefer amber-tinted or rose-colored glasses, just as for some we want candlelight or moonlight, and just as for some the cinema cameraman may have us view the face of an aging actress through a soft-focus lens. These however are not the optical resources we seek to employ if we wish to determine whether the filament in the light bulb broken, not the kind that is wanted for the desk of the accountant or for the surgical operating room. What is illustrated here in a very simple way is the fact that the recognition that we learn about the revelatory capacity of instruments by employing them does not commit us to some kind of crude pragmatism that identifies truth with pleasant disclosures or indiscriminately satisfactory views. The machinery we employ in divining the character of objects we are concerned with, including ourselves, is a vast physical, psychological, technical, cultural, historical, and social complex. Part of the history of man is a history of the ways we have learned and continue to learn to discriminate what is satisfactory, successful employment for cognitive purposes from what is not. The history of science, philosophy, theology, and the social studies (including, not least, history itself) amply testifies to the related facts that learning to discriminate genuinely revelatory results is an immensely complicated and seemingly unending task, but one nevertheless in which in some areas great achievements have been made and more surely remain possible.

10. In particular cases many serious and sometimes insuperable difficulties are encountered in the project of testing the veracity of our revelatory machinery. But as in the case of what we refer to literally as spectacles in everyday life, there is no reason in principle why it is not possible for us to appraise the revelatory quality of one lens even though in the process of appraisal we employ this lens and others. There is no philosophical bar preventing our judging, by employing them, which of several pairs of binoculars best reveals the kind of characters in birds, landscapes, or seascapes, which we are interested in discriminating. When the figurative binoculars are the Bohr theory of the atom, the theory of the structure of DNA, or, say, the view of the matters under investigation that is implicit in the batteries of tests employed by psychologists to test for psychological aptitudes or by sociologists to sound public opinion, the manner of testing the tests by employing them and others is vastly, almost incomparably more complex. But though difficulties there are, and though in some cases these may prove to be insuperable, there is not the slightest reason for supposing that they must always be so. There is no good basis for rendering a philosophical judgment that a project in which in some cases we have succeeded so strikingly must be regarded as a hopeless

venture. There is no reason for judging that at best all that such testing of a test can reveal is either our general personal or social satisfaction in using the test—which might diverge from that of individuals or groups with dissimilar appetites or mores —or the general congruence of tests, of one part of our intellectual machinery with others. The kind of difficulties that are met and in a variety of degrees surmounted in distinguishing what are sometimes referred to as the "validity" and the "reliability" of psychological tests, and in making judgments about this validity, testifies amply that the distinction between these aspects of tests is not some kind of large-scale intellectual illusion.

11. The kind of seemingly insoluble philosophical difficulty to which a theory of knowledge is thought prone which insists that the revelatory power of our intellectual agencies can and must be tested by employing them is exemplified in the threatening regress of tests which some writers have thought they detected as a necessary and fatal flaw in such a theory. Thus A. N. Whitehead, commenting upon this defect in what he took to be the pragmatic test of truth, judged that such a test

can never work, unless on some occasion—in the future, or in the present—there is a definite determination of what is true on that occasion. Otherwise the poor pragmatist remains an intellectual Hamlet, perpetually adjourning decisions of judgment to some later date.[4]

And Russell, developing a similar vein of criticism in his essay on Dewey's *Logic,* urged against what he took to be a possible interpretation of Dewey's view of knowledge, namely, that it is "belief leading to success," that in such a case,

When you see a man eating salt, you cannot tell whether he is acting on knowledge or error until you have ascertained whether he wishes to commit suicide [and takes the salt under the impression that it is arsenic]. To ascertain this, you must discover whether the belief that he wishes to commit suicide will lead to your own success. This involves an endless regress.[5]

[4] *Process and Reality*, p. 275.
[5] "Dewey's New Logic," in P. A. Schilpp, ed., *The Philosophy of John Dewey*, pp. 152–153.

12. This is not the place to engage in a discussion of the virtues and vices of that protean philosophical thesis which has been the topic of discussion at various times in the recent past under the general title of the pragmatic theory of truth. What is of principal interest here, emerging in both Whitehead's and Russell's comments on that theory, is something by no means peculiar to discussions of it, namely, the paralysis of judgment about the revelatory power of our intellectual agencies, typified by the threatening endless regress, thought by many to infect any theory of knowledge which rejects the possibility of appealing in such judgment to some kind of direct revelation.

By this time the sensitized reader may perhaps already have discerned some of the philosophical preconceptions that are being expressed in the reasoning leading to the charge about an endless regress of judgments of success. Agreeing at once that a commitment to complete such a regress is fatal to any theory that entails it, one must ask from what that commitment derives. The answer to this question is presumably, first, that a view according to which judgments of veracity are always open to question about their own veracity provides the possibility of an endless repetition of the veracity question, and, second, that if the question can always be repeated, one who is interested in making a judgment of veracity must always answer. And since he must keep going to the end of a sequence that has no end before his judgment is made, he is thereby rendered incompetent to make any judgment whatever.

Perhaps a brief return to the metaphor of the spectacles will help. The reason why philosophical views holding that all revelation is indirect seem to some to lead to the untoward consequence of endless regress is illustrated in the view of a man who, noting the indirect character of the revelations of spectacles (or even eyes), concludes that therefore without some other more direct source of revelation concerning the character of material things, judgments of the veracity of deliverances of spectacles (or eyes) can never properly be made. This man is not without supporters, as discussions of the causal theory of perception make plain. But at first view, at least, the consequence of endless regress and incapacity to judge the results of observations made with spectacles (or eyes) is much less plausible. For in thinking of visual inspection of tables, chairs, trees, houses, and so on, we have much less inclination to think ourselves into a situation in which, having put into question the veracity of spectacles (or eyes) altogether, we set out to determine independently of these, without reliance upon any of the supposed revelations we may have through them, whether spectacles (or eyes) are good for seeing.

In the broader philosophical case, correspondingly, what lies behind the supposed commitment to an endless regress of judgments of veracity—indeed what is required in order to make the threat of such a regress conceivable, let alone a valid consequence of the theory—is the supposition that it is possible, and, for certain philosophical purposes, necessary for us in some wholesale way to put into question the veracity of our intellectual spectacles. And the character of the philosophical purpose to be served in this way is not difficult to discern. The purpose is that of entertaining, whether for ultimately intended skeptical purposes or not, hyperbolic doubt about our spectacles. No one who conceives himself engaged in a wholesale questioning of the veracity of all spectacles is going to be satisfied with answers to his questions which already presume the veracity of some. Similarly no one who, for whatever philosophical purposes, regards himself as engaged in a similar wholesale investigation of the veracity of our means of indirect revelation, can accept, as satisfying, answers which presume the veracity of any such means. Conceiving himself to have divested himself of all trust in such organs or instruments of intellectual vision, he must seek for answers in some extraordinary means that will enable him to look upon some entities, states, or processes, however limited these may be, in an immediate, direct way. A threatening endless regress has an ominous sound. But in this case the threat is but the formal expression of the fact that no one who professes to put a question about the veracity of all spectacles is logically permitted to begin to answer his question by trusting any. The case for direct revelation as a necessary means for avoiding the threatened regress is no stronger than the case for the possibility of entertaining for philosophical purposes this kind of wholesale, veracity question, the kind which, if they could be asked but not answered, would precipitate those who ask them into philosophical skepticism.

13. The hyperbolic questions about the veracity of all the intellectal lenses that we employ in our efforts to secure reliable information about ourselves and the world bear a familiar resemblance to less extreme ones we commonly entertain concerning various aspects of our intellectual optics and for which often we are capable of providing secure, reasonable answers. This resemblance contributes to the plausibility of these expanded questions as ones which it is proper to ask (as if there were not some gigantic fallacy of composition involved here in the passage from "each" to "all") and also to the difficulty of dealing with them when they are asked. It helps to obscure the intellectual peculiarity of the questions and, with that, the fact that this peculiarity calls for equally peculiar philosophical treatment.

At any point in time the legacy of cognitive optics with which human beings operate is a complex mixture of features of highly various degrees of perfection. Some of the less perfect features are due to the obsolescence of what were at one time well-ordered ones; some were sources of opacity, narrow vision, and distortion from the start. One who inherits preconceptions from ancestors, close or remote, or from earlier versions of himself, inherits prejudgment, prejudice in the wide sense of the word that implies no reflection upon its quality. Without such prejudgment each person would have to discover with each new encounter that fire burns, that ice is cold, and that velvet is softer to the touch than cockleburs, or, for that matter, that what he had encountered *was* fire, ice, velvet, or cockleburs, supposing *per impossibile,* he could still know what such things are. Without such prejudgment men would also not have to divest themselves of vast amounts of error, distortion, cant, nonsense, and pure superstition. The story of achievement in this regard in some areas of our cognitive institutions is one of the more heartening chapters in the history of mankind. But this story, for reasons already given, is not altogether germane to, and its recounting not directly effective in, dealing with the kind of large-scale questions from the posing of which the need for direct revelation seems to derive. The demonstration that limited questions about aspects of our cognitive institution can be effectively and profitably dealt with in limited ways, that the possibility of error, distortion, confusion is also, in more than a tautological sense the possibility of enlightenment, is not sufficient to meet large-scale, unlimited philosophical challenges. For this kind of philosophical question, challenge, and eventual would-be doubt, a different response is called for, the aim of which is not to show that the questions can be answered, and in this direct way what seems to be doubt allayed. Rather the aim must be to make plain that the questions and challenges are in a fundamental way misconceived, and the doubts to which they seem to lead not ones that can be consistently entertained.

14. The connection between the doctrine of the need for direct revelation and the raising of large-scale questions about the totality of our cognitive practices reveals this doctrine to be another expression of a very familiar one already elaborated upon in the preceding discussions of justification theory and the relations between this theory and philosophical skepticism. In spite of the plausible way in which the alleged need for revelation sometimes makes its appearance—seeming to ensue from a more thorough prosecution of activities ordinarily engaged in in the scrutiny of limited features of our cognitive practice, and seeming to show that such revelation remains the sole means of avoiding the philosophical perils of either accepting congruence of judgment or pragmatic ministering to our needs as substitutes for objective validity—what these philosophical specters represent is not sound logical consequences of the rejection of such revelation, but rather consequences that would follow if in the philosophical scrutiny of knowledge there were the need or even the possibility of entertaining the kind of question raised. Such consequences would follow if the task of philosophical scrutiny could be and were what it is conceived to be in Cartesian or justification theory, if in performing this task one could and needed to accept the challenge of these questions in the way

which has been characteristic of this tradition in the modern philosophy of knowledge.

15. In the treatment of the relations between Cartesian or justification theory and philosophical skepticism in the preceding chapters, the primary aim has been to expose these relations and utilize the clarification which that exposition brings for illuminating the justification problem in general and, among its important speciations, the philosophical problem of induction. Justification theory has been viewed as a skeptically impregnated endeavor to meet skeptical challenges by finding satisfactory answers to the skeptic's questions. The intellectual obduracy of the problem of induction, and of a plentiful set of similar problems that have emerged in the development of the empiricist version of Cartesian theory, has been accounted for as a manifestation, at a certain level, and in a certain context, of a fundamental weakness in the theory. These more prominent problems are accompanied, at the level referred to as "construction," by other less well-attended difficulties, some of which were discussed in connection with the revision phenomena. And at the "foundation" level there are the difficulties attending the quest for first cognitions, particularly, in the empiricist version of the program, the first cognitions of sense.

The accumulation of considerations deriving from these topics weighs heavily against any theory that tries to give an account of our knowledge as the outgrowth of direct revelation, as a branching system of claims that depends for its fidelity to its objects upon the guarantees of some kind of revelatory intuition. But the exposure of the impossibility of one of a pair of alternatives does not by itself invalidate the assessment of possibility represented by the pair. Rather, if the exposure succeeds, in the case of an alternative as desperate as the one under examination, and if the posed alternative is valid, it serves to emphasize this desperate character. But is the assessment valid? The supposition that it is, as has just been observed, depends upon a further supposition, implicit in the justification program, that it is possible for us, without fundamental logical inconsistency, to raise questions in a wholesale way about the possibility of human knowledge, about the world and our position in the world which renders knowledge possible.

The question is not, it should now be very clear, whether philosophical challenges should be responded to, but how the responses should be made. Challenges of an extreme skeptical nature, which seek to call into question our capacity to attain any substantial knowledge of ourselves and the world, beyond a few possible fleeting apparitions or deliverances, are a very special kind of challenge and require a correspondingly special kind of response. This being so, it is very important in determining what response is appropriate to a philosophical challenge, problem, or question, to be able to discriminate those which are animated by deep skeptical motives, express deep skeptical presuppositions, from those of a different nature.

16. The primary purpose of the examination of the skeptical motives in justification theory that has been carried on in this book has been to expose this character, not to respond to it in a thorough, systematic way. Nevertheless enough has been said, in making plain the considerations that ensure the elimination of the kind of revelatory knowledge conceived in the fateful pair of alternatives under consideration, to indicate what the basic response must be. The very same considerations which have been employed to eliminate the possibility of basic incorrigible cognitions of sense, and of similarly irrevisable inferences or constructions proceeding from these cognitions, ensure, when their significance is fully appreciated, that, in spite of the fateful pairing, the result of this elimination cannot be skeptical disaster. For the way in which the elimination of the supposed revelatory knowledge is effected is by grounds which show that, not merely in knowing the character of objects of knowledge, but also in the very activity of thinking about such objects, wondering about them, and hence entertaining doubts about the possibility of our knowing them, we are dependent upon these objects. In our very activity of wondering about the character of some X, in forming the very thought of that character, we presume, whether we are aware of it or not, that we do know something about the character of some Y, or set of Y's which in many cases, though not all, will even include X itself. Therefore, a perfectly proper query

or doubt about the existence or character of this X, or that Y, when generalized into a hyperbolic doubt about the existence or character of all X's and Y's, is often rendered improper by its extreme generality. By the endeavor to stretch the doubt too far, its character as a doubt has been destroyed, not in any sudden, shattering collapse, but by a less perceptible generation of inconsistency within it. What one is endeavoring to succeed in doing with all X's and Y's is what can only be accomplished with some of them. That levers can be detached from particular fulcrums, that no lever is necessarily attached to any, does not warrant our supposing that there is a universal lever that can be employed without any fulcrum whatever.

One cannot, to revert to the now familiar example, wonder about or doubt that all John's sons are bald without in some way taking it for granted that John has sons, or even children. If John has no sons, we may *take ourselves* to doubt whether they are bald. But the fact that we may say the words with feeling, with indeed feeling that we cannot by inspection differentiate from that which we have when we speak of Joseph's actual sons, does not mean that we have succeeded in formulating and entertaining what it would be right to refer to as a doubt that all John's sons are bald. For that achievement we needed a certain objective complement to or, rather, setting for our activity which for one reason or another was wanting, and the wanting of which subtly distorted or diluted the sense that can properly be attributed to this activity. The moral of this, expressed as an answer to the question implicit in the title of *Meditation I*, namely, "What things is it possible to bring into doubt?" is, as Peirce among others has now well taught us, "Not nearly so much (for the achievement of a genuine doubt is not nearly so easy) as many philosophers have hitherto thought."

17. The challenge of hyperbolic doubt, or of what is advanced as such a doubt, is but one of the kinds of challenge to which our settled cognitive practices and established cognitive institutions are open, and to which some response must be possible in an adequate philosophy of knowledge. As was emphasized earlier, challenges to what are recognized as accepted practices in the cognitive institution are not met by repeating their identification

as practices or displaying again their settled character. One does not meet a challenge to the accuracy of the clock indicating the time to be nine o'clock by reading again its face. For various reasons, the kind of broad, wholesale challenges to our cognitive practices that threaten to ensue in some kind of hyperbolic doubt with respect to these practices has exerted an especially strong appeal upon philosophers with interests in philosophical questions about knowledge. It is of the greatest importance in the philosophy of knowledge, not only that it be made clear that such challenges can be met, but also that the manner in which they can be met be spelled out in some detail. This task has been performed repeatedly through the years of philosophical debate by many eminent writers. It is one which no doubt needs to be performed again and again, utilizing somewhat different means, speaking in the somewhat different idioms that new occasions, new developments in the cognitive institution, and new forms of life, repeatedly call for.

18. That further efforts have not been expanded upon this task in the present book is due, not to any lack of appreciation of this task, but rather to a devotion to a different though closely related one. For there is not just one task to be performed in the philosophy of knowledge, but many. And important as is that of blocking the incursions of that thin, haunting specter of disbelief that passes as skeptical doubt, it should not be permitted so much to pre-empt the limited time available for philosophical reflection, to so greatly monopolize philosophical energies. There are a great variety of important, though less transfixing challenges to philosophical reflection about knowledge. These challenges and the difficulties they represent are often tractable to reflective thought; and their successful treatment, or at least progressive amelioration, is of great assistance to our lives and activities within the institutions of human knowledge, both in furthering the understanding of the institution and its practices, and in their preservation, cultivation, and development.

19. No one sufficiently informed to be interested in the philosophy of knowledge needs to be instructed that cognitive principles and practices are important, though, to be sure, the degree, nature, and grounds of that importance vary from age to age,

depend upon the character of prevailing cognitive institutions and their relations with others. In the latter half of the twentieth century the nature and position of the natural sciences in civilized societies renders almost incomparable the significance of the philosophy of science in comparison with that of such predecessors as the metaphysics of natural philosophy at the times of William of Ockham and Thomas Aquinas. A very concrete and prominent sign of this difference of significance is the difference of organization of the universities, the difference of subjects of instruction and those in which degrees are awarded, between those times and the present day. The theory of knowledge takes on a very different cast when the urgency of its cultivation arises less from a desire to understand the ground and the nature of natural theology than from a corresponding desire directed toward nuclear physics, microbiology, or the principles of scientific linguistics.

20. An interesting feature of the philosophical enterprise of attempting to work out a theory which will provide us with general, systematic understanding of certain activities in which we constantly engage, is the ease with which any considerable failure of the enterprise leads those who engage in it to the conclusion that since they have not succeeded in achieving the understanding of what they took themselves to do, therefore they must not really do it. It has been many centuries since any natural philosophers of note showed a disposition to conclude that because there were difficulties in achieving a mathematical understanding of how Achilles could win a race with the tortoise, that therefore he could not, and that, furthermore, on the same grounds it could be shown that these imagined contestants could not race, because neither they nor anything else could move. Few philosophers have been inclined to deny that there are external objects like tables and chairs, and other living creatures, including human beings. But there have been not a few who, in the face of the difficulties encountered in developing a theory for accounting for our knowledge that there are such entities or beings, while eschewing denial that there are such, are prepared to defend the theses that we cannot know that there are and can have no real knowledge of their character. Similarly some philos-

ophers, frustrated in their attempts to understand how it is possible to draw reasonable conclusions concerning unobserved objects on the basis of knowledge of the observed, have been led to conclude that we cannot draw such conclusions, and that in consequence, for example, it is impossible for us to form rational judgment of whether, or in what respects, the future will resemble the past. Similarly, in other areas of philosophical inquiry, and sometimes with most unfortunate practical results, frustrations in the project of understanding how ethical and political judgments can be reasonably formed have led to the conclusion that they cannot, and to theories that echo in one way or another Hume's dictum that in such matters reason is and ought to be only the slave of the passions.

If reactions such as this be rightly regarded as falling in the domain of the pathology of philosophical inquiry, they are not less important for that reason; and the pathology dealing with them is correspondingly an important branch of philosophical inquiry. Because the problems dealt with in this pathology seem to call into question the very feasibility of the philosophical enterprise, they have a capacity to displace other philosophical topics in many serious minds. The imbalance and displacement of attention thus produced would be perhaps a matter of no serious concern if these did not have a tendency to become chronic. One of the unfortunate aspects of justification theory in the theory of knowledge is the extent to which it contributes to this tendency. The theory of knowledge when practiced in accordance with the tenets of justification theory resolves into an enterprise concerned solely with this one kind of difficulty. Interest and energy in the philosophical scrutiny of knowledge are pre-empted for this one purpose, and the incapacity of justification theory to succeed in the enterprise ensures that the pre-emption and fixation of purpose will become permanent, creating a bottomless pit of intellectual appetite constantly calling to be filled.

21. One benefit to be gained, therefore, from an examination of justification theory in philosophy is some sense of balance between the concerns to which this theory is directed and others which also have legitimate claims for attention in the philosoph-

ical examination of knowledge. Likewise one dividend that accrues from an understanding of how this one concern can adequately be dealt with is a release of time and energy which can be devoted to the others. There are other challenges to be met in the cognitive practices of our lives, which, no less than the skeptical challenges, promise to repay careful consideration with increased illumination that is of great value, not only to those who are privileged to engage in this activity as a vocation, but to their fellow men.

Probability

1. The widely conceded failure of some philosophers and philosophically minded mathematicians and statisticians to achieve in one or two abstract formulae a "definition" of probability counts, of course, not as a weakness in the theory of probability and its technical applications, including those of statistical theory, but as a weakness in a certain way of approaching this theory and achieving a philosophical understanding of it. That is to say, the weakness is not in what is normally studied and taught under the title of "theory of probability" by mathematicians, specialists in mathematical statistics, and others, but in something discussed under this title by certain philosophers.

2. There are several sources of this weakness. One is a common, often unexpressed assumption that whatever it is that the term "probability" signifies, it is something that might also be identified substantially as "good reasons" or evidence: the kind of reasons that are reasons for "belief," theoretical reasons, as distinguished from reasons for action.

A second source of weakness is the assumption that the project of elucidating philosophically the significance of expressions like this and the intellectual practices and institutions in which they are employed requires for its successful completion the formulation of definitions of these expressions, definitions of the kind that provide at one and the same time a noncircular explication of the expressions in question and an adequate operational guide or manual for their correct application. A third source of weakness is an attempt to understand the construction of the desired definitions in terms of the crude but now comfortable rubrics of "test" and "meaning."

3. For reasons that should now be fairly clear, an essential feature of empiricist philosophy was the drive to close the gap between test and meaning. Applied to probability, in conjunction with the other presumptions just cited, this drive led easily to the identification of probability with frequency, to some version of the relative-frequency theory (read: definition) of probability. For though the earliest work on mathematical probability had emphasized that we estimate probabilities by counting things like the sides of dice, or the possibilities these sides represent, no one wants to construe the statement that the probability of getting a six in a toss of a die is $\frac{1}{6}$, as simply a statement about the ratio of the numbers of sides or of possibilities.

But the difficulties of identifying probability with relative frequency were multiple and serious. Some of these sprang directly from the view that when probability is literally identified with relative frequency, it quickly becomes clear that the relative frequency in question cannot be interpreted as something that will be realized in a sequence of trials of any determinant finite length, but rather will be realized eventually in a sequence of trials that is indefinitely long. This led to the problem of the maturation of the chances alluded to in Chapter 2, Sect. 12, in connection with Peirce. It also led to the exacerbation of an already serious difficulty with which Hans Reichenbach, one of the leading protagonists of this theory, struggled manfully in his writings on probability and induction, namely, the problem of induction itself as it applies to the determination of probabilities. In spite of certain differences produced by the introduction into the discussion of probability of the idea of a limit of an indefinitely extended sequence, there was in the case of statements conveying probability estimates and statements conveying necessary or causal connections the same problem of how to construe the rationality of such statements themselves and how to determine whatever rationality they are conceived to have. In short, when good reasons themselves are explicated in terms of more or less constant (probability) or strictly constant (necessity) associations of events, characters, or objects, what does it mean to say, and how does one determine, that one has good reasons for statements conveying such associations? The problem of a regress of statements which seemed to be implicated in such a theory was met in Reichenbach's philosophy by the view that the regress did properly end in estimations of frequency which stood by themselves without reasons. Such estimates were termed by Reichenbach "blind posits."

4. The publication of Rudolf Carnap's paper "On Inductive Logic" in 1945, followed within a few years by his two books on probability and induction marked a startling reversal in orthodox empiricist philosophy. It was misleading to think of this as a liberalization of the empiricist program for explicating good reasons, effected by enlarging the cabinet of probability to include a representative of "logical" probability; for from a philosophical point of view, this new entrant into the intellectual cabinet was entrusted with the most important portfolios. It was now in terms of a version of the theory of probability as a logical relation—a version which, in comparison with that of Keynes, was much more rigorously defined and vastly limited in scope— that the beginnings were now to be made in explicating the concept of good reasons for statements, hypotheses, suppositions, and the like. Empirical or statistical probability was now regarded as a kind of physical, or at least natural entity, like mass, energy, and entropy, and to be investigated scientifically like them. Logical probability was identified with degree of confirmation relative to evidence, an epistemic entity to be investigated and defined by logical, and primarily, semantic means. So viewed, the move to inductive logic thus represented not a minor concession to rationalistic principles in the investigation of good reasons, but rather capitulation.

5. But the apparent victory of rationalist principles was short-lived, and its shortness of life was itself due in part to the carefulness with which Carnap had elaborated his version of the principles in his treatment of inductive probability and its applications. Some of the difficulties which had attended previous, looser versions of these principles were circumvented temporarily by Carnap by specifying that their application be confined to language systems that are both highly formalized and of a severely restricted kind. Critics were quick to point out that to

the extent that the need to specify the character of the language system to which the principles applied represented the possibility of different choices in the definition of probability, the definition could not be regarded as complete unless supplemented by a theory accounting for the particular choice represented by the language system specified. Furthermore, in order to preserve the rationalistic character of the definition, this theory, hard as this may be to conceive, would have to be rationalistic as well. And to the extent, which was considerable, that the restrictions on the richness of the language systems were dictated by a need to exclude predicates of a kind fundamental to science, namely, quantitative and continuous ones, these restrictions were a sign of a fundamental difficulty in this and other versions of the a priori theory of probability. For, as one critic observed, "no one has yet given the least indication" of how assignments of probability can be made for such predicates in a theory of probability of this kind.[1]

6. Even if one restricts one's efforts to definite and severely restricted language systems of the kind indicated, a further serious difficulty lies in wait for this attempt to construct an a priori definition of inductive probability (inductive good reasons). This difficulty resides in the rich number of possibilities of definition which still remain and which were referred to by Carnap as the "continuum of inductive methods."

Suppose one is given a conclusion in the form of a law, or at least an unrestricted generalization, to the effect that A's are uniformly B, and the evidence for this is simply that all the known A's, these being a relatively large number, have been such. One of the most striking aspects of Carnap's theory of probability is the emphasis it gives to the conclusion that it is quite consistent with the program of providing a priori assignments of probability to possible states of affairs that the determination of the probability of the above conclusion in relation to the cited evidence should be any one of an indefinitely large set of numbers ranging from 0 to 1. In this theory the indeterminacy

[1] A. W. Burks, Review of Carnap's *Logical Foundations of Probability*, *Journal of Philosophy*, XLVIII (1951), p. 533.

appears in a plurality of measure-functions, each of which determines a different number to be assigned as the probability of an inductive conclusion like the one above.

7. In the history of the discussion of probability and induction this conclusion is by no means a novel one; but no one has paved the way to it with the abundance of hard, technical detail provided by Carnap. Suppose for the moment that one fixed upon a measure-function that would enable one to show that an inductive conclusion of the above sort has a high degree of probability, as defined by this function. One would still not have succeeded in providing an a priori "justification" of this conclusion: this because of the unfinished business of providing reasons for the choice of this out of the vast set of possible defining functions. Once the choice has been made, in the restricted kind of situation to which this general logical apparatus applies, the decision about the probability of the inductive conclusion is determined. But over the choice, and over what counts as decisive reasons for the choice, there are still, as Carnap recognized, "irreconcilable differences," which affect the above results in a most radical way.[2] It is conceivable, Carnap himself thought, that at some future time, on the basis of better knowledge of the field of inductive logic, these differences will dissolve in agreement upon one specific function, and hence one specific inductive method. But we do not know whether this will be the case, he said, do not know whether the number of admissible functions "will always remain infinite, or will become finite and possibly even reduced to one."[3] Therefore, at the present time, one cannot assert that there is only one rational method and function. One must not exclude the possibility that "the multiplicity of mutually incompatible methods is an essential characteristic of inductive logic," and that it is hence "meaningless to talk of 'one valid method.'"[4]

8. If, in the face of these difficulties in executing the project, one remains convinced that the understanding of probability, in

[2] *The Continuum of Inductive Methods*, Part I, Sect. 1; cf. also A. W. Burks, "The Presupposition Theory of Induction," *Philosophy of Science* (1953).
[3] "The Aim of Inductive Logic," in E. Nagel, and others, *Logic, Methodology and Philosophy of Science*, p. 316.
[4] *Continuum*, Sect. 1.

its inductive applications, is to be achieved in the construction of some defining formula—short, as in the case of von Mises or Reichenbach; long, in the case of Carnap—the form that the next attempt should take is not difficult to anticipate. First steps toward it are already made in Carnap's view about the real and possibly permanent sources of a division of opinion concerning valid inductive methods. It is but a few short further steps from his concession that the choice of measure-function cannot be made upon "purely theoretical" grounds to the view that the difference between possible measure-functions is not an essential matter for the definition of probability. If the choice of measure-functions introduces a possibly inescapable element of subjectivity, intractable to theoretical decision, into the definition of probability, why not recognize this element and confine the philosophical exploration and elucidation of probability to those aspects of it which are tractable? One will then not expect of probability theory, no matter how industriously it may be cultivated, a complete definition of inductive good reasons, but rather only a theory of that aspect of the assessments of probability that is not subjective, not in any degree idiosyncratic, but rather logically required of any assessments whatever if they are, when taken together, to meet the standards of logical consistency or coherence.[5] This alternative in the philosophy of probability, like the frequency theory and the logical theory, has a long ancestry, leading back, in modern times, through the work of Frank P. Ramsey and Bruno de Finetti, to Augustus de Morgan and perhaps also James Bernoulli. The professional expertise with which this alternative has been developed and discussed in recent years is impressive.[6]

5 "Coherence" is a term favored by some writers to distinguish the logical requirements of consistency of *assessment* of beliefs, propositions, hypotheses from the more traditional requirement of the consistency as applied to these logical objects themselves.

6 *The Encyclopedia of Philosophy* entry on "Probability," written by M. Black, contains a good brief introduction to this theory and a brief bibliography. Some further valuable beginning references are: H. E. Kyburg, Jr., and H. E. Smokler, *Studies in Subjective Probability;* R. Jeffrey, *The Logic of Decision;* H. E. Kyburg, Jr., *Probability and Inductive Logic* (this book contains a very extensive bibliography); L. J. Savage, *The Foundations of Statistics.*

9. If by a subjectivist view of probability is understood one that in one way or another identifies probability with strength of belief, then the view here is one of subjectivism mitigated by certain logical considerations, and specifically by the requirement that the assessments of probability, and hence the degrees of strength of belief associated by the believer or assessor with statements or hypotheses must as a totality be logically consistent. One cannot, to take an obvious case, suppose that the probability of heads is $\frac{1}{2}$ and the probability of tails $\frac{2}{3}$, in a toss of a coin. As two recent writers say,

Perhaps the simplest way to characterize the subjectivist conception of probability is to say (a) that any degree of belief in any statement is permissible, but (b) that there are restrictions placed on the distribution of degrees of belief among sets of related statements.

In this respect the theory contrasts with both the relative-frequency and the logical theories, according to which

there is one and only one degree of probability that can be correctly assigned to an event of a certain sort in a given sequence, or to a statement relative to a given body of evidence.[7]

An analogue in ethical theory would be a theory of good which said that any valuation whatever is possible with respect to any object, state of affairs, or human act, so long as certain restrictions hold for sets of related valuations, restrictions dictated by the need for logical coherence.

10. There are several points to be kept in mind in judging the philosophical significance of the controversy over these three alternative views about probability and in appreciating the present state of the controversy. The chief of these points were mentioned at the beginning of this discussion. If one's view of theoretical considerations is so restricted that nothing counts as theoretical that is not amenable to treatment in the highly abstract way in which subjects in pure mathematics and mathematical logic are treated, then it is perfectly obvious that the correct conditions for the application of the term "probable" and related expressions cannot be sufficiently specified by purely theoretical

[7] Kyburg and Smokler, *Studies*, p. 7.

means. Further, if what lies beyond the fringe of the theoretical are "pragmatic" considerations, and if the reactions of individuals and groups to such considerations display irreducible variations, then the specifications of the conditions for the application of this term, the definition of probability, will in this respect be irreducibly relative or subjective in relation to the individuals and groups exhibiting these variations.

11. A continuing undercurrent of presumption in this reasoning is the supposition that the philosophical understanding of a term like probability is achieved through the explication of the meaning of this and similar expressions, where meaning is thought of as something the exploration and illumination of which can be effected principally by paying attention to usage, in the way that we should explain or define the meaning of "probabilis" in giving instruction in Latin, or "τὸ εὔλογον" in Greek. The criticism of this supposition is not a simple matter, since it involves in the end an evaluation of a whole and still very influential genre of philosophical work. Though an important aspect of the usage of the term "probable" is the variety of the conditions of its correct use, another important aspect is that amid the great variety of conditions, tests, and criteria of use there is a common element of personal act and expression of the general kind that J. L. Austin came to designate in other connections as "illocutionary force." This aspect was emphasized by certain British philosophers, and with particular effectiveness by Stephen Toulmin. Why, he asked in his criticism of the two-species-of-probability views of men like Kneale, Urmson, and Carnap, should one suppose that the term "probable" has a different meaning when one is talking of outcomes in games of chance and when one is talking of scientific hypotheses? Is the case for different senses of "probable" here any stronger than the case for different senses of "know" in such contexts, e.g., in "I know that Hodgkin's explanation is correct" and "I know that if I throw this die twenty times, a six will turn up at least once," or even in "I know that the square root of 2 is not a rational number"? Toulmin said:

Of course, if you are considering the correctness or incorrectness of a scientific hypothesis, the evidence to which it is appropriate to appeal is different from that which is relevant if you are concerned with the results of dice-throwing. But, unless we are once again to confuse *the grounds for regarding something* as probable with the *meaning of the statement that it is* probable, we need not go on to say that there are consequently a number of different senses of the words 'probable' and 'probability.' [8]

The common significance of these and like words, persisting through the variety of evidential contexts, Toulmin argued, could best be conceived as that of guarding or restricting the commitment of a speaker considered to be advancing predictions, statements, hypotheses in these contexts. The probability that a speaker attributes to a hypothesis or a future event is a reflection of the way he restricts or guards the way he advances the hypotheses or predicts the event, or *would* advance or predict these things, in the light of his reading of the evidential situation. This view led to difficulties, some of them in relation to attributions of probability in the past tense, and in relation to utterances other than those of the speaker. To these more or less specific difficulties of the theory in practice it is not necessary to give consideration here.

12. For interesting as some of these specific difficulties are, they are less significant than certain more fundamental defects in this whole approach to probability to which the exploration of these specific difficulties eventually leads. In the first place, the separation of inductive from statistical probability is but a first primitive step toward the recognition that good reasons, even reasons of a theoretical or cognitive kind, come in a great variety of forms, some of which (think of theories now in astrophysics, or of what may or may not be genuine instances of religious knowledge. Is transubstantiation *more probable* than consubstantiation?) do not associate in easy logical relations with terms like "probability" and the rest. And if we remind ourselves of what the assignment of probability to a hypothesis (e.g., the hypothesis that Lee Harvey Oswald did fire three shots from the window of

[8] "Probability," *Aristotelian Society Supplement Volume XXIV* (1950), p. 61 (italics in orig.). This article is reprinted in A. Flew, ed., *Essays in Conceptual Analysis*. Toulmin's criticism of Carnap appeared in *Mind* (1953). Portions of both writings are combined in the chapter on Probability in his *The Uses of Argument*.

the Texas School Book Depository Building in Dallas) implies concerning the truth of that hypothesis, as it stands, how comfortable can we feel in speaking of reasons for accepting or holding scientific hypotheses as grounds rendering these probable, when the evidence suggests that in the most highly developed disciplines the mortality of theoretical elements as literal truths in the relevant domains of application during the next fifty or a hundred years may be expected, if our hopes for scientific progress are realized, to be extremely high?

13. More important than this question, however, is the broader one concerning the rationale of the project of seeking philosophical enlightenment concerning probability by means of constructing definitions, of the kind specified above, of this and similar terms. Even if the project is restricted to those domains in which there is a close congruence between good cognitive reasons and probability, there is the question of how much is won if the project is achieved. If we look for a common significance that can be attributed to probability expressions throughout the wide variations of use, we may indeed succeed in finding and formulating a plausible candidate, perhaps in the illocutionary force emphasized by Toulmin or in degree of belief or confidence expressed, presuming this degree to be subjected to the restrictions of consistent distribution in relation to other assessments. There is no reason why a meaning of this kind cannot be precipitated out of a variety of uses and linguistically isolated. In order to do this we must, as the discussions of the matter by Toulmin and others illustrate, concentrate upon a certain aspect of the use of the expressions, namely their use in conveying avowals of belief, signaling strength of assertion and therewith also perhaps some personal assessment of strength of grounds for the proposition or statement conveyed in the assertion. And we may defend our concentration upon this aspect of the expressions by emphasizing, as already indicated, that what we are concerned with is the meaning these expressions convey when we use them rather than with what grounds we may have, or may need to have, in order to determine that our uses are correct.

14. To identify test and meaning is unquestionably an error. But the proper correction of the error of simply identifying these

aspects of the use of expressions is not their intellectual separation. "Obviously meaning and verification *are* connected," Waismann remarked many years ago, "so why say they are not?" [9] It is, fortunately, not necessary to revive the debate about test and meaning and to try to provide some settlement of it in order to say what needs to be said concerning the definition of probability, though in understanding what needs to be said it is helpful to have some appreciation of the fact that the intellectual categories and framework in which the debate arose were infelicitous, and the issues joined in the debate ones which call more for reinterpretation and transcendence than for definite decision one way or the other.

15. The development of linguistic theory in the past twenty years has realerted philosophers to the fact that there are very important ways in which the meaning of linguistic expressions can be scientifically construed and explored that are very different from the ways in which philosophers proceed in trying to achieve an understanding of these expressions and of the social practices in which the expressions are employed. One reaction to the discovery of this fact might be a declaration to the effect that to the extent that philosophers have conceived of their activity as an exploration of meaning they were mistaken; and that the way out of this mistake is by way of a recognition that what they are investigating, when they take themselves to be exploring the meaning of "space," "time," "cause," "number," "courage," or "virtue," is, rather, the nature of these entities, relations, or qualities. Another reaction, as has already been suggested, is that although from certain restricted points of view it is possible and valuable to distinguish questions about the meaning of the expression X from questions about the character of X's, it is much less possible and valuable to do this from the broad point of view that is taken in philosophy. The insistence upon absoluteness in the distinction between real and nominal questions is part of the broad, philosophical thesis that there is such a distinction between the analytic and the synthetic in truth, and the a priori and the posteriori in knowledge.

One of the benefits of a more relaxed, less absolute view of

9 "Verifiability," paragraph 2.

such distinctions is the way it enables one to recognize, in the case of terms like "probable," that one aspect of their use is to indicate in certain contexts, not only the strength of grounds for assertions or possible assertions, but also something of the character of the grounds themselves (sometimes a matter of counting or measuring possibilities; sometimes a matter of actual frequencies), because here as elsewhere in the employment of expressions to make assertions or to consider assertibles, the distinction between what we are saying and the grounds we have for saying it is far less tidy than fits certain kinds of philosophical theory. On the other hand, while recognizing this, one can still allow for a certain aspect of meaning that is relatively context-free, an aspect that is in consequence of the greatest significance for linguistic theory and for the explanations that can be provided in this theory of how we learn to employ in the way we do these and other expressions. The admission of *this kind* of relatively context-free meaning for the term "probable" and related terms does not commit one to the admission that in the philosophical exploration of the significance of these there must be, as a goal, a common *designatum* of the term probability, and that it is in the identification and isolation of this that a great part of the philosophical illumination consists. One may, in the philosophical exploration of this term, remain as firmly convinced as Toulmin that, notwithstanding the important role that things like frequencies or proportions of alternatives have for probability, they need not be considered as "rival claimants to a tinsel crown" that is thought to mark the "real *designatum*" of the term.[10]

16. Allusion has already been made to one analogy between the conception of probability in the theory of knowledge and the conception of good in ethics. Though the matter may not be expanded upon here, there is a most interesting and illuminating comparison to be made between the fortunes of attempts at the definition of "good" in empiricist-minded philosophies and the fortunes in the case of probability. Naturalistic views of good which tend to translate judgments about what is good into what

[10] "Probability," p. 54.

is desirable and what is desirable into what men desire, as illustrated in the ethical writings of such figures as Hume, Mill, and, more recently, Schlick, are the close analogue in this line of inquiry of the constancy theory of laws and the frequency theory of probability in the theory of knowledge. Another analogy holds between the a priori view of probability, especially those forms of it, like that of Keynes, in which probability is viewed as a relation between propositions, which is only in a limited way, and in certain contexts, capable of further analysis and which ultimately depends for its apprehension upon a logical intuition, and those forms of ethical intuitionism in which good is viewed as a non-natural quality (hence not analyzable in terms of the desired, the satisfaction-bringing, etc.), similarly dependent for its discernment upon intuitive means. One cannot read the early philosophical discussions in Keynes's *A Treatise on Probability* without being repeatedly reminded of the parallels in Moore's *Principia Ethica*.

But disagreements of apprehension have always been a problem for theories of intuition; and what shall one do about the cases in which one man's good, or probable, is another man's evil, or improbable? Is it not still the case that between *A*, who identifies the good as *X*, and *B*, who identifies it as *Y*, there is nevertheless some common meaning conveyed by the term "good"; else how could they be disagreeing? Taking a clue from the identification by the *Oxford English Dictionary* of the word "good" as "the most general adjective of commendation" in the language, may one not, in defining good, fix upon this general commending, advising, enjoining (and expressing) use? [11] And conceding the wide differences of commendation, and so on, which may be given the very same objects by different persons, groups, parties, and societies, together with the insufficiency of purely scientific or logical means to determine any one of these differing commendations as valid over the others, may one not say that so long as the set of related commendations of anyone is logically consistent, they are not from a theoretical point of

[11] Cf. P. H. Nowell-Smith, *Ethics*, Penguin ed., p. 95. The smaller *Oxford Universal Dictionary* correspondingly says of "good" that it is "a term of general or indefinite commendation."

view criticizable or corrigible? Then the theory of good may be regarded as the theory of consistent commendation, as an elaboration of the characteristics in related commendations that such consistency requires. The idiom in which the view has been just expressed, chosen as it was to accentuate its analogies with developments in the philosophical theory of probability, is in some respects divergent from that employed by the exponents of subjectivist–emotivist ethical theory in recent and contemporary philosophy. But the congruence of the basic thought expressed with that of a variety of writers in the field—e.g., A. J. Ayer, C. L. Stevenson, P. H. Nowell-Smith, R. M. Hare, and Paul Edwards—seems plain.

17. In view of the general deprecating tone taken in the preceding pages in speaking of philosophical definitions of probability, it may be well, before this comment is concluded, for the object of deprecation to be more exactly identified. The object of criticism is of course not a word, but a practice; nor is it every practice to which the name "definition" can be applied. There is an enduring tradition of philosophical usage in which the quest for philosophical understanding of a large domain of human concern is spoken of as a matter of seeking to define certain broad terms that refer in an embracing way to the objects of that concern. In Plato's *Republic* Socrates is represented in his highly various discussions of psychology, politics, education, aesthetics, knowledge, and metaphysics, as providing a definition of justice as it applies both to the human soul and to the city. It is likewise perhaps not inaccurate to think of the *Nichomachean Ethics* as a project of defining that kind of happiness for man that consists in living well and doing well. And the usage is not restricted to those domains that are in a full-blown way philosophical. It is not unreasonable to think of the theory of numbers as providing an elaborate definition of number, and Euclid's geometry as defining in detail the character of a certain kind of space.

18. It is not, therefore, the project of defining "good" or "probable" that is the object of criticism here, when, in contrast with the nominal, linguistic connotations of this way of referring to the project, what is sought under the title of "definition" is

nothing so restricted as the isolation of some linguistic fact. This title is also sometimes employed to refer in a compressed way to the project of developing a comprehensive view of a whole domain of human practice, a whole institution or set of institutions, which, not in any narrow, strict way, but in a genuine philosophical way, may be thought to be the *designatum* of the terms in question. Then the term "definition" itself refers to the endeavor to develop a systematic critical view of these practices and institutions which will serve to provide, not only understanding of them as they stand at any given time, but also, and closely consequent upon this, a basis for the criticism and rectification of these institutions, as the need for these repeatedly arises. Definition, so understood, signifies a process and result that are indispensable, and indeed central, to the philosophical vocation.

19. This does not commit one to the deprecation of other kinds of definition pursued and achieved in the philosophical vocation, except insofar as this pursuit and achievement interferes with, or, more seriously, supplants the kind of definition that requires not merely a refined understanding of words but an equally refined understanding of things. It is unquestionably of some service to this latter more-embracing understanding to have made plain that, persisting through the variety of contexts, statistical and otherwise, in which we make assessments of probability, and in which the significance of the assessments is itself affected by these varying contextual circumstances, there is an isolable residue of meaning such as that discriminated by Toulmin's more or less Austinian analysis. Similarly it is of value to have the identification and clarification that modern semantic analysis can provide by precipitating, from the mixture of philosophical and linguistic theses that were often advanced not very discriminatingly in pronouncements about good and desire, the linguistic conclusion that "apart from certain minor, derivative, or deviant cases, 'good' in English means answering to certain interests." [12] Analytic results of this kind, though valuable, and even perhaps necessary for some philosophical purposes, are for others very deficient. Deficient they are if what is being sought

[12] P. Ziff, *Semantic Analysis*, p. 247.

under the title of "definitions" of the probable or the good is a broad, critical understanding of the human practices and institutions of which these general terms stand as linguistic representatives, one which will in a substantial way contribute to the continuing project of trying to penetrate, comprehend, and help resolve some of the serious disagreements that arise concerning the significance and correctness of general practices of assessment of probability and of goodness in the various domains of theoretical and practical life in which these practices have their homes. And the same must be said of a philosophical definition of probability that restricts itself to the conditions of consistent probability assessments, to the requirements that such assessments must satisfy "in all possible worlds," as we say speaking loosely, in Leibnizian terminology, of the way in which certain theoretical systems may be developed independently of a consideration of the conditions of their application. Such independence is always purchased at a price, and in this case a price that may be reasonable for mathematical purposes is for philosophical ones excessive. For it is a price that renders the theory of probability encapsulated in this definition constitutionally incapable of providing answers to the large-scale questions of principle which constantly arise in disputes that far transcend issues over what is required for the consistent ordering of assessments of probability, but concern the principles we employ to judge the material adequacy of assessments that need to be ordered.

Bibliography of Works Cited

Austin, John L. *How to do things with Words,* J. O. Urmson, ed. Oxford, Oxford University Press, 1962.

——. "Ifs and Cans," *Proceedings of the British Academy,* Vol. XLII, 1956, pp. 109–132. Reprinted in *Philosophical Papers,* pp. 153–180.

——. "Other Minds," *Aristotelian Society Supplementary Volume XX,* 1946, pp. 148–187. Reprinted in A. Flew, ed., *Logic and Language,* Second Series, pp. 123–158, and in *Philosophical Papers,* pp. 44–84.

——. *Philosophical Papers,* J. O. Urmson and G. J. Warnock, eds. Oxford, Oxford University Press, 1961.

——. "Truth," *Aristotelian Society Supplementary Volume XXIV,* 1950, pp. 111–128. Reprinted in *Philosophical Papers,* pp. 85–101.

Ayer, A. J. *Philosophical Essays.* London, Macmillan and Co., 1954.

——. *The Problem of Knowledge.* London, Macmillan and Co., 1956.

Beck, L. J. *The Method of Descartes.* Oxford, Oxford University Press, 1952.

Berlin, Isaiah. *Historical Inevitability.* Oxford, Oxford University Press, 1954.

Black, Max. *Models and Metaphors.* Ithaca, N.Y., Cornell University Press, 1962.

——, ed. *Philosophical Analysis.* Ithaca, N.Y., Cornell University Press, 1950.

——. "Probability," in *The Encyclopedia of Philosophy,* Vol. 6. Paul Edwards, ed. New York, Macmillan Company and The Free Press, 1967.

Bosanquet, Bernard. *Implication and Linear Inference.* London, Macmillan and Co., 1920.

Brown, Roger. *Words and Things.* New York, The Free Press, 1958.

Burks, Arthur W. Critical review of Rudolf Carnap's *Logical Founda-*

tions of Probability, Journal of Philosophy, XLVIII, 1951, pp. 524–535.

——. "The Presupposition Theory of Induction," *Philosophy of Science*, Vol. 20, 1953, pp. 177–197.

Burtt, Edwin A. *The Metaphysical Foundations of Modern Physical Science*. New York, Harcourt, Brace and Co., 1932.

——. *Types of Religious Philosophy*, rev. ed. New York, Harper and Brothers, 1951.

——. "The Value Presuppositions of Science," *Bulletin of the Atomic Sciences*, XIII, 1957, pp. 99–106.

Carnap, Rudolf. "The Aim of Inductive Logic," in E. Nagel, P. Suppes, and A. Tarski, *Logic, Methodology and Philosophy of Science*, pp. 303–318.

——. *The Continuum of Inductive Methods*. Chicago, University of Chicago Press, 1952.

——. *Logical Foundations of Probability*. Chicago, University of Chicago Press, 1950. Reviews: see Burks, Arthur W., and Toulmin, Stephen.

——. "On Inductive Logic," *Philosophy of Science*, Vol. 12, 1945, pp. 72–97.

——. *Philosophy and Logical Syntax*. London, Kegan Paul, 1935.

——. "Testability and Meaning," *Philosophy of Science*, Vol. 3, 1936, pp. 419–471; Vol. 4, 1937, pp. 1–40.

Chisholm, Roderick M. *Theory of Knowledge*. Englewood Cliffs, N.J., Prentice-Hall, Inc., 1966.

Chisholm, Roderick M., and others. *Philosophy*. Englewood Cliffs, N.J., Prentice-Hall, Inc., 1964.

Cornford, Francis M. "Greek Natural Philosophy and Modern Science," in J. Needham and W. Pagel, *Background to Modern Science*, pp. 3–22.

Descartes, René. *Descartes: Philosophical Writings*, ed. and trans. by N. Kemp Smith. New York, Modern Library, 1958.

——. *Discourse on Method*, in E. S. Haldane and G. R. T. Ross, and in N. Kemp Smith translations of Descartes's philosophical writings.

——. *Meditations on First Philosophy*, in N. Kemp Smith translation of Descartes's philosophical writings.

——. *Philosophical Works*, Vol. I, trans. by E. S. Haldane and G. R. T. Ross. London, Cambridge University Press, 1967.

——. *Regulae: Rules for the Direction of the Mind*, in N. Kemp Smith translation of Descartes's philosophical writings.

——. *See also* Smith, Norman Kemp.

Dewey, Jane M. "Biography of John Dewey," in P. A. Schilpp, ed., *The Philosophy of John Dewey*, pp. 1–45.

Dewey, John. "Experience, Knowledge and Value: A Rejoinder," in P. A. Schilpp, ed., *The Philosophy of John Dewey*, pp. 515–608.

——. *The Quest for Certainty*. New York, Minton, Balch & Co., 1929.

Edel, Abraham. "Naturalism and Ethical Theory," in Yervant H. Krikorian, ed., *Naturalism and the Human Spirit*, pp. 65–95. New York, Columbia University Press, 1944.

Feigl, Herbert, "De Principiis Non Disputandum. . . ?" in M. Black, ed., *Philosophical Analysis*, pp. 119–156.

Feigl, Herbert, and Wilfrid Sellars, eds. *Readings in Philosophical Analysis*. New York, Appleton-Century-Crofts, Inc., 1949.

Flew, Antony, ed. *Essays in Conceptual Analysis*. London, Macmillan and Co., 1956.

——. *Logic and Language*. Oxford, Basil Blackwell, 1951.

——. *Logic and Language*. Second Series. Oxford, Basil Blackwell, 1953.

Galileo. *Dialogues Concerning Two New Sciences*. New York, Macmillan Company, 1914. Reprinted New York, Dover Publications, n.d.

——. *Le Opere di Galileo Galilei: Edizione Nazionale*. Vol. X, 1604.

Garrigou-Lagrange, Réginald. *God: His Existence and His Nature*. Vols. I–II, trans. from 5th edition by D. B. Rose. St. Louis and London, B. Herder Book Co., 1936.

Haldane, E. S., and G. R. T. Ross, trans. *Philosophical Works*. See Descartes, René.

Hart, H. L. A., and A. M. Honoré. *Causation in the Law*. Oxford, Oxford University Press, 1959.

Hempel, Carl G. *Aspects of Scientific Explanation*. New York, The Free Press, 1965.

Hospers, John. *An Introduction to Philosophical Analysis*. New York, Prentice-Hall, Inc., 1953.

Hume, David. *An Abstract of a Treatise of Human Nature* (1740), J. M. Keynes and P. Straffa, eds. Cambridge, Cambridge University Press, 1938.

——. *Enquiry Concerning Human Understanding*, in L. A. Selby-Bigge, ed., *Hume's Enquiries*, 2nd ed. Oxford, Oxford University Press, 1902.

——. "On Miracles," in *Enquiry Concerning Human Understanding*.

——. *A Treatise of Human Nature*, L. A. Selby-Bigge, ed. Oxford, Oxford University Press, 1896.

James, William. *Pragmatism.* New York, Longmans, Green and Co., 1925.

Janik, Allan, and Stephen Toulmin. *Wittgenstein's Vienna.* New York, Simon and Schuster, 1973.

Jeffrey, Richard C., *The Logic of Decision.* New York, McGraw-Hill, Inc., 1965.

Kant, Immanuel. *Critique of Pure Reason,* trans. by N. Kemp Smith. London, Macmillan and Co., 1929.

Keynes, John Maynard. *A Treatise on Probability.* London, Macmillan and Co., 1921.

Kneale, William. *Probability and Induction.* Oxford, Oxford University Press, 1949.

Koyré, Alexandre. *Études Galileénes.* (*Étude II,* "La Loi de la chute des corps: Descartes et Galilée," in *Actualités Scientifique et Industrielles,* No. 853.) Paris, 1939.

——. "An Experiment in Measurement," *Proceedings of the American Philosophical Society,* Vol. 97, 1953, pp. 227–237.

Kuhn, Thomas S. *The Structure of Scientific Revolutions.* Chicago, University of Chicago Press, 1962.

Kyburg, Henry E., Jr. *Probability and Inductive Logic.* New York, Macmillan Company, 1970.

Kyburg, Henry E., Jr., and Howard E. Smokler, eds. *Studies in Subjective Probability.* New York, John Wiley & Sons, Inc., 1964.

Leibniz, Gottfried Wilhelm. *Opuscules et fragments inédit de Leibniz,* L. Couterat, ed. Paris, Félix Alcan, 1903.

——. *Leibniz: Selections,* P. P. Wiener, ed. New York, Charles Scribner's Sons, 1951.

——. *Monadology and Other Philosophical Essays,* ed. and trans. by P. Schrecker and A. M. Schrecker. Indianapolis, Bobbs-Merrill Co., 1965.

——. *New Essays Concerning Human Understanding,* trans. by A. G. Langley. Chicago, Open Court Publishing Co., 1916.

——. *Die Philosophischen Schriften von G. W. Leibniz,* Vol. 7, C. I. Gerhardt, ed. Berlin, Weidmann, 1875–1890.

Levi, Edward H. *An Introduction to Legal Reasoning.* Chicago and London, University of Chicago Press, 1948.

Lewis, Clarence Irving. *An Analysis of Knowledge and Valuation.* La Salle, Ill., Open Court Publishing Co., 1946.

Lipton, Michael. Letter, *re.* Wittgenstein and Rilke, *Encounter,* Vol. XXXII, No. 5, May, 1969, p. 97.

Locke, John. *An Essay Concerning Human Understanding,* Vols. 1–2, A. C. Fraser, ed. Oxford, Oxford University Press, 1894.

Lorenzen, Paul. "Methodological Thinking," *Ratio,* Vol. VII, 1965–1966, pp. 35–60.

Macaulay, Thomas Babington. *Francis Bacon.* New York, Cassell Publishing Co., n.d.

McMullin, Ernan. *Galileo, Man of Science.* New York, Basic Books, 1967.

Marx, Karl, and Friedrich Engels. *The German Ideology,* R. Pascal, ed. New York, International Publishers, 1947.

Mill, John Stuart. *A System of Logic,* 8th ed. London, Longmans, Green and Co., 1872.

Mises, Richard von. *Probability, Statistics, and Truth.* New York, Macmillan Company, 1957.

Moody, Ernest A. "Galileo and Avempace: The Dynamics of the Leaning Tower Experiment," *Journal of the History of Ideas,* Vol. XII, 1951, pp. 163–193, 375–422.

Moore, G. E. *Principia Ethica.* Cambridge, Cambridge University Press, 1903.

Murphy, Arthur E. "Dewey's Epistemology and Metaphysics," in P. A. Schilpp, ed., *The Philosophy of John Dewey,* pp. 193–225.

Nagel, Ernest. Critical review of Hans Reichenbach's *Experience and Prediction, Philosophy of Science,* Vol. 6, 1939, pp. 212–253. Reprinted in Ernest Nagel, *Sovereign Reason.* Glencoe, Ill., The Free Press, 1954.

——. Critical review of Donald C. Williams's *The Ground of Induction, Journal of Philosophy,* XLIV, 1947, pp. 685–693.

——. *Principles of the Theory of Probability.* Chicago, University of Chicago Press, 1939.

Nagel, Ernest, Patrick Suppes, and Alfred Tarski. *Logic, Methodology and Philosophy of Science.* Stanford, Stanford University Press, 1962.

Needham, Joseph, and Walter Pagel. *Background to Modern Science.* New York, Macmillan Company, 1940.

Neurath, Otto. *Anti-Spengler.* Munich, G. D. W. Callwey, 1921.

——. "Protokollsätze," *Erkenntnis,* Vol. III, 1932–1933, pp. 204–214. Republished in translation by F. Schick in *Logical Positivism,* A. J. Ayer, ed., New York, The Free Press, 1959, pp. 199–208.

Nowell-Smith, P. H. *Ethics.* Baltimore, Penguin Books, Inc., 1954.

Peirce, Charles Sanders. *Collected Papers,* Vols. 1–6, C. Hartshorne and P. Weiss, eds.; Vols. 7–8, A. Burks, ed. Cambridge, Mass., Harvard University Press, 1931–1935, 1958.

Perelman, Ch. *The Idea of Justice and the Problems of Argument.* London, Routledge and Kegan Paul, 1963.

——. *Justice.* New York, Random House, 1967.

Plato. *The Republic,* in *The Dialogues of Plato,* 3rd ed., trans. by B. Jowett. New York, Random House, 1937.

Quine, William Van Orman. *Methods of Logic,* rev. ed. New York, Henry Holt and Co., 1959.

Quinton, Anthony. "The Foundations of Knowledge," in Bernard Williams and Alan Montfiore, eds., *British Analytic Philosophy,* pp. 55–86. London, Routledge and Kegan Paul, 1966.

Reichenbach, Hans. *Experience and Prediction.* Chicago, University of Chicago Press, 1938. For critical review see Nagel, Ernest.

——. "Kausalität und Wahrscheinlichkeit," *Erkenntnis,* Vol. I, 1930–1931, pp. 158–188.

——. "Die Logischen Grundlagen des Wahrscheinlichkeitsbegriffs," *Erkenntnis,* Vol. III, 1932–1933, pp. 401–425. Trans. in H. Feigl and W. Sellars, *Readings in Philosophical Analysis,* pp. 305–312.

——. *The Theory of Probability.* Berkeley, University of California Press, 1949.

Russell, Bertrand. "Logical Atomism," in J. H. Muirhead, ed., *Contemporary British Philosophy,* pp. 357–383. New York, Macmillan Company, 1924.

——. "My Mental Development," in P. A. Schilpp, ed., *The Philosophy of Bertrand Russell,* pp. 3–20.

——. *The Problems of Philosophy.* New York, Henry Holt and Co., 1912.

——. "Why I Took to Philosophy," in *Portraits From Memory,* pp. 13–18. New York, Simon and Schuster, 1956.

Ryle, Gilbert. *The Concept of Mind.* London, Hutchinson & Co., 1949.

Sabine, George H. *A History of Political Theory,* 2nd rev. ed. New York, Henry Holt & Co., 1950.

——. "Rationalism in Hume's Philosophy," in G. H. Sabine, ed., *Philosophical Essays in Honor of James Edwin Creighton,* pp. 42–60. New York, Macmillan Company, 1917.

Savage, Leonard J. *The Foundations of Statistics.* New York, John Wiley & Sons, Inc., 1954.

Scammon, Richard M., and Ben J. Wattenberg. *The Real Majority.* New York, Coward-McCann, 1970.

Scheffler, Israel. *Science and Subjectivity.* Indianapolis, Bobbs-Merrill Co., 1967.

Schilpp, Paul A., ed. *The Philosophy of Bertrand Russell*. Evanston and Chicago, Northwestern University Press, 1944.

———. *The Philosophy of John Dewey*. Evanston and Chicago, Northwestern University Press, 1939.

Schlick, Moritz. "Causality in Everyday Life and in Recent Science," in *University of California Publications in Philosophy*, Vol. XV, 1932, pp. 99–125. Reprinted in H. Feigl and W. Sellars, *Readings in Philosophical Analysis*, pp. 515–533.

———. "Die Kausalität in der gegenewärtigen Physik," *Die Naturwissenschaften*, 1931, pp. 145–162. Reprinted in *Gesammelte Aufsätze, 1926–1936*, Vienna, Gerold, 1938, and in *Gesetz, Kausalität und Wahrscheinlichkeit*, Vienna, Gerold, 1948.

———. *Problems of Ethics*. New York, Prentice-Hall, Inc., 1939.

Settle, Thomas B. "An Experiment in the History of Science," *Science*, Vol. 133, 1961, pp. 19–23.

———. "Galilean Science: An Empirical Source for the Odd Number Rule." M.A. thesis, Cornell University, Ithaca, N.Y., 1963.

———. "Galileo's Use of Experiment as a Tool of Investigation," in E. McMullin, ed., *Galileo, Man of Science*, pp. 315–337. New York, Basic Books, 1967.

Smith, Norman Kemp, ed. and trans. *Descartes: Philosophical Writings. See* Descartes, René.

———. *New Studies in the Philosophy of Descartes*. London, Macmillan and Co., 1952.

Toulmin, Stephen. Critical review of Rudolf Carnap's *Logical Foundations of Probability*, *Mind*, Vol. LXII, 1953, pp. 86–99.

———. "Ludwig Wittgenstein," *Encounter*, Vol. XXXII, No. 1, January, 1969, p. 62.

———. "Probability," *Aristotelian Society Supplementary Volume XXIV*, 1950, pp. 27–62. Reprinted in A. Flew, ed., *Essays in Conceptual Analysis*, pp. 157–191.

———. *The Uses of Argument*. Cambridge, Cambridge University Press, 1958.

Train, Arthur. *My Day in Court*. New York, Charles Scribner's Sons, 1939.

"Trial—The City and County of Denver *vs*. Lauren R. Watson," NET Journal, March, 1970. New York, National Educational Television.

Ueberweg, Friedrich. *History of Philosophy*, Vols. I–II. New York, Charles Scribner's Sons, 1909.

Waismann, Friedrich. "Verifiability," *Aristotelian Society Supplemen-*

tary Volume XIX, 1945, pp. 119–150. Reprinted in A. Flew, ed., *Logic and Language*, pp. 117–144.

——. *Wittgenstein und der Wiener Kreis*, B. F. McGuiness, ed. Oxford, Basil Blackwell, 1967.

White, Leslie A. "The Locus of Mathematical Reality: An Anthropological Footnote," *Philosophy of Science*, Vol. 14, 1947, pp. 289–303.

Whitehead, Alfred North. *Process and Reality*. New York, Macmillan Company, 1929.

Will, Frederick L. "Consequences and Confirmation," *Philosophical Review*, Vol. LXXV, 1966, pp. 34–58.

——. Critical review of D. C. Williams's *The Ground of Induction*, *Philosophical Review*, Vol. LVII, 1948, pp. 231–247.

——. "Justification and Induction," *Philosophical Review*, Vol. LXVIII, 1959, pp. 359–372.

——. "The Preferability of Probable Beliefs," *Journal of Philosophy*, LXVII, 1965, pp. 57–67.

——. "Thoughts and Things," *Proceedings and Addresses of the American Philosophical Association*, Vol. XLII, 1968–1969, pp. 51–69.

Williams, Donald C. *The Ground of Induction*. Cambridge, Mass., Harvard University Press, 1947. For critical reviews see Nagel, Ernest, and Will, Frederick L.

——. "On the Derivation of Probabilities from Frequencies," *Philosophy and Phenomenological Research*, Vol. V, 1944–1945, pp. 449–484.

Wittgenstein, Ludwig. *Philosophical Investigations*, trans. by G. E. M. Anscombe. Oxford, Basil Blackwell, 1953.

Wright, Georg Henrik von. *The Logical Problem of Induction*, 2nd rev. ed. New York, Macmillan Company, 1957.

Ziff, Paul. *Semantic Analysis*. Ithaca, N.Y., Cornell University Press, 1960.

Index